Music Direction for the Stage

Music Direction for the Stage

A View from the Podium

Joseph Church

OXFORD
UNIVERSITY PRESS

Oxford University Press is a department of the University of
Oxford. It furthers the University's objective of excellence in research,
scholarship, and education by publishing worldwide.

Oxford   New York
Auckland   Cape Town   Dar es Salaam   Hong Kong   Karachi
Kuala Lumpur   Madrid   Melbourne   Mexico City   Nairobi
New Delhi   Shanghai   Taipei   Toronto

With offices in
Argentina   Austria   Brazil   Chile   Czech Republic   France   Greece
Guatemala   Hungary   Italy   Japan   Poland   Portugal   Singapore
South Korea   Switzerland   Thailand   Turkey   Ukraine   Vietnam

Oxford is a registered trademark of Oxford University Press
in the UK and certain other countries.

Published in the United States of America by
Oxford University Press
198 Madison Avenue, New York, NY 10016

© Joseph Church 2015

All rights reserved. No part of this publication may be reproduced, stored in
a retrieval system, or transmitted, in any form or by any means, without the prior
permission in writing of Oxford University Press, or as expressly permitted by law,
by license, or under terms agreed with the appropriate reproduction rights organization.
Inquiries concerning reproduction outside the scope of the above should be sent to the
Rights Department, Oxford University Press, at the address above.

You must not circulate this work in any other form
and you must impose this same condition on any acquirer.

Library of Congress Cataloging-in-Publication Data
Church, Joseph, 1957–
Music direction for the stage : a view from the podium / Joseph Church.
pages cm
Includes bibliographical references and index.
ISBN: 9780199993406 (hardback; alk. paper) 9780199993413 (pbk; alk. paper)
1. Musicals—Production and direction.   I. Title
MT955 .C59 2015—2014
782.1/4145   2014017176

9 8 7 6 5 4 3
Printed in Canada

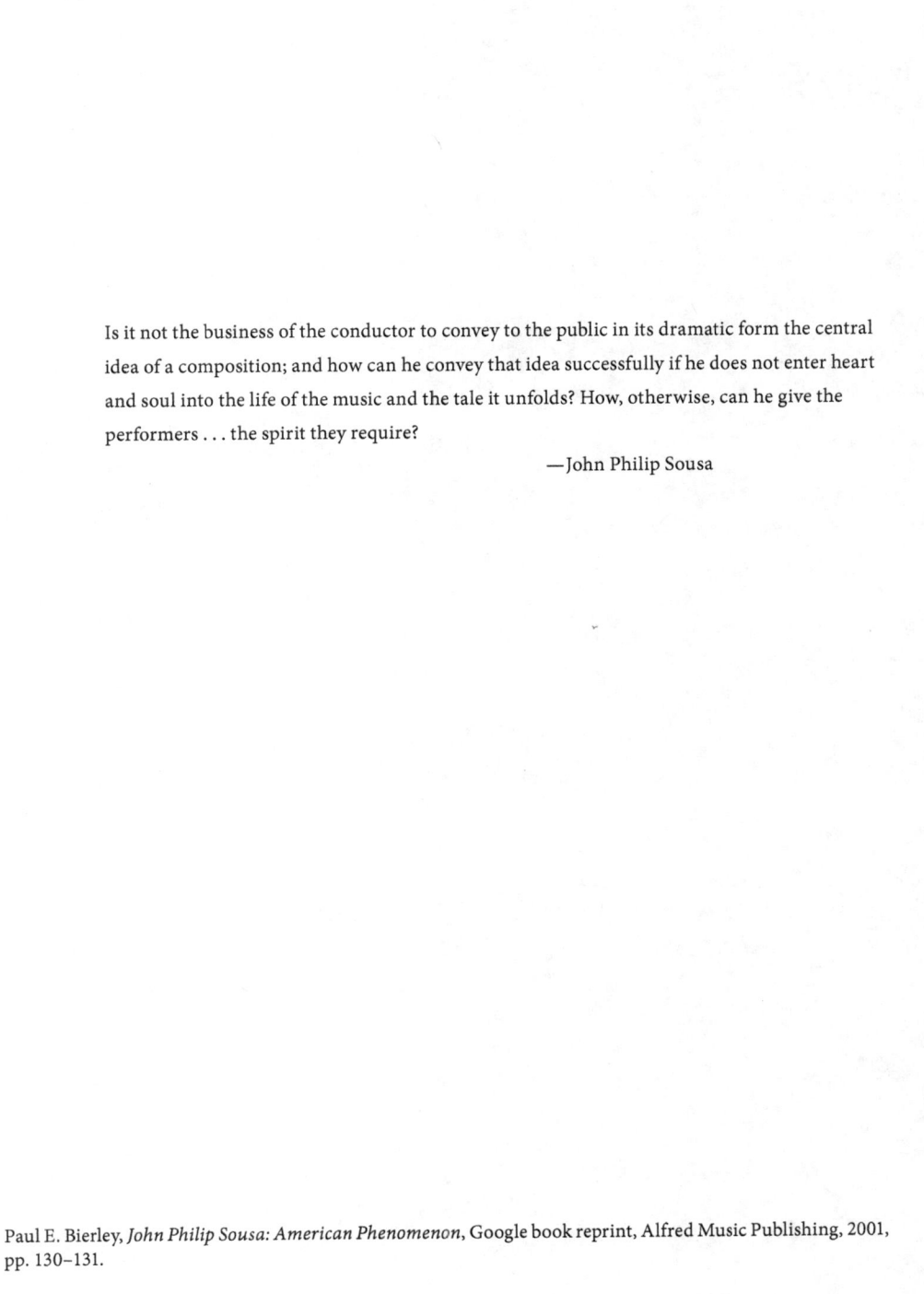

Is it not the business of the conductor to convey to the public in its dramatic form the central idea of a composition; and how can he convey that idea successfully if he does not enter heart and soul into the life of the music and the tale it unfolds? How, otherwise, can he give the performers . . . the spirit they require?

—John Philip Sousa

Paul E. Bierley, *John Philip Sousa: American Phenomenon*, Google book reprint, Alfred Music Publishing, 2001, pp. 130–131.

Contents

Foreword by Alan Menken — xiii
Acknowledgments — xv

Introduction: The View from the Podium — 1

PART I   Music Direction: A Job Description — 11

1. Music Direction Today and Yesterday — 13
   What a Music Director Does — 13
   Historical Survey of Music Direction — 19
   Technology and the Shrinking Orchestra — 22
   Looking to the Future — 27
2. Musical Stage Production — 34
   Songs, Musicals, and Opera — 34
   A (Very) Brief History of Music for the Stage — 38
   Production in the Twenty-First Century — 42
3. Job Opportunities for Music Directors — 45
   Broadway and Off-Broadway — 45
   National Tours — 49
   Regional (Local), Repertory, and Stock Theater — 51
   Nightclubs, Cabarets, and Concerts — 57
   Revues, Special Events, and Industrials — 62
   Academic Theaters and Events — 63
   Amateur and Community Performances and Talent Shows — 65
   Workshops and Developmental Productions — 67

PART II   Personnel   71

4. The Production Team   73
   Producers   74
   Stage Managers   76
   General Managers, Company Managers, House Managers, and Production Managers   79
5. The Creative Team   81
   Composers and Lyricists   81
   Directors   84
   Choreographers   88
   Designers and Technicians   90
6. The Music Team   93
   Conductors, Associates, and Assistants   94
   Contractors and Music Coordinators   96
   Orchestrators and Copyists   98
   Vocal and Dance Arrangers   103
   Synthesizer Programmers   104
   The Orchestra   108
7. The Performers   110
   Singers and Dancers   110
   Singers and Actors   113
   Star Performers and Nontraditional Casting   115
   Casting Directors   116

PART III   Preproduction   119

8. Mounting a Production   121
   Meetings and Agendas, Planning and Scheduling   121
   Casting   126
   Determining the Orchestration: Three Scenarios   132
        Scenario 1: Voice and Piano, or Maybe More   132
        Scenario 2: Small Ensembles   133
        Scenario 3: Orchestra Reductions   136
9. The Music: Assessment and Analysis   138
   Learning and Practicing Scores   139
   Preparing Scores for Rehearsal   141
   Transcribing   145
   Practical Analysis for Music Direction   148
10. Arranging for Music Directors   154
    Starting an Arrangement: Approaches and Rightness   156
    Technical Fundamentals of Arranging   159

		Distribution, Registration, and Voicing	160
		Dynamics and Articulation	161
		Key	161
		Feel and Style	162
		Tempo	163
		Structure	163
		Notating Arrangements	163
	Arranging for Voices		164
	Arranging for Movement		174

PART IV Rehearsals 1: Singers and the Stage — 179

11.	Overview of Rehearsal Process		181
12.	Individual Vocal Rehearsals		187
	Coaching Singers		187
		Rehearsal Process and Conduct	188
		Background, Analysis, and Style	190
		Key	194
		Tempo	195
		Vocal Technique	198
		Accompanying and the Accompaniment	199
	Text and Singing		202
	Acting and Singing		203
13.	Ensemble Vocal Rehearsals		207
	Ensemble Rehearsal Process		208
	Choral Techniques for the Stage		213
		Dynamics and Articulation	213
		Breathing and Phrasing	216
		Vocal Production and Technique	217
		Intonation	218
		Text and Diction	219
		Acting and Characterization	220
		Movement	221
		Choral Conducting for the Stage	221
14.	Rehearsals with Directors and Choreographers		223
	Staging and Dramatic Rehearsals		223
	Movement and Dance Rehearsals		227
15.	Adapting Music to the Production		230
	Cueing		231
	Underscoring, Transitions, and Incidental Music		235
	Overtures, Bows, and Exit Music		239

PART V	**Rehearsals 2: Musicians, Technicians,**	
	and the Venue	241
16.	Orchestras and Orchestrations	243
	Organizing the Musicians	243
	The Orchestra: Sections and Setup	246
	Rhythm Sections: Keyboards, Drums, Bass, and Guitar	247
	Woodwinds and Brass	253
	Strings	255
	Orchestration: Notation and Parts	257
17.	Instrumental Conducting for the Stage	262
	Rehearsal Process	264
	Conducting Styles	267
	Visibility and the "Field"	269
	Baton, Head, and Hands	269
	Conducting Techniques	271
	Meter, Beat Patterns, and Subdivisions	272
	Preparatory Beats and Cutoffs	278
	Rests and Holds	282
	Safeties and Vamps	284
	Free Tempo, Recitative, and Following Singers	286
	Tempo and Tempo Changes	289
	Feels, Grooves, and Syncopations	291
	Dynamics and Articulations	293
	Cueing and the Stage	295
18.	From the Studio to the Stage	297
	Run-throughs, Dress Rehearsals, and the *Sitzprobe*	297
	Load-ins, Seatings, and Sound Checks	302
	The Podium	308
	Technical Rehearsals, Previews, and Brush-ups	312
	Giving and Receiving Notes	315
PART VI	**Performance**	321
19.	Conducting in Performance	323
	The Pre-Show Routine	324
	Showtime	326
	Repeated Performances: Variations on a Theme	327
	When Things Go Wrong	329
20.	Maintaining a Production and Preserving a Show	334
	A Day in the Life	334
	Keeping the Performance Fresh	335
	Rehearsing after Opening	337

	Subbing in the Orchestra	340
	Subbing on the Podium	341
	Disputes	343
	Original Cast and Other Recordings	344
	Repeatability and the Rehearsal Score	347
21.	Working as a Music Director	359
	Starting Out	359
	Career Philosophy	361
	Maintaining a Career	364
	How to Get a Gig	367

Appendix A Putting It Together	373
In The Heights #1: "In The Heights"	374
The Lion King #1: "Circle of Life"	378
Appendix B Bibliography, Suggested Reading, and List of Musical Works Cited	383
Index	387

Foreword

by Alan Menken

It's about time someone wrote a book about the world of the music director. And Joe Church is just the right guy to do it. We met and first worked together back in the early 1980s, with Little Shop of Horrors, and our association has lasted well over thirty years, through his years as a musician, conductor, professor, and as a music director for all kinds of projects: from developmental readings and concerts to long-running Broadway shows. As a composer of songs and scores, whether for stage, screen or recording, I liken myself to an architect. I create a structure that others can live in. I develop a basic musical concept with which to tell a story, a style, a vocabulary, an attitude, and a musical palette. Along with a lyricist and book writer, I design a structure in which songs and score can push story along, illuminate, amuse, and move emotionally. Like a house, a musical theater score has a flow and a purpose, an entrance, a variety of rooms that serve different functions and windows to allow light in.

Actors, singers, musicians, and audiences inhabit those works, the houses we design. They move in and make them their own in the end and if I've done my job well, those structures can withstand the test of time; surviving through varied interpretations, differences in languages and culture, and all levels of performance.

In the center of all of this is the music director, who builds the house and maintains all the systems. As every architect relies on a contractor to turn blueprints into a finished house, I rely on my music directors to turn my notes on a page or my MIDI files or recorded demos into a living, breathing finished experience. I trust them to creatively interpret my wishes and communicate them to arrangers, orchestrators, singers and dancers, culminating at last with the audience.

On any given production, the music director might adjust keys, tempos, phrasings, or dynamics to best suit the skills of individual actors. He or she will stand in the back of the house to coax the best mix decisions from a sound designer. A music director will monitor the physical and emotional condition of singers and do whatever it takes to support them and enhance their performances. Music directors are traffic cops in rehearsals and performances; the crossroads of notes from the composer, the stage manager, the director, and the producer. They have to be aware of every note of the score and every performance on the stage, never burying their noses in the written score or drifting into self-indulgence.

When a production is a new work, being developed for the first time, the music director's job is intense, exhausting, and exhilarating. In my studio, when I'm creating a work, I am at one with the notes, the harmonies, the words, the characters, and the story. That is the peak of the experience for me. In the theater, before, during, and after a performance, my work lives in my music director's hands, face, intellect, and heart. It belongs to him or her every bit as much as it belongs to me in those moments. He or she interprets audience reactions during previews and, along with the rest of the creative team sitting out in the house, decides how to adjust the next night, and while we experience that adjustment, he or she creates it.

It's no coincidence that I, and so many of the other composers I know and respect, learned the craft of writing musicals from the great music director Lehman Engel. He taught so many of us through the BMI Workshop, in a program based on his observations from the pit of so many of the great musical theater works of the 1940s, 1950s, and 1960s. It's also no coincidence that so many of the great music directors I have worked with were fellow composers in those classes. We are cut from the same cloth and we serve the same end.

If you're interested in the world of musical theater I know you'll enjoy and learn from Joe Church's *Music Direction For The Stage: A View from the Podium*.

Acknowledgments

Music Direction for the Stage: A View from the Podium was a long time in the making, and could not have been written without the invaluable assistance of several members of the musical community, who, through interviews or conversations, helped me see through more than my own eyes. My deepest gratitude to John McDaniel, Jeffery Klitz, Alex Lacamoire, David Chase, Donald Pippin, Galt MacDermot, Michael Kosarin, Michael Keller, Constantine Kitsopoulos, Adam Ben-David, Henry Aronson, Jeff Marder, Randy Cohen, Howard Joines, Andrew Schwartz, Jeffrey Seller, Eric Cornell, Doc Zorthian, James Harvey, Tom Barney, and Owen Wang. Thanks also to Disney Theatrical Group, the company managers and stage managers at Rock of Ages on Broadway, the American Federation of Musicians Local 802, and the photographers who generously contributed their beautiful artwork.

This book would not exist without two people, editor Norman Hirschy, and the person who led me to him, David Hahn. Their industriousness fortuitously collided with my persistence to make sure the book reached its readership. One could not ask for a kinder, more thoughtful, or better informed guide than Norm. Thank you for believing in this book, and for sharing my dream of making it come to life. Special thanks, too, to copy editor Leslie Safford, for her very helpful suggestions and kind support, and to production editor Molly Morrison for guiding me and holding my hand through publication. Thanks, too, to Constance Ditzel at Routledge Press for helping me decide what shape this text should take.

I have often thought my encyclopedically knowledgeable research assistant, Daniel Sefik, to be more qualified to write this book than I, and I have no doubt I will be petitioning him for a job someday soon. Sincerest thanks to him. My love and gratitude to my mother, Alexandria Church, who is not only an incisive judge of quality and a fine editor, but also stayed on my back for all the years this book took to complete. The groundbreaking writings on psychology and political and behavioral science by my late father, Joseph Church, are my inspiration. I know he is always looking over my shoulder with a discerning yet loving eye.

Above all, I must acknowledge a lifetime's worth of magnanimous, insightful mentors and colleagues, too numerous to fairly mention any one, who through their tutelage or collaboration entrusted their ideas to me to pass on. I hope to be as good a teacher as they. In keeping with this, I must also acknowledge my talented students, who, over many years of teaching, helped me put this information into focus, and insisted that I write it down.

Finally, everything I do is for my daughter Susannah Jane Church and my partner Susan Aquila. Without them I would have given up long ago. Thanks to Susan and Susie for their unyielding patience, and their love.

Music Direction for the Stage

Introduction
The View from the Podium

Finally the big night has arrived. We bought our tickets months ago. We put on our Saturday night best. We arrive at the theater, and settle into our seats. The house lights dim. Slowly the curtain rises. A spotlight shines on a stunning figure in a dazzling sequined outfit. The audience's anticipation is palpable. Then . . . silence. And then . . . more silence. Wait a minute, silence? Okay, back up. Lower the curtain. Bring up the house lights. Refund the tickets. What is wrong here? I know. Where's the music? What happened to the music?

On every Broadway musical stage, whenever a musical show is put on at the local high school or church or community theater, every time a nightclub performer appears in Las Vegas or on a cruise ship, for every musical performance of any kind in any venue, there is musical accompaniment. The music that accompanies whatever is happening on stage originates somewhere, and from someone. Someone starts the music, someone plays the music, and someone stops the music. It may come from an orchestra pit, or through a sound system, or there may be an orchestra in full view. Regardless of its outward presentation, there are human beings performing or otherwise executing every accompaniment. Traditionally, live musicians have done the job, but in recent years recordings have begun to supplant them. Even when an accompaniment is pre-recorded, someone played it to begin with, and someone has to turn it on and off at the right moment in performance.

The term "accompaniment" might imply that the music is somehow subordinate. In some ways it is, but that does not make it any less essential. It does not renounce its identity because it is an appendage to something else. Rather, musical accompaniment is a form of collaboration. Music conservatories teach accompanying as a discrete area of study, and in recent years have renamed it "collaborative piano." This politically motivated correction is especially apt in a stage music setting, where a music director is not just an accompanist, but also a collaborator, performer and co-creator.

For any musician, fruitful and enjoyable collaboration is among music's richest rewards. I got an early taste of it on one of the first shows for which I was music director, and my first with a big orchestra, my college production of *West Side Story*. For fifteen weeks (!) we klutzy undergraduates collectively figured out how to put on a musical, and we rehearsed. Boy, did we rehearse. There were fifteen three-hour orchestra rehearsals, months of dramatic rehearsals with the director and actors, dance rehearsals, dialect rehearsals, vocal coachings, you name it. And we talked, and we analyzed. We exhaustively dissected the text and the score, made charts of Bernstein's musical motifs, lost sleep over the thought of transposing Tony's music to a range singable by our sophomore baritone, and doted on authentic recreation of the Robbins stage movement. I caught the bug. I dreamed of doing the same thing with Lenny and Steve at my side. (I even wrote Sondheim a letter with a numbered list of questions specific to our production, and he wrote back, obligingly and eloquently replying to each in a correspondingly numbered list of answers.)

Twenty years later, my wish came true (actually it came true a few times before that, but twenty makes better reading) when I was hired as music director of Broadway's upcoming production of *The Lion King*. The excitement I felt merely at landing the job—I remember driving home from the interview, my heart pounding, with Lebo M's extraordinary *Rhythm of the Pridelands* CD pumping in the car stereo, the first time I had heard the South African sound that was to become the musical DNA of the stage show—was surpassed at every turn during the mounting of the Broadway production. It was a near-perfect collaboration of talented, imaginative, and diligent individuals, under the munificent yet firm leadership of director Julie Taymor and producers Thomas Schumacher and Peter Schneider of Disney Theatricals. The show was grown from a seed (the story from the film) in workshops and in extended rehearsals, and matured into a piece that outshone its already imaginative and beloved source material. Each person on the very large creative and music teams worked at his or her strength, but there was constant and welcome crossover among departments and specializations. Seldom are so many different processes and personalities planted in one stage production, and seldom are they given such a well-subsidized breeding and testing ground. The collaboration, while at times unruly, could not have been healthier. The price tag was exorbitant, but the payoff, creatively and financially, was and continues to be enormous.

My love for making music for a living in such highly creative melting pots was what led me to a career in music direction, and what now brings me to writing this book. There is agreement among many of my colleagues that an attempt to share the occupation of music direction with others is overdue, and I am pleased to have their support and contributions in making the attempt in this text. From the unique point of view of the music director on the podium, this book will observe musical productions and make accounts of music directors in action within them. I hope to strike a balance between description and instruction that makes this text both entertaining and useful. My intent is to enlighten anyone interested in the profession, purveyors and observers alike.

It is mostly the lack of understanding of music direction (and what may be an immodest desire for its proper recognition) that creates space for a study of the subject. A music director is not an interchangeable part, or just someone who plays the piano really well, or just someone who happened to be available when a music director was needed, but rather an individual who can provide a unique and significant creative contribution to a production, as well as absolute musical and accompanimental proficiency.

If I have a loftier goal, it is the desire to improve upon the discipline and its execution in both professional and amateur situations. Music direction has a bad reputation in some circles, and deservedly so. Some music directors and conductors achieve their positions not through musical excellence or extreme stage savvy, but simply by convenience, timing, or chance. This is a reality that skilled musicians live with and, for the most part, tolerate. (Heard any good conductor jokes lately?) The outcome of subpar music direction will not be necessarily perceived, or even perceptible, to less discerning audiences. This may be good news for musicians who have an interest in the field of music direction and whose musical chops are not of the highest caliber, but whose talents in other areas are very strong. More competent musicians can bolster and obscure those who are less so, even those in leadership positions (this covering for questionable competence is no less prevalent in any professional organization). Still, when paying any significant amount of money for a show on Broadway or for any commercial production, every audience member is absolutely entitled to consistent musical execution of the very highest order. That is the standard to which this book holds.

What qualifies this author as an expert? In no way whatsoever do I profess to be the sole or utmost authority. It is not boldness, but rather inquisitiveness that motivates this work. The only assuredness I put forth is that all music directors can improve their work with thoughtful and thorough study of their knowledge and methods. I also know for certain that I am not alone in my quest for organized information on the topic. Many people enter into music direction situations with little or no experience. As a teacher and an active professional, I receive dozens of phone calls and emails each year from young and aspiring music directors wanting to know more about the craft, the profession, job opportunities, and formal study in the subject. Of course, there are no simple answers—and there are answers that may differ from mine—if for no other reason but that music direction is too great a conglomeration of too many disciplines and varies too greatly from job to job. Therefore, seasoned music directors will probably find some of the information I present secondary or obvious, while to others it may be revelatory.

In researching this book, I interviewed and observed several of the finest music directors in the profession, and have tried to represent their views as well as mine. Much of the time, the experiences and advice they related to me were shared among us all. Yet each point of view offered another unique perspective to a professional experience that is by nature multilayered and multifaceted. It is inevitable, however, that in a first-person account some statements I make will meet with dissent, which I not only expect but I encourage. I am well aware that other music directors have different ideas. Any disagreements, I hope, will initiate open and lively discussion and more profound scholarship in the field.

During my career I have done both good and bad work as a music director, and I have benefited from both. For those who might denigrate my authority on the grounds that I was not entirely in the Broadway mainstream, I respond that this book is not intended just for the mainstream, but for all corners of the profession. I hope that my many years of experience in a variety of musical styles and professional situations, in many different occupational capacities, and in vastly divergent socioeconomic entertainment strata, have furnished me with a firm enough knowledge base to justify my offering at least a seasoned perspective. I also hope that I have been sufficiently thoughtful and unbiased to pass on responsibly that which comes from personal experience as something to be learned from, and worth learning. Beyond that, achieving expertise and success will be up to the individual, not the textbook.

Some of what I present reflects the guidance I have given to students of music direction, conducting, and composition, in university courses and private lessons, professional seminars, and master classes. When I am speaking directly to interested listeners, my thoughts emerge with less structure. Organizing such a massive body of freeform thought into a readable and useful state was a long and painstaking process, but has already has helped me to improve my own work as a music director. It has also helped me understand why music directors have been so reluctant to codify their work in writing, and why several of my colleagues have been openly skeptical of any purportedly useful guide to the profession.

Music directors experience the excitement of privileged access to music of all sorts, in all genres, and in all phases of composition. Stage music—Broadway show music in particular—is not style-specific. It is show-specific, and production-specific. There is a false but commonly held notion that theater music, or Broadway music, is a style of its own. Indeed, harmonically tame, bouncy, brassy two- or four-beats, cakewalks and foxtrots and marches, plus an occasional waltz, have pervaded the scores of many stage musicals. That sound and feel originated in Tin Pan Alley, vaudeville and British music hall, and moved on to Broadway early in the 1900s in works of musical stage writers such as George M. Cohan and Irving Berlin. It has characterized or influenced the styles of many theater composers since, whether they are purposefully derivative or not. (The purposefully antique sound has also persisted in songs by progressive popular artists such as the Beatles, Genesis, and Queen, and even in hip-hop and its offshoots.) Later in the 20th century, Broadway brought this predilection somewhat up to date by incorporating light or generic swing and jazz, and later soft rock beats, but the mild, conventional harmonic and rhythmic vocabularies of its forbears endured. Whereas there are many stage scores that reflect this conservatism, there are just as many that purposefully break the mold. The best of show music has style and content that surprise and challenge its audiences.

My bias toward less derivative, more remarkable and substantial music and musical theater will be obvious. I much prefer music and theater that are aesthetically interesting, in some way original or notable, and worth the effort and investment of writing and producing. There is a great deal of interesting musical work out there being done every day in our overpopulated musical world, and some of it is indeed extraordinary. Yet today's commercial musical theater industry tends toward the complacent and predictable. If this opinion puts me slightly out of touch with the realities of my profession, so be it. Despite any high-minded aesthetic ambitions, I have also spent a lot of time in the trenches, and I believe I can speak to the needs of any music director working on any sort of production anywhere. I also love good music of all kinds, regardless of its style or sophistication.

If theater music is indeed largely stagnant, it is not Broadway's fault in particular; rather, it is the general cultural condition. Branding, packaging, star power, demographics, and salesmanship are more dictatorial than ever. Monetary success or a semblance of artistic success at times supersedes genuine artistic success. Musical theater and its offshoots have been very prone to this syndrome. Some Broadway offerings that in years past would have been run out of town by critics or audiences now last for extended periods. They play to theatergoers who are aggressively marketed to and buy a ticket for a show because they recognize its title, or are too easily drawn in by the latest technological wizardry. (Twenty-five years ago it was a helicopter landing on the stage of *Miss Saigon*; today it is *Spiderman: Turn Off the Dark*.) One might have hoped that the sustained box office bounty would have resulted in an outpouring of fresh, sophisticated writing, but unfortunately, originality has not consistently been the case, though the last decades have seen some brilliant, cutting-edge new work on musical stages.

The silver lining of this lingering overcast, and a very bright one it is, is that the financial boom in stage music has generated far more and far more professional opportunities in all related fields, including music direction. Jobs are popping up everywhere, and even if the music that music directors are leading won't always alter the course of music history, it is still usually very skillfully written and enjoyable to perform. And music directors can always help make it better. Music directors also reap profit from a task list that has lengthened over the last few decades to include transcribing, arranging for piano, orchestrating, additional composing, and otherwise completing a score, activities that all represent increased earnings opportunities.

Quite often being a music director entails making others happy, putting the needs of others above his or her own, and whoever mounts the podium may be the first to hear complaints. There is an old quip that the conductor of an orchestra stands in the middle because that makes him or her the easiest target. This is not far from the truth. The best music directors are masterful diplomats as well as musicians.

Yet in spite of its precariousness, the conductor's podium is one of the best seats in the house. A music director positioned there has a reasonably unobstructed view of the stage, can turn around and see the audience, and can even catch some of what's happening in the wings and the rafters. It's the best place to hear everything, too, at least in principle. The singers are right there, the orchestra is right there, and there you are, the music director, right smack in the middle of it all.

In spite of your central placement, what is evident to an audience is your work or, more accurately, the result of your work, not your presence. The audience doesn't hear the music director; they hear the music. Most aspects of a music director's work, if the work is done well, will be absorbed into the work of others, woven seamlessly into the fabric of the production, and the music director is invisible, as he or she should be. In a manner of speaking, the music in a stage production should materialize as if by magic, or at least without undue effort. This effect is not unlike a great concert musician who during a great performance allows his or her own persona to disappear, and becomes purely a vehicle for the vision and expression of the composer.

For these and other reasons, there seems to be an impenetrable mystery surrounding what music directors do. The contribution they make may be greater than anyone other than their closest colleagues know. In a few cases their involvement may be only menial, but more often the position requires great artistry, skill, and always cooperation. Assimilation into the fabric of the production may be the ideal, but it does not make the work any less challenging, or sometimes even any less visible. No one said that being invisible was easy.

A few matters of background and procedure are worth mentioning at the outset.

To begin with, I apologize for the length of this volume. It was my intent to be thorough, and omitting discussion of any of the sub-disciplines of music direction would have defeated the purpose. I also wanted to be somewhat anecdotal, and that approach, too, requires more words. So does working within a new scholarly context, one in which I often had to state the obvious in order to effectively look beneath it. Though the many topics in the book are very much interconnected, I have separated them as best I could by chapter and subheading. If you are a music director working on a show, you might keep this book at your side; the text is organized to take you from hiring through opening night and beyond. If you are a music director early in your career, this book is designed to tell you things you'll need to know to get a good start. If you are an interested bystander, feel free to skip around.

Another justification for my lengthiness is the dearth of existing literature on music direction. The profession is as undocumented as it is often unnoticed, so there are many holes to fill. Besides a few basic handbooks, there is virtually no scholarly inquiry into the subject, and at present music direction is part of only a few college or university curricula. There are few anecdotal writings, a paucity that is surprising, considering how freely stories and gossip are swapped backstage and in orchestra pits everywhere. One of the most important scholars of the musical theater, and a music director by trade,

Lehman Engel, wrote several books about songs and lyrics for the musical theater and a handbook on producing musicals that included a chapter on music direction. Steven Suskin's marvelous *The Sound of Broadway Music* includes a few brief but very informative biographies of music directors. There is a good deal of critical, biographical, and autobiographical writing about the master composer-conductors of earlier centuries, including the work they did as music directors, but these works are not really relevant in the contemporary environment. There are several excellent texts on conducting, orchestration, and arranging. I will speak to these specific disciplines as they are relevant to music direction, but I will offer little basic conducting or orchestration instruction; the book is already long enough.[1]

Each music direction job differs in time span and size, in expectation and responsibility, and in required abilities and specializations. In a study of a profession so typically atypical, an organizing principle for presenting the information was difficult to devise. In my doctoral dissertation in composition I followed in detail and kept a journal of my creative process in composing a new musical work. This book follows a comparable methodology, a series of case studies, some real and some hypothetical, that illuminate an array of preproduction, rehearsal, and performance situations from the music director's point of view. Because music direction unfolds over time, the chronicle is in pseudo-chronological order. For the most part, I follow the order of events as they would unfold in a production. Occasionally I take excursions outside the loose organizational model to focus on specific topics. My intent is for the examples and their contexts in different phases of the production process to be inclusive enough to represent musical stage production of all sorts. I bring up specialized tasks as they arise in the methodological production schedule.

The focus of this text is music direction for the "stage," and that is a broad appellation. By my definition, a stage can be anything from a Times Square theater presenting musicals, revues, concerts, or variety shows, to a noncommercial house doing the same, but not for profit, to school and municipal auditoriums of all sizes, to dance recitals, vocal recitals, outdoor arenas for festivals and such, corporate events, special events, holiday parties, nightclubs, and cruise ship, hotel, and casino lounges, anywhere the music is live. (Prerecorded music played back in performance barely fits in.) Whereas I am using Broadway musicals as the paradigm for stage productions of all kinds, I refer extensively to other productions of all kinds in all venues.

The term "musical theater" includes dramas and comedies set to music, as well as organized revues. "Productions" encompass all types of stage entertainment, including concerts and events as well as dramatic shows. The term "musical" refers to Broadway-like entertainments of all sorts, including ones that never made it, or were never intended to make it, to Broadway. (Arguably, the flagship of the stage music fleet is the Broadway stage. Although equally lavish and musically sophisticated endeavors

---

1. Please refer to the bibliography and list of additional readings in Appendix B.

are presented in major cities such as Las Vegas, Chicago, and Los Angeles, New York takes center stage in American theater production. Los Angeles is the home of many popular artists who employ music directors for their concerts, and Las Vegas is as busy a live music community as any.) Similarly, the job of theatrical music director is my starting point or focal point for discussing music direction in all settings. The Broadway model is useful in that the diverse responsibilities and challenges of music directors in musical theater apply to music direction in almost all other settings, though a Broadway budgets will of course far exceed most other productions, which I account for. My intent in choosing musical examples is to represent a balanced and useful cross-section of the theatrical song literature.

I was tempted to designate some shorthand for the bulky term "music director," such as "MD," but in the end I resisted. I refer specifically to any of the variety of tasks that can fall under the job title, when it makes sense to do so. I staunchly refuse to use the incorrect adjectival forms "music directorial" or "music directional," though they have regrettably invaded the lingo. Nor did I, or will I, use the verb form "to music direct" or the gerund "music directing" (or worse, "musically directing"), though I can see why one might want to. (Directors can; why can't we?)

Of late, the term "music supervisor" is a frequent replacement for or colleague of a "music director." Here in 2014, the work I describe in this book as music direction is just as often done on Broadway by someone holding the title of "music supervisor." Within a typical modern Broadway music department (though in reality there is no typical music department) one might find a music supervisor, a music director, and a conductor, as well as several associate and assistant conductors, and more. Occasionally the term "music producer" has also made an appearance. The title was transplanted, one might infer, from record producers, and in some way from theatrical producers. These are not inappropriate borrowings; indeed, music direction shares a good deal with these professions. More careful examination reveals that the different duties ascribed to the different job titles are as changeable as they are under the title of "music director." They are merely different levels, or subsets, or permutations of the many duties that fall under the umbrella term "music direction." The job title disorder will assuredly continue on the professional scene, as will the interchangeable use of the term "music*al* director" (a title that implies at least to me and most of my colleagues a stage director with good musicianship rather than someone directing the music).

The term "score" denotes the music of a show. "Arranging" is the transformation of an existing piece of music (some part or all of a score) into a related but new piece of music, called an "arrangement." "Orchestration" is a subset of arranging, denoting arranging for a specified group of musical instruments. Arranging is among the tasks that music directors often perform in some fashion, and in recent years this activity has increased. This upsurge is partly attributable to the arrival on the musical theater scene of many "pop" writers, who contribute songs rather than completed scores, and leave their manipulation—their arranging—to the music director or other music staff.

In addition, smaller, rhythm-section- and keyboard-based orchestras, more common in contemporary stage music, afford music directors the time to arrange as well as rehearse; large orchestrations usually occupy too many hours for a music director to do both jobs effectively.

The sorts of jobs that will *not* be included this book are the music director of a symphony orchestra, who is its principal conductor and to various degrees its artistic director; the music supervisor of a film or television show, who is the person responsible for choosing and placing the music to be used in a film or video; and the music director or supervisor or producer for an advertising, video production, or video game, whose responsibilities are primarily organizational. There are conductors for film and television and video game recordings, but conducting is their sole duty, and often composers conduct these sessions. In recordable media there is much more specialization. I must also unfortunately exclude the fascinating non-Western traditional and contemporary music for the stage in China, Japan, Korea, Indonesia, and India, among other non-English-speaking regions. My knowledge of those musical traditions is simply too limited to responsibly write about them, though they are certainly worthy of discussion, particularly in a global society.

As in many musical professions, and in many professions in and out of the arts, the cultural and technological times are rapidly changing. These days the view from the podium can be "partial view" seating, and the music might be heard only through a sound system. Orchestras are placed upstage, backstage, under the stage, almost anywhere except the pit, and when they are in the pit, they are often covered by the stage, acoustically baffled, and/or buried more than six feet deep. On top of that, today's music directors are always looking over their shoulders, fearful that the machine built to replace them is right at their heels. The stalking has already begun, and the full force of the invasion may not be at all that far in the future. Synthesized orchestra designs for musical theater performance can now automate entire scores for performance, and the "conductor" might be no more than a box with chase lights drawing beat patterns in preprogrammed tempos. (In these designs, if a single instrument does happen to be available to a certain performance outfit, then that instrument's computerized voice can be silenced in the playback. What a twist—real musicians replacing synthesizers!) Whether these trends represent advancements will be a frequent topic of this book.

With all those bumps in the road, why be a music director? There is little glamour in it, and seldom is there prestige, either, except for a very few. The potentially generous paycheck alone may be sufficient motivation to make such an unusual and risky career choice. Some music directors may be in it for the cachet of rubbing shoulders with the artistic elite; a few are more expert shoulder-rubbers than they are musicians, and they get by just fine. Overall, though, it is not a well-celebrated profession; the music is mostly, and rightly, taken for granted, except perhaps for its composition. Where is the music director's reward? Are the joys of collaborative effort enough?

For most music directors, the work itself is the payoff. The career choice springs from an irrepressible passion and devotion to expanding their artistic horizons and growing as musicians. With every new production, music directors upgrade their musical, organizational, and collaborative skills. Each new project represents a new musical adventure, and, not surprisingly, most musicians prefer working on new music to repeatedly performing pieces from the repertoire. Therefore, the very act of music direction is a highly desirable state of musical being. The unpredictable and sometimes impossible complications of the job balance out with a love of making music with other dedicated musicians and artists. Music directors embrace the energy and conviviality that come with stage performance. The impetus is their love of music and their love for creating and performing and sharing it with others. I hope that the following text will adequately convey my own joy in music and making music and my drive to continue making it, and making it better and better, for a lifetime. I hope to inspire others to do the same.

For those who have wished for this book's existence, I hope it will become a companion, the diary of a fellow tradesperson, a guidebook, an informative and amusing source of answers to FAQs. Music direction has always been unnoticed and underappreciated. If it has become undistinguished, I hope that with rigorous examination it may regain some of its distinction.

Just for fun, and as a first step toward defining a profession that evades definition, let's see what happens when a music director fails to do the job properly in performance. It's something like the scenario I imagined in the first paragraph, where the music was missing.

Just out of college, I worked in a summer stock theater as a music director. We were doing the Marvin Hamlisch–Carole Bayer Sager–Neil Simon musical *They're Playing Our Song*. The show is more like a play with a handful of songs here and there, and in the middle of the first act, there was a twenty-plus-minute break between numbers. A door led out of the pit through a short vestibule to an outdoor deck behind the stage. The rest of the six-piece band and I had it timed so we could adjourn to the patio during the extended break and be back in plenty of time to play the next song. That is, until one matinee, on a particularly lovely afternoon, when as we luxuriated in the fresh air, the actors skipped several pages of dialogue, about five minutes' worth. We, or more culpably, I, did not hear the cue line for the song until the actor delivering it repeated it several times very loudly, loudly enough for us to hear it on the veranda. We scrambled back into the pit, the drummer nearly knocking over her kit in the process. The actor, seeing us now in position, calmly walked downstage, leaned over, and dryly said to me, perched behind an upright piano on the conductor's podium, beads of sweat forming on my brow, "So nice of you to join us."

PART I

Music Direction

A Job Description

1

Music Direction Today and Yesterday

What a Music Director Does

The way in which music is directed and performed has a potent and immediate effect on how a listener perceives it. To demonstrate this, one need do no more than compare one's impression of the sound of an amateur high school musical to that of a professional, polished Broadway show. Nonetheless, even music directors themselves acknowledge that what constitutes music direction can be hard to pin down.

The basic process of putting music on stage goes as follows. A composer or composers, and perhaps other writers, create a song or songs or a piece of music, or an entire score, and that music becomes part of a production, that is, a public presentation. Implementing music into a production is the occupation of a music director. On its way to the stage, the music may stay pretty much as the writers wrote it, needing only to be rehearsed and performed as intended. Far more often, however, the music undergoes some manner of remodeling, and sometimes a complete metamorphosis. In certain instances, it is difficult to draw a line between the writers' work and the music director's.[1] Here is a proposed working definition: *a music director is responsible for all aspects of preparing and performing the music for a musical production.*

What a music director does, the job *description*, is a varying, fluid combination of creative, technical, and administrative functions. He or she is the nominal head of any music department that might exist within a production organization.[2] Among the duties are accompanying (usually, but not always, at the piano), conducting, rehearsing,

---

1. For an example, see Sheryl Kaskowitz, *God Bless America*, New York: Oxford University Press, 2013, pp. 21–32.

2. Again, in the current Broadway environment, the title "music supervisor" may be equivalent to the "music director" who is the subject of this book.

arranging, composing, giving notes, coordinating with technicians and designers, hiring and firing, and many others. I have also heard music direction referred to as a combination of an active performance role, like an actor, and a stage design element, such as costume or scenic design. This is a fitting summation. Only on rare occasions is music direction itself the focal point of a production, such as when an orchestra is part of the staging, or in a production in which musicians are characters or participate in the action (*Ain't Misbehavin'* is one Broadway hit that prominently featured its music director). The case studies to follow will demonstrate music directors' functions in different combinations and situations.

The *definition* of music direction depends what the music director is hired to do in each job, that is, on the needs of each production's unique musical element and on the expectations of the production team. Beyond being a skill set, music direction is the application of different skills to different problems under different circumstances at different times. There really is no one definition; the job is simply different each time. Music direction is the combination of musical jobs that coincide on any given production, artistic and administrative stewardship of the music, and leadership of the music team in rehearsal and through performance. The lack of a single decisive definition will not impede this study.

The possible duties also include instrumental and vocal conducting; explaining or demonstrating music to others; teaching singing; instruction in harmony and counterpoint; composing harmony and counterpoint; creating piano or other accompanimental arrangements; vocal and dance arrangements; orchestrations; arranging or composing incidental and transitional music; determining music cues; contracting and managing music staff and instrumentalists; overseeing the physical and technical aspects of the music; maintaining and revising performances over time; and acting as a supporter, mediator, counselor, psychotherapist, and executive decision maker when musical indecisions and disputes arise. (In professional stage productions, music direction is usually separated from at least some of the arranging work and credit.) To prepare for each job, music directors acquire a comprehensive understanding of every aspect of the musical score, and of the onstage content—including the story and the style. They must execute their work in an effective union with many other creative and production personnel.

It would be remarkable for any one person to be equally skilled in all disciplines; yet the best music directors working on the field today are more than competent, often expert, in many or all the areas previously listed, and more. Others may specialize in one or a few. In keeping with historical tradition (as described in this chapter and in Part 6), many music directors are not exclusively music directors by trade. They are also composers, arrangers, instrumentalists, singers, actors, and stage directors. Perhaps they began in one of those fields and moved to music direction. For some it is a temporary state, perhaps even a onetime digression, and for others, a career.

Music direction is often assumed to be equivalent to what is called "conducting" in "legitimate" music (also known as "art" or "serious" music), music composed for listening and not necessarily connected with other art forms. Indeed, conducting an orchestra (or leading a band), when there is one, is a large part of the job, but not the whole job. I bring this up to clarify the terminology, and because in symphonic conducting, the issue of "interpreting" a score is of primary interest. "Interpretation" in music direction is not the same. To begin with, music directors are much more likely to be working with music of living composers, who may be providing original music for the production, and may be present in rehearsal. A music director *adapts* a score to a production as much as interpreting in the classical sense. Legitimate music would never permit the sorts of cuts and additions, rearrangements, and other revisions that are standard music direction practices with popular stage scores.

In rehearsal and in performance, stage music directors do exhibit unique interpretive voices and, as in the classical world, there are debates over authenticity and definitiveness. Also as in classical music, the differences among interpretations may be very subtle even to a trained ear. Because of the inherent variety of music directors' work and the malleability of the material, their contribution may be more tangible and conspicuously "interpretive" than a symphonic conductor's. A music director "owns" the music direction in the same way that a stage director owns the direction of a stage show. There is a musical "vision" to a music director's work, made up of organizing principles and stylistic preferences and performance practices, as well as arrangements and addition composition. This is the "direction" part of music direction. A stage director may decide to set *Henry V* in World War II; likewise, a music director might choose to add a modern feel to a traditional song. The music director, however, makes choices primarily in service of the production's and the director's vision, while the director envisions and mounts the entire production. The director is the functional and artistic "superior," but that role does not negate the interpretive activity of the music director.

Music direction is an arts profession, a paid position (except, of course, in amateur productions, and even there, musicians are often compensated when others are not), and many musicians, including me, began their music direction work as a way of making a living in music. The relation between professionalism and the work itself is complex and constantly in play. Music directors walk the fine line between manager and artist. As managers they are expected by a consortium of individuals who are vested rather than salaried (the producers or other employers) to act like a manager and put in extra time, go above and beyond, without overtime pay; that's what managers do, and that's why their salaries are higher than non-managers'. Under union coverage, there is compensation available to music directors for only some of the various specialized tasks they perform: in particular, conducting, and any musical work that they commit to paper as writers, arrangers, transcribers, and copyists. There is none for the extra administrative hours. Most music directors work freelance, but there are some resident music director positions at theaters and academic institutions.

In music direction, perfection of musical execution is the norm. It is also the expectation, conscious or not, of colleagues and audiences alike. Imperfection results in visibility; people generally do not notice the workings of the music until they go wrong. Writers and directors espouse absolute musical proficiency because fluency ensures maximum believability and comprehension. The better a language is spoken, the more communicative and emotional power it has. If stage music is supposed to appear from nowhere, it certainly should not trip and fall on its way in. For example, any audible flub by the accompanist at a vocal recital (who is by my definition the music director of the recital) is sure to turn the listener's attention to the piano when it should be on the singer, and the pianist's error might well throw the singer off. Take another example: if an excessively loud music cue is suddenly heard in the midst of a quiet, tender dramatic moment of a play (or film), the intent of the drama will be compromised. When music does encroach on a dramatic or entertainment setting on a stage, it should sound as if it belonged there, it should sound musically right, and it should leave a good impression. It is the music director's obligation to properly assimilate the music, to oversee its quality control, and to connect the material with its listeners.

The idea of music direction, in the sense of someone shaping and leading a musical performance, goes back to the beginnings of music. Even the gamelans of ancient Indonesia had leaders who would signal to the group changes of meter and tempo, beginnings and endings, and transitions from piece to piece. Yet listening audiences are rarely aware of any musical leadership, and for good aesthetic reason. They need not be aware to fulfill their experience; indeed, the unnecessarily conspicuous presence of a musical leader will detract from it. An audience is better off, for the most part, taking in the whole of a stage work rather than being party to the techniques that go into realizing it. This is not to say that when an orchestra plays alone the audience members' eyes are not fixed on the conductor for the majority of the time; they probably are. When music is accompanying something happening on stage, however, all eyes turn to the stage, and so do everyone's ears, too (including the music director's).

The following accounts demonstrate the obscurity and inscrutability of music direction.

In 1964, the last Tony Award for Best Conductor and Musical Director was given to Shepard Coleman for his work on the original production of *Hello, Dolly!* on Broadway. Mr. Coleman died in 1998. His obituary in the *New York Times* cites his work as a "pit musician for Broadway musicals from 1946 to 1960" and states that his *Hello, Dolly!* Tony was for his "vocal arrangements" for the show.[3] In truth, Mr. Coleman had been let go early on in the production, and his position was taken over by dance arranger Peter

---

3. "Shepard Coleman, Musical Director," *New York Times*, 25 May 1998, http://www.nytimes.com/1998/05/25/arts/shepard-coleman-musical-director-for-theater-74.html/.

Howard three months after the show opened. Historian Steven Suskin puts forward the very plausible notion that in bestowing the award on Coleman, "the Tony voters simply voted for the biggest hit musical."[4] It is unknown what contributions Coleman made to the production, or why he was fired.

Other recipients of the Best Conductor and Musical Director award included such highly respected maestros as Maurice Abravanel and Thomas Schippers, who were far better known for their work conducting major symphony orchestras than for Broadway shows. After 1964, the Tony for Best Conductor and Musical Director was dropped from the awards roster.

In 1994, a group of Broadway and Off-Broadway music directors formed a new committee within their union local (New York's Local 802 of the American Federation of Musicians, or AFM) to define and address issues specific to their profession. (I was among the founding members.) Among our objectives was the reinstatement of the Tony Award for Music Directors, and we also sought the creation of a Tony for Best Orchestrations.

The impetus for forming the committee was the concern among the participating music directors that they were making significant creative contributions to shows (that is, arranging and composing) as well as providing the usual conducting and coaching and technical and administrative functions, but that their work was neither acknowledged nor understood by their employers and by their audiences. Furthermore, there were few guidelines for compensating the music directors for their work. Local 802 recognized "conductors" as members of their rank and file, but nowhere in the union bylaws did the term "music director" appear. In many cases the music that music directors had composed or arranged or otherwise contributed to on a production was not paid for at all. The reluctance of employers to begin budgeting for something they had never had to in the past was understandable.

The extent of the theater community's lack of comprehension of music direction became much more evident when the new union committee expressed its concerns to the Tony Awards Administration Committee. The American Theater Wing, which administers the Tony Awards, has progressed over time into an organization that purportedly dedicates all of its efforts to promotion of and education in the theater arts. Its Administration Committee determines eligibility for nominations in all awards categories, reviews the rules governing the awards, and appoints the Nominating Committee.[5] The Administration Committee consists of ten members designated by the Wing, ten by what is called the Broadway League (formerly the League of American Theatres and Producers, a more descriptive title), and one each by the Dramatists Guild

---

4. On the Record: *No Strings* and *Peter Howard's Broadway*, Playbill.com., 5 September 2004, http://www.playbill.com/news/article/on-the-record-no-strings-and-peter-howards-broadway/.

5. The Tony Awards®. Rules and Regulations of the American Theater Wing's Tony Awards®, New York: Jean Kroeper. 2011–2012, brochure, pp. 1–2.

of America, Actors' Equity Association, United Scenic Artists, and the Stage Directors and Choreographers Society (all unions or other organizations of theater professionals). There is no representative required from the field of music, nor is there a musicians' union delegate. Yet musicals, rather than straight plays, garner the vast majority of the income of today's Broadway theater industry, and the production numbers and excerpts from musicals are what the Tony Award television viewers tune in to watch.

The music directors' committee presented its case in person and with a meticulously detailed and well-produced demonstration video about music direction, showing the transformation of a raw piece of music into its final form. The Tony committee members were apparently unmoved by our impassioned plea. They still expressed bafflement at a music director's work, and were unable to remember the criteria by which they had judged the award up until 1964, even though some of them had been on the awards committee then. The effort was not entirely fruitless: thankfully, the Tony committee established the award for orchestration as a result.

We were an enthusiastic group, and one whose purpose was objectively well justified. Considering how the entertainment industry loves to bestow accolades, extolling its own excellence as a proven marketing tool, it is surprising that the Tony committee did not accede to a music direction award.[6] There is a Tony Award now for Sound Design. Perhaps the explanation for the omission is in the invisibility of music direction. A respected stage manager friend once told me that he believed neither music directors nor stage managers should receive front-page billing in theater programs, as they were the deliberately nameless pilots of the ship, the captains sequestered on the bridge, the drivers of the bus whom no one should disturb while operating the vehicle. Our expertise was presumptive, and our contribution most valuable when completely unseen. Of course, in some ways he was right, but it seemed only natural for music directors to seek the same sort of recognition for their work afforded to nearly all of their colleagues.

Our committee sought recognition of and payment for our work mostly because we saw arranging and composing music as outside of the traditional job duties, which we were already performing very conscientiously. This was a legitimate concern. Writers of successful show music garner very robust royalties, while music directors are for the most part salaried. Historically, music directors had already been working without the standards and protections given to stage directors, technicians, and managers by their guilds and unions. When the position started to regularly involve new responsibilities, it became critical that their work be acknowledged in a more substantive way, and immediately, to avoid precedents of nonpayment. There was a brief attempt by the music directors' committee to ally itself with the stage directors' society (SDC, formerly SSDC, the Society of Stage Directors and Choreographers), but eventually the committee gave up that effort as well.

---

6. In 2013, the Society of London Theatre, the group that gives out Olivier Awards, London's equivalent of the Tonys, pledged to honor music directors, supervisors, orchestrators, and composers of incidental music, beginning in 2014.

Instead, music directors looked to their own individual contract negotiations, with varying degrees of alacrity and of success, to ensure that the original creative work they did was fairly compensated.[7]

Historical Survey of Music Direction

The existence of musical leaders, as noted, traces back to the origins of performance ensembles. A music director exercising the sorts of skills previously described emerges with the advent of musical-dramatic performance. Greek choruses, whose members also danced, were accompanied by instruments; it's quite likely that the *choregos,* or chorus master (although the term could also refer to a play's sponsor), acted as music director, organizing, programming, and leading the music and dancing at the performance. Later, in the Middle Ages and Renaissance, itinerant minstrel groups performed music in a predetermined manner, like a modern touring production. A music director organized, programmed, and led their musical performance.

Many a major composer of the 15th through 20th centuries served as music director of a church or royal court (*Kapellmeister* or *maestro di camera,* for instance), or later to a symphony orchestra. To this day many music directors find gainful employment in the church. Other music directors for courts or churches may not be best remembered for their compositions, yet were required to be occasional composers. There were always professional opportunities for those willing to serve the upper and ruling classes in several musical capacities: conducting, arranging, composing, and otherwise presenting the music for any or all purposes dictated by their employers. There was music for entertainment, music for the constant variety of religious services, music for rich amateurs to play on their given instruments at their given levels of ability, music for the glorification of an individual or a holy figure, music for holidays, and music of all shapes and sizes. One reason Mozart's life was so brief and tragic was his difficulty holding down a job as a music director. Mozart and other masters often depended on the income derived from their positions as music directors. And they were kept very, very busy at work. It is no wonder that as composers they were so prolific; they had to produce a huge volume of material to satisfy their patrons and hold onto their jobs. This demand did not make them any less meticulous, as shown in J. S. Bach's manuscript page in Figure 1.1.

Figure 1.1 is the full score; Bach also copied all the individual orchestra parts and, unfathomably, was in the habit of writing the clef and key signature on every staff of every part, using no shortcuts or shorthands. There might also have been a staff of composers, arrangers, copyists, and performers working under him or with him, not unlike a modern music department in a large production company or a Broadway show.

---

7. In late 2013 Local 802 began discussing the possibility of paying pension and health contributions on Broadway music supervision fees.

FIGURE 1.1 "J. S. Bach, manuscript, soprano aria from Cantata BWV 105. (The Bach example is from Wikipedia Commons, "BWV105-wie-zittern" by Johann Sebastian Bach, Bach Digital Archive, Leipzig, Germany. Licensed under Public Domain via Wikimedia Commons, http://commons-wikimedia.org/wiki/File:BWV105-wie-zittern.jpg.)

The greatest of these music directors rose to near "star" status. Handel was a particular favorite of the general public, Beethoven of the aristocracy, the latter despite a well-documented abrasive personality, the former sporting the utmost charm and social grace. Most music directors operate today, mostly contentedly, in relative anonymity. They are active members of the musical and theatrical communities, but are largely unknown outside those circles. There are the occasional "stars," but they are rare, and even the best-known music directors are far from being household names like the performers they accompany or the productions they work on.

As music intended for artful entertainment took an increasingly firm hold in the Western cultural musical consciousness, beginning late in the 18th century, composers became more independent and more often self-employed, and engaged music directors as performers, leaders, and organizers of their musical presentations. The separation of composer and performer grew wider, though it has never become complete. Although many composers continued as performing musicians, and though many conductors, pianists, and instrumentalists continued to write their own music, a greater number specialized in either writing or performing.

In the mid-1900s the variety of types and styles of stage music exploded, and with it the field of music direction. Popular music and musical theater burgeoned into profitable industries. Producers and presenters bet their bankrolls on their shows, and impresarios found a new home in show business. Audiences flocked to theaters and auditoriums, and countless performers, technicians, and creative specialists found work there, including musicians. An expert who could handle large amounts of music in different styles with relative facility, and with the intelligence or intuition to make the music work effectively in many situations, was a huge commodity. Specializations abounded, with conductors, pianists, arrangers, orchestrators, copyists, and others steadily employed and, around 1900, unionized. Singing and dancing on stage were nothing new; music direction was nothing new. Now, as in history, music directors were the generalists, the "multitaskers." What was new in the modern age were the stylistic scope of music that music directors worked on and the conditions under which they were employed.

In the world of contemporary commercial music, which encompasses music for the stage, the composer is seldom also the music director. Some pop singers and singer-songwriters (James Taylor, Bette Midler, and Miley Cyrus, to name just a few) employ music directors, especially when the arrangements are specific and the accompaniment needs to be well controlled in a live setting. Usually these music directors are members of the onstage band—the drummer, perhaps, or bassist, guitarist, or keyboard player; it really doesn't matter—and are responsible mostly for distributing and updating set lists, making sure everyone is on stage at the right time, starting and stopping the songs in a concert, perhaps counting off the tempos, and helping to maintain the quality of performance over time.

The leading stage music directors of the past gained their reputations through proven virtuosity (often at a young age) on one or more instruments or a flair for composition and improvisation, or both. Improvisation, which is in effect spontaneous composition, was a requirement simply because of the sheer volume and immediacy of music to be composed. If a composer's deadline could not be met or the composer was not on site, the music director could always fake something or elaborate on existing music. This is still the practice today.

But prodigal talent or impeccable musicianship is not necessarily requisite to working as a music director in today's environment. Some music directors have achieved success just because of their understanding of a particular musical style, their singular skill at a particular instrument, some nonmusical ability such as outstanding organizational acumen, an unbreakable connection to a star performer, or perhaps just being in the right place at the right time. If a certain music director's skills are precisely in line with the needs of a particular production, then he or she need not be multitalented. Some music directors have a long-term association with a certain writer or director or a perceived sensitivity to a certain type of material.

Though some may lack the virtuosity of music directors of earlier eras, today's music directors are direct occupational descendants of their musical ancestors. Their methods have evolved a great deal (most conductors no longer beat the tempos on the floor with a large stick, as was practiced in 18th-century conducting, and seldom do they write their music by hand in ink anymore), but there are still employment opportunities anytime someone needs music for the dancing and singing, or whenever someone is putting on a show.

Technology and the Shrinking Orchestra

The following is a "help wanted" ad posted on an online theater website in 2011:

> [Unnamed theater] requires a musical director/arranger to m.d. and create custom tracks for a summer season of 3 cabaret musical revues with four-member SATB cast. The shows are a Sinatra tribute, an Elvis tribute and a celebration of 'One Hit Wonders'. The candidate will rehearse the cast through the opening of the final of the three shows [sic]. Theater provides a Yamaha Motif XS for rehearsals and building tracks—experience with that line or similar is a plus. Duties include creating vocal arrangements, charting certain songs by ear, and the creation of MP3 accompaniment tracks with complex rhythm/orchestration ranging from american [sic] standard to pop. The right candidate will have the computer software technology (Logic, Cubase, ProTools, or a similar program) to build quality MIDI tracks before rehearsals begin and to modify those tracks during rehearsals as needed.[8]

---

8. Retrieved from http://www.theproducersperspective.com/my_weblog/2011/02/musical-directorarranger-new-huntington-theater.html.

For music directors, there is gainful employment in technologically oriented positions, but the music direction position advertised here largely ends on opening night, when the machines take over. In many fields, computers are now performing many functions formerly done by humans, and music is not exempt. The reaction of audiences watching shows with mechanized accompaniment runs the gamut from ignorance to outrage. In music, as in other areas, the information age has brought with it an unfortunate tendency toward superficiality, enough so that listeners sometimes can no longer discern live music from its electronic emulation, or make no such value judgment. This is not to say that electronically produced music is all bad or entirely unacceptable in live stage productions. Rather, it can be very useful, from allowing low-budget productions to sound more grand to creating musical and sound effects that would be otherwise unperformable. (Even Respighi's *Pines of Rome* is rented to orchestras with an audiotape of nightingale song to be played during the last segment.)

Like it or not, permanent groundwork for further dilution of realistic sound may already have been laid. Music directors are among those in the industry who will decide whether replacing live music with electronically simulated sound is a threat to the long-term health of music, or a new and useful technology. If audiences can no longer tell the difference between the real thing and a fake, or if they believe a recording to be a live band, should it matter to those who produce the music?

Even putting aside the argument that electronics replace human jobs, my answer is almost always a resounding yes. Audience members who do know the difference find the replacement unacceptable. Professional musicians, and all performers, avow to satisfy the keenest listener in the audience, not the one who will love the show regardless of its production values. This pledge is even more sacrosanct when considering the high cost of tickets. On the other hand, all professional musicians must appreciate the importance of thoughtful budgeting. Unfortunately, the most popular means of cutting budgets is by reducing orchestra (and cast) sizes and replacing real instruments with synthesizers. The practice continues on Broadway despite its increasing profits. This can be a disheartening state of affairs for music directors doing their best to serve the music, and for those who aspire to conduct a full orchestra.

Compounding their gradual diminution, orchestras are being hidden away under stages, behind set pieces, and in offstage rooms. Traditionally, an orchestra would occupy an orchestra "pit" in front and below the level of the stage. Pits are a holdover from opera (venues for musicals and concerts are often converted opera houses, or modeled after opera houses) that help balance orchestra and singer, both without amplification (pits, of course, preceded microphones). Now many orchestras are being evicted from their dens and relocated, reducing their visibility and live audibility. Many are isolated in separate, acoustically treated compartments, similar to a recording studio.

The podium of this book's subtitle may in the future be a chair in front of a computer screen and an electronic keyboard in a dressing room backstage. For the 2013 Tony Awards show, held at Radio City, the orchestra was piped in from a recording studio several blocks away, despite the Hall's spacious, mobile pit, and a generous but ironic nod to live orchestras from Harold Prince in his acceptance speech for a lifetime achievement award. Music directors continue to pursue the best possible performance and sound, and can either work within the given constraints, or protest them. It seems, however, that these technologies are here to stay, so it is probably wise to work with them, one would hope not exclusively, but always creatively.

Music directors can, if they like, "sequence" a production's accompaniment, that is, record it on a hard drive as digital data, and replay it with remarkable flexibility in factors like key, tempo, and instrumentation. The reliability and realistic sound of such an accompanimental approach, however, are different matters. Although one or two computers can (arguably) do the work of a full orchestra, and the sound of some digital samples is now astonishingly real, in performance these data streams still run with varying degrees of dependability and authenticity. They are contingent on electric current and complex connectivity as well as human skill, and are prone to breakdown. The best electronic music designs now operate more reliably, but when they do fail, the effects of their failure can be catastrophic—if the accompaniment ceases to play, the curtain will have to come down. With intelligent and limited usage, digital emulation and synthesis are acceptable, but as proxies for large musical textures, they range from problematic to mildly disappointing to abrasive. Most importantly, they defeat the purpose of live accompaniment; the point of onstage entertainment is that human beings are the entertainers.

Music directors (and producers) should keep in mind that synthesized music incurs costs of its own, some of which might be hard to foresee (computer crashes, power outages). Synthesizer programming itself, the plentitude of gear and the maintenance thereof, and the reconciliation of electronic and acoustic sound sources are all expensive undertakings. Keyboard players whose synthesized and sampled sounds unseat musicians also receive a significant premium on their salaries, a concession by producers to the union, intended to regularize the total amount of money passing through the union payroll and offset the unemployment of live players. One might think the expense would be a deterrent to replacing musicians, but clearly it is not. Shows with sufficient technical layouts have gone so far as to integrate the musical synthesizer programming into the larger technical plot, using click tracks and MIDI channels to synchronize lighting, sound, and special effects, as well as music.

The trend toward synthesis is empowered by the predominance of amplified sound design, which has reached a point in full-blown commercial stage shows where now virtually no acoustic sound at all reaches the listener. What audiences now mostly hear comes from microphones and direct lines, processed and sent through speakers placed strategically through the performance space. The finished musical product, that is, what the audience hears, may not at all resemble the music at its source. Inexplicably, even some pit or onstage orchestras that would be acoustically vivid without amplification now reach the audience only through a sound system.

The dispute over shrinking orchestras and digital replacement has become increasingly controversial and antagonistic in recent years, coinciding with the improvements in synthesizer technology. For decades, the musicians' union had enforced minimum orchestra sizes in most Broadway theaters, based on the seating capacity of each. The minimums ostensibly kept Broadway orchestras large and lusty, and guaranteed employment for a steady pool of theater musicians. The minimums ranged from five musicians to twenty-five or more in theaters seating from about seven hundred to two thousand; the smallest houses had no minimum. If the orchestra required for a production happened to be smaller than the theater's minimum, the producers would engage "walkers" to fill the remaining spots. These were union members who were paid to attend every performance as if performing, but did not perform. (Some conductors, including me, tried to find some value in employing walkers by using them as orchestra understudies, but more commonly they could be found watching sports on television or playing cards in a secluded room of the theater.) These sorts of policies held sway in other performing venues throughout the country as well, and some still do.

Broadway producers began challenging the minimums in the 1980s, and rightly so, as the system had become manifestly dysfunctional, and a source of unnecessary expenditures. The producers' rationale, however, was not based on correcting the flawed system from an artistic standpoint; rather, it was an undisguised attempt to reduce personnel and increase profits. The effort has since then persevered, with considerable resistance from the union and its membership. In 1998 the union allowed producers some relief, by way of an utterly confounded system of disproportionate personnel reductions, by adding the aforementioned premiums paid to synthesizer players, and by establishing an untrustworthy case-by-case examination body called the Special Situations Committee. The escalation reached a climax in March 2003, when Broadway musicians went out on strike, and were supported by Actor's Equity (the actors' union), shutting down Broadway for two weeks during the height of the pre-Tony theater season, as shown in Figure 1.2. In true muscle-flexing New York fashion, the mayor and city government eventually stepped in and forced an agreement.

The current contract leaves a system of reduced minimums in place until 2016. The compromise is disappointing for both sides, especially for the musicians (and the music), and the true issues have never been properly understood by anyone except those at the higher levels of production. The media has done little to clarify the underlying conflict, instead reducing the problem to a simple disagreement over minimums or no minimums. Far more thoughtful solutions are called for, and are possible, but at the time of the strike the atmosphere was so hostile and the pressure to reconcile so intense that they were politically infeasible. The idea behind the Special Situations Committee—good-faith meetings of producers and artists to reach informed agreements on orchestra sizes—was a sensible one. Nonetheless, producers, with their managerial acumen, have since then kept the upper hand.[9]

---

9. In the case of *Priscilla, Queen of the Desert*, the presentation to the committee to compare real and synthesized violins with prerecorded ones was so slanted by the sound design and threadbare live orchestral forces that the acoustic sound never had a chance. The show closed before the lengthy appeal process, endlessly postponed by the producers, was ever completed.

FIGURE 1.2 Broadway musicians on the picket lines in 2003. (*Credits:* A: Photo courtesy of AFM Local 802; B: Photo by Michael Minn/michaelminn.net/newyork.)

If orchestral sound continues to give in to more rhythmically based music, the controversy may die down simply because of the shift in the language. In popular music, acoustic and electronic music have been more cooperative. But for musical works whose writers intended them to have full-sized, living orchestras, is not a high-priced ticket worth the human-based superiority that the art form demands?

An audience member deserves to hear the energy of a living horn player blowing into a metal mouthpiece or bamboo reed, deserves to hear the sound of the player's spit, and even deserves the musician's mistakes, which confirm the sound's reality, its personality, and its immediacy. Surely the few dollars that might be saved with reduced and synthesized orchestras cannot be worth the loss in humanity. When synthesis is called for, so be it, but humanity is the essence of live stage performance. Audiences pay often exorbitant prices for Broadway tickets so that they can experience this essence.

On stage, casts have shrunk as well, but obviously an actor or singer's stage performance cannot be synthesized (though it can be permanently captured, by recording it). Larger vocal arrangements may suffer from reduced casting, but it is usually more problematic for stage directors than for music directors. The reality is that music directors simply don't conduct big orchestras as often anymore, as most want to. Striking keys and pushing buttons have to some extent taken over wielding a baton. The charm and allure of the large orchestra and chorus will never fade, but meanwhile, and especially while working their way up the ladder, music directors might have to be content leading smaller ensembles.

Looking to the Future

In 2011, nearly fifty years after Shepard Coleman's brief moment of Tony glory, there were four Tony nominees for best orchestrations: Doug Besterman for a revival of *How to Succeed in Business without Really Trying*, Larry Hochman for the critically acclaimed *The Scottsboro Boys*, Marc Shaiman and Larry Blank for the ill-fated *Catch Me If You Can*, and the eventual winners, Larry Hochman and Stephen Oremus for *The Book of Mormon*. The first three were fine orchestrations, if unadventurous; one (*How to Succeed*) was a fourteen-piece reimagining (with no strings) of what had been a fuller orchestral grouping (twenty-two in the 1996 Broadway revival and twenty-seven in the original Broadway production). In what may be seen as a sign of the times, what distinguished the orchestration of *The Book of Mormon*, other than its victory, was that it was mostly an electronic facsimile of an orchestra and an orchestration. There were four acoustic instrumentalists (trumpet, trombone, a violin-viola double, and multi-reeds) and a rhythm section (guitar, bass, and drums) complementing two elaborate keyboard synthesizer parts. The synthesizers emulated (with varying verisimilitude) a host of orchestral and other instruments, everything from African drums to concert bass drum rolls and tympani crescendos to alto flute and baritone sax. Whereas the faux instrumentation is clever at times, the score is less orchestrated than it is synthesized. As in 1964, when voting on the season's best orchestration, the Tony voters again seemed merely to have filled out the ticket of their favorite musical (*The Book of Mormon* took home a total of nine Tonys, including Best Musical). Furthermore, the recording of *Mormon* that Tony voters heard, the original cast recording, complements the orchestra with real instrumentalists, an inaccurate representation of what is played and heard in the theater.

One might well contend that a musical aspiring to such a large and varied orchestral sound should achieve that sound with a real orchestra, rather than with two keyboards and a few real orchestral instruments as fill-ins, especially on a hit show of this magnitude. In these situations music directors can and should invoke their influence and insist on those real strings, more brass and woodwinds, and real tympani and other percussion. Luckily for *The Book of Mormon*, its synthetic onstage reality takes a cartoonish view of the world, and permits this synthetic musical approach. No listener really seems to mind.

If a production really cannot afford or has no access to large ensembles, the music director has the choice of acceding either to reduced orchestrations or to synthesized or prerecorded music. Often the former is the better choice; for instance, a well-played two-piano version of a Broadway score, perhaps with bass and drums, can be far more exciting and responsive in performance than a CD playback or a second-rate digital sample. Or if a college has only half the orchestra needed, but the players they do have are very good, there may be a way to feature those instruments in a cleverly reduced orchestration that does not sacrifice the composer's intention, and fills in the rest on piano or a keyboard. For more contemporary, rhythmically oriented music, greater use of electronic synthesis is probably a more suitable option.

Let's say that a score for a musical requires an expressive bowed string sound (something a synthesizer does reasonably well) for only one of its sixteen musical numbers, and uses strings only minimally elsewhere. In that case, hiring a string section might be fiscally unwise and musically unnecessary. Certain instruments and certain qualities of instruments, however, are more difficult to duplicate than others. Use of a pizzicato (plucked) string sample is not as distasteful as keyboard player struggling to play a sweeping chromatic run of twenty-four violins. Strings may seem an overused example, but string sections have been among the first targeted by producers for elimination, or at least drastic reduction. The orchestra of the Broadway version of the string-heavy movie musical *Mary Poppins* had one lone cello player, and the 2011 musical *Priscilla, Queen of the Desert* used a live orchestra of only nine players to represent a large recording studio orchestra, heavily augmented as it was by string samples and prerecorded tracks, with no real string players at all. These are artistic choices that may be without merit, yet music directors, and all musicians, often have little recourse but to go along.

On the other hand, in a large-budget show with music that calls for a large orchestration, it is difficult to defend the use of a reduced or artificial orchestra, unless as part of the director's vision (such as the recent Sondheim revivals in which the actors played the instruments themselves, though one might suspect that this artistic conceit began as an avaricious twinkle in a line producer's eye). A music director, however, cannot enter into a contractual agreement and then complain because he or she does not like the terms. Music directors who do not want to work with a synthesized orchestra should not accept a job that entails leading one. They must make the best of every work situation because they are involved in a collaborative, commercial enterprise. Cooperation is always within reach as long as neither Scrooge-like penny pinching nor unbridled musical zeal rules the day.

Problems caused by sound amplification are particularly difficult for today's music directors to solve. When on the modern-day podium, they do not necessarily hear what the audience hears, especially if the podium is not downstage center, which increasingly it is not. Only when music directors observe a performance as audience members can they find out if the music sounds as they intend, and often they cannot leave the podium, at least until after a show opens and is running. For this reason many Broadway music directors stipulate in their contracts a salaried viewing of one performance per week. Somehow music directors must be determined and vigilant in their efforts not to sacrifice the music to misrepresentation through amplification.

There are clearly issues yet to be resolved in modern Broadway sound design, ostensibly the paradigm for all theatrical sound design. Critics and audiences alike openly express their inability to hear properly at many musicals, or complain that the sound is too loud (usually), or too soft (rarely), or that the words are unintelligible. Music directors can help, and should help, for the sake of the music, and for the long-term aesthetic well-being of the art form.

The purported philosophy of Broadway sound design is absolute clarity of the sung and spoken word, which is indeed the most important facet of the work. Quite often, however, in attempting to achieve this goal, it is defeated. Because the sound operator of a Broadway show mostly "rides the faders" on the vocals, that is, brings up and down different singers' levels, the orchestra is left out of the mix, so to speak, and the entire balance is left to up one individual. It is hard to hear the orchestra at all in many Broadway shows, not to mention the detail within them. In others, the entire mix is simply too loud. Singers rely on their microphones and their lyrics are therefore not distinct. Furthermore, the musical attributes that composers, music directors, and orchestrators prize as the audible substance of their work are often inaudible, or amplified indelicately.

There are, of course, exceptions, and some sound designers are entirely devoted to faithful reproduction of acoustic sound. A shining example is the recent Broadway production of *The Bridges of Madison County*. Its masterly score was orchestrated by composer Jason Robert Brown for eleven pieces. The pit was wide open, and the singers were strong. Sound designer Jon Weston smartly let the music play and sing itself, giving the sound just enough of a boost to make it clearly and evenly audible throughout the theater.

Historical perspective helps clarify the issues. The whole notion of sound design for a show is relatively new, and there are few remaining vestiges of the original approach to stage music. Nonetheless, the music of past eras and newly written music rooted in the music of past eras receive many modern performances. The musicals of Rodgers and Hammerstein, Lerner and Loewe, and Cole Porter are performed in some of the same Broadway theaters audiences visit today, but without modern sound designs. When that music was composed, people still sang on stage augmented at most by foot microphones placed far downstage along the floor, and maybe an auxiliary vocal microphone overhead. Amplified sound for the stage became more widely accepted when popular music and recorded music gained prevalence in post–World War II culture; a singer's voice needed reinforcement to be heard over the accompanying electric instruments, brass, and drums. As rock and pop music took to the theatrical stage and pit, greater reliance on amplification came with it. To restore balance *within* a pit orchestra, sound designers had to put acoustic (non-electric) instruments through microphones to bring them up to the level of the amplified instruments. Consequently, the singers on stage could not be heard over the amplified orchestra. Before long everything was going through microphones, amplifiers, and banks of processors, each altering the essence of the sound. The modern-day sound design had been born, and grew up fast, big, and strong.

Complicating matters further in the present day is that there are few remaining Mermans or Streisands with self-amplifying voices (Kristen Chenoweth, Brian Stokes Mitchell, and some others still possess them), and opera singers less frequently cross over to popular stage performance, as they do in classic musicals. A pop singer with a natural voice that can be properly heard only through a microphone now has as much of a chance at success on the musical stage as a singer with powerful pipes and a master's degree in voice. The understanding that all voices will be amplified on stage makes these disciplines more acceptable to undervalue. (Musical-theater-singing training programs may also be deemphasizing the importance of stage projection and enunciation.) Just as importantly, modern stage production rejects old practices of musical staging that allowed voices to be better heard when unamplified, in particular, moving downstage and turning toward the audience when singing, in favor of dramatic realism (not to mention singing while swinging from a rope or a vine or when perched on a catwalk high above the stage).

It has become virtually impossible to eliminate amplification; it is too central to modern music and stage performance, and audience members' ears have been trained to expect it. Rather, the solution lies in using it sensibly. Instead of amplifying all elements of the music, just because that is the current convention, why not amplify for balance and audibility, as the philosophy of good audio design states? It is possible to work from the premise of amplifying only that which needs amplification, and then balancing other elements accordingly. The multi-speaker, souped-up, tricked-out, up-to-date systems that sound shops spend countless dollars on are only necessary for a production whose size and style call for that sort of design. A singer who needs a close microphone to be heard should still sing dynamically, and can be reinforced just enough to be heard over the accompaniment. If an accompaniment is orchestral, the music director should balance the orchestra naturally, then reinforce individual players or sections as needed: this strategy will reveal the features of the orchestration while keeping the orchestra at a manageable volume level. Nightclubs often get a beautiful sound from a good piano with some gentle reinforcement through the house speakers, a pickup on a bass or guitar, and a very high-quality vocal microphone. The sound is strong, vivid, and resonant, an excellent model for Broadway, which is often tinny and muddled.

When music directors work with repertory and revival musicals and traditional stage music, they should consider that modern audiences have become less tolerant of the sound of the past, the rougher, grainier, truer sound of minimally processed music. Today's listeners respond more readily to the slick, shiny sound quality they have become accustomed to over two decades of digital playback. Modern music directors can implement ideas that update the sound of older music and thereby enhance the audience's enjoyment of it, while assuring authentic interpretation (assuming it is desired) and retaining the performance practices that characterize the style. Again, they require the sound department's cooperation to attain this ideal.

Today's music directors are just beginning to develop strategies through which to effect a positive outcome on the way the music they produce is generated and amplified. Foremost in the effort are, first, their knowledge of technology and sound design, so that they are justified in adding their voices to the discussion of instrumental emulation and sound reinforcement with producers and designers, and, second, constant and thorough communication with and monitoring of the synthesizer and the sound design, and their personnel, through all phases of preproduction and production, so that the designs are properly and musically executed. Under ideal circumstances, music directors and informed producers together will decide to employ the number and type (real or imitation) of musicians that are right for the production, good for the music, and in line with the available talent. They will choose their sound team carefully and with the intent of the score in mind: a designer's or operator's proficiency in one style does not guarantee excellence in another. If as music director you want your opinion to count, and if you are in a situation in which sharing your musical desires and philosophies with those in charge is acceptable (without jeopardizing your job), you should express yourself early on, while the production is still taking shape. You can help formulate strategies that give producers what they need (savings and quality), and still be faithful to the music. Artistic quality will generate financial success, and good producers know it.

The theater-going and music-listening public will require re-education if the voice of aesthetic reason is to be heard over the screaming sound systems. Only by regularly experiencing the unfiltered glories of an appropriately sized and properly amplified (or unamplified) orchestra and cast will audiences retune their attention and regain their appreciation. Ticket buying is the most powerful tool available to music's defenders, but how can musicians hope to influence the busloads who are shuttled into Times Square if their viewing choices are predetermined by a media blitz or a travel agency? Critics regularly express their affection for live sound, when it happens. The 2008 revival of *South Pacific* at Lincoln Center's Vivian Beaumont Theater was highly acclaimed for, among other things, its large thirty-piece orchestra, barely needing or using amplification in the open pit of the three-quarter-style house (where the audience surrounds the stage on three sides), as seen in Figure 1.3. The orchestra sounded lush, beautiful, and natural, and the music director on the podium expertly led a tasteful, convincing, and moving production.

FIGURE 1.3 The stage retracts to reveal the orchestra for *South Pacific* at the Vivian Beaumont Theater, 2008. (*Credit: New York Times*/Sara Krulwich/Redux.)

The following is the opening paragraph of Christopher Isherwood's New York Times review of the 2013 Broadway revue *After Midnight*:

> The band takes the last bow in *After Midnight*, the sparkling new jazz revue that opened at the Brooks Atkinson Theater on Sunday night. This may be unusual for Broadway, where the players are normally in the pit—and the music often sounds as if it could have been piped in from Hong Kong—but it's entirely as it should be.[10]

Music directors in future working environments must continue to approach all their work with respect and integrity, toward the music, their collaborators, and their employers. Regardless of whether something is right or wrong with a show or a production, in spite of limitations put upon them, or with freedoms given them, music directors must do what is appropriate to do under any set of circumstances to make the music fit into a production correctly and sound the best it can. It is unlikely that a music director can save a show from disaster; what leads to the demise of most stage failures is not their music, as long as it is well performed, but something amiss on stage. Unimaginative or uninteresting stories don't work, nor do interesting stores told in unimaginative or

---

10. Christopher Isherwood, "Review: After Midnight on Broadway," *New York Times*, 4 November 2013, http://www.nytimes.com/2013/11/04/theater/reviews/after-midnight-on-broadway-fetes-the-heyday-of-an-era.html?_r=0/.

uninteresting ways, nor concepts that do not warrant musicalizing. (In spite of the craft that went into making them, *Footloose,* the musical; *The Wedding Singer,* the musical; and dozens of others were simply misconceived. Inversely, there was no point in making *A Chorus Line,* the movie.)

To me what is most fascinating about integrating music and theater is exploring the possibilities of the integration. Familiar combinations done with excellence and original thinking are commendable, too, and always welcome, but discovering new, unexpected, striking fusions of music, theater, dance, and all elements of live performance is more enriching still. My desire for innovative works of substance and my pioneer spirit for the future of musical theater may be more at home in the worlds of serious music and the noncommercial stage, but without a serious approach and attitude toward commercial music for the commercial stage, the moneymaking machine would soon grind to a halt with creative inertia. Audiences have seen how marvelous the possibilities of combining art forms can be, in stage productions as varied as Cirque du Soleil's magnificent *O,* John Adams and Alice Goodman's minimalist opera *Nixon in China,* well-crafted book musicals like *The Light in the Piazza, Spring Awakening,* or *Matilda,* in stage extravaganzas at Coachella or Madison Square Garden, or concerts by Justin Timberlake, P!nk, Madonna, or Madonna's 2010s incarnation, Lady Gaga. They have experienced the (all too infrequent) moments when great composers or inventive popular musicians have revitalized a tired musical vocabulary. This is the true excitement of uniting music with words and action on a living stage. May it flourish in a society that in the future may care less and less about art and more and more about its own continued existence.

2

Musical Stage Production

There are three essential elements of all theatrical and popular music, indeed, of all music: creation, execution, and reaction. Writers create, performers execute, and audiences react. Production connects a creative product with an audience by organizing, managing, staffing, casting, and directing it. A production defines a show, locates it, associates it with certain people for a certain period of time; it brings it to life. It takes the written words, if you will, off the page and onto the stage. To talk about stage shows as written works, as scores or scripts on a library shelf, denies them most of their existence. Instead, one must talk about shows in *production* to understand them and their operation, and to specify a music director's part in them. It is in production that the music director makes his or her entrance, usually in a very early phase.

Songs, Musicals, and Opera

All musical productions begin with musical material, or the intent to create it as part of the process. When text and music are combined in an organized fashion, they form what is called "song." Song is the basic stuff of stage music. Yes, there is other music onstage, such as dance music, instrumental music, and underscoring (music that, as in a film, plays under dialogue or action), but as often as not they are derived from a correlative melody, feel, or theme. This is the material that music directors work with.

In song, melody rules. Words are set to music and become melody, and that melody is usually accompanied. Sometimes melodic content is deliberately vague, and what a performer "sings" lies somewhere between song and speech. Examples include recitative (a form of vocal writing intended to mimic dramatic speech in song), *Sprechstimme* (literally, speech song: a type of vocal performance between speech and song), and rap. The accompaniments to stage melodies tend to be far more elaborate than the melodies they join with, and they are created to give context and additional meaning to the melody and text. The relationship between words and music is essential to a stage score, and to the music director. As early as ancient folk song, later in the *lieder* (songs in the German vernacular) of classical composers, and still in today's popular song, the connection of text and music has been of prime concern to writers, performers, and audiences in equal measure.

Songs tell stories, short and long. They divulge character, reveal feelings, or otherwise bring ideas to life in a manageable and attractive way. Music and text enrich each other, and writers craft each to suit the other. For example, music is assembled into phrases, sections, and standard forms that delineate textual syntax and meaning, and words are repeated over music as they would never be in conversation. Song forms have always been subject to expansion and experimentation, in art music, popular music, and stage music alike.

A successful marriage of music and lyrics is almost universally understood and embraced. Songs become part of the collective culture, and are cherished for their recollective or sentimental value as well as musically appreciated. As Dick Clark famously phrased it, "Popular music is the soundtrack of our individual lives."[1] Individual songs can be tiny pieces of theater, even when simplistic:

> Welcome to the jungle
> It gets worse here everyday
> Ya learn ta live like an animal
> In the jungle where we play[2]

They can be innocent statements of affection:

> The kiss my lover brings
> She brings to me
> And I love her[3]

Or they can be poetic balladeering, like Paul Simon's "Boxer," who

> . . . carries the reminders
> Of ev'ry glove that laid him down
> And cut him till he cried out. . . . [4]

None of these highly effective lyrics to popular songs are all that remarkable on paper: the first is raw and overstated, the second naïve and vernacular, the last rambling

---

1. Michael Arkush, "Q & A With Dick Clark," *Los Angeles Times*, 2 July 1994, http://articles.latimes.com/1994-02-07/entertainment/ca-20043_1_dick.clark/.
2. Guns 'N' Roses, "Welcome to the Jungle," *Appetite for Destruction*, Geffen, 1987.
3. John Lennon and Paul McCartney, "And I Love Her," *A Hard Day's Night*, Parlophone, 1964.
4. Paul Simon, "The Boxer," *Bridge over Troubled Water*, Columbia, 1969.

and perhaps a bit inflated. But when set to music they take on new qualities, forming their own rationales and establishing memorable, discrete worlds that a listener easily enters into and identifies with. "Welcome to the Jungle" brings out a crowd's animalistic side; The Beatles made their fans swoon with their charismatic delivery of "And I Love Her," and Paul Simon's "The Boxer" is sheer folk poetry that touches its listeners even after decades and countless hearings. In the words of aesthetic philosopher Suzanne Langer, ". . . art penetrates deep into personal life because in giving form to the world, it articulates human nature: energy, passion, and mortality."[5] Nowhere is this philosophy more evident than the primitive impulse of song.

Songs in compilation make up a show, and when the compilation is performed before an audience, a stage production. Compilations take any number of forms. With unrelated groups of songs in concert, the performer may be the only common thread. There may be a theme to a group of songs, having to do with their style, their era, their tone, a societal trend, a product for sale, or any number of possible organizing principles. This thematic treatment is a revue, or perhaps a song cycle (a form with roots in Romantic art song that has reincarnated in works such as Jason Robert Brown's *Songs for a New World*).

The most complex and difficult song compilations are those in a dramatic work. In these "book musicals," music and lyrics have a dramatic function equal to dialogue (and movement), and thus the songs do not always fare well when performed out of the show's context. Combining drama and songs is inherently problematic because of the fundamental dissimilarity of music and drama as art forms.

Drama, that is, stories told by actors on a stage, span from the realistic to the absurd, but are by nature representational. Drama represents events that occur in human life. People on stage represent other people, or themselves, or things (animals, trees, candelabras, fairies). Drama is a portrayal of our actual human experience; its meaning is a portrayal of our reality. In music, by contrast, meaning and emotion are not actual; they are abstract. Music can refer to, or in its own way imitate, things in reality, such as a repeated staccato octave pattern imitating the tick-tock of a clock, and in depicting actions and events on stage it often does. Still, it cannot represent them in the same way as dialogue represents conversation. Music is an abstraction of one person's experience (the composer's knowledge and feeling) into a sonic entity. That entity, when performed, is open to the reaction of others, a reaction that will be subjective to each listener. A composer may intend a proud military march as heroic and uplifting, but a listener may instead hear only the fearsome sounds of war. A work that evokes tragedy to one person may sound passionate or ecstatic to another. Music has significance only on its own pseudo-syntactical terms, each piece forming its own unique emotional fabric. "Embodied musical meaning is . . . a product of expectation. If, on the basis of past experience, a present stimulus [a musical event] leads us to expect a more

---

5. Suzanne Langer, *Feeling and Form*, New York: Scribner's, 1953, p. 401.

or less definite consequent musical event, then that stimulus has meaning."[6] In other words, what music makes us feel as we listen is of our own making, a reaction to the unfolding of the music. Musical matters can only refer to other musical matters, and cannot denote anything beyond the musical. Our knowledge and prior experience of music and the feelings music brings out in us inform our experience of each new work we hear. Our accumulated experience leads to increasingly deeper "understanding" of musical connotation and communication, but they can never approach the directness and specificity that are conveyed by words and actions.

Because of the representational nature of drama and the abstract nature of music, the writers and directors of musical-dramatic works run headlong into a conflict. When music and drama are forced into coexistence, there is a risk of patent artificiality. In reality, people do not sing their lives, or about their lives. The lyricism of the language and the content of text, however, can be effectively and beautifully paired with music by applying certain constructs.

The easiest combination is in a single song, in which the work is more temporary and its scope more manageable, for the writer and listener both. More difficult is a full-length musical play, in which the fusion must be maintained over a long period and with a wide range of emotion and energy. In dramatic musical theater (which includes comedic works) the audience members invoke what is called "suspension of disbelief." They put aside what they know as realistic and give in to the approximate reality of a performance that communicates with them on unique levels of emotion and meaning. Suspension of disbelief is not absolute. The audience members are aware that they are in a theater and watching a form of entertainment, and have some knowledge of its operational methods, but they are complicit with the writers and performers in agreeing to ignore their awareness. The responsibility for the audience's ability to suspend disbelief ultimately rests with the writers and performers, and thus writers and directors craft and rehearse dramatic musical work with the utmost attention to detail, and to a semblance of truthfulness. It is also why rewrites and experimentation (and workshops; see "Production in the Twenty-First Century" in this chapter) are so much a part of writing a stage show; writers and performers are concerned above all with what works and what doesn't on stage. Only very rarely is the combination successful on every level; almost every stage musical is flawed in some way, yet these flaws seldom upset an audience's perception, despite their fragile surroundings.

There is endless discussion of what differentiates an opera from a musical. Both are varieties of musical theater, and the gradient between them is replete with sort-of operas and sort-of musicals. Historically speaking, the two collided in late-19th-century and early-20th-century light opera and operetta. In these pieces (mostly comical) the musical conventions of opera and the theatrical conventions of comedy shared the

---

6. Leonard Meyer, *Emotion and Meaning in Music*, Chicago: University of Chicago Press, 1956, p. 35.

stage with equal time. The dividing line is, in my opinion, quite clear: in opera, the music is the driving force; in musical theater, it is the drama, the story, and the text.

As advocates of both the writers and the director, music directors discern the balance of text and music and determine how to best bring out the enhancements one provides the another, including when to favor one over the other. For the most part, they treat operatic music with due reverence and perform it authentically, whereas the music of a musical may be perpetually in rewrite or revision. Musical values in an opera cannot be compromised because of a technical or dramaturgical need of some production. The sextets and septets of *opera buffa* in which the same lyrics are repeated endlessly in spectacular counterpoint are purely musical constructs (though they do tend to emphasize important story points in those repeated lyrics). Though there are moments like these in many musicals, all aspects of the music (and the entire production) are subject to the storytelling: elements like song structures, arrangements, dynamics, and modulations all depend on what is happening on stage. A music director's interpretive guide in a musical is not the score, but the director (or performer) and his or her vision of the musical material.

A (Very) Brief History of Music for the Stage

Somehow, live popular music for the stage has weathered the storms of faltering economies and encroaching technologies better than other art forms. It did so during the Great Depression, and is doing it again now. Here in the early 2000s, there is far more employment for stage music directors than for conductors of legitimate music. Painful though it may be to accept, it seems possible that the era of concert music is waning. Major orchestras are revealing their financial insolvency and vying with their memberships over plummeting pay scales, and even the Grammy Awards have excised the category of Best Classical Album. Ironically, many symphony orchestras today, to improve lackluster ticket sales, are programming musical theater and popular songs (and film music) along with their classical staples, or scheduling as many "pops" concerts as traditional ones. Music for the stage is by nature more catholic. It welcomes serious as well as light music—indeed, music of any taste or breeding—provided that it works on stage in the production. Its formula for continued success lies in its diversity.

Especially in the modern era, music for the stage—music, that is, for public entertainment—has not necessarily been the product of the "masters." Just as often it is the music of populist composers and songwriters. Hoagy Carmichael and Mel Brooks inhabit the same theatrical pantheon as Jerome Kern and Leonard Bernstein. Yet opera and musical theater of all kinds have always been favorites of many great composers. Mozart's *The Magic Flute* and Bizet's *Carmen* bring song, dance, and dialogue together in much the style of modern musicals, Wagner was obsessed by his notions of *Musikdrama* and, along with Puccini, Verdi, and many others, devoted the majority of his *oeuvre* to operatic pursuits. Drama and music seem natural and eternal bedfellows, albeit uneasy ones.

Though until recently music for the stage—indeed, all music—was not a reliably sellable commodity, from its onset it has been impelled by affluence. The aristocracy or the church commissioned and financed great works such as the madrigals of Gesualdo, the cantatas of Bach, the operas and oratorios of Handel, and the symphonies of Haydn, Mozart, and Beethoven. Unlike today, those financiers were not investors. Rather, they controlled such a disproportionate percentage of the collective wealth that they could easily afford music as a means of, in the case of organized religion, worship and aggrandizement and, in the case of the noble upper classes, prestige, diversion, and intellectual exercise. Interestingly, much of modern music for the stage, artful and commercial both, is still financed today by moneyed individuals and groups (more so as the socioeconomic gap between rich and poor widens), a truth that music directors cannot help being cognizant of.

Musical theater is an ancient art form. Greek dramas using music were presented as early as the 5th century BCE. Medieval minstrelsy and musical liturgical dramas were akin to modern popular stage performance, in particular touring productions. Beginning in the late Renaissance, music and drama were more formally and elaborately combined in, for instance, English masques. This combination culminated in oratorio and early opera, in which dramatic material was sung to orchestral accompaniment in extended form, also much like modern stage musicals. Beginning in the late Classical period (*c.* 1750–1800) and continuing into the present, dramas and comedies set to music have diversified into many genres, with appeal to both the ruling classes and the bourgeoisie. Although music and lyrics had been paired as a means of expressing any number of utterances—mythological, ritual, communicative, personal—for as long as anyone had known, in the modern age they became a purposeful musical-dramatic art form, a means of artful entertainment. Performances took place in theaters or concert halls before audiences who attended either by choice (buying a ticket) or by invitation. Consequently, music for the stage, in particular, song, opera, and musical theater, became a preferred form for many of the finest and most successful composers.

Late in the 19th century, as art music began to veer from its accessible diatonic traditions, audiences not ready for musical departures such as tonal extension and chromaticism turned to composers writing in a more orthodox classical vocabulary that was easier on the ears. The operettas of Friml, Herbert, Gilbert and Sullivan, and Lehar epitomize this style and, along with British Music Hall numbers, are perhaps the immediate European progenitors of early Broadway musical theater scores. As the country grew, America also bore several informal yet pervasive sorts of staged entertainments, such as variety shows (olios), burlesques, folk dances, ballets, dance extravaganzas devoted to exalting the female form, and even some attempts at dramatic storytelling. The first works of modern musical theater are variously attributed to John Gay's *The Beggar's Opera* (1750), or in America *The Black Crook* (1866, written by several composers).

Of additional importance to modern musical theater was Romantic ballet music that began to tell stories entirely through dance and music. Most notable were the works of Tchaikowsky, Stravinsky, Prokoviev, and other composers born in Russia, where ballet has thrived since the mid-18th century.

As American culture took on greater identity early in the 20th century, the traditions of European classical music, now including Eastern European and Scandinavian nationalistic traditions, merged with African, African-American, Central American, South American, Caribbean, and Caribbean-American music. The resulting amalgamation transformed into the very accessible vocabulary of modern American popular music. The most obvious features passed down from its ancestors are diatonicism interspersed with purposeful excursions from it, emotionalism, and, perhaps above all, an insistent rhythmic pulse. In legitimate theaters and concert halls and music halls and burlesque houses all over the English-speaking world, the forms and sounds of popular song still purveyed today had begun to coalesce.

Through the 20th century, the mass appeal of popular song rapidly proliferated among listeners and amateur musicians, who could now purchase the sheet music and a recording of their favorite songs and re-experience them at home. (The bourgeoisie had now acquired the privilege once reserved for aristocrats.) Comedic and dramatic musicals and musical revues that introduced or featured these songs formed a new and hybrid musical niche. These humble musicals and musical acts blossomed into elaborate stage spectacles. Later, song form and the preeminence of melody and rhythm took even greater hold with rock music (another style with roots in African-American culture and expropriated by zealous European-American businessmen for a mainstream audience).

To some extent, modern musical theater and popular song have always reflected the mood of their times. In the financially carefree 1910s and the roaring 1920s there were vaudeville shows and revues with music that still unmistakably wore their European (opera and operetta) and African-Caribbean (ragtime/Dixieland) cloaks. The Great Depression and World War II brought with them upbeat songs and love songs with conversational lyrics that soothed and amused during difficult times. The prosperity and population boom of the postwar years not surprisingly coincides with the "Golden Age" of the Broadway musical and the rise of rock 'n' roll music. In the 1960s there were the antiestablishment *Hair* and *Oh, Calcutta!* and in the 1970s the urbanity, cynicism, and wit of Stephen Sondheim. In the 1980s was the splashy faux symphonic rock of Sir Andrew Lloyd Webber, and in the 2000s a profusion of pop genres geared to mass audiences (among the many, *Taboo*, *Billy Elliot*, and *Memphis*, but indeed, like the 2000s themselves, Broadway has, since the millennium, been nothing if not eclectic).

The 1942 musical *Oklahoma!* is generally held as a benchmark for the start of the modern era of musical theater, a Golden Age indeed. The show is said to be the first to integrate music, dance, and drama in a seamless whole, called a "book musical." Under scrutiny, *Oklahoma!* is not entirely seamless, and there are in truth earlier examples that fit the same bill, such as *Of Thee I Sing* (1931) and *Porgy and Bess* (1935). Nonetheless,

Oklahoma! does seem to be a landmark production, and it inspired many similar efforts. Music directors found a gracious new home in the musical theater. It particularly suited their combination of skills, adding to their list an understanding of text, drama, and acting.

The 1940s through 1970s were truly four decades of wonderfully imaginative and artful musical theater. Those years ushered in such timeless masterpieces as *West Side Story, My Fair Lady, Cabaret,* and *Follies,* to name just a few, as well as many fine but more forgettable shows, and hundreds of others long forgotten. Since then the quantity of musical theater works equaling the originality and excellence of the "classics" has declined. Since the 1980s there have been fewer new musicals mounted on Broadway overall than there used to be (there have been exceptional years), but the ones that get there tend to run much longer, even without critical backing.

In the 1980s the "Great White Way" ushered in the "mega-musical," a high-budget, large-scale, heavily hyped production (such as *Starlight Express, Jekyll and Hyde,* or *Miss Saigon*) designed to move and please a wide audience and run as long as people would keep buying seats. Starting in the mid-1990s or so, theatergoers saw a parade of skeletally constructed "jukebox" musicals, which use the catalog of a certain artist or songwriter(s) with a theme or semblance of plot fabricated around the songs, and at the same time Broadway became a destination for recognizable, mostly comedic movies transferred to the stage as musicals. In the 2005–2006 Broadway season alone there were the jukebox shows *Good Vibrations, All Shook Up, Lennon, In My Life, Jersey Boys,* and *Ring of Fire,* and in 2011–2012 the movie transfers *Priscilla, Queen of the Desert; Catch Me If You Can; Sister Act; Spiderman; Once; Newsies; Ghost;* and *Leap of Faith.* In 2013 producer Kevin McCollum signed a deal with Fox to transfer nine to twelve movies to the stage,[7] thrusting Fox into the limelight already shared by Disney and other large entertainment conglomerates. Producers are now capitalizing on the population bubble of baby boomers and the songs and stories that this demographic and their children most easily recognize.

Broadway's profits rise every year, as does attendance. The Broadway scene pre-1980s was typified by far modestly scaled productions and shorter-term profit ambitions than today's stage spectacles and title value transfers. Producers of musicals in earlier years would hang on by a shoestring, pay back their investors first, and try to take home enough to keep their company afloat until the next project. Nowadays, most shows are carefully market-tested before they go up. Large corporate enterprises such as DreamWorks, ClearChannel, and Universal regularly produce works for the stage (so-called "Mousicals" like *Tarzan* and *Shrek*), and tourists flock to shows that the hype and the crowds lead them to.

---

7. Brooks Barnes and Patrick Healy, "20th Century Fox Enlists Help in Bringing Its Properties to the Stage," *New York Times,* 11 July 2013, http://www.nytimes.com/2013/07/12/business/media/20th-century-fox-opening-division-for-live-theater.html?_r=0/.

Outside the confines of Broadway, though, less commercially oriented musical theater continues to thrive. Likewise, genres such as dance, nightclub performances, concert performances, and special events manage to sell tickets through all economic climates and shifting stylistic tides. As in the nation's economy, the disparity between upper and lower financial classes of stage production persists and deepens. (This economic gap is no less evident in the recording industry, in which only a handful of major labels and venues rake in the vast majority of profit.) It is the quantity of stage performance that characterizes where stage music has arrived in the early 21st century. There are fewer shows on Broadway now than in years past, but far more shows and other staged events elsewhere. Furthermore, Broadway shows now tend to run longer and often proliferate into multiple subsidiary productions. The repertoire has been amassing for a century now, too, and revivals abound, meaning more opportunities for music directors. In the changing scene, versatility is a huge asset.

Production in the Twenty-First Century

Here's how a modern Broadway-bound original musical production (or one with Broadway hopes) typically gets under way. Let's say a composer and lyricist have gotten together with a playwright to write a musical. They write some songs and a draft of a script, but they're having trouble finishing the piece, and they want to find out how the material that they have so far will look and sound with real performers. As noted music director and professor Lehman Engel explains in his essay "Production Values": "The writer of a musical show . . . must 'see' it on the stage and attempt to feel what the audience's response will be. It is certainly true that when or if his show is actually put on the stage, its look will be considerably altered by the interpretive talents of the stage director and his collaboration with scenic and costume designers."[8] And, I would add, it will be altered by the "interpretive talents" of the music director and performers. Visualization enhances composition by inspiring ideas that, rather than having been generated purely musically (as in developing a motif), arise from the stage content, dramatic, choreographic, or otherwise visual. When music and action are conceived of concurrently, they are more believable when fused in performance. Our composer, lyricist, and playwright can't visualize their work without having it in front of them, so they seek out collaborators.

There are several avenues they might follow. They could find a director or a producer or theater, and a music director, especially if the music requires preproduction work (see Part 3). A director would begin getting the show into performable condition. A director's specialty is enacting written or composed material; directors are often said to have a "vision" of a play. A producer would raise money, hire other personnel, and coordinate all the elements of the show's continued forward movement. A theater would

---

8. Lehman Engel, *The Making of a Musical*. New York: Macmillan, 1977, p. 142.

give the show a performance space, and help it find its audience. A music director would fashion the musical material into a stage score, interweave the music with the script and the stage action as they develop, and help establish musical production values such as instrumentation, arrangements, sound, and vocal style.

Until the early 1970s, by the time a score and script left the authors' hands they were in a near completed state, and once the director and producer had come on board, the production process would soon accelerate. The rest of the staff would be put in place, the show cast, and a theater rented; the rehearsals would begin and within few months the curtain would rise on opening night. All of that changed around the time of the musical *A Chorus Line*. For years that show was the longest-running musical in Broadway history, and its acclaim and longevity were instrumental in making New York's Off-Broadway Public Theater, its original producers, permanent dignitaries in the show business domain.

A Chorus Line is a backstage story of a group of aspiring dancer-singers auditioning for a new musical. The personal testaments of several of the performers form the backbone of the drama. So that the writers could authentically portray the characters, they held interviews with actual performers and developed the dramatic material and musical numbers around their stories. The effort required more than a traditional rehearsal period, so a series of "workshops" were arranged. The workshop process infused the show with a measure of sincerity and realism that undoubtedly contributed to its huge success. Some of the same producers and creative artists reunited a few years later to begin workshops of a new musical, *Dreamgirls*, which of course has gone on to many successful productions of its own over the years, including the 2007 film. (I was among the audition pianists for the show, one of my first jobs in New York, and I regret to this day having turned down a job offer as associate conductor of one of the early workshops.)

Out-of-town tryouts were nothing new to the Broadway scene when *A Chorus Line* came along. Shows had traditionally prepared for their Broadway openings with runs in cities such as Boston and New Haven, where critics and audiences could not sully long-term Broadway potential with bad reviews or unfavorable word of mouth. In a modern workshop or reading, however, the understanding is that the work is still incomplete, and will benefit from experimentation at a quasi-performance level, as well as perhaps from an informal presentation before an invited, trusted audience. Workshops ease the hurriedness, and the cost, of later phases of rehearsal processes by allowing work that was once done while in full production to be begun in advance, including arrangements and orchestrations, script rewrites, and recasting. Workshops became the darlings of the industry in no time.

The workshop approach has also somewhat altered the popular music concert production model. Modern pop and rock concerts, even when they do not incorporate visual, physical, and technical elements (as they often do), now more frequently carefully work out and rehearse their shows, the arrangements, the transitions, their set lists, and any special material (now it seems as if every concert has a surprise guest star), unlike the more freeform concerts of years past.

Outside of the commercial theater, production models have not changed as drastically, mostly because there is less original work done there. When amateur and academic theaters do present original works, they are not necessarily intended for eventual commercial production, though they may have developmental phases or productions. More often, a group of people who want to put on a show choose material from the rental catalogues and, much as in the mold of a professional production, the cycle of preproduction, rehearsal, and performance begins.

The musical and textual content of modern commercial productions has undoubtedly succumbed to the conspicuous consumerism that dominates popular culture. Producers are mining the same audiences that flock to Disney movies and watch endless hours of television, and have prospered wildly as a result. The core appeal of musical theater has spread to a younger demographic, and writers and producers are paying attention. Perhaps the epitome of the phenomenon, as well as the harbinger, is *Wicked*, a musical that survived overspending, mixed press, muddled out-of-town tryouts, and adult indifference to become a monumental success. Stage musicals have also overflowed into and assimilated with other divisions of popular entertainment, and vice versa. Recent television reality shows have made public the process of auditioning leading players for revivals of *Grease* and *The Sound of Music,* and show tunes are heard belted out on the many offspring of *American Idol,* itself a very stagey enterprise (and one that, thankfully, has a music director—in fact, a few music directors—and a live orchestra).

Disney Channel musicals, the sing-offs, and of course *Glee*, some of which have been transferred to the stage, are now many children's and adolescents' introduction to musical theater as an "art" form. As these teens become adults, their tastes feed back into production choices and methods. Serious-minded commercial entertainment is feeling the squeeze. One wonders if producers today would refuse to finance *Fiddler on the Roof* or *A Little Night Music* because their subject matter was too serious or sophisticated. (For all we know, product placement may be next. Broadway theaters are already getting corporate names.) Music directors may be riding the tide of a permanent change in the profession that reflects the disposition of intellectual entertainment, as is taking place in concert music. Regardless, musical proficiency with music of all styles, including those which are disappearing, will more readily help them secure work.

3

Job Opportunities for Music Directors

This chapter surveys different types of productions that employ music directors, starting with those with the most visibility and the highest price tag and moving to more modest and spontaneous productions, and what as a music director you might expect from each.

Broadway and Off-Broadway

Broadway shows vary so widely in content and style that they can hardly be considered a genre, though they often are. In reality they cover the range from the purely presentational to the dramatically profound. To some extent they can be categorized: book musicals, revues, dance musicals, plays with music, and concert performances are among the classifications.

The term "Broadway" conjures up any number of images, in the same way as does "Hollywood" or "Vegas." The word seems to come with an exclamation point attached (!). Broadway is bright lights, big voices, energetic dance numbers, teeming crowds, the kind of place where one's entertainment dollar will assuredly be well spent.

Like Las Vegas and Hollywood, however, the imagery is something of a facade, and everyone knows it. Yes, there are bright lights, but they are mostly advertising. Yes, there are big voices, but partly because there are microphones amplifying those voices. In truth, Broadway is many different things, some very bright and brassy, some smaller and subtler, some memorable, and some misguided. But the public has adopted the toe tapping and belting, the glitter and splash, the air of sophistication, as Broadway's emblems, and those are the qualities that promoters exploit when marketing Broadway as a product. The best of Broadway is innovative, moving, exhilarating entertainment. When the opulence afforded by big Broadway budgets translates to artistic force, and the gifted writers and performers the industry attracts are encouraged do their most imaginative work, Broadway is the pinnacle of the stage industry that it deems itself to be, and its music can be at once intelligent, compelling, and accessible.

The decline of the recording industry in recent years as a source of steady income has led many pop artists to seek out new earnings, and the musical theater has proven its ability to perpetuate the careers of and offer new creative ground for veteran songwriters and performers. Artists of no lesser stature than Randy Newman, U2, and Cyndi Lauper have recently forayed into the theater. This influx of talent has increased stage music's appeal to musicians and music directors, who get the chance to arrange, conduct, and play newly minted melodies and great grooves from the world's premier pop writers. The tireless Sir Elton John is now as active as a theater composer as he is a recording artist. Music directors and supervisors from outside the usual Broadway circles have become involved in theatrical productions, including Stuart Malina, music director–conductor of the outstanding Harrisburg (Pennsylvania) Symphony, music supervisor and orchestrator of Billy Joel and Twyla Tharp's *Movin' Out*, and Oscar Hernandez, the brilliant bandleader and arranger for the Spanish Harlem Orchestra, and music director for Paul Simon's *The Capeman*. Heralded comedy writers venturing into musical theater territory, such as Mel Brooks, the *Monty Python* gang, and Trey Parker and Matt Stone, have also relied heavily on the expertise of music directors to realize their stage scores for Broadway musicals.

For music directors—indeed, for all musicians—the allure of Broadway is obvious, and for music directors it perhaps represents the highest achievement in the profession. Broadway is first class; it is the major leagues; it is . . . well, Broadway, a metaphor in itself. Broadway salaries are generous, the working conditions are outstanding, and almost everything extramusical related to your work is taken care of for you. You can merely step on the podium or sit at the piano or take a chair in the conference room, and begin work; you don't have to organize the band, bring the keyboard with you, or decide on a place to meet. Many Off-Broadway productions are miniatures of their Broadway siblings, and are equally well appointed and well staffed. Others, however, are more homespun and require music directors to be more resourceful and adaptable, providing for themselves and their music departments in lieu of the personnel and materials provided for them in higher echelons.

The pull of a Broadway (and to a lesser extent Off-Broadway) salary is obvious, especially considering the bleak earnings forecast that goes with a career in music. All Broadway and most Off-Broadway musicians are under union coverage. In 2013 base union scales for playing a single non-keyboard instrument in a Broadway pit are upwards of $1500 per eight-performance week; keyboard players receive an additional 25 percent, associate conductors an additional 30 percent, conductors an additional 75 percent, and "doubles," or premiums for playing additional instruments, are available to all. (Again, the term "music director" is not recognized by the union, so in rehearsal, you must either be paid as a rehearsal musician—you can be a conductor in rehearsal, too, and receive the overscale—or you can negotiate a rehearsal salary with the producers, independent of the union.) So are the benefits and perks, with pension funding, insurance benefits, talk shows and cast albums, lenient substitution policies, and swanky parties. Off-Broadway salaries lie anywhere from about one-third to two-thirds of a Broadway salary, but the jobs there still attract musicians because they are (at least temporarily) steady, and offer some extras. Music directors who are most in demand can negotiate salaries above union rates, or "overscale" (their lawyer or agent usually does the negotiating), and receive preproduction fees to cover meetings, casting, and some of the other preparatory work. Those who originate a show also often receive a small royalty, or a weekly "maintenance" fee, usually equivalent to a stage designer's share, or perhaps a choreographer's. It is hard to specify the numbers, because there are so many ways that producers divvy up any profits.

In New York, other than working for the Philharmonic or perhaps a high-end steady hotel or club date job, Broadway is by far the most lucrative music gig in town. The pay Off-Broadway is not bad, either, and the work can be more interesting, fun, and less restrictive than Broadway. Naturally, all these jobs are highly coveted, and the competition for steady work, though polite on the surface, is fierce.

For the record, the official definition of Broadway productions is geographical, and is relevant mostly to unions and their pay scales. Shows that play in certain theaters (mostly seating a thousand or more, with exceptions), within a certain boundary—essentially what is called New York's Theater District—are considered Broadway shows. Off-Broadway theaters are outside that line, and unofficially seat about two hundred or more, with exceptions. Off-Off-Broadway is used loosely to refer to anything else theatrical in Manhattan, or in New York City's outer boroughs. It exists, geographically and artistically, on the fringes. The work there might be very unusual and enjoyable, but production values, resources, and compensation are minimal or nonexistent. These shows can be a good opportunity for a music director to get in on the ground floor; *Rent* is one of several commercial musicals that began Off-Off-Broadway. Strongly reminiscent of New York's Off-Off-Broadway are the local Los Angeles theaters. Innumerable original productions are done in that sprawling metropolitan area's smaller (ninety-nine-seat) houses. L.A. has a particularly widespread and lively theater scene. The stage is an excellent place for its overabundance of aspiring actors to perform when they are not doing movies and television or auditioning for movies or television; many are trained as stage actors and love performing live. Only a relatively small percentage of these shows are musicals or use live music, but they are so plentiful that many opportunities exist. Salaries and fees, however, are minimal. Music directors based in L.A. include working on these sorts of shows among the many musical assignments they take on to earn a living.

As noted earlier, many Broadway musicals capture the music and *zeitgeist* of their times. Still, Broadway is musically quite conservative, sticking to what has succeeded in the past. Its experimentation is cautious, adapting very gradually to current trends, which usually has it lagging a few years behind the cultural times. Even newly composed music for the Broadway theater draws freely and frequently—indeed, it dwells—on sounds of its past. One is as likely to hear a throwback as an original composition. Revivals of musicals, too, are now almost as common on Broadway as are new shows. Inasmuch as Broadway theater is tuned to a mass audience, this phenomenon is not surprising. Producers are more confident in presenting known properties, and with their profits rising consistently year after year, they have no reason to doubt that their approach is a smart one.

Music for the Broadway theater has over the years been considered by many musicians and music lovers to be decidedly uncool and unhip, despite attempts to shake that image (*Bye, Bye, Birdie* in 1961, *Hair* in 1967, *Company* in 1970, *Rent* in 1996). Musical theater music has always been slow to catch up with the cultural trends and, at least until recently, was aimed at an older audience who supposedly preferred their music easy on the ears. Learned music lovers and writers who prefer modernistic rock, jazz, contemporary classical music, world music, crossovers, experimentations—music that expands the mind rather than feeding it the expected—were there on the scene in the 20th century and are still there today. Now, however, the progressive contingent is far outnumbered by a young theatergoing generation that prefers mass-produced radio hits and middle-of-the-road pop, and in addition have a penchant for musical theater. So "hipness" becomes a matter of perspective. If defined by the preferences of the younger generation and by what sells, musical theater is now hip.

If, musically speaking, Broadway does not always make room for work that takes risks or defies traditional expectation, that is one reason there is an Off-Broadway. Ideally, Off-Broadway is an arena where musical progressiveness may thrive, and a place where shows can be mounted with a smaller investment and operate at a lower budget. If a production fails, the financial loss is more bearable. If it succeeds, its success may be more modest, but that is the expectation. The most promising shows often move to a venue with greater potential for financial gain, that is, to Broadway.

Off-Broadway production is viable because of a constant stream of producers, writers, performers, and theatergoers who cannot or will not pay the higher price of Broadway but still want to produce, write, perform, and attend high-quality musical productions. Although Off-Broadway has spawned many shows that later succeeded on Broadway (among them *A Chorus Line, Sunday in the Park with George*, and *Rock of Ages*), it is just as notable for its native body of work. Off-Broadway shows that stay Off-Broadway may not be as streamlined and certainly not as mainstream as their Broadway siblings, but can be very profitable. Profit is not always the goal, though. Experimental theater has always found a home there, and in recent decades so has "performance art," theatrical or musical or choreographic presentations or installations that combine music, movement, and often some specialized or unusual talent in a nontraditional milieu, such as *Stomp!* or Blue Man Group's *Tubes*.

Contemporary Off-Broadway is also the home of much fluffy, comedic entertainment, such as *Potted Potter*, *Silence!* (the *Silence of the Lambs* musical spoof), and the many incarnations of *Forbidden Broadway*. It also houses many unostentatious yet sophisticated shows, among them revues such as Maltby and Shire's *Starting Here, Starting Now* and *Closer Than Ever* and Sondheim's *Marry Me a Little*, book shows such as *March of the Falsettos* and its sequels and prequels, and intriguing works by composers such as Michael John LaChiusa and Jeanine Tesori. There are also the marvelous in-betweens such as *Hedwig and the Angry Inch*, *Passing Strange* (both of which have transferred to Broadway), and the long-running *Fuerza Bruta* and its predecessor, *De La Guarda*. Music directors can find great reward in the variety.

National Tours

National tours of Broadway shows used to be quite a glamorous thing, and at times they still are. If a show is a big hit on Broadway, a tour is the chance for everyone outside New York to see what all the buzz was about. Therefore, the best touring productions are as just as thoughtfully cast, extravagantly produced, elegantly designed, and intelligently directed as their Broadway versions. Sometimes these secondary productions even surpass their originals, as directors, writers, and designers have another crack at tying up any loose ends or making any improvements they may not have had time for the first time around, or that they discovered by observing the first production's run.

Touring Broadway shows can also be quite profitable for presenters, but increasingly the productions are somewhat watered-down, or at least downsized, versions of their Broadway originals. Producers pre-sell a certain number of tickets for their tours, so they estimate the financial outlook and keep costs in line with their forecast. One of the reasons that producers of Broadway shows of moderate artistic value now promote them so fervently, and allow them to run despite flagging attendance, is that their road companies can generate better profits, as long as the shows have a Broadway pedigree, a Broadway run of a year or so under their belts, some positive word of mouth, good title value, and perhaps a star in a leading role.

To the dismay of music directors, recent tours use far more reduced orchestrations and synthesized instruments than in the past. It's much less costly to set up and break down a few electronic devices than it is an orchestra with multiple microphone feeds and a sizable physical footprint. The AFM's control over touring orchestra sizes and salaries is weakening, except with regard to the numbers required in each particular venue.

The AFM's *Pamphlet B* outlines wage scales and work conditions for touring productions whose highest scales are comparable to Broadway's. This once ironclad document has taken several hits in recent years, and salaries and perks are in decline. Several "tiers" of touring agreements have superseded the original. In the upper tiers with higher per diems, companies will offer the staff a choice of luxury hotels and travel at deep discounts, but in the lower tiers, salaries are half or less of Broadway scales, and the production company, rather than the employee, books transportation and lodging, often choosing midrange chain hotels. Stays in each city are usually much shorter. These lower-budget tours, formerly called "bus and truck" tours after their humble means of conveyance, have become the norm (though there have been rumblings in 2013 that some of the tier structure will be eliminated and some old *Pamphlet B* requirements restored). There is an arm of the AFM, called the Theater Musicians' Association, or TMA, with chapters in several cities, that helps to set touring and resident standards outside of New York, and music directors interested in touring should protect themselves by allying with this group and whatever other resources and organizations may become available.

Nonunion production companies, formerly relegated to the bottom of the barrel of touring shows, draw larger audiences than in years past, and are now sometimes the first to take out a recent Broadway title. These are the least advantageous situations for a music director. The presenters of these shows egregiously decimate orchestras and casts and employ low-fidelity electronic emulation, yet they bill their productions as "Broadway" shows. Musicians on these productions can be worked at will, going weeks without days off and traveling nightly by bus to the next stop, all at paltry wages. On the road, when not under a union contract, with many or all of their belongings in tow, including perhaps their instruments, exploited musicians have little remedy should their circumstances become dire, such as a sudden cancellation. In my opinion, music directors (and all musicians) should avoid these productions entirely, even when looking to build a résumé. The experience gained will not be typical of your work life (unless you intend to do nonunion work forever), and by allowing employers to take advantage of you, you undermine the value of your profession and set a harmful precedent for other working musicians. One of the AFM's motivations in making deep concessions to union-sponsored touring producers is to allow nonunion producers a chance to unionize and still operate at low cost. Notwithstanding, nonunion productions continue unabated. There are exceptions, including some well-run theme parks and cruises, companies that employ nonunion workers with working conditions and contractual guarantees comparable to what the union stipulates.

All salary cuts and deteriorating working conditions aside, union road shows offer long-term, steady contracts and a chance to see the country (or the world) on someone else's dime. It is a good proving ground where less seasoned music directors can go through the full rehearsal process, performance, and long-term maintenance of a full-scale project. For more seasoned musicians, it has many advantages as well, such as building retirement funds and paying off mortgages and college tuitions, along with any artistic rewards. Concert tours, as opposed to theatrical tours, tend to be shorter, or broken into sections with a hiatus between sections. They have fewer total performances, but usually pay much better, often by the performance, with no per diem but all expenses prepaid or reimbursed, and with more upscale travel and accommodations.

Tours can be grueling work, but there is great practical knowledge to be gained by working in different venues, familiarizing yourself with personnel and management through an extended run, and delving so deeply into a single score. The psychology of touring with others can be tricky, with many people locked into a demanding routine while living out of a suitcase. Yet tours can also be enjoyable, especially when they visit interesting places and you meet interesting people along the way. Sometimes, especially when the bookings are longer, music directors on a tour spend very little time on the job outside of performance, and maybe a little rehearsing. As usual, every job is different. Figure 3.1 shows three different "roadhouses."

The title "music supervisor" originated (in its stage meaning) in touring companies. It denotes overseeing, rather than performing with, the music and music department of the production. A music supervisor of a tour is the musical commander-in-chief, regardless of whether he or she is on site. A tour music supervisor does essentially what I have defined as music direction, but does not perform, and perhaps does not attend to every musical detail of a production, as there is a music director on board as well. The shorthand is "setting up" a company of a show. Music supervisors customarily attend casting calls, at least for principal and important singing roles, take some part in production rehearsals, which may include teaching and coaching but not conducting (unless it's planned that they might do it temporarily), and visit the show periodically to maintain or re-rehearse as necessary. This sort of work can be lucrative, with fees, royalties, and various incentives all available under the right contractual conditions. The position is mostly managerial, and there is no union protection or standard contract. As it is with performing musicians, paychecks have dwindled as of late, as have expense allowances and luxury travel (no more business class).

Regional (Local), Repertory, and Stock Theater

Let me not be so New York City–centric to imply that Broadway and Off- and even Off-Off-Broadway entertainment belong only to us New Yorkers (yes, I am one, for most of my life). For one thing, out-of-towners make up a good chunk of New York's theatergoing audience. More notably, musical theater is flourishing outside New York City, and overseas, beyond its other primary hub, London. It may not have the staying power elsewhere that it has in those two cities, where theatergoing is a linchpin of the local economies. Nonetheless, stage musical performance is ubiquitous in America, with regional theaters in every state, touring companies making stops in cities large and small, and pockets of active theatrical and performance life in such places as Los Angeles, Chicago, Nashville, and Dallas.

FIGURE 3.1A–C Three grand, historic theaters, with views of their orchestra pits: (A) Loew's Jersey in Jersey City, New Jersey; (B) Shea's Buffalo (New York); and (C) the Atlanta, Georgia Fox Theater, decked out for *The Nutcracker*. (*Credits:* A: Photo by John D. Woolf; B: Photo by Scott Hendershot; C: Photo by Alex Koloskov.)

Regional theaters around the United States mount productions that are often comparable in technical values and artistic quality to Broadway and touring productions, and do them on more limited budgets. Most of these theaters are members of LORT, the League of Regional Theaters (a unit similar to the Broadway League), which standardizes practices and expectations. There are several levels of LORT theaters, depending on

FIGURE 3.1A–C Continued

seating and seniority. The best regional theaters have superb reputations (for example, the Guthrie Theater in Minneapolis, the Goodman Theater in Chicago, Hartford Stage, Denver Center Theater Company, and New York's Roundabout and Lincoln Center Theaters, which also have Broadway ties) but are also known as less commercially motivated than Broadway. Most are not for profit, and some are governmentally funded (the Kennedy Center in Washington) or are associated with a university (such as the American Repertory Theater in Boston on the Harvard campus). See Figure 3.2 for a look at two other theaters.

Music directors for productions at regional theaters are sometimes hired locally, and sometimes come along with the show. Some theaters have resident music directors, who work on many but not all the musical events at that theater, and might also work outside that theater. Many outfits are rightly proud of their musical theater traditions, and take their musical rigor and scholarship very seriously. Goodspeed Opera House in East Haddam, Connecticut is a fine example. It has an extensive and well-maintained music library, attracts an intelligent audience and staff, and unearths many forgotten shows that deserve at least a second look. For some years Goodspeed also published *Show Music,* the only magazine devoted entirely to theater music.

For music directors, regional theaters can be a chance to attach oneself to an original work, often with the writers on site, while a score is still being written. Revivals, too, often get a fresh look in regional theaters, which are the stomping grounds of free-thinking directors and open-minded executives who are true theater lovers and themselves patrons. Salaries for music directors in regional theaters range from minimal to excellent. Many of these theaters, especially those in good-sized cities, have a union

FIGURE 3.2 (A) The Old Globe in San Diego, birthplace of several Broadway shows, and (B) the stage and orchestra pit at the Royal Court Theatre, Bacup, UK, set for a Christmas pantomime. (*Credits:* A: Wikipedia Commons, Bernard Gagnon; B: Photo by Victoria Christina Johnson.)

agreement in place, but at times the union makes concessions ranging from slight to significant to not-for-profit or cash-strapped theaters.

If after its regional run a show later transfers to a larger commercial setting, such as Broadway (the ambition of many regional productions), the producers might supplant a locally hired music director with someone with Broadway experience. Music directors for regional shows can try to negotiate a "first right of refusal" into their contracts, that is, the option of being involved in future commercial productions. Yet producers view a regional production of a show on its way to Broadway as an opportunity to audition and, if need be, replace personnel before their financial risk grows higher. If you have secured first right of refusal in your contract and you are replaced, you will be entitled to any buyout you have negotiated with the theater or the show's producers. Music directors and their reps will negotiate similar terms for developmental productions (see the section "Workshops and Developmental Productions").

Larger than regional theaters in audience size are Broadway-like theaters and concert halls in various cities that house musical events of all kinds—*Shen Yun*, the Rockettes, Elvis Presley tribute shows, ice shows, variety shows—and employ music directors when the event calls for one, but those music directors usually work with the production and are not affiliated with the theater. These theaters are mostly union houses with in-house salary scales. Often these arenas double as Broadway tour venues.

Smaller than the regionals are many local unaffiliated theaters, often called stock or repertory theaters, some seasonal (summer stock theaters thrive in resort areas), some year round. They are professional theaters, but may be only partly unionized or entirely nonunion. Some stock theaters put on a new show every other week or even every week. In that short time the music team must teach, rehearse, and often re-orchestrate an entire score. Seldom do these theaters present original works; mostly they do shows from the rental catalogues, one at a time or in rotation. Fewer changes are made to existing material, because fewer changes are feasible, given the time constraints.

Among the smaller regional and stock theaters (one might as well call them all "local" theaters; they are "regional" only from some outside perspective, presumably that of New York, and "stock" only because "stock" is a slang term for "repertoire"), one finds good places and not as good places, good productions and not as good productions, some that approach the high quality of the LORT regionals or better, others less polished and less well cast and staffed. Cruise ship and theme park productions also fall within this category. For a music director the often reduced or nonexistent orchestra forces (sometimes just an upright piano) and less expert players and singers may be less gratifying, but these shows can also be exhilarating challenges. What you gain by mounting productions in rapid succession while performing nightly is as valuable as boot camp to a soldier. Many music directors, including me, have held jobs of these kinds while working their way up the ladder. Two stock houses are shown in Figure 3.3.

Salaries for these jobs vary widely, from next to nothing upward, and are not often very high, though they can be steady. Established local theaters might offer modest travel allowances and better housing along with small fees and slightly better salaries, while others may operate on a shoestring budget and offer minimal pay. Unfortunately, many amusement park, theme park, and cruise ship employees are nonunion, and working

FIGURE 3.3 (A) The Gateway Playhouse in Bellport, Long Island, and (B) the Ogunquit Playhouse in Ogunquit, Maine, two East Coast stock theaters. (*Credits:* A: Wikipedia Commons, Dan TD; B: Wikipedia Commons, B. Lee Mannino.)

conditions vary widely. Still, there are many employment opportunities, and much experience to be gained, in all sorts of local situations. What's more, the young actors and singers and musicians you might work with there may be upwardly mobile like you; a few months later you may be coaching one of them, or one of them might mention your name to a potential employer.

Nightclubs, Cabarets, and Concerts

Beyond musical theater, there is a cornucopia of events in which music directors find employment. Performers (primarily singers) nightly grace the stages of nightclub and cabaret stages nationwide. Cabaret, literally, is a subset of nightclub performance, one of French and German origins that features a variety of acts and implies risqué conduct, on and off the stage. In actual modern usage the terms "nightclub" and "cabaret" are virtually interchangeable. Nightclub or cabaret acts are not to be confused with "club dates," which are single-service engagements such as weddings or bar mitzvahs. (Club-date music directors have protocols and rules of their own, and often they front the band as a singer or master of ceremonies. I wish I had had a guidebook to help me on my few awkward attempts early in my career to venture into this specialized and potentially lucrative field, and I do not claim here any knowledge whatsoever of that arm of music direction, nor do I offer advice in that specialization.)

Certain districts are centers for nightclub and cabaret performance, such as midtown Manhattan and the West Village, the Sunset Strip vicinity in Hollywood, South Beach in Miami, and of course, Las Vegas, a city of hotels and restaurants. In these and other locations, performers pay the "room" (the venue) a fee, or share the "gate" (what the room makes on ticket sales alone), for the right to play there. The room provides basic amplification, sound and lighting and the technician(s) to run them, usually a piano and sometimes other instruments (a drum kit, an upright bass), and whatever services and amenities the room may offer (such as backstage space, food and drink, servers, seating, hosting, and a warm-up act). Performers are usually given time for a brief sound check or rehearsal in the space. A nightclub can be anything from a rundown low-ceilinged dive with a piano missing some keys, an outdated P.A. system, and a closet to dress in, to a huge, lavish four-star restaurant with jacket and tie preferred, a Steinway grand tuned each morning, state-of-the-art tech, fresh flowers on the stage, and comfortable pre-show digs. (I have played both, and enjoyed both.)

What distinguishes stage performance in a nightclub or club date setting is the breaking down of the "fourth wall," the invisible barrier between audience and performer that separates their realities. The audience's disbelief doesn't have to be suspended for more than the length of a song, if at all (though a good nightclub performance may be quite hypnotic). A performer still has tales and feelings to share, but they won't be shared in as rigid a manner as they would in a drama or musical theater setting. Nightclub performers connect with the audience by reaching them directly, looking into people's eyes and telling their stories—the songwriters', their own, and the audience's—in song. Sometimes they are known as "song stylists." As music director you support or help to develop the singer's style, in individual songs and for the act as a whole.

Performers (or performing groups) in these venues run the gamut from hopeful to big name. Nightclub performance is a specialty for some singers, such as Karen Akers or Nina Simone, while others are successful actors who pursue it as a sideline, such as Jane Krakowski, Idina Menzel, and perhaps the paragon of the art form, Liza Minnelli. (The reader will note the predominance of female performers on these lists. Indeed, far more women than men visit the cabaret stage, if one is to judge by the listings in newspapers and magazines on any given day in any given city. Cabaret is also a darling of—and I hope I am not stereotyping—many gay male attendees, for whom nightclub singers in the tradition of Liza, her mom Judy, Barbra Streisand, and others, are musical godheads.) Many musical theater actors perform on cabaret stages to showcase themselves, try out material, make extra money, or just to keep their careers active "between jobs."

As music director in a nightclub or cabaret setting you will usually be the accompanist, probably at the piano, sometimes an arranger, and sometimes a coach and collaborator. Most nightclub bands are very small: piano, sometimes bass, maybe a small drum kit, or a guitar, or a solo reed or string player, but not much more. Nightclub stages are too small to fit large complements of musicians; the band cannot be too loud, for the focus of cabaret is the singer, not the accompaniment. Arrangements are likewise usually kept simple, though at times, with the singer's sanction or commission, they can be more adventurous, particularly in jazzy harmonic extensions and rhythmic reinvention. Occasionally the pianist will not be the music director of a small ensemble; instead, another band member will take on those duties.

A good part of the music heard in nightclubs is standard popular song (jazz standards and the so-called Great American Songbook) and theater music repertoire, with a cache of original material, some written expressly for the nightclub circuit, mostly comedy songs, novelty songs, and the occasional torch song. The performer, for the most part, determines the set list (the songs being sung and their order), sometimes with the music director's advice. Some acts are largely ballads and romantic material, others are personal, soul-searching character explorations, some are topical, some are themed, some are mélanges of all sorts of material, and some are just silly and lighthearted. Cabaret performance can be impromptu, such as in piano bars, improvisational comedy, and, to widen the genre, karaoke.

More than any other stage music form, in cabaret and nightclubs the performers themselves are likely to help shape the musical arrangement. Because the production is their showcase, performers might outline to the music director what they seek in genre, tempo, sound, and feel. They may specify musical modulations, digressions, medleys, and so on, that best serve their voices and their onstage identities. The music director then usually translates the performer's desire to notes and notation. (A few performers do write down their own arrangements.)

Most performers, however, entrust the arranging to the music director, or to a separate arranger, or their arrangements already exist. Simple chord and rhythm charts (rudimentary or makeshift parts) are as common in nightclubs as specific orchestrations.

Cabaret and nightclub production budgets are very tight, especially when the performer is "backing" the show, so detailed written music is simply unaffordable. Because rehearsal time with a band is also extremely limited, to some extent "faking it" is customary. Nightclub musicians are expected to be at least competent improvisers, capable at least of transforming a chart, especially one of a familiar tune or in a familiar style, into a finished performance. Of course, this ability is also a requirement for a music director. Underscoring during a performer's patter with the audience might be improvised as well.

In rehearsal for a cabaret act you are the singer's confidante, an even-handed practice audience, and a supportive critic of the performance's quality and believability. Sometimes a performer will ask for coaching and, if the situation is right, you may offer it. A singer may need musical help, such as in learning new songs, choosing a key, phrasing, rhythmic interpretation, and intonation, or maybe even with character or acting choices.

Nightclub work, like most music direction, holds little glory for music directors, even if they exercise their full creative powers as performers or arrangers. The spotlight will always be on the headliner, and as music director you remain contentedly (or at least cooperatively) in the background. The pay offers little consolation. The performer might offer you a predetermined fee, or might share his or her fee. The percentage varies: a performer getting a hundred dollars might give all of it to the music director, but another headlining at ten thousand dollars a night may only pay the music director a thousand or less. The majority of these shows fall at the lower end of the scale, but most nightclub performers know (they may have to be reminded) to take care of the music director properly. Upscale clubs can have greater financial reward, but such jobs are scarce. In good situations, music directors will reap the reward of playing good music with other good musicians and stage performers, doing interesting, sometimes spontaneous arrangements, and, unique to this sort of musical performance, very closely interacting with an audience. Good music directors often remain associated with a nightclub singer over a long period. Some relationships have lasted for decades, such as Barbara Cook and her music director, Wally Harper, also a veteran music director of Broadway shows.

Collections of songs performed on a larger stage, with an audience not at tables but in seats, are concerts. Concerts share many of the musical qualities of nightclubs, but the instrumental forces may be larger and the arrangements more specific. Orchestrators and orchestra contractors (we'll meet them in chapter 6, "The Music Team") are more likely involved. Some contact with the audience is sacrificed, but not all. Concert stages require a broader persona in the performer and less spontaneity in the music. (The more complex the environment, the more that can go wrong, the greater the need for careful planning.) A music director in a concert setting is more likely to come out from behind the piano and conduct from a podium, or might conduct from the piano. In pop performance, a music director's duties are much lighter. So confirms Tom Barney, music director for Steely Dan: "That gig required very little in terms being music director. We had the best musicians, so all I had to do was run sound checks and an occasional rehearsal, and go get the singers."[1]

As is true of all stage music, musical style in a concert or club act will vary with each performer and possibly within each act. Music directors who travel easily in multiple styles, who can both conduct and play well, have an advantage in nightclub and concert performances. Others may find work because of a particular stylistic affinity or association with an individual or property.

The pay for music directors in concerts depends on who is paying, and on the experience and expertise of the music director. If a performer pays the music director out of pocket, it is similar to what I described previously in nightclubs, but with higher figures. In other cases a venue or a producer will pay the music director. Some concert venues and most orchestras are unionized, and guarantee the conductor a per-concert minimum based on the local scales. Music directors can receive guest conducting or

FIGURE 3.4A AND B Music Director Rob Mathes leads the orchestra. (*Credit:* Photos by Joseph Deruvo.)

1. Tom Barney, telephone interview, 7 December 2013.

JOB OPPORTUNITIES FOR MUSIC DIRECTORS | 61

FIGURE 3.4A AND B Continued

single engagement fees anywhere from a few hundred to several thousand dollars. As a rule, the bigger the audience and the bigger the star, the bigger the paycheck for all.

One final word about cabaret and concert performances. Performers will occasionally involve their music directors in the stage action, or banter with them, or in some manner force upon them more of a stage role. Music directors might be an Ed McMahon–like sidekick, a foil for jokes, may have a few one-liners of their own, or may be asked to sing a harmony part, or possibly participate in a skit. This contradicts the tendency of music director to be unobtrusive, but with the fourth wall already down, it makes more sense. Obviously some music directors are better cut out for this sort of thing than others. (I myself am *not*, but I am willing when asked. Willingness, I believe, is more crucial than charm.) If this is the sort of personality a performer is seeking in a music director, he or she will usually vet music directors for their "stageworthiness" as part of the hiring process. If you really don't want to have to talk or sing on stage, steer clear of these jobs. In Figure 3.4, a guitarist is the music director.

Revues, Special Events, and Industrials

A "revue" is a collection of songs or musical material grouped around a single theme or purpose and put on by a group of performers. (I suppose there are solo revues, but they are likely termed "one-man" or "one-woman" shows.) Revues have many subcategories. Some appear on Broadway; the jukebox musicals mentioned in chapter 2, "Musical Stage Production," when they are thematic rather than dramatic (*Smokey Joe's Cafe*, for example), are revues. Revues are produced in much the same way as dramatic musical theater works, but they omit the overriding element of dramatic storytelling.

Themed performances for ceremonial events—among them tributes, awards, holidays, weddings, and charitable fundraisers—aren't always called revues, yet can be considered revues. Each is called what it is, event by event. Theatrical revues or special events can cross over into the concert and nightclub fields, depending on the venue. Commercially profitable revues have flourished in large auditoriums in Las Vegas and overseas in Hamburg, London, and Tokyo, among others, including burlesques featuring showgirls and male strippers, celebrity imitators, and the highly popular *Riverdance* and *Cirque du Soleil* and their many offshoots.

Revues presented for sales purposes or to entertain corporate clients and employees are called "industrials." Most industrials have short rehearsal periods in a secondary space, perhaps in another city, then move to the performance venue with a quick load-in and sound check. There are some very artistically done industrial shows, with exemplary music and other design elements, and some feature professional or celebrity performers. Less elaborate corporate productions might simply present a group of old musical favorites as background music for their sales pitch. Spoofs of standard songs are commonplace; the writers substitute for existing lyrics phrases that are relevant to the product for sale (or maybe a jab at a boss or coworker). Industrials are a natural match for synthesized and electronic music. More than just the savings that an electronic orchestra can provide, the cleanliness and modernity of the digitally produced sound can help a product seem up to date. Sometimes industrial shows contain original material, some written by corporate employees.[2] Although there are particular conventions in each situation and each locale, a music director's work in a special event or industrial is most influenced by three things: the performance venue, the size of the orchestra, and the needs of the production. You and your employer, or client, will lay out your duties in advance.

---

2. One of my favorite jobs in this wide-ranging field was at New York City's 1999 *Inner Circle* show, an annual event in which the city administration lampoons the press corps by using the year's most popular musical as a starting point. (The press has a night of its own, in reverse.) Rudolph Giuliani portrayed the majestic "Scar" in the year of *Lion King*; as articulate and impressive a man and as obviously gifted an attorney and politician His Honor might be, he's not the quickest study as a vocalist.

Most special events have severely limited rehearsal time, perhaps a few hours, if any at all, or just a sound check, and technical aspects may be makeshift. Special performances often take place in venues that, rather than ideal, are available or within budget. The technical staff of some of these spaces may not be as reliable as in a more professionally managed event, and the functions that the staff members of a special event perform may not be their usual vocations. Production companies for special events are formed ad hoc and by nature are disorganized. As music director you might end up taking on more than what you bargained for, and the decisions you make may not be motivated as much by music as by the need to simply get the job done, or to ingratiate an organization or client. Your duties may well extend past the musical. For instance, a guitarist's cable doesn't reach his amplifier (you're a gofer). There are fewer inputs on the sound board than there are instruments and microphones (you're a sound technician). There are no lights for the music stands, or enough outlets (you're an electrician). There is not enough coffee to keep the drummer awake (you're a gofer again). In one industrial show I did, I realized that in certain songs the singers could not sing together unless I sang with them, so I quickly rewrote those charts without my keyboard part and conducted from the stage, as a member of the choir.

Special events range from well-funded productions planned months in advance by experienced presenters to benefit concerts thrown together overnight by a group formed on Facebook. A music director is a key component of all. A confident, capable, creative leader on the podium will especially benefit a marginally planned event by keeping the proceedings on schedule with a calm yet commanding rehearsal and performance approach in a chaotic environment. The music directors of the Tony and Academy Awards shows are perpetually rehired at least in part because they know how to make what happens on stage and in the broadcast go smoothly from a musical standpoint.

Benefit and specialty concerts usually pay nothing or perhaps an honorarium. Music directors do them mostly as favors, for fun, and for networking, and many are for a good cause. This practice can be a deterrent to some music directors, as are the headaches that hastily or faultily planned productions carry with them. These shows are, however, excellent opportunities for exposure and meeting others. Many fine performers get involved for the same reasons, and of course are charitable when charity is involved. The exception is industrials, which music directors negotiate individually, but can pay quite well. The musicians' union oversees some of them, again depending on the performance venue. Revues of any kind that are performed in unionized theatrical houses pay the equivalent of any other production in those spaces.

Academic Theaters and Events

Despite what *Glee* and the *High School Musical* television films might have viewers believe, academic productions do not come equipped with customized, pre-rehearsed, pre-mixed vocal arrangements, autotuned voices, studio-quality sound systems, and eminently skilled side musicians and vocalists capable of morphing into any size and style of ensemble at will. Music direction in secondary schools and colleges presents unique challenges. Musical productions for the stage in academic institutions are staffed mostly in-house, though on occasion outside professionals ("ringers") are brought in to help out. High schools and universities usually have sufficient musical faculty and aspiring music students to handle music direction duties. Academic ceremonies such as commencements and other occasional events also sometimes require music direction, and again, music faculty, students, and the occasional ringer usually do the job. Depending on the institution, these ceremonies can be quite extravagant, and of high musical caliber.

The main singularity of academic music direction is that the duties may be divided among a few people. With orchestral, vocal, and piano specialists on most faculties, a vocal director and an orchestra conductor often replace a single music director, with an accompanist–rehearsal pianist perhaps rounding out the music team. This approach makes sense, for the combined skill sets of the musically divergent specialists is probably stronger than those of any individual as a music director for the stage. Also, given the unavoidable scheduling difficulties of academic production rehearsal, it allows for the music director to be, as it were, in more than one place at a time.

When presenting existing works of musical theater, academic production and creative staffs conform mostly to the printed scores and scripts that they rent from publishers. There are exceptions, but adapting repertory works is time consuming and involves permissions. Academic institutions also sometimes present original works, especially at the college level, many of them topical variety shows or satires of campus life, such as Harvard's renowned *Hasty Pudding Show*. An adventurous high school or college director or producer might also try to revise an existing work, time and talent permitting.

One sector of academic performance stands out from the rest. Universities and music conservatories that house training programs for stage performers and musicians, or those with diverse music, theater, and dance departments, mount productions that can rival their professional counterparts, with the anomaly of casts made up of students. These schools are also reliable feeders of talent to professional stages, pits, and podiums.

Student-run productions such as those put on by drama clubs are staffed and administered by students, while officially sanctioned university events are probably managed or at least supervised by the faculty or administration. A music director (or music direction team) often has greater autonomy in academia than in professional productions, because a drama teacher who is directing a high school or college production will more freely give in to a lack of understanding of music than would the director of a commercial musical. Some of the jobs available on these productions pay modest fees to the ringers, and sometimes also to students.

When professional music directors are engaged for any sort of academic engagement, they should keep in mind that they are working with students. What you can expect most in an academic production is to learn, have fun, make friends, and yes, of course, put on a good show. This philosophy is especially true with younger students. Regardless of whether your Tony hits his high note in "Maria" cleanly, even if your Mimi forgets the lyrics to "Light My Candle," even if your Tevye's beard falls off in the middle of "Tradition," the reviews, such as they are, will assuredly be positive. Parents attend the show to root for their kids, and friends to root for their friends. The director and music director will get flowers from the cast. Sometimes it is very frustrating trying to corral or conduct a rambunctious group, but you can still try to instill in students a professional attitude. It is completely unnecessary to drive them slavishly or berate them, as has been known to happen in these situations, though it is wise to encourage a rigorous work ethic. Implicitly, even with all hands doing their best work, there is rarely an ideal performance in a student performance (an exception might be a show in which all characters are of the same age range as the actors).

In preproduction, academic production teams assess the limitations of their resources in relation to the show they want to present, and plan accordingly. Simpler material or a smaller quantity of material performed well is often preferable to overreaching. Yes, everyone would love to put on *Sweeney Todd*, but *You're a Good Man, Charlie Brown* might be better, for any number of reasons, from propriety to castability. On the other hand, if a school has a commanding dramatic baritone, a virtuoso singer for Mrs. Lovett, a strong choir, a skilled orchestra, solid technical resources, and plenty of rehearsal time, *Sweeney* might be an appropriately challenging educational experience. The choice of repertoire might be hotly debated among those in charge. Administration, department heads, and faculty from every department might be involved in the decision, along with alumni, fundraisers, students, and parents.

As in all amateur performance, cuts and reductions may be needed, and in schools, content may also be called into question. Some shows are available from publishers with their adult themes toned down for general audiences. A creative team might edit a show themselves (the rental houses do not permit editing but in practice it is not uncommon; I recommend strongly against it without permission), customizing their production to their academic outfit. Academic theater is another fine example of how music directors must work toward the production's success within its format above all else, including any undue musical idealism.

Amateur and Community Performances and Talent Shows

Modern community theater is theater performed by amateurs for a limited, local audience for no reason other than the desire to perform and view performances. Could its persistence be evidence of some innate need in people to share their stories in a creative way, a vestige of ancient societal rituals? There is no honest expectation of professional excellence; the process is more important. People get involved in amateur productions for any number of reasons: just for fun, because they have no other outlet for their creative urges, because their friends do it, to get away from the spouse and kids for a while, to impress the neighbors. And perhaps because it is in their blood.

Community theaters put on plays and musicals, revues and concerts, and the odd special event such as a Christmas pageant. They perform in churches, high school auditoriums, wherever there is a stage or something like one. Often the same people participate year after year; some come and go, but a core group remains in place. The regulars might include producers, stage directors, performers, designers, and music directors. A regional professional or academic music director will at other times be jobbed in. Community productions, like academic productions, are usually straightforward versions of existing shows, but again, production limitations may dictate cuts or simplifications. Sometimes community theaters will produce an original show.

There is a more relaxed pace to most community-theater production schedules. There may be months of planning and rehearsal periods just as long. There are still scheduling challenges, but usually they have more to do with people's work and family obligations than with restrictions imposed by the production.

Some professional music directors cut their teeth in community theater, and some professional music directors still retain their loyalties to certain companies, returning periodically to work at the places that got them started and gave them their first jobs in the profession. Music direction positions of these sorts pay minimally, and sometimes the staff even contributes to the production and the producing organization. People often work on a volunteer basis, and with a lot of assistance from friends, family, and donors, sewing costumes, painting scenery, making posters, printing playbills, and holding bake sales.

Amateur stage performance in the last few years has found a new friend. A few years back, the notion of a singing contest seemed the outdated practice of women's societies and opera clubs, or maybe for a talent night at the local VFW hall. I was in Japan in 1999 and saw on television some very bewildering, yet soothing, ballad-heavy singing competitions, and thought how they might catch on elsewhere if they were only to pick up the tempo a bit. Before that experience I had been vaguely aware of a lively British musical subculture dedicated to sing-offs. A few years later, American television screens were inundated with reality shows, one of whose most enduring sub-genres seems to be the talent tournament. When it comes to singing "talent," whether it's the best, the flashiest, the loudest, or the riffing-est voice doesn't seem to matter; the genre has exploded in popularity. The original *Pop Idol* formula from England, made fashionable in the United States first by *American Idol* in 2002, has since spawned many imitators. Devoted fans have enthusiastically approved the format with sky-high ratings and phone-in rushes. As a result, amateur performers, good ones and so-so ones and not-so-good ones, have stepped into the spotlight, assisted by YouTube and social media. They sing for friends and family and clubs and societies all over the country, especially in suburbs, smaller urban areas, and rural centers. Our notion of community theater now must now expand to meet this new form of presentational vocal performance, which is inclusive, inexpensive, and diverting, the perfect sort of entertainment for talented and aspiring amateurs.

This sub-genre is a wellspring for music directors. Every show and every individual performer needs someone to play or record the music. *American Idol*'s music directors and team of coaches and arrangers create elaborate, customized orchestrations and arrangements weekly. And on YouTube, whether it was the singer's brother or sister or someone who posted a flyer on a bulletin board at the local recording studio, there is accompaniment on that video, created and performed by YouTube's equivalent of a music director.

Workshops and Developmental Productions

As noted in chapter 2, "Musical Stage Production," since the 1970s almost every new major musical goes through at least one, and often several, developmental productions before being presented to the public. These "workshops," or "readings," or "staged readings" can also serve as backers' auditions, and producers and investors are regular attendees, trolling for new material. A huge upsurge in these productions has followed the increase of contestants wanting and vying for a chance to write for the commercial stage, and has provided many new ground-floor opportunities for music directors.

Workshops are quite inexpensive by comparison to a full production. They take place in a bare rehearsal room, with no design elements, using creative personnel working at drastically reduced rates. Since the increase in production costs that resulted from out-of-control economic inflation beginning in the 1970s, investors have been far more comfortable putting their money into a show that is not just tried out, but very carefully worked out. Actors' Equity and eventually the AFM got on board and created contractual agreements with concessions and enhancements for workshops. Certain regional and repertory theaters are active in development, such as the Norma Terris Theatre at Goodspeed (East Haddam, Connecticut), and there are dozens of festivals and retreats and other hatcheries of new musicals, such as the National Alliance for Musical Theatre (New York City), and the Eugene O'Neill Festival (Waterford, Connecticut), that produce workshops for shows in progress.

Music directors covet the chance to become involved with a show at the workshop phase. It has become the surest way, and probably the most artistically satisfying way, to become attached to a production for the long term. When a show is in its infancy, the music director is more likely to be called upon to perform any number of interesting creative tasks, such as arranging for piano or voices, orchestrating, creating a rehearsal score, and writing incidental music, and becomes identified with the work. The money

FIGURE 3.5 Director Kevin Albert directing the company in a workshop of *Mediterranean Voices*, and a table reading of the musical *Mask*. (*Credits:* A: Photo by Joseph Church; B: Photo by Barry Mann.)

at first is usually negligible; that is the tradeoff. You can, however, negotiate right of first refusal, and the union contract includes this protection. Although many workshops are quite intense and involve a huge workload, less experienced music directors might find a place to grow with a piece of music under more relaxed conditions, and seasoned music directors can help a new show set off on the right foot. See Figure 3.5.

Professional music directors now stand on fertile ground. The entertainment industry is currently energetic, even hyperactive, and opportunities are bountiful. There is a lively repertoire, there are diverse and prolific writers, and there are ambitious producers. As of 2014, Broadway has continued its economic escalation, and Off-Broadway is robust, too. At the same time that insurmountable financial crises and corporate greed are bringing down opera companies and symphony orchestras, popular stage performance thrives. Writers and producers are testing and tinkering with a host of new ideas for shows, on their own, in workshops, in regional theaters, and online. Songwriters are everywhere, given a boost by GarageBand and Logic and other software that turns composing into a sideline. The Disney and Universal parks have live shows; Branson, Missouri still brings in audiences in by the busload and cruise ships by the shipload for their live shows. Even the film musical has experienced a revival in recent years, with big-budget movies such as the endless stream of animated film musicals, stage musicals made into movies (*Chicago, Nine,* and *Les Miserables*) and the occasional live-action original film musical (*Burlesque, Idlewild,* and *Moulin Rouge!*). Almost every children's show on television or on the stage (and there are many) seems to include songs and extensive musical scoring. There has even been an episodic operetta on television for children (*Wonderpets!*), and a reality show that paired composers and lyricists to write popular songs. The landscape is shifting, but music directors are still in the picture, busier than ever.

PART II

Personnel

4

The Production Team

Every day, all over the world, people are organizing their musical performances into productions, dramatic or thematic, competitive or casual, richly subsidized or homemade. Every one of those productions needs someone to handle the music.

Congratulations, music director. You're hired. Introductions are in order.

The person responsible for your hiring in any professional situation was most likely a producer, a director, or a composer, or, once in a great while, a music contractor. A colleague or friend or teacher or relative may have recommended you, but it was probably a producer, director, or composer who made the final decision to give you the gig.

Every creative participant in a production, including the music director, is foremost a team member, all contributing to the piece and the production as a whole. The music may be a greater or lesser factor in a production than any other element of that production, but regardless of its standing, it, and you, as music director, will often be called upon to adapt to the work of others.

The multidisciplinary personnel working together on a production are grouped by department. Departments join up to form larger units, referred to as the "production team" and the "creative team." The creative team, those working on the artistic side, are a subset of the production team, which has representatives from all departments. Music directors are members of both teams.

Many of your creative collaborators will possess some musical sensibility even if they are not musicians by calling; music is a craft more universally practiced and partially understood than other art forms, by amateurs as well as pros. Most music directors, by contrast, have only an observer's understanding of stage direction, but a director or producer might know a fair amount about music. Therefore, during the life of a production, you might have to contend with the musical opinions of collaborators who are not entirely musically aware or articulate. By nature, the stage is a director's and choreographer's realm, and unless the music takes a very prominent role, most of the time you will be following their creative lead. You might have to perform your job under strictures or conventions dictated by your employers, especially when you are first starting out in your career. At times you will have to adapt your thought process to an unorthodox, that is, nonmusical, mode of musical thinking, and somehow make that approach productive. You should not necessarily perceive this mode as destructive to the music, or as a hindrance to the integrity of the performance, or as an affront to the music or you, its caretaker. Rather, it is an explicit demonstration that music is but one cog in a larger production machine. Your goal as music director is to adapt the music to extramusical or even anti-musical needs as expertly, smoothly, and musically as you can.

Producers

For creatively oriented music directors, there is something of a veil drawn around the business end of the entertainment business. Most music directors have little interest in or aptitude for handling significant amounts of money, especially other people's money. In order to responsibly represent producers' points of view, therefore, I have solicited descriptions from working producers and managers of what they do, and how they view their interactions with music directors.

Producers are the ones (usually there is more than one) who assemble and oversee a project and its staff, including its funding. This is why I introduce them first. They are the music director's bosses, insofar as music directors have bosses. Producers do not necessarily invest money, but organize and look after those who do. Producers are different from managers; managers, or general managers, preside over the day-to-day finances of a production (see the section "General Managers, Company Managers, et al."). Producers are in charge of management. Simply phrased, producers put on the show. Sometimes it is a producer's initiative to mount the show, while other producers seek out shows to produce, and a few shows are the producer's artistic conception. Another term for producer is "presenter," but the latter can also refer to someone who books productions into certain venues.

According to Jeffrey Seller, producer of several hit Broadway musicals, including *Rent*, *La Bohème*, and *Avenue Q*, few currently active Broadway and major tour producers exclusively produce theater for a living. Many are instead "people from the outside who come to Broadway . . . to play, participate, to make something happen, and maybe to express themselves with money that they've made in other areas, and for them it's a hobby."[1] Some are wealthy individuals with disposable income; others are corporate entities. The Max Bialystock–like fantasy figure of a crusty number cruncher always on the prowl for the next big score has gone extinct; many rock producers fit this mold as well, among them Bill Graham and Ron Delsener, and they too are mostly gone. Just as often on today's major commercial productions, music directors will have more contact with a middle manager from a large corporation assigned to the project than they will

---

1. Jeffrey Seller, in-person interview, 20 December 2012.

with a producer in the historical sense. In regional theaters and local theaters, production is the sole occupation, so there is none of the dilettantism of Broadway, though wealthy local citizens and merchants still might be the ones endowing the theater.

Producing is above all a business venture. (That's why they call it show business.) Money matters can cause difficulties for musicians motivated by creativity and artistry. Nevertheless, I reiterate that music directors, in signing on to receive financial reward for their work in a commercial venture, acknowledge their commitment to an organization whose reason for being is mostly to earn money, and thus they consent to work toward that collective goal.

One might think that the not-for-profit, academic, and amateur worlds are exempt from budgetary motivation, but they are not. In amateur and academic theaters, producers, liberated from their fund-raising capacities, function more like managers. Still, even when less money or no money changes hands, and even when all the people involved in a production concurs that they are not in it for financial gain, the fiscal realities of staging a production are inescapable. Not-for-profit organizations that need to recoup their expenses keep watch over their purses even more vigilantly than those who hope to make a profit. Amateur and educational productions, as well as professional ones, beg and borrow labor and materials by way of favors, sponsorship (such as a mention in the program or with an executive producer credit), or barter, all of which are merely forms of financing in different costumes.

Though their eyes are always on the bottom line, the finest producers encourage and underwrite excellence in new work. "When I produce a new show, I'm hoping to bring something fresh in the way it sounds to the audience," Seller adds.[2] Indeed, freshness of sound has proven to translate into profit by way of artistic interest, as has authenticity when working with music requiring a certain sound and style (like successful recent versions of *Carousel* and *Follies* on Broadway). Profit may come in the short term or the long, and to some extent it may be paid out in prestige as well as in currency. That is to say, good productions breed more productions by earning investors' trust in producers to continue to do good work.

Much of the interaction between music directors and producers occurs in preproduction. Once rehearsals have started, music directors more often deal with representatives or other employees of the producer. Producers are among the few who do not routinely attend production meetings, because the operational specifics that are covered there are not of interest to them; they are looking at the bigger picture and entrust their staff with the operations. Most conversations between music directors and producers are about either facilitation—casting, scheduling, setting up meetings, securing an outside vendor, staffing—or expenditures. If there should arise a music-related dispute or problem within the organization, a music director might solicit help in solving it from a producer, or a producer from the music director, if either party cannot settle it alone.

2. Ibid.

Music directors require a producer's approval on any costs that exceed the proscribed budget. Indeed, all requirements of the music department that incur costs of any kind are subject to the producer's assent. The higher the echelon of the production, the less privy he or she will be to a production's music budget. Music directors are expected not to overspend, and to balance quality with affordability, according to each situation. Occasionally a producer will consult a music director regarding the budgeting of a show, especially when the budget is low; this practice is more common in amateur and academic shows. Most communication between music directors and producers, however, is about specific music-related spending decisions, such as how big a keyboard rig is needed or if three tympani and a real celeste are absolutely necessary. The music directors I know, including me, are happy to entrust money management to the experts, as long as they get what they need and the musical result is good.

Music directors must recognize that many elements of their work constitute significant budget line items for a producer, who is balancing many such significant line items. Music on stage cannot happen without funding, but it also cannot succumb to parsimony. The commercial production approach that is healthiest for the music is to forecast earnings against expenses and to make budgetary choices accordingly. This is the strategy of many current productions. Most producers, despite reputations or mythology to the contrary, are not wanton cost slashers, or blackguards who take pleasure in firing musicians and replacing them with computers. In an ideal situation, producers take into account the musical needs of a production and decide what they can afford within a given financial outlook. They will most likely promote ways of doing it for less; that is in the nature of businesspeople. If their proposals are unacceptable to the creative team (of which the director is chief and the music director the musical chairperson), all parties involved can work toward an acceptable compromise.[3] Music directors will not have final say, but they can rationally and respectfully express their opinions and exert some influence through education and persuasion, toward an aesthetically workable solution.

Stage Managers

Problem solving is a music director's stock in trade, as it is for one of his or her closest colleagues, the stage manager. Veteran Broadway stage manager Frank Hartenstein described a stage manager's job to me as such: "Stage managers are responsible for everything and everybody from the proscenium upstage. Everything in the pit is yours. Everything from the pit wall behind you to the back of the house is the house manager's."[4] This is a valid summary, as long as one keeps in mind that pits have become movable objects. Hartenstein's reference to "responsibility" is an understatement. Even in

---

3. Ibid.
4. Frank Hartenstein, in-person interview, 15 December 2008.

a small production with only a few performers, the operations of a show in production are demanding and neverending. What's more, stage managers act as onsite spokespeople and surrogates for producers, directors, technicians, designers, and Actors' Equity. A music director's congested agenda looks measly in comparison to a stage manager's.

Lawrence Stern's authoritative text on stage management specifies duties of stage management that extend into virtually every aspect of production—technical, personal, financial, logistical, dramatic—but makes almost no mention of music, and little mention of sound.[5] Stage managers are indeed in charge of all these matters, and the music, too, but Stern's omission makes sense, because stage managers run the show along with, or alongside, the music director. The music runs parallel to their work; they do not control it as they do some other theatrical elements, such as scene shifts or understudies or the rehearsal schedule. They do not give the music any more attention that they do anything else; for them it is another item on a checklist.

A musical production typically carries at least two stage managers, more often three, and sometimes more. The head of the team is called the production stage manager; below him or her are stage managers and assistant stage managers. The hierarchy is relatively unimportant except for executive decision making; most duties are shared equally among the team members. Stage managers' desks and offices are beehives of activity, and almost everyone involved in a production checks in with the stage managers daily, if not more often. Music directors are regulars there. Almost every part of a music director's administrative output passes through stage management.

Stage managers turn out a slew of documentation: rehearsal schedules and reports, show schedules and reports (Figure 4.1), contact sheets, memoranda. By referring to this paperwork and through their conversations with stage management, music directors disseminate relevant information to the music staff and performers.

Two parallels between the professional nature and creative function of music direction and stage management in production are particularly interesting and noteworthy. First, in the eyes of Actors' Equity, stage managers are strictly rank and file, as conductors are in the AFM; otherwise, it would be illegal for either to be represented by a labor union. In reality, though both stage managers and music directors (conductors, too) function quite managerially. They may not sign the hiring and firing slips, but they do make hiring and firing decisions. They most certainly supervise, and tell others what to do. Like music directors, most stage managers handle their managerial duties collegially rather than autocratically. They acknowledge the collaborative effort and make a point of promoting mutual respect and good will in the workplace, even in difficult situations.

Second, along with the music director, stage managers copilot the performance of a musical show. One stage manager "calls" the show, that is, gives cues to the actors and technical operators from a desk offstage or in a booth, and one or more are positioned

---

5. Lawrence Stern and Alice R. O'Grady, *Stage Management*, 10th ed., Upper Saddle River, NJ: Pearson, 2013.

ROCK OF AGES BROADWAY
Performance Report for **/**/****
Helen Hayes Theatre
Performance Number ****
Broadway Performance ****

Act 1 Up: 8:05:47

Act 1 Down: 9:09:52

Act 1 Elapsed Time: 1:04:05
Intermission: 0:18:46

Act 2 Up: 9:28:38

Act 2 Down: 10:26:05

Act 2 Elapsed Time: 0:57:27
Elapsed Time: 2:20:18
House Count: 579

OUT/IN

***** OUT (sick) - ***** ON as Drew - Vocal Booth CUT

***** OUT (vocal rest) - ***** ON as Stacee Jaxx - ***** as Joey Primo
***** (swung out) - ***** ON as Young Groupie

***** OUT - ***** ON Conducting
***** OUT - ***** ON Bass

TODAY'S SCHEDULE
1 p-5p - Work Call

TOMORROW'S SCHEDULE

5p-6p - Onstage Rehearsal w/ Piano - no Props (Lonny/Dennis understudies)
7:15p - "Motorin" Vocal Brush Up (Ensemble)
8:00p - Performance #1173

TECHNICAL

CARP: The SL stripper curtain got caught on the wall of the Bourbon Room on its way offstage after Hate/Heat. It was hung up at the top of Hit Me With Your Best Shot and in the middle of the number, The Head Carpenter was able to bring both sides in a hair to release the snag and then page both sides up.

WARDROBE: The zipper on one of *****'s Joey Primo boots broke and we can't get it repaired until Monday.
He will wear his Act One shoes for the full show for the rest of the weekend.

REMARKS

Very solid and tight performance tonight! It was a hot one on and off stage, but the cast muscled through (minus a couple jackets here and there). Nice responses from the crowd who seemed to really enjoy the show. ***** had a strong performance as Drew and ***** was a vibrant and fiery Young Groupie, as always. We got another big standing ovation before "Don't Stop" was over.

FIGURE 4.1 A stage-management performance report from *Rock of Ages*. Because the musicians in the show are on stage, substitutes in the orchestra are listed; most reports list only the conductor's name. (Report authored by Matthew DiCarlo, Production Stage Manager, *Rock of Ages*.)

elsewhere or rove backstage. The myriad performance elements that work in sync in performance—actors on stage, musical accompaniment, lighting, scenery shifts—are synchronized by the stage managers calling cues and directing the backstage traffic. Some calling stage managers use the score as well as the script and technical plot to call a show. Similarly, the music director on the podium cues the musical elements and synchronizes them with the nonmusical ones, in conjunction with the stage manager. Because many stage events are accompanied by or pertain to musical cues, stage managers count in rhythm, like conductors, to prepare and indicate their timings to all parties listening on the headsets, such as "Lights one hundred twelve . . . one-two-three-and-*go*." (I have listened in befuddlement and wonder to stage managers counting into cues in patterns of four or eight even when the music was in three-quarter or six-eight time.)

General Managers, Company Managers, House Managers, and Production Managers

General managers of Broadway shows handle a production's finances. They write and sign music directors' checks, and approve or disallow significant expenses. General managers, like producers, will always appreciate a music director's efforts to defend the budget lines. As something akin to a junior executive or middle manager in a corporation, a music director is wise to treat respectfully and make friends with the folks in the payroll department. Yet other than the occasional exchange regarding expenses and the production-wide issues (schedules, personnel, logistics) that they discuss at production meetings, music directors and general managers have only irregular contact during production. For certain production organizations, general managers take on producer-like functions, particularly when the general manager has an artistically based background or education.

Company managers are employees of the general manager and work with the entire production staff as representatives of the producer. Unlike producers and general managers, company managers are in contact with music directors almost daily. They handle the needs of all of a production's personnel, including the music team. They field complaints, fulfill requests, secure tickets, and arrange special events. Company managers on Broadway track performances and rehearsal hours for the music director and pay him or her accordingly. Company managers are also the equivalent of a human resources department. Inevitably, issues and conflicts arise during production, and company managers are the first to step in to resolve them. The music director, the stage manager, and the company manager form something of a managerial association once a show is up and running. "It is imperative for the Music Director, Company Manager and Stage Manager have a tight working relationship during a show's run. Together, the three watch over the show each day to ensure that a consistent show is presented every time the curtain goes up."[6] Music directors treat company managers, whose job it is to make everyone's professional situation as positive as can be, with more than due regard. Doing so is easy, as most company managers are affable, efficient, and here to help you.

6. Eric Cornell, email interview, 13 January 2013.

House managers look after the theater, the box office, and the audience. The reason they are relevant is that on Broadway, they also distribute paychecks to all orchestra musicians, except the conductor, checks written against the theater's account. This is an arcane system dating back to an era in which each Broadway theater had a resident orchestra (each theater still has resident technical personnel). Only if a production somehow spills over from the pit or stage into the house will the music director deal directly with a house manager.

A producer often designates or hires one or more people to coordinate the different departments and see to their diverse and chaotic needs. Someone holding the title of production manager or supervisor or coordinator might organize the creative and design teams; a technical director leads the stage crew. These managers are excellent liaisons between music directors and their production colleagues and are often the most expedient route to solving urgent technical problems. With smaller production outfits, a stage manager or producer might perform a similar organizational function.

Acting as a manager of anything other than music is counterintuitive to me and many of my musical cohorts, but the best music directors embrace their managerial and administrative work. Good business and working conditions make for better musical output, and as music director you can help to create a healthy atmosphere with an obliging attitude toward your paperwork, and your fellow paper pushers, as well as your musical work. In a production organization there are many thankless jobs, and the sincere dedication and care of those who work far behind the scenes—assistants in the cubicles at the producer's office, ushers in the aisles, music copyists, dance captains, costume menders—are truly impressive, admirable, and inspiring. The sense of community that develops within a production begins (and ends) with the people behind it, and their relationships have a tangible bearing on the success of the artistic product. Music directors, as a key part of this production organization, can contribute to the collective good will with commitment and enthusiasm at least comparable to those who get far less applause.

5

The Creative Team

A music director's primary collaborators are the director, the choreographer (if there is one), and the composer. Though producers employ and pay music directors, the production belongs to the creative principals. It is their vision under which music directors work, and whom they report to, as it were. Music directors can better execute their work by apprehending their teammates' processes, and how music direction fits in with what their collaborators do.

Composers and Lyricists

Most composers are on site only if a show is a new work or a significant new production of an existing work. As often as not, the composer is absent, and the music director is his or her staunch and perhaps sole exponent. Relationships between composers and music directors are mostly smooth and symbiotic, the evidence for which is that many composers employ the same music directors regularly. The two jobs are interdependent, and mutually beneficial. As will be evident in chapter 10, "Arranging for Music Director," and chapter 15, "Adapting Music to the Production," when arranging or adapting music, music directors think very much like composers, so the two processes move comfortably in tandem. The composer and/or lyricist knows what is best for the music, but not always what is best for the music in context of a production, and relies on the music director as a liaison and custodian. Some composers articulate their intentions and needs very clearly, in notation, in words, or by demonstration, and others do not, or cannot. It is up to music directors to develop a rapport or system that helps them interpret composers' intentions and translate them to any others who need to know.

Music directors cannot think separately of the lyricists and librettists who collaborate with composers on stage music, because words and music are inseparable, at least in their ideal state. A stage composition includes anything textual; that is to say, the score encompasses the lyrics and any spoken text that falls within musical numbers. For a music director, long passages of unaccompanied dialogue may merely be breaks in the music. Whereas most non-composing lyricists are quite musical—writing lyrics is, after all, a skill dependent on music—not all of them are, and some are but are not musically conversant. (A lyricist once approached me in rehearsal, independently of the composer, to express her concern that the words in a certain passage of an up-tempo rock song were unintelligible, and asked that I slow down those measures "twenty clicks or so.") On the other hand, there are some lyricists who are the prime creative force behind a songwriting team, going so far as to dictate sung rhythms or grooves and even melodies to their partners. In rehearsal, they may be the more outspoken spokespersons of the songwriting team, or at least are equally interactive with the music director.

A composer present in production becomes the de facto head of the music department, but typically does not take the reins in this capacity. Composers may also take an informal but important role in coaching singers, demonstrating feels, or advising the music director and musicians. Their presence is informative and enriching for performers and the music staff, but there can be pitfalls. Without an ongoing performance relationship with a performer, a composer's offhanded remark or suggestion can mushroom into a problem. Composer to performer: "I love when you belt that high note, even though I know you can get the same power when you mix it." Two months later, singer to music director: "I'll be out for a few weeks. Belting that high note has really blown out my voice, and I know the composer really wants me to belt it." Music directors mediate and interpret composers' remarks, as long as they accord appropriate respect to the composer and the music. Sometimes it is wiser for a music director to reserve any strenuous exhortations for those issues that are most crucial. A well-known or "star" composer may also assume the mantle of leadership of the entire creative team. When a star's voice is heard, other voices in the room go silent, even the heavyweights'. Only a few well-known composers I have met seem to like it that way; most are bewildered because no one else is speaking.

When creating a show, whatever form it takes, writers take tremendous care with the details of construction of a score, on small and large scales both. The music director bears at least partial responsibility for the correct execution of what the writers have so meticulously crafted. The composer, lyricist, and librettist are likewise entrusting their work to the stage performers, under the leadership of the music director (and of course the director). All are relying on the music director to properly incorporate the music into the production and to encourage approaches to and techniques of rehearsal and performance that will best serve the material.

The majority of writers for the stage, especially those who preceded the predominance of pop and rock music, are quite well versed in serious music, yet they write music that is purposefully uncomplicated. Good stage songs tend to be straightforward and not overfilled with ideas. Serious composers tend to think on a grander scale, in which formality, prolongation of motivic ideas, and interconnection of material take precedence over spontaneity and universality. A theater audience cannot be bothered with working too hard musically; they are absorbed in the story or the performer, and they have access to the show only once for the price of their tickets. Thus music for the stage is usually accessible, and is immediate in its effect. But it is also detailed, intelligent, and above all relevant and constantly attuned to what is happening on stage, in content and concept. Music directors work with the writers to keep the music comprehensible and relevant and to make its detail vivid.

Some composers scrupulously arrange and notate their scores, and some continue to edit them throughout production, working with the music director to make changes as needed. Some composers will also make instrumental choices as part of their compositional process, and work closely with an orchestrator, if not orchestrating the score themselves. Obviously in these cases, the music director's and orchestrator's roles are reduced. Other composers leave more up to the production music team, and just oversee their work; others remain detached from production entirely.

Music directors deal mostly with musical material that is linked to a broader purpose or another form of entertainment, unless it is presented in pure concert form. Concert music is customarily presented unedited and unchanged, and if it is edited or changed, the change is announced. A performance of an art song that has been rearranged will credit the arranger as well as the composer. Pop artists, too, publicize that their music will be heard in an unexpected fashion, such as *Led Zeppelin Unplugged* or, conversely, *Brahms Rocks!* (either hypothetical production will probably need a music director). Whereas music directors are respectful of a composer's work for a stage show or production, they view all music as wholly adaptable. This is true both with living composers, whether they are present during production or not, and with composers past. Composers are usually not overly protective of their work (though their heirs can be, as the Gershwins were notorious for, at least until recently), and are aware of the need to adjust it to the stage and production. They also know that adjustments and adaptation inspire new ideas, ones that are organically connected with the onstage story or theme and are thereby more effective.

Music directors work with all brands of composers during their careers, from pop artists to schooled artisans, living and departed. Irving Berlin was perhaps the archetypical pop stage songwriter[1], and the tradition continues through to Freddie Mercury, Bono and The Edge, and Dolly Parton. The stage has also welcomed works by Bernstein, Puccini, Weill, Sondheim, and other musicians of more vaunted artistic repute. Straddling the line between the popular and legitimate musical realms is a time-worn practice. Mozart and Bizet wrote musical theater, Schubert and Bartok wrote folk dances, Ravel and Satie and Milhaud dabbled in jazz, and Billy Joel, Paul McCartney, David Byrne, and Brian Eno have all written concert works. Charles Strouse, the composer of *Annie* and the score for the acclaimed film *Bonnie and Clyde*, also composed

---

1. One also hears the term "melodist" applied to an untrained composer, but I believe the word gives songwriting short shrift: important as the melody is, there's much more to songwriting than melody.

an atonal opera, *Nightingale*, and Stephen Schwartz, the composer of *Godspell* and *Pippin* and many other a hit show, had an opera performed at the Metropolitan Opera in New York. The experimental quasi-operas of Phillip Glass and others walk a thin line between intellectualism and transparency. Some stage composers, such as (the late) Marvin Hamlisch and Rupert Holmes, are also superb arrangers and producers, as well as erudite musical thinkers. Some writers stay true to their style when writing for the stage, while others do their best to write stagey music or music that is sonorically evocative of the stage context. Because stage music is specific to each production, it accommodates composers of all ilk, from the most cultured to the imaginative amateur.

One can draw a dividing line by saying that a songwriter is concerned mostly with melody, rhythm, basic harmony, basic structure, and how music and lyrics go together. Arranging, routing, rewriting, and many other matters are left for someone else to attend to. On the other hand, a composer takes command of most aspects of the music. He or she will be far more specific with melody, rhythm, harmony, and structure, and will add to the compositional process matter such as counterpoint, voicing (the relative placement of tones within a chord), registration (high and low placement of tones), instrumentation, and articulation, along with sharing the more basic concerns of songwriting. Moreover, originality is among a "serious" composer's overriding concerns, but songwriters, including stage composers, are more derivative of one another, and themselves, purposefully or inadvertently. This is not to say that originality is never a songwriter's concern, too, but in many cases, it patently is not. One should in no way infer that composers possess a greater talent than do songwriters; it is just a different one. Songwriting is among the most difficult musical endeavors of all, and many excellent composers of other musical forms have trouble doing it well. Many do not try. (If every musician knew how to write great songs that sold millions, then all musicians would be doing it.)

Is it necessary for music directors to make a distinction? It is, because they must account for how each writer wants and expects his or her music to be handled, how specifically he or she has notated or recorded or otherwise communicated the music to them, and the extent to which he or she has pre-customized the score to the production. These considerations will help predict the scope of the music direction work. Music directors collaborating with serious composers will very likely do more coordinating and less creating, while music directors working with songwriters can take a far more creatively decisive role, manipulating material with far greater freedom.

Directors

The director of a stage performance is responsible for all creative elements of a production, including the music. In musical theater, the director is the central figure in a production, and the undisputed leader. This balance of power differs from opera, in which the music is the dominant force, and the stage director will defer to the music director and to the opera itself; regardless, all visual aspects of the production are the director's.

In a concert or ceremony, stage direction is minimal, including putting people in place, coordinating entrances and exits, and bringing the lights up and down.

> In the most basic terms, the director is a production's primary storyteller. A play has only one plot (including subplots), but it contains many potential stories. The interpretation of the primary characters largely determines the story, so in effect, every production of the same play will inevitably tell a different tale. One of the most important functions a director fulfills is determining, with the actors and designers, which story to tell and how to tell it coherently.[2]

As I have repeatedly noted, every stage production is different in nature, purpose, and meaning. According to noted stage director Harold Clurman, "Every director makes his own 'law,' depending not on his own temperament or artistic inclination, but on the circumstances of a production."[3] A director will not do *Camelot* on Broadway as he or she would with an amateur company, nor will a music director. A director and music director will not hold the singers in a topical cabaret revue to the same high vocal or acting standards as he or she would a Broadway *Camelot* cast.

A director does more than envision a play for the stage. That is only half the job; the other half is realizing the vision, artistically and physically, in production. This is a considerable undertaking for one individual, to say the least. Yet there are directors who take on even more: choreographing, producing, or writing book or lyrics. Though they bear the ultimate responsibility themselves, a crucial part of directors' success comes from assembling the right group of people to share it. Among a director's closest associates in a musical is the music director; often the director, choreographer, and music director are thought of a creative triumvirate, and ideally they work in unerring sync with one another.

Like a conductor ignoring the seemingly absurdly fast metronome markings on the *Urtext* of Beethoven's Third Symphony and other works, the director acknowledges and attends to the area between the composition (the play) and its fruitful execution (the production). Clurman again writes

> [t]here is perhaps an analogy with performances of music. We do not hear Bach or Mozart as they were rendered in their day. Our audiences would probably not enjoy them if we did. . . . The director discerns a script's style—the production method best suited to convey its quality and meaning—not through stage directions set down in the script or through discussion with the author himself, but by what the author has actually written: his plot line and his dialogue. The director translates his understanding of the material into stage language.[4]

2. Michael Bloom, *Thinking like a Director, a Practical Handbook*. New York: Faber & Faber, 2001, p. 5.
3. Harold Clurman, *On Directing*, New York: Fireside, 1972.
4. Ibid., p. 47.

In dramatic musical theater works, music is an element of the storytelling, and as music director, you align your musical interpretation to the director's interpretation of the whole. If a director's approach seems unmusical or musically impossible, you must respond with creative thinking and compromise. Some friction between the needs of the direction and the needs of the music is inevitable. The priorities of the two departments will sometimes simply differ, and aesthetically, music and drama already have an uneasy fellowship. Furthermore, an excusably preoccupied director may think of music as only one item on an overcrowded agenda, while the music director holds dear the music as the heart of the production.

Administratively speaking, the director is the creative chief of staff, and in this capacity is further overwhelmed with information and responsibilities. Some directors bear this load with authority, while others are more passive, and allow their team to work without interference. Very weak directors jeopardize a production with their timidity or reticence. Often, music directors' communication with busy directors must be very succinct. Music directors should keep in mind that no matter how vital an issue may seem to them, the director may not view it that way. Music directors must think both autonomously and as a director would think. They may have to figure out how to fit their contribution to the director's vision even without the director's involvement; the director's lack of comment on what they have done is probably a sign of approval.

Certain directors freely confess their lack of understanding of music, and empower the music director to take care of all things musical. Still, the music director ensures that the music remain in line with the director's overall purpose. Other directors are very hands-on with the music in their productions. Let's use two examples, first fictional, then one from an actual production.

Let's imagine that in a regional theater in a city of 100,000 in the Midwest there is a very extroverted, very proud, very loud former leading man with a couple of Broadway musical credits who is now doing what he has always wanted to do: direct. In this scenario he will be directing an "extravaganza" of show tunes to be presented in quasi-concert form at the local concert hall, featuring the local semiprofessional symphony orchestra, some guest artists who also have a couple of Broadway credits, and the State University choral society and jazz band. This overeager director might very well commandeer the music director's role and personally coach each singer. He might demonstrate with his own stentorian voice the correct vocal production, enunciation, and proper vowel formation on a list of songs that includes "Some Enchanted Evening" from *South Pacific*, "Gethsemane" from *Jesus Christ Superstar*, and "Out Tonight" from *Rent*. A blowhard or bully of a director will be only a blowhard or a bully; as music director you can usually disregard the bombast, keeping in mind that you will still be conducting the performance. Let him do his thing, offer advice when solicited, and conduct or accompany to the best of your ability, no matter how misguided or outlandish the process. Regardless of any director's difficult personality or untenable opinions, the musical performance is always subject to his approval. I include this scenario not, of course, to mock directors, or to reinforce a stereotype, but to stress that the director is in charge, and music directors are best off working from the assumption that a director always has good intentions.

In a much better world, and the real world, I had the great pleasure of working with director Des McAnuff on the musical *Tommy* on Broadway. A fine and knowledgeable musician himself, Des was very involved in creating the score for the show, as indeed was every member of the creative team. *Tommy* was a dramatic stage show adapted from a "concept" album by The Who, with most of its music and lyrics by Pete Townshend. For its adaptation to a dramatic stage form, the story required specification and clarification, as the story on the album is tremendously evocative, but vague. In Des's conception, the tale would be told largely visually, with music throughout.

The creative team assembled the score for the musical, as well as revising the story and outlining the staging, in a series of meetings in Des's living room. These meetings were intense at times, due to the very brief time we had available to put the score, libretto (the verbal part of the musical, also known as the "book"), and visual elements together. The theater that housed the show's première production, the La Jolla Playhouse, a not-for-profit regional theater, could afford only so much preproduction time to import a staff from all over the country to San Diego. So we wrote the first act in the few weeks leading up to rehearsal, and the second act in the evenings after daytime rehearsals of the first act. Each day we generated new music, new scores, and new staging and choreography.

In attendance were the choreographer, Wayne Cilento, and his assistant, Lisa Mordente; the music director (me) and my associate conductor in La Jolla, the brilliant pianist Ted Baker (also our primary rehearsal pianist and eventual keyboardist in the pit); orchestrator Steve Margoshes; two assistant directors, Michael Wilson and Lisa Portes (both of whom have since gone on to illustrious careers); the occasional visiting designer; and a lot of other people I no longer can remember but probably should.[5] The composer was sometimes available via telephone (in an era before cell phones) and fax (email was just coming into vogue). The La Jolla unit would usually save up our questions for Pete Townshend and include them in periodic longer phone calls. With a model of the stage and plastic miniatures of the actors and set pieces on the coffee table, the director and choreographer storyboarded the musical in three dimensions. As I played the music at the piano, they and their assistants would "act out" the staging, or we'd all sing along with several different recorded versions of the music, pausing the CD or lifting the needle temporarily off the vinyl if we were inserting music. We would determine durations of such elements as phrases, scenes, dances, onstage activities, and scene shifts, one by one, adding new music and restructuring old, until everything worked in

---

5. It was important to me to get all those names in; all of them contributed significantly to the writing of the show, and they and others in similar positions are not always properly recognized for their work. They deserve more than a footnote.

synergy. The seamlessness of the show's staging and of its reconstructed, refitted score was in large part due to this highly collaborative effort, and to the high level of musicianship of the director, who capably and confidently guided the team through a very time- and budget-constrained process.

Early in production, much of the interaction between director and music director will be readying musical material, as it was with *Tommy* and, just as important to the production and the job, planning—planning the musical approaches, planning the casting, planning production schedules, planning the sound design, and mapping out all procedural and technical aspects of rehearsals and performance. As the production moves forward, the director and music director may begin to operate more independently, but they keep closely and regularly in touch. Directors might or might not attend music rehearsals; it is their choice. If they do, they are entitled to run the rehearsal. Most will not; they will allow the music director to lead, and will chime in along the way.

Only on rare occasion do directors overstep a music director's rehearsal jurisdiction, as in the previous fictional scenario. During a staging rehearsal for one production for which I was the music supervisor (I was not at the rehearsal but orchestrating in a studio nearby), the director gathered the chorus on stage and conducted them through an *a cappella* number from the show, making changes in the vocal arrangement as he went. Understandably, the music director was beside himself with anger, and I was rushed in to intervene. Instead of openly voicing his disapproval in rehearsal, the music director probably should have done so in a private conversation with the director, but this was a particularly egregious intrusion. Fortunately, most directors think of their staff not as employees but collaborators, and most, when they breach a musical boundary, do it innocently, if perhaps insultingly. If as music director you do run up against a malicious or insensitive director, simply finish out the job and don't work with him or her again. Unfortunately, some directors who behave despicably have been tolerated, as a trade-off for being talented, though in the new age of political correctness and harassment lawsuits, it is less common than it once was.

Choreographers

The line between dance and naturalistic movement on stage can be very blurry. For the purposes of this study I will define choreography as any kind of stylized movement that is part of a musical number (more on this topic in chapter 10, "Arranging for Music Directors," and chapter 14, "Rehearsals with Directors and Choreographers"). Of course, not all musical productions for the stage involve dance, but many involve some form of movement, for which the choreographer is responsible, in the same way a music director is responsible for the music. One might call a choreographer a "movement director."

The energy generated by music and dance working together is powerful and captivating. No one can escape the emotional wallop of *West Side Story*'s "Rumble," or be unimpressed by the precision of the Rockettes' formations in Victor Herbert's "March of the Wooden Soldiers." The ideal marriage of dance and music departments in a production is perfectly collaborative, with free exchange of ideas, plenty of give and take, and mutual trust. Unlike drama and music, the meeting of dance and music in stage productions is an auspicious one, as they share an abstract and lyrical core. A successful alliance of music and dance on stage merges the two forms of expression into a cohesive entity.

In a musical, the substance of dance and music, alone and in combination, ideally stems from the storytelling, and in a revue or concert, from the style and content of the material. Music is the impulse for dancing, and the nature and detail of the music are reflected in the dance. Inversely, the shapes, phrases, and accents that the choreographer creates are accounted for in the music. Choreography quite commonly uses "dissonance" between dance and music for deliberate dramatic effect. As was true with stage direction, any incompatibility between music and dance may turn out to be a source of unexpected creativity, a new idea better than the old, one that because of its composite essence is more effective than either element individually.

Musicians and dancers have collaborated throughout history, but it is no secret that their collaborative process is at times turbulent. When they work in sync, the similarities of the art forms and their integration in practice take precedence over any discord between them. Still, any personality conflicts aside, a basic dilemma underlies the disharmony. Is the music being danced to, or is the music accompanying the dance? In stage productions, the answer is far more often the latter. Visibility and physicality are more immediately impressive to the audience than sound. The music comes out of nowhere, but the dance unfolds right before your eyes.

Some choreographers have had the reputation of being quite imperious, if not despotic. This trait could be a result of dance's visual primacy in a stage show, or might be a vestige of the iconic switch-wielding dance teachers under whom choreographers earned their calluses as neophyte students. Jerome Robbins's vicious and unpredictable temper and Bob Fosse's megalomania and self-destructive philandering are the stuff of backstage legend. Choreographers can certainly be taskmasters with their dancers—just ask any dancer—and at times they view the pianist in the room as an interchangeable minion, there only to obey the choreographer's methodical strictures. This perception sometimes extends to music directors, who are much more than accompanists. Luckily for music directors, choreographers cannot get by without the music (whereas, music directors like to remind themselves, the music doesn't have to be choreographed), and thereby require music directors, and pianists for rehearsals and classes.

Often during a production rehearsal process, a music director will dedicate a single accompanist to all dance rehearsals, for consistency and to give the choreographer a sense of security. Productions also often employ a separate dance arranger, someone whose undivided attention can be given to working with the choreographer to create music that will accompany danced portions of the score. Sometimes a music director will assume the role of dance arranger, particularly when the quantity of dance music needed for a production is manageable. See chapter 6, "The Music Team"; chapter 10, "Arranging for Music Directors"; and chapter 14, "Rehearsals with Directors and Choreographers" for more on dance arrangers and dance rehearsals.

One inevitable topic of discussion between music directors and choreographers is tempo. Tempos will constantly be under the microscope of a choreographer, and of dancers, too. Historically, ubiquitous tempo disputes in professional theater are partly the reason for the increasing, now almost pervasive, use of metronomes and click tracks in stage performance. I have much more to say on this issue throughout this book.

Designers and Technicians

Music directors interact with stage designers primarily on practical matters relating to the music. The business they conduct together is usually amicable and to the point. Much of it involves planning and scheduling in preproduction. Most pivotal to the music is the sound designer, but music directors also work with other designers of, for instance, lighting, scenery, and costume. Lighting design extends to the lighting used by musicians to read their music, stand lights, and overhead or "work" or utilitarian lighting. A scenic design may spill over into orchestra territory, or an orchestra might be built into the scenery. Occasionally the music director might have to wear certain clothing in performance. Most music directors and orchestra members generally prefer not to be in costume; tuxedos are perplexing enough. When a production specifies something other than typical pit wear (concert black, casual black, dinner jacket, tails, or street clothes), a costume designer will create their costumes.

On Broadway and in most professional productions, crew electricians ably set up and maintain the lighting for the orchestra. There are many clever lighting options available on the market today for musicians, including cordless lamps that mitigate the eternal quandaries of how to dim the pit lights and where to find enough outlets. (Soon, I suspect, electronic tablets and readers will eliminate the need for stand lighting altogether.)

Set designers are very respectful of the music for a show. They are, however, subject to the director's vision, and the music might be a casualty of the designer's compliance. Music directors working with nontraditional pit setups that result from unorthodox direction and scenic design choices should proactively connect with the director and designers early on in the process. If the pit is to be covered over by stage extensions or squeezed in tightly by space-eating machinery under the deck (the stage floor), or the orchestra is to be situated where hearing or balancing them properly will be an issue, good planning and staking an early claim will go a long way. This is one reason that as music director you must never miss a production meeting, even though the topic there is almost never the music. When it is, you want to be there to have your say.

The furnishings of a Broadway orchestra—the chairs, music stands, microphone stands, the carpeting on the floor, the conductor's podium, and any other equipment owned or leased by the production—and their setup are the responsibility of the props department. In my experience a props crew are the music director's best friends on the spot. They work miracles with their ingenuity, elevating the use of items like gaffer's tape, glue guns, and two-by-fours to a science. When a stand is wobbly, a floor is creaking, a power cord lurks like a trip wire, a piece of music won't stay on the shelf, or the conductor needs to be six inches taller, the props crew are the ones to call. Creativity is not confined in the theater to the "talent," and properties "masters" live up to their superlative honorific.

Costumes are only a minor nuisance for musicians working with a stage production, but they tolerate them, and are paid a little extra (at least under union guidelines) for wearing them in public. Costume designers and wardrobe personnel are aware of the inconvenience. Dressing musicians is inconvenient for them, too. So music directors' dealings with costumers are usually informal, friendly, and fast. I have tolerated playing such diverse costumed roles as Beethoven in Hell (Randy Newman's *Faust*, with a Beethoven wig, no less), Jenny Lind's conductor in *Barnum*, and Harvey, the singing bass player in Cy Coleman's charming *I Love My Wife* (I did the show in stock, so I was the singing piano player instead). In *Sister Act*, the conductor makes an enjoyable cameo appearance in the finale as the Pope, levitating on the podium from the pit to bless the singing nuns (a Pope costume was preset in the pit, and during the number, while the band played to a click track, the conductor put on the robe). As I, along with every other conductor of the show on Broadway, reported, the comments they received from friends and fans after the show never had anything to do with the fine vocalists or orchestra, or their conducting; it was always, "I loved you as the Pope!"

From specializations in modern stagecraft come new designers and new relationships. I have worked with, among others, projections designers to synchronize video imagery with music, fight captains to arrange music for boxing and fencing, and a special effects wizard, who, after singeing my eyebrows with an exploding piece of scenery, moved it six feet further upstage.

The design element that musicians are most dependent on and most concerned with is sound. The sound of a human voice or a cello or French horn is fundamentally changed the moment it is sent through a microphone, an amplifier, or speakers. All the care that composers and arrangers devote to their music and the music director puts into its presentation is subject to the manipulation of the sound designer. Broadway sound designers do not remain on site after opening night, and the very important work of mixing a show is the job of a sound operator, or board operator, often referred to simply as the "sound person." Sometimes, especially in concert settings, there may be more than one operator at the board, and in some situations the sound designer will also be the operator.

Because their work has such a powerful effect on the music, as music director you should think of the sound designer and sound operator as key players on the music team. Only some professional music directors, however, have a say in hiring a sound designer, though you may be able to express a preference. On Broadway, producers generally make their hiring decisions on the basis of past work experience and the most cost-effective bid.

The sound designer consults with the director, producer, technical director, and music director to decide how and to what extent a production will be amplified; there are many options. (Though wireless microphones have come way down in price, they are still not easy to get right.) Music directors should work closely with sound designers, especially amateur ones, to make the best of the available personnel, equipment, and knowledge. In lower-budget or amateur situations, sound design will probably be simpler, perhaps a few overhead or hand-held microphones. As in many musical disciplines, the profusion of computer-based software has made some of the basic skills of sound design accessible to a greater population. It is in music directors' best interest in this amplified, digitized universe to keep up with these technologies. The introduction of the synthesizer programmer in the next chapter, "The Music Team," will corroborate the wisdom of this recommendation.

In all your relationships with directors and other creative staff you reap the rewards of collaboration. The music mutates to something greater as a result of your interactions; the collaboration is at the essence of a music director's work. At the essence of the accompaniment for a production are the other musicians with whom a music director works, and they are the subjects of "The Music Team."

6

The Music Team

The roster of musicians who work with and under the music director are specific to each production, as are the manner in which they are hired, by whom, and in what order. The music director may not be the first person on board. Music team members often come in bunches. The producer of a new Broadway musical, for example, might engage a music director, contractor, and orchestrator independently of one another but at the same time. A composer might prefer to always work with the same orchestrator, who in turn might favor a certain music director. If the music director is hired first, then he or she might be responsible for hiring some or all of the remaining music team, and takes into account prerequisites or endorsements from producers, directors, contractors, fellow musicians, and others. In the majority of cases, music directors will select their own associate and assistant conductors and rehearsal musicians. Although in my experience, music departments and orchestras function better when the music director is involved in, if not in charge of, music staff hiring decisions, this protocol will only sometimes be in effect. Larger and more expensive productions will generally have bigger staffs, and more people will have a say in the staffing.

The music director is a music department's chairperson and informational hub, as well as its artistic governor. He or she is responsible for properly conveying to the music team all necessary information—material, direction, alterations, explanations, procedures—originating from many sources and passing through many channels, constantly and instantaneously. The stream is perpetually overflowing, and sometime backlogged. As music director you may choose to delegate some administrative responsibility to an associate music director or departmental assistant. The ultimate accountability for information handling, of course, is always yours, so your designated assistant should be very organized and reliable. The results of improper communication can be troublesome or even calamitous in production. Musicians, for instance, cannot have on their stand for tonight's performance yesterday's version of a part that was rewritten overnight. A rehearsal pianist cannot miss a dance rehearsal that the stage managers rescheduled last minute at the choreographer's request. A singer needs to know that the director has denied the request to transpose her song to another key. Fortunately, computers, email, smartphones, and texting have made communication easier, and are immensely useful in production, where instantaneous exchange is obligatory.

Conductors, Associates, and Assistants

A conductor is one who leads a chorus or orchestra through a piece of music in performance and in rehearsal. Music directors usually assume conducting duties in any production that requires a conductor (a majority do). There are also times when they choose not to, or cannot, conduct, and delegate the conducting to an associate or assistant conductor. As noted in chapter 3, "Job Opportunities for Music Directors," on the current Broadway scene, music supervisors—those doing much of the music direction work described in this book—often hire a "music director" or "conductor" to lead the orchestra in performance. As noted in chapter 1, "Music Direction: Today and Yesterday," Local 802's Collective Bargaining Agreement (CBA) with the Broadway League, covers conductors, but not music directors or supervisors (though in a 2013 article in their journal the union expressed interest in attaching benefits to supervision fees[1]).

There are many reasons that as music director you might not conduct certain performances. You might want to observe from the house to hear a show from the audience's perspective or to work with the sound operator on the balances. You might be unavailable because you are working on a different project, or you may simply be unavoidably detained. The associate is your primary substitute, or "sub," and an assistant is a secondary cover. There can be only one associate, but there may be any number of assistants.

The CBA specifically delineates the titles "associate" and "assistant" conductor. Associate conductors act as understudies for conductors, might or might not play in the orchestra, and are paid a salary premium whenever they perform in the orchestra, regardless of whether they are conducting (on Broadway, the premium is 30 percent over scale). Assistant conductors are full-time members of the orchestra, and receive additional compensation only when conducting. They supposedly conduct fewer performances than associates, though in reality the vagaries of Broadway conducting organizations and schedules make this clause virtually moot. The music director or primary conductor determines the conducting schedule of a Broadway show, with the approval of the producers or director or stage managers. Union bylaws stipulate five substitutes for each orchestra member in an extended run, but the rule is only loosely applied to conductors. Obviously in a production with only one or a few musicians, the associate is likely a sub whom you have trained solely as your cover, does not perform nightly as

---

1. Tino Gagliardi, "President's Report: We're Getting Our Message Out," *Allegro* 113:4 (April 2013), http://www.local802afm.org/2013/04/were-getting-our-message-out/.

a member of the orchestra, and might or might not have been part of the rehearsal and creative processes.

My definitions of associates and assistants add some detail to the union's. An associate conductor might function in several ways, in line with or in place of the music director. Like a music director, an associate's job can range from one or two simple duties to full creative participation. Distributing those duties is up to you as music director, and in some cases the line between the jobs can be quite thin. Associates can play a very important role in rehearsal, covering anything on your agenda that you cannot accomplish or you wish to delegate. (Associates may unfortunately end up with some of the less exciting musical tasks.) An associate may have a particular talent that you want to exploit, perhaps one that you lack, or time constraints may require your splitting up the workload. Some associates lack the full array of skills needed to be a music director, instead excelling in one or more sub-disciplines. Some are first-rate accompanists or arrangers or conductors. If an associate does take on a significant portion of the music director's creative or managerial duties, he or she would certainly merit the title "associate music director," and a commensurate bump in pay.

Assistant conductors are backup conductors, and do not necessarily perform any other musical functions than playing in the orchestra and conducting when needed, though you may assign them to take notes, work with subs, cover a rehearsal, or attend a meeting in your stead, as long as you make sure they are compensated for the additional time and work. Whenever music directors delegate any responsibility to another party, it is only with the approval of the director or producer or his or her designees.

A music director might hire the same associate on every job, as the comfort of the affiliation and full comprehension of each other's strengths and weaknesses can be invaluable. Others choose associates on the basis of each project's particular needs. In any case, an associate (and sometimes an assistant) is your representative, your confidante, and often your *consigliere*. He or she will interact with the same people you do, and his or her performance and behavior will reflect yours and the whole of the music team's.

Many associates and assistants are aspiring music directors, either content being temporarily second in command or very eager to take over, and indeed some form of promotion is often forthcoming. In the short term, an associate conducts in the music director's place, but down the line, he or she may take over as music director of a long-running show if the music director moves on. Some associates prefer being associates to being music directors, because the job entails less responsibility and less stress, and sometimes a greater emphasis on the musical than the extramusical (and the wages are still good). I have enjoyed being in both positions, and I appreciate the advantages of each.

Music directors do not always choose their covers on the basis of conducting ability. They might base their selection instead on a substitute's familiarity with the score, because a sub conductor who knows the score thoroughly will react more astutely if something goes wrong on stage or in the pit. The choice is preventive. Keyboard players from the pit are quite often next in line to the podium. If they were involved in rehearsals as accompanists, the music director may have designated them as associates or assistants from the outset. Other pit players will take the baton, too: drummers, woodwind players, violinists, or anyone with conducting skills and a knowledge of the score, and who is present, ready and willing, might be a good assistant or even associate. Above all, the show must go on.

Rehearsal musicians, especially pianists, are crucial members of the music team; do not underestimate their value. Reproducing orchestral music and popular styles accurately and consistently at the piano is quite difficult, yet essential for stage rehearsals. Moreover, especially with a new score, the way an accompanist plays the music in rehearsal becomes to everyone in the rehearsal room (directors, choreographers, performers, stage managers) the "definitive" rehearsal version. It is also what orchestrators may hear as their source material during production. Rehearsal accompanists are usually pianists of the highest order. Drummers and percussionists make frequent appearances in rehearsals, too, and, less commonly, guitarists, bassists, and sometimes players of exotic instruments specific to the material. Any of these participants might also make significant creative contributions to a production. Richard Rodgers's favorite rehearsal pianist, Trude Rittmann, wrote many of the ballet and incidental arrangements in the classic Rodgers scores. Drummer Tommy Igoe and I were among the arrangers of the "Kickbutt" dance in "Be Prepared" from *The Lion King*, and guitarist Kevin Kuhn had a major part in recomposing and arranging the iconic solo guitar parts of *Tommy*.

Contractors and Music Coordinators

Another bewildering job title is "contractor." Like their counterparts in construction, music contractors recruit, bring together, and manage teams of workers. A music contractor's basic functions are to hire the performing musicians and oversee their implementation into a production, and then manage them in production. The contractor of stage production rarely hires the music director—often it is the other way around—but sometimes advises the music director in hiring conductors, associates, and assistants.

The contracting of a modern Broadway show is in practice divided between two positions. One is a playing member of the orchestra, called a "designated" contractor; this title is from the CBA, but pit musicians use the term "in-house" contractor. He or she is the equivalent of a union shop steward, keeping track of and turning in the payroll, logging orchestra substitutes and rehearsal hours, calculating benefits, keeping watch on standards and practices in the workplace, and making sure everyone is in the right place at the right time. There is a 50 percent premium on an in-house contractor's salary for these very time-consuming and at times demanding or delicate tasks.

The title given to the person who hires and manages a Broadway theater orchestra is "music coordinator." This designation is presumably to avoid any confusion with the union's term, even though everyone, musicians and non-music staff alike, including producers, still refer in conversation to music coordinators as "contractors." It is the music coordinator who receives billing on the front page of *Playbill* and on the poster outside the theater, not the in-house contractor. The music coordinator hires the in-house contractor, with the producer's and music director's sanction. Early in production, the music coordinator handles the musicians' day-to-day business affairs; after opening night the in-house contractor assumes those duties.[2]

Most music coordinators and contractors are musicians (or former musicians) themselves, often excellent ones, and they can be among music directors' closest allies when they are juggling many complex musical, managerial, and personal issues. The administrative functions of the two positions often overlap. Music coordinators make only periodic appearances at the performance venue after opening nights; most of their duties are accomplished in preproduction, production rehearsal, and in the week or two leading up to the opening. As music director, however, your relationship with a music coordinator continues after opening. Together you keep watch on and solve problems of the musicians, the physical setup, and to some extent the performance quality, throughout the run of a production.

Though the position of music coordinator was birthed in the union, and though music coordinators maintain their union affiliations, they are more management than union. Music coordinators are employees of producers, and producers count on them as liaisons or buffers between management and union personnel. Given the antipathy of the two factions over the last few decades, producers understandably feel better protected under this arrangement. As the tensions have heightened, the managerial bent of music coordinators has become still stronger. A successful music coordinator's income is very handsome. He or she can have many productions running simultaneously, in different locations, all of which pay a separate royalty or ongoing maintenance fee, along with preproduction fees.[3]

There are only a handful of music coordinators contracting most of the productions in any given geographical area or in any given genre of music. There are no more than a dozen music coordinators contracting virtually every Broadway and major Off-Broadway show, as well as the touring shows that originate on Broadway, and this has been the norm for decades. Musicians are preternaturally respectful, even obsequious, toward music coordinators. They know where their next job will most likely be coming from. If a musician is late for a performance call, or makes an atrocious musical error, the last person he or she wants knowing about it is the music coordinator (the second to last is the music director).

---

2. Michael Keller, in-person, phone, and email interviews, 20 November 2012.

3. Some music coordinators put themselves on the orchestra payroll as a means of compensation, sometimes to suit a minimum, but other times, just to pay themselves. I question the scrupulousness of this practice. The orchestra payroll should be for orchestral musicians, union rank and file, not for their "boss."

When music directors work outside of their usual geographical territory, or in an unfamiliar style of music, music coordinators or contractors can be particularly helpful. Contractors introduce the music director to musicians, and explain any conventions or peculiarities of the locale, venue, or genre.

Contractors accomplish their primary task, assembling a band or orchestra, through their knowledge of the available players, and by recommendation, by reputation, and sometimes by audition. The union doesn't officially permit auditions for Broadway orchestras, but it happens sometimes anyway. (Radio City, under its new corporate structure, now auditions annually.) Presumably any union member should be competent, or better; after all, the mission of the union is to provide mutual protection for employee and employer. Yet competence may be specific to a certain type of music. For union stage jobs, therefore, auditions usually take the form of informal meetings at which a less experienced or known musician has the chance to show his or her musical skills to someone in a position to offer a gig.

Most music directors select at least some of the orchestra musicians for a production, often all of them, and inform the contractor of their choices. The contractor may suggest changes to a music director's selections, but will always defer on final decisions. In some cases, contractors recommend hiring a group of people as a unit that would disqualify a certain individual musician of the music director's choosing. Let's say the music director wants to hire his or her one-and-only first-call lead trumpet player for a show with a big-band musical style. The contractor thinks a particular group of three trumpets and three trombones who play together regularly would be perfect for this particular score. In this instance the music director might put aside individual taste aside in favor of an improved ensemble.

After the hiring is done, contractors inform musicians of rehearsal and performance schedules, locate rehearsal space and ensure proper rehearsal gear and outfitting, provide the production team with music department updates, attend production meetings, and at rehearsals count heads and call for breaks. They work with the music director to plan the physical layout of the orchestra. They supervise the load-in and the seating of an orchestra when the orchestra moves into a rehearsal studio or performance space. These are tasks most music directors are happy to divest themselves of. In conjunction with the sound and props departments, music coordinators oversee renting or purchasing equipment and make sure it is delivered to the right place at the right time.

Orchestrators and Copyists

Orchestrators are among the arrangers of a stage score. Orchestration is the distribution and assignment of different lines and segments of a piece of music to an ensemble of instrumentalists, in idiomatic fashion. Orchestration brings a score to life, because it puts the music in the hands of the musicians. One can define an "orchestra" however one likes, but orchestration is at play in every definition. For a solo, duet, or other very small ensemble, the term "arrangement" will probably replace "orchestration." All forms of arrangement freely and frequently cross over into others. For example, a dance arranger might conceive a certain musical idea as being played on a particular instrument. An orchestrator may add counterpoint in the instrumentation of the dance arranger's work. The vocal arranger might double the orchestrator's contrapuntal line in the singing, or change a chord inversion (the position of the root of a chord relative to its other factors, or notes) to suit the vocal line.

The line between composition and arranging, and orchestration in particular, is a fine one. Historically, composers of serious music orchestrated their own material. As music became more commercialized, it became more susceptible to interpretation and reconstruction. Arrangers more frequently customized songs to suit performers. In musical theater, a composer's songs and dances were (and still are) arranged and orchestrated expressly to accompany the stage. Only a few composers did their own orchestrations for production, and this is still the case in the present day.

The orchestrator orchestrates, or "scores," all music in a production, such as accompaniments, dance arrangements, incidental music, transitions, and overtures. Some instrumentation will be part of the composition and, as noted, certain composers will specify instrumentation (a very few will do the entire orchestration). When that is the case, the orchestrator fills in and notates the details and, with the music director, other arrangers, and copyist, readies the score and orchestra parts for performance. The extent and content of an orchestration, including the number of instruments, the choice of instruments, the style of the writing, the specificity of the orchestration (notes versus chord symbols, for example), and the expected or desired creative contribution of the orchestrator, are, as usual, specific to each production. In all productions, however, it is expected that the orchestrator will deliver on time to the copyist a complete score from which all individual parts can be extracted merely by copying them; in other words, the orchestrator's completed score should contain every piece of musical information, and as much stage-related information as he or she has access to, ready to be put before the musicians. It is the music director's job to communicate to the orchestrator whatever stage-related information will affect the orchestration, or that should be included in the orchestra parts (such as a lyric cue, the predicted length of a vamp, or a possible cut).

Assigning music to instruments is not the same as filling out a checklist. Orchestration requires exceptional musical knowledge, creativity, taste, and, as much as anything, speed. It can be a demanding, exhausting job. On a Broadway show, as much as three hours of music may have to be orchestrated in as little as a few weeks. When I worked in a summer stock theater as a young music director, my associates and I would re-orchestrate four or five shows per summer for our piecemeal orchestras. We would reassign the parts of larger orchestrations, cutting and pasting our hand-copied additions and subtractions (with scissors and masking tape, not Command/Control-X and -V), retooling the published music for ten or so instruments, while at the same time incorporating changes coming in daily from the director and choreographer at rehearsal. In retrospect, I have no idea how we possibly could have had the time and wherewithal to accomplish this miracle, but somehow we did, and we did it every two weeks. (One can only imagine the endurance of Bach, who did much more than all that in half the time, and oh yes, he was composing the music, too.)

When orchestrating a new score, an orchestrator can work on only as much of the score as has been finalized in rehearsal, meaning that he or she may have a very short time in which to complete a large body of work. Of course, there is rarely such a thing as "final" in stage productions; there are constant changes that will require the orchestrator's continual involvement up to and sometimes beyond a show's opening night, and players in the orchestra might tweak their parts to their liking, and, one would hope, to the benefit of the show. Orchestrators usually begin work early on some sections and leave others for later. But until keys are determined, song orders and structures are set, and vocal and dance arrangers have completed their work, an instrumental arrangement cannot be finalized. As music director, you'll have among your jobs making sure the orchestrator has the material that he or she needs to meet all deadlines.

The composer, music director, producer, director, choreographer, other members of the music team, or any combination will decide whom to hire as orchestrator. Different styles of music are definitely the specialties of certain orchestrators, but others are able to cover a wide range with equal mastery. There are, like music coordinators, a very small number of orchestrators who seem to dominate the professional scene at any one time. Skilled and specialized as these musicians are, it seems odd that the net is not cast more widely. There are, however, special preconditions in orchestrating for the stage, in particular, support of the wider artistic vision, and conveying to an instrumentalist in notation that which is musically essential to the whole of the production.

The traditions of orchestration in stage music are, as in the music business and in music itself, being rewritten with each new trend. Orchestrations for the stage now tend to be smaller and more rhythm-section- and percussion-based, and many have a significant electronic component. Nevertheless, the larger textures of music for film, television, and video games and some stage productions have required that modern orchestrators maintain their legitimacy and stylistic versatility. Most orchestrators who write for the stage make their livings from more than just stage music.

After the music for a production has been written, arranged, and orchestrated, so that it can be accurately communicated to the performing musicians and stage performers, it has to be written down, or "copied." Good copyists do not specialize in one particular musical style, and there is no notational challenge too great for most to handle. There are different conventions in different genres of music, but a good copyist effortlessly negotiates all conventions of the trade.

Music copying, like other aspects of music for the stage, has changed drastically over the last twenty years. Most music preparation firms have been put out of business or shrunk to their bare bones by computer notation software. Finale and Sibelius (which has suffered through corporate upheaval), and a few competitors, have allowed any amateur copyist to create notation as good looking as a professional's; professionals and amateurs use the same applications. More and more commonly, composers and arrangers simply write their music directly into these applications, and their "sketches" are just steps away from a finished, copied product.[4]

Music is naturally far easier to alter and to archive, and of course to read, when copied on computer. One should always keep in mind, however, that notation software is a graphics program, one that depicts and organizes a language of symbols, and to some extent their meanings, quite dexterously, but its actual understanding of musical substance is nonexistent. Only a human can make music software notation work, but irrefutably it is a tremendous convenience. The era of Broadway and film music copying by hand has largely disappeared, though the basic manuscript style they originated in preserved and honored in some materials provided by rental libraries, and in several computerized fonts (Figure 6.1). It is interesting that the new, computer-based trend in copying harkens back to the Baroque and Classical periods, when composers would not only compose prodigious amounts of music, but also copy all the parts for the orchestra by hand and in ink, as Bach did, with clefs and key signatures on every staff of every page, which are the stock in trade of computer notation.

It was a tremendous thrill to walk into a busy music preparation office in New York or Burbank in the 1980s, where a throng of scribes hunched anxiously at their desks and put calligraphic pens to paper, each with a distinct and identifiable yet perfectly legible hand, the smell of cigarette smoke, ink, and the "repro" machines thick in the air. The whine of electric erasers, movie music or Mahler from a cassette tape player, and energetic banter among the copyists provided cacophonous underscoring. The work done there seemed to embody the energy that all members of a production team would put into their efforts of getting a project on its feet.

The few professional copyists who survive as regulars on Broadway are under the same time constraints in production as orchestrators, but of course, computers help to mitigate the pressure (it does for orchestrators, too, of course). The music director, arrangers, orchestrator, and copyist get together early in production and determine what music needs to be ready by when. The copyists with the most knowledge of stage music are very busy, and handle multiple projects at once, so securing their time and commitment well in advance is essential. Nowadays, however, the field is wide open, with steady professionals, semiprofessionals, and amateurs who need not even live in the city where a production is mounted. Music directors are in charge of making sure all arranging and copying deadlines are met, but the orchestration and music preparation units of most music teams are very prompt; meeting deadlines is their hallmark.

---

4. A program that allows the writer to enter music on a touch screen as if writing on a piece of manuscript paper, the computer translating the writer's hand to a beautiful and functional piece of written music, seems the logical next step. This small advancement will again revolutionize the act of music copying. There may soon even be tone-recognition software that takes down music as a speech-recognition program transcribes the spoken word.

FIGURES 6.1 (A) Hand-copied manuscript ("Politics and Poker" from *Fiorello!*) and (B) the Finale "Broadway" font in the "Handwritten" document style ("Honky Tonk Merry-Go-Round" from *Always . . . Patsy Cline*).

Copyists are union members, and the union posts an extensive, elaborate price list for the various kinds of work they do. Their agreement in the CBA also includes the scales for orchestration, arranging, and transcription, under the heading of "music preparation." If a music director does any work in any of these areas, he or she submits a bill through the music preparation payroll, as do the arrangers and copyists. Roughly speaking, arranging and copying are paid by the bar, or group of bars, such as a four-bar "line," or system. Rates vary according to the complexity and forces of the work, but arrangement and music preparation costs can add up and be significant, and there is no discount on rewrites. The top professional orchestrators receive overscale, as well as fees and royalties similar to a music director's.

Vocal and Dance Arrangers

Vocal arrangers determine the most communicative and attractive vocal assignments, registration, harmonies, and counterpoint for any material sung on stage. Because the voice is such a flexible instrument, uniquely innate and expressive, capturing it in notation can be perplexing, and subjective. The two main reasons for notating vocal arrangements are to provide a learning aid and to preserve the music as performed. It is possible to learn vocal music perfectly well by ear (one might argue that it is better learned by ear), but written music is still useful in rehearsal. Particularly in dramatic musical theater, in which characters sing, the stage director partly determines vocal arrangements, and collaborates with the vocal arranger in preproduction and rehearsal to make choices that work within his or her vision.

Vocal arranging and music direction frequently go hand in hand. Though the division of arranging duties is different in every production, the pairing of vocal arranging and music direction makes sense. Because music directors are already rehearsing the singers, it falls conveniently into their process. Furthermore, music directors, as the conduits from the writers' and director's intent to the performance on stage, are to in an excellent position to determine who should sing what, and how, and when, and sometimes why.

The same argument can be made for the music director–orchestrator combination, in that the music director, who is in charge of the music overall and is the orchestra conductor as well, would be the best judge of the best choices for the orchestra. Orchestration, however, is such an enormous job (at least with larger orchestras), and a talent that a select few musicians carry out so ingeniously and brilliantly, that it is often best left to a specialist. Good vocal and dance arrangers likewise enjoy a specialized, higher level of facility with voices and dance music. Yet vocal arrangement for stage shows is more manageable because, among other reasons, vocalists do some of the arranging merely by singing, and the music director has only to transcribe, refine, and codify what they sing.

Dance arranging is specialized as well but, like the general notion of "arranging," deals as much with musical content as a whole than with one specific aspect of it, as with orchestrating and vocal arranging. This attention to both generality and specificity makes it more akin to composing than to either vocal arranging or orchestrating. When dance arrangements are plentiful or complex, productions usually have a separate dance arranger.

Dance arrangers (who may not be credited, especially when the dance arranger is also the music director) write music for any staging and dance sections of a stage score that a composer has not composed. They work directly with choreographers to customize the music to the dance, and the dance to the music. Some music directors take on the job, but choreographers often have preferences and will have a significant say in hiring. Dance arrangers might also double as rehearsal musicians (pianists, probably, or drummers). Stage directors, too, will be involved in dance arrangement choices, and again, all areas of arranging will overlap. Dance arrangers also consider scenic, lighting, and costume designs in their writing, because these elements affect the choreography and the stage picture that the arrangement is accompanying. How long the train of a gown is, how long it takes a dancer to climb a flight of stairs, or how long it takes a piece of scenery to revolve might determine the length or some other quality of a musical phrase. For an arranger these parameters can be challenging but satisfying, similar to scoring the dramatic and visual beats of a film.

Music directors will usually find it impossible to do all the arranging for a production while working through an already long list of rehearsal, performance, and administrative duties. The team effort makes it possible to accomplish everything musical, and the music director formulates and coordinates the arranging team, whatever form it takes. He or she supervises the team members' work, contributes as needed, and keeps them connected with the material, the stage direction, and the rehearsal process.

Synthesizer Programmers

Synthesizers seem the antithesis of the vibrant atmosphere in the bygone copyist's office. They are cold and impersonal, programmed by an individual in a studio in front of a keyboard, some sound modules, and a computer. Instead of an impassioned effort to meet a deadline by sheer human will, the programmer coolly draws sounds from a library, adjusts them as needed, and sets them in the right order with software designed for that purpose. Regardless, here in our technological age, music directors welcome to the music team a person whose short history is somewhat tainted and whose work is at times tolerated as much as it is appreciated: the synthesizer programmer. The composer, music director, or orchestrator usually decides whom to hire in this capacity, with approval from the producer. As with everything else musical, the proper execution of the synthesizer programming is ultimately the music director's responsibility.

When synthesizers first caught the ear of musicians, they sounded like what they were—electronic instruments. To emulate sound, they copied and manipulated the observable sound waves of a real instrument, but had trouble capturing the sound itself. Therefore, their use was limited to music in which electronic sound was the aesthetic. Computer music had been a fixture in the work of some serious composers and in academic circles since the 1940s, and made its way into popular music around the 1960s. Through to the present day, the technology has advanced steadily. As time passed, electronica increasingly conquered mainstream music, and eventually took hold of live music for the stage. (Even symphony orchestras now engage programmers to synthesize their keyboards—celeste, harmonium, clavichord—instruments that are often expensive to own and maintain, especially when on tour.)

Most consequentially, as computer processing speed and power increased, so did the resemblance of synthesized sound to its acoustic ideal. The technological advance that had the most profound effect was digital sampling, which was in widespread use by the 1990s. Digital sampling is the recording of a sound source (an instrument, a voice, a sound effect) and its transformation into digital data that can then be manipulated at will. Sampling can involve the conglomeration of a number of different samples to that together form a "sound," or a "patch," or a "voice." A sample can be played back from any number of "controllers," most routinely a piano keyboard, through MIDI (musical instrument digital interface) or other digital interfaces. For example, if each note that can be played on a clarinet is sounded by a real clarinetist and sampled, those samples can be collected into a clarinet patch. This capability allows a keyboard player, who can play several lines simultaneously, to do the work of multiple clarinet players, or of several different instruments.

Of course, synthesizers are not used only to replace actual instruments. They are used for their native electronic sounds, keyboard sounds, to augment other sounds, for sound effects, and for many other purposes. Synthesizer programming may include drum programming and other MIDI rigs, as well as loops and effects. The best programmers I know are also excellent musicians, using the synthesizer as a musical instrument rather than as a robot, and when imitating real instruments, they provide the player as much control as possible over the sonic outcome. Synthesizer programmers who understand the sensitivity of their effort will balance their attempts at realism and quality with the acknowledgment that their product is a facsimile, sometimes a transparent one. They find a way to keep the synthesized instruments well blended with the real, and when a real instrument does need to be emulated or enhanced, they seek out the finest and most appropriate samples.

By nature, digital replacement has several drawbacks. Most profoundly, synthesized instruments forfeit a large part of their humanity. Every time a note is struck, the same sample plays, and despite a range of dynamics and articulations programmed into some sounds, there is still no way to reproduce the instantaneous, contextual choices of how to play a note that a musician makes afresh in each performance. In real playing, no note will ever sound precisely the same twice, unless the player wants it to, and each has infinite subtleties. But in sampling, sound reproduction options are limited. Furthermore, passing along the synthesizer programming design of a score beyond an initial production or productions is problematic. Because technologies change so rapidly and new gear is constantly replacing the old, it is hard to preserve programming from one production to the next, particularly as productions of a show proliferate into the stock and amateur markets, and the original programmer is not a participant. Music directors of repertory shows rightfully complain of having no access to existing electronic designs for existing orchestrations, only patch lists or obsolete storage media that contain data no longer usable. As music director you may have to engage a programmer to reprogram a show already to some extent synthesized and, if your production calls for it, recreate the original programming with only any available recordings of the sounds as reference. (I often field phone calls and emails from music directors wondering about the cryptic synthesizer patch names in *Tommy*, originally programmed on synthesizers now considered "vintage.")

Finally, of course, sampling also robs musicians of employment and performance opportunities. This problem is not new in any field. The difference is that a machine can install a car part with greater accuracy than a human, whereas a synthesizer can never achieve human expressiveness. The human element in any art form is its essence. Systems have been devised that can emulate the performances of entire orchestras (yes, including the conductor, but not the music director, yet . . .). Their use has become widely accepted, in educational settings, in smaller, lower-budget productions, and, as discussed throughout Part 1, in some Broadway and major touring productions, as Figure 6.2 depicts. Sometimes these computerized versions are offered by music publishing houses as part of their performance licensing packages.

Programmers are paid fees and a maintenance stipend, and some receive a designer's royalty. Currently there are no specified standards, union or otherwise, for a synthesizer programmer's job description, duties, or compensation. It is obviously expected that the work will be completed on schedule and in line with the needs of the production. Programmers or their delegates attend load-ins, seatings, and sound checks (see Part 5, "Rehearsals 2: Musicians, Technicians, and the Venue"), and should remain on call to maintain the synthesizer setups during the run of a production, an important safeguard, given the proclivity of the machines to malfunction. Technicians and designers count synthesizer programmers among their number, as do the music team, particularly sound designers and electricians, as their work intertwines in technical setup and rehearsals.

In a smoothly running production, the music director, composer, orchestrator, and programmer correlate their needs and efforts. The music director or composer or orchestrator indicates to the programmer what sounds are needed, the programmer finds or programs sounds that satisfy the need and makes what the orchestrator has

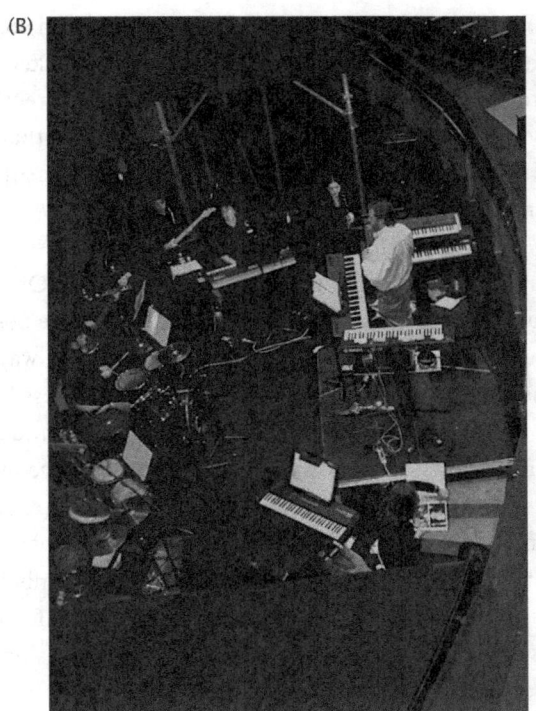

FIGURES 6.2 Lots of keyboards—but no strings. (A) The *Priscilla, Queen of the Desert* tour pit, and (B) a high school production of *Aida*. (*Credits:* A: Photo by David Clarke; B: Photo from the collection of Conrad Askland.)

written sound good, and the orchestrator writes parts that sound good on the patch that the synthesizer programmer has devised.

The Orchestra

It is a timeworn and correct adage that an athletic coach is only as good as the players on his or her team. This is no less true for a music director leading an orchestra. Not even the most proficient conductor on the planet can turn an inexperienced band of musicians into the Metropolitan Opera Orchestra. It is obviously in a music director's best interest to work with the best possible musicians and, perhaps less obviously, to work with those who best fit into a production. Fine musicianship is not the only necessary attribute of a good musician for a stage show; a strong ability to collaborate musically and communicate effectively with others is just as essential. Sometimes one or more of these strengths may to some extent have to be sacrificed, but at least in urban centers, there are enough solid musicians who are also productive coworkers available for a music director and contractor to convoke a good stage ensemble.

Among the many qualities that are assets for musicians in a stage production are familiarity with and appreciation for a wide variety of music, so that they are not befuddled by unorthodox modes (scale or melody type), jumbled meters, or extremes of stylization; patience, acuity, and adaptability, so they are not taken aback by the quick pace of changes in rehearsal, ambiguous notes and chords, or directions scribbled illegibly in pencil; interest in the production beyond the music, so that a connection with the stage is real and palpable in performance; and, of course, considerable skill on one's instrument(s) and in ensemble playing.

Yet an ability to coexist with others, personally and musically, in a sometimes tense working environment may take precedence over all else. One must put the right musician for the team in each chair, rather than necessarily the best musician in each chair. Music coordinator Michael Keller, a veteran of many Broadway shows and concert tours, suggests, "The most important aspect of the hiring process is to hire good/great musicians who also are great colleagues and, most importantly, understand what the gig is, namely, that after the initial rush of creation the job is 'creative repetition.'"[5]

The so-called submarine mentality that comes from congregating nightly in the close quarters of an orchestra pit seems to routinely induce petty bickering. For all the creative thought put into perfecting an ensemble, if its members do not get along, the effort is for naught. Broadway pit orchestras are notorious for their ability to find sources of internal strife, especially in long runs. Despite witnessing it and hearing of it in several situations, I still find it surprising and appalling that a member of a Broadway orchestra could at any time be anything other than absolutely content, and display any animosity whatsoever at work. The gig is highly desirable and steady; it has stylistic

---

5. Keller, interview.

variety, excellent pay, full benefits, and reasonable hours. Nonetheless, pit battles are fought all the time. And once the first salvos have been fired, it is very difficult to end the war. The union protects musicians from actions against them by employers and fellow musicians, and producers do not want to incur costs by entering the fray, much less firing misbehaving musicians and risking litigation. The best way to avoid conflict is preemptive, that is, hiring the right group.

Music directors' and contractors' most important hiring criteria, beyond musicianship and personality, are consistency, reliability, and professionalism. Music directors are more comfortable when they know that musicians will always show up on time, and always play their best in every situation, and if they do not, will rectify matters immediately. Certain productions might require musicians who are particularly virtuosic, or well versed in a peculiar musical style, and at times music directors might need to venture outside of their usual spheres. Some music directors and contractors simply hire the same orchestras again and again. Whereas loyalty to musicians is valuable, and the togetherness and dependability of a certain group may be impeccable, it is hard to imagine that precisely the same combination of people will serve equally well in a wide variety of musical contexts. Loyalty is long term, and your closest musician colleagues will understand if you do not hire them for every job, as long as you frankly explain your rationale and prove your allegiance over time.

In situations in which the pool of musicians is smaller or a production's budget is restricted, of course, music directors may have fewer choices, but they can still be discerning, and think creatively. For example, if the music director of the holiday Christmas pageant at the local community center knows that the seventeen-year-old lead alto sax player in the high school jazz band is a far better saxophonist than the person who has played lead sax in the pageant for the last fifteen years, the music director can insist that just for this year, because the young player will soon be going off to college, she should play the lead alto this year. Or the music director can leave the regular player in the first chair, but in the arrangements sneak in a few extra solos or features for the talented young musician playing second.

Everyone introduced thus far works behind the scenes. What brings the production into the public eye are the performers: the singers, dancers, and actors who populate the stage. If music direction is an elaborate form of accompaniment, the onstage performer is the one being accompanied. We'll meet them next.

7

The Performers

Besides the director and his or her fellow musicians, a music director's closest allies in a production are the players on stage. As fellow performers, the ones who realize the music in performance, the music director and cast form a strong bond. Singers and actors flourish in their time in front of an audience; some say they live for it. Music directors share these treasured moments with them and support their very heartfelt efforts. As accompanists, they listen to the singers and follow along, doing all they can to make them sound good.

More than anything else, good performers strive for believability. Believability is what makes people and events on stage come to life, or a meaningful representation thereof. When a singer performs a song, the audience must believe, or feel, or identify, with the singer. Dancers must convincingly use abstract, expressive movement to have the audience believe in and feel along with the story they are telling or with the emotions they are acting out. A good actor has the audience members set aside their awareness that he or she is an actor, and be complicit in the pretense that he or she is instead a character in a drama. Music directors, positioned in front of the performers and fully attendant to their musical needs, collude in the effort at believability.

Singers and Dancers

Many relationships between music directors and performers begin at auditions. Some productions do not hold auditions; instead, the creative and productions teams hire performers on the basis of previously shared work experience or knowledge of their work in other productions. (In theater communities large and small there is a great deal of familiarity.) Some performers spearhead their own productions, and sometimes performers perform as or are hired as a group. Sometimes a leading or star performer will have a say in hiring a music director, and some will bring to a production his or her own music director, orchestrations, and music staff.

As with musicians, when one is choosing stage performers for a production, the other performers' ability to get along with the creative team and one another does factor in, though perhaps less so than in an orchestra. Someone who is exactly right for a part might be cast in spite of his or her lack of "people skills," and it will be up to you as music director to be agreeable.

Most stage performers have big personalities and big hearts. They are effortless centers of attention, gifted in their ability to display their feelings and talents openly and generously and control them with mastery, for public enjoyment. Many are extraordinarily intelligent, perceptive, warm, and witty, as well as disciplined and diligent. On the other hand, stage performers have been known to be insecure, moody, narcissistic, histrionic, and very demanding of their coworkers—in short, full of themselves. These more negative characteristics are not unexpected, given the profession. The stage performers' job is to convincingly inhabit the stage, and therefore they must be very self-aware. They may need a hand to hold—it really can be scary out there in front of an audience—but only when they say so. As the focal points of a production, they carry the weight of its success largely on their shoulders. But it is unfair to generalize. Performers are human, and every human is unique. There are shy, retreating performers; quiet, businesslike ones; serious, focused ones; class clowns; the whole spectrum. Without these diverse personalities, there could be no believability, and audiences could not be entertained. Love them or tolerate them as colleagues, stage performers are the ones people pay money to see.

Singers get an especially bad rap, as do dancers. Again, the reasons behind this reputation are understandable. Their voices and bodies are taxed and twisted and tired, and sometimes for pitiful wages. Their workday continues outside the theater or rehearsal hall, in classes and warm-ups, and their careers may be brief and irregular. So to some degree all performers are justified in discharging anxiety or letting off some steam. There is no music director in the business who cannot regale you with a tale of woe brought on by a performer's unreasonable demands or irrational behavior. Likewise, there should be no music director who cannot appreciate, or at least accept, that being in the spotlight so much of one's life might lead one to believe that the spotlight is on permanently. There is also no listener who can deny the potential beauty and power of the human voice or the human body in performance.

Most singers and actors and dancers are genuinely and outwardly appreciative of musical assistance, and are a pleasure to work on music with, but a few do take music directors and accompaniment for granted, or can even be contrary and difficult at times. I worked on a Broadway musical in which a principal actor was leaving the cast after a year. His featured solo song was accompanied by a very difficult, long, and exposed instrumental solo at a very emotional moment in the show. The accompaniment was played beautifully and flawlessly by an orchestra musician who almost never hired a substitute, assuring the actor of consistently superb musical support. The musician insisted that his subs be equally perfectionist with that passage in the score, and if they were not, they were not rehired. Before the actor's final performance (he had been hired for another show), he gave a pre-curtain thank-you speech in the green room to the company. He said the usual things actors say in these speeches; he talked about his lifelong journey and his growth as an actor and a human being, and he fervently expressed his deepest gratitude to his fellow actors, to the directors, the producers, the writers, the stage manager, the company manager, his dresser . . . but not, of course, the musician in the orchestra. Or the orchestra. Or, for that matter, the music director or sound operator.

Music directors' relationships with singers are usually closer than with dancers, simply because they work more closely with singers, especially in rehearsal. The best relationships between singers and music directors are those of genuine respect, affection, and mutual encouragement, not just a kiss on the cheek and an "Oh my God, you were *fabulous* last night!" and a greeting card on opening night. Those courtesies are important, too, but a strong artistic relationship is evident in performance. In rehearsal, as music director you can hear objectively what a singer cannot, right and wrong (believable and not), and help improve the bad and build on the good. For the singer, you are a musical guide and an informed set of ears. The sensitivity of singers' emotions and their hyper-awareness of their "instruments" (their voices) and their own uniqueness require that you offer help and criticism with appropriate sensitivity, and tailor your work to each unique performer. In group rehearsals, obviously, this task is not as easily done, but the group dynamic also offsets some of the cumulate egoism.

Some singers will not need or will not be as open to a music director's help. This situation is more common when a performance has already been thoroughly rehearsed (even then you can tactfully offer assistance, under the right conditions), or when a performance is prepackaged and you are jobbed in. Some performers require only a good organizer, or a strong accompanist, or a good arranger, as in presentational shows.

Although music directors may not relate as readily in production to dancers, music and dance are interdependent, too, and personal and musical fellowships between musicians and dancers can be strong, and are similarly manifest in the work. Music directors should study dance history and theory as part of their education and take dance classes as part of their physical regimen. Knowing how dance works and how choreography treats the body and its movements helps music directors to conceive and lead dance music more effectively. The physical confidence and movement skills that dance training offers are also very helpful in conducting technique.

Many dancers are not trained in music, and for some reason do not have natural singing or musicality. (I have always found this odd, given dance's artistic alliance with music, but I also understand the demands of dance as a discipline, and how they might disallow musical absorption.) Many dancers openly profess their lack of vocal ability and musicianship. Non-singing dancers who are willing to learn music, and who have the facility for learning music (which is almost every one), can be a pleasurable challenge for music directors, but may require committing extra time.

Singers and Actors

In a way all singers are actors. Singing is acting. Most singers know that they are acting when they sing, and some do it quite naturally, whether they know they are acting or not. On the other hand, many actors do not think they are good singers, and some become very withdrawn and self-deprecating when it comes to having to sing.

Singing is acting of several kinds. It can be very intense, specific, and consuming, it can be very generalized and casual, or it can be just having a presence on stage, a convincing state of "being there," or "being in the moment." The following are three of a myriad of possible approaches to acting in vocal performance, and a music director's relevance to and activities in each.

In one scenario, a singer delivers a lyric and melody detachedly, without internalizing the song's text. His manner implies that he is reading or relating a story rather than living it, and that he has a point of view. He half sings, half speaks the written contours of the melody. (Imagine a country narrative, such as Johnny Cash's "A Boy Named Sue," or on the musical stage, Noël Coward performing "Mrs. Worthington" or any of his patter songs, or Harold Hill and "Trouble" or "The Sadder but Wiser Girl.") In a different case, a singer draws on her own life and feelings in interpreting a song, deeply connecting personal experiences with those alluded to in the text. This personal investment imbues the melody with specificity, intensity, and divergence from the written notes (Bernadette Peters singing "Children and Art" from *Sunday in the Park with George*, or Diana Krall's version of "I've Got You under My Skin"). In a third scenario, the singer sings a song very legitimately and with musical rigor (Pavarotti singing the "Soliloquy" from *Carousel*, or William Warfield's version of "Ol' Man River.") He interprets the melody literally, making each tone beautiful and musical, and enunciates the text with an operatic version of clarity. (Again, these are only three among countless ways to render a work.)

In the first case, as music director you go along for the ride. You provide solid, stylistically and musically accurate and characteristic accompaniment, stay in the background, and let the singer make his points and get his laughs. In the second, you become a musical acting coach and stylist. Together you and the performer analyze the material and use your conclusions to inform the performance. You incorporate the singer's feelings and intent into the arrangement and accompanying style. In rehearsal you listen critically to the singer for truthfulness and convincing application of the textual values to the music, and for musical values and vocal technique appropriate to the interpretation. When the situation calls for it, you advise or correct. In the third scenario, you might help the singer, if the situation makes it acceptable, to apply more specific acting values that will enhance the performance. You can also be a monitor of musical correctness and diction, joining in the singer's effort at musical accuracy, and perhaps work off some of the musical stiffness.

It is possible for a music director to coax an attractive or at least convincing enough singing voice out of actors who are unaccustomed to singing or do not have "good" singing voices (a subjective judgment, to say the least), but it is not always an easy task. I have held several jobs teaching songs in straight plays and musicals to non-singing actors, and all I have learned is that there is no one reliable way to help non-singing actors sing reliably. Those actors were far more concerned with truth of character, and to many, music seemed like a technical burden or an interruption of their absorption in a role. So-called method actors live their roles in their daily lives; their characters don't take singing lessons.

Some non-singing actors don't mind singing, but are uncomfortable or lack experience. At times they may give their all, but their vocal shortcomings can threaten their believability. On the other hand, speak-singing has been a highly effective outlet for certain actors in musical roles, such as Rex Harrison, Robert Preston, and Lin-Manuel Miranda. Other actors do sing very well (Hugh Jackman, Nathan Lane), and others make the best of what they have, and are quite convincing (Johnny Depp, Robert Morse, Andrea Martin). Composers of musical theater know that some of the best actors may not be the best singers, so they factor that knowledge in when writing certain roles. The vocal range of the splendid melody of Richard Rodgers's "Shall We Dance" is a mere minor seventh, to suit its star actor-singer Gertrude Lawrence in the original production of *The King and I*. Kurt Weill composed the *Sprechstimme* role of Jenny in *Die Dreigroschenoper* (*The Threepenny Opera*) for his actor wife Lotte Lenya. If necessary, you can adjust stage music to suit a non-singer, usually by simplifying it in some way, and you can employ the same pedagogical techniques as you would in any music rehearsal, but more systematically. Your encouragement and tolerance are especially important to actors who are intimidated or challenged by singing. Also important are doubling their melodies audibly in the orchestration, helping them understand basic music theory (which they may have forgotten the next day), and rehearsing them right up to and after opening night, the same thirty-two measures that have been rehearsed again and again and again, and still are correct in performance only about half the time.

"Triple threat" performers are the opposite, in that they need little personalized care. These actor-singer-dancers are consummate music professionals and well trained, and they constantly improve and expand their abilities. They learn music quickly and thoroughly, take direction well, and work effortlessly with others. These performers have always been and still are the backbone of the commercial theater industry. They put in more hours and put out more sweat than anyone else in the production, with the least job security. Their love for and commitment to their performances irradiates and enlivens them and the stage.

Star Performers and Nontraditional Casting

One of producers' pet reasons for mounting a production is signing a star performer, especially in a culture of celebrity. Stars put butts in seats, as producers say. Recent Broadway musical revivals have featured teen heartthrobs Daniel Radcliffe and Nick Jonas as J. Pierrepont Finch in *How To Succeed. . .*, Disney Channel alumnus Corbin Bleu in *In The Heights* and *Godspell,* and Raven Symoné in *Sister Act.* On a smaller scale, local theaters have local stars who are local fan favorites.

Music directors bend to the musical needs of a star, even one who twinkles dimly, for in a way the star *is* the show. A "headliner" can rejuvenate the box office of a dying production, or be the impetus behind one. Either way, chances are that he or she will enter into a project with a strong idea of how a role should be interpreted, including the music. You might need to customize keys, tempos, arrangements, and orchestrations (not just for a star, of course; music directors often customize music to performers), even music that is normally left alone, such as in a "classic" musical. Whether in the accompanist's chair or on the podium, you are an unswerving acolyte and advocate, there to make the star musically content and secure, especially if he or she is out of his or her element, such as a television star appearing or singing on stage for the first time. Stars who are inexperienced with stage performance are often unaware of the demands of an eight-show-per-week schedule. Even the brilliant and durable Julie Andrews, in a return to Broadway in the 1995 stage version of the film *Victor, Victoria,* exited prematurely from her scheduled run because of vocal fatigue. "American Idol" vocal whiz Jordin Sparks, too, missed many performances when appearing as the juvenile female lead Nina Rosario in *In The Heights* because of unforeseen wear and tear on her young singing voice.

A music director dispensing coaching or advice to a star performer should do so with the utmost tact and deference, much more than is usual. Celebrities, like all performers, have insecurities in spite of outward confidence. The special burden they bear is that they are widely admired and therefore presumed always to be in top form. Even when you feel that you have an open, honest, and entirely friendly and collaborative relationship with a star performer (or composer, or director, for that matter), and that some violation of formality might be permissible, you still should tread lightly. To some extent this rule applies with all performers, in that everyone in a workplace deserves to be treated with respect and support. In truth, many star performers are just regular working folks who neither need nor expect special treatment. It can't hurt to give it to them anyway.

The way an existing show is cast may call for other sorts of musical changes beyond those related to its leading performers. So-called nontraditional casting has historically produced many fruitful theatrical ventures, and musical variations. Rethinking repertory musicals with African-American casts became something of a fad in the 1960s and 1970s (*Hello, Dolly!* and *Guys and Dolls,* among others), and freely mixed-race or "color-blind" casts started appearing in the 1990s. It was in part the discovery of South African vocalist Tsidii LeLoka that led director Julie Taymor to change the gender of the character Rafiki in *The Lion King* to a female, a decision that in turn opened up many new developments for the character, and the score. On the extreme end of casting adventurousness, there have been, among others, all-male productions of *The Sound of Music*, animated film musicals transferred to the stage with the use of roller-skate sneakers and vine- and web-swinging through the audience, and of course translations of several musicals into the languages of the countries in which they were newly produced. (Fitting the Japanese lyrics into the songs of *The Lion King* was an enlightening musical-linguistic experience.)

Casting Directors

According to Mark Brandon, a casting director with New York's Binder Casting, finding and bringing in performers to be considered for professional productions is the link, the "marriage broker" between performers and producers, directors, choreographers, and music directors. At the professional level, casting directors are chosen and hired by producers, in consultation with the director. With extensive archives of working performers' headshots and résumés in their filing cabinets and ongoing searches for new talent, they assist the creative staff in turning a vision into a living work. Along with a production's creative team and the director in charge, the casting director narrows down the choices and arranges for auditions, the logistics of which he or she manages as well. Casting is so crucial to a production's success that the work can be grueling and very prolonged; the casting director is essential in moving the process forward and organizing the complex decision making. The work continues throughout a production, as changes are made, actors move into other roles or jobs, and replacements and covers become necessary.[1]

Casting directors themselves sometimes achieve something of a star status because the outcome of their work can turn a good show into a great production and even maybe a not-so-good show into a bankable venture. If believability is indeed the greatest of stage virtues, then the work of casting directors is even more vital. Casting directors have access to most performers in and around the stage industry, from child actors to recent graduates of music schools to recording artists and movie stars. The creative team usually imagines ("fantasy casting") and auditions many performers before finally judging which are best for the production, but some choices are clear in advance, and a meeting or a job offer replaces an audition.

Because casting directors work with people "on both sides of the table" (the creative staff sitting behind a table and the performers auditioning in front of it), they are exceptional go-betweens, agreeable and available to both sides as facilitators, counselors, and

1. Mark Brandon, phone interview, 11 December 2012.

partisans. Many are former actors or other theater personnel, who enjoy being close to the stage but not on it. They are lovers of stage production (why else would such a career choice occur to someone?) and are intelligent, critical, considerate, constant theatergoers, very much in touch with all aspects of the industry, including music. Many casting directors have at least a passing understanding of music, especially stage music performance, more than enough to articulate their directions to a performer and comprehend the needs of the music and music director in casting and in production.

As is true with music contractors, music directors and casting directors are of benefit to one another, and work jointly to assemble the best people for a production. In their hiring process, they unite their resources to compile lists of potential performers, and in auditions, they work together with a performer to evince an audition that will best determine the performer's rightness for a part. The relationship between performers and casting directors is likewise not far from that of musicians and contractors. Also as with contractors, only a few major casting houses handle a majority of commercial theater productions, but casting directors will reach out beyond their localities to a nationwide pool. Actors, rather than being obsequious toward casting directors, as a musician might be to a contractor, try to always present themselves in their best and most employable image, not just when auditioning. More details of the actual casting process, and more on the relationship between music directors and performers, follow in later sections.

The overwhelming volume of work undertaken in a large production in all its facets requires independent motivation and self-monitoring from each individual, perhaps most of all the directors—the music director, stage director, and choreographer. Of equal priority, though, is the smooth functioning of all efforts collectively, characterized by frequent and clear communication among colleagues. Once the stage performers and musicians are added, the production and creative teams can begin to truly envision the work on its feet. It may have taken many years, a few months, or just a few days to prepare a show, and the completion of the cast and staff marks its graduation into production. Each project has a lifetime, and a lifestyle, of its own. Each one really does represent a new journey, and once they are united, the production team, the creative team, the music director, the music team, and the performers can embark upon it.

PART III

Preproduction

8

Mounting a Production

In music direction you learn best by doing, because each work situation has its own conditions. The doing begins with preproduction, the period that precedes scheduled production rehearsal. Preproduction gets underway for you as music director the moment you become associated with a show, and officially when you sign a contract for a production. Occasionally, when a production is not imminent, you are put on call, and occasionally on paid retainer.

A good portion of both your nonperforming creative work (preparing and writing arrangements and scores) and your organizational and technical work (staffing, physical planning, rehearsal preparation) will probably take place in preproduction. Sometimes phases of production overlap. For example, directors and music directors often begin work with actors during or immediately after casting, and singers often approach music directors before rehearsals begin to learn music (and they might well have learned some of it for auditions). During the *Tommy* process I recounted earlier in chapter 5, "The Creative Team," rehearsals overlapped with writing: we rehearsed Act I in a studio during the day, and completed Act II in the evenings and on days off.

Meetings and Agendas, Planning and Scheduling

The personnel introduced in Part 2, "Personnel," the members of the production and creative teams, along with technical department heads, crew chiefs, and some members of the music team, convene somewhat regularly during preproduction (and continually throughout rehearsal) for production meetings. At these often very entertaining sessions—it is gratifying, and often amusing, to see so many very talented people from so many creative disciplines gather in a room to talk shop—the production staff strategizes, exchanges progress reports, makes requests, solves problems, and airs grievances.

Almost all departments, including music, have multiple members, including associates, assistants, specialists, consultants, and interns.

The importance of good planning for a production, musical and otherwise, cannot be overstated. It is essential because of the effect every department's work has on others', including, of course, the music. Production meetings promote interdepartmental communication. Purely musical issues seldom occupy more than a small fraction of production meeting time, if any. Yet the music director's presence is essential because so many issues come up that might have a bearing, even a faint one, on the music.

Let's say that a wig designer announces that the director has ordered a certain hairpiece, and because of its cut, a wireless microphone can be placed in only one of three locations on the actor's head. The sound designer takes note of the restrictions of the microphone placement, and the music director notifies the sound designer that the actor has a thin voice, so the closest possible placement of the microphone to the singer's mouth will be best. The stage manager consequently schedules a sound check with the actor, the hair designer and the wig, the sound designer and the mic, and other relevant staff—including the wig supervisor and the sound operator. The stage manager consults the producer to find out if the actor will need to be paid for the wig and mic call, and the director says that he or she wants to attend to make sure that the wig looks right for the character and that the mic is invisible. The music director attends the meeting to ensure that the mic placement and hairpiece do not impair the singer's already marginal tone. Dozens of such issues will arise at each production meeting.

Some sort of chain of command within the production team is usually evident early on, at least insofar as running the meetings, but differs in each production. A hierarchy may be predetermined, such as when a group has worked together before, or if a managing director or corporate executive dictates an organizational structure. A production manager or stage manager often leads production meetings, or sometimes the director does. Some production meetings are very loose, with plenty of laughs and anecdotes and cookies and amiable anarchy. Others are quite formal, with reports to be filled out and copied in triplicate and on the supervisors' desks by the next morning. It can be difficult for a creatively oriented music director to fall in line with some rigid administrative systems, but at some point in a successful career it will probably be a contractual stipulation.

There are also many meetings of subgroupings of the production team. The music director meets with, for example, the dance department to discuss dance arrangements and specify when during the show the dancers are available to sing; the set designer and carpenters to wheedle one more square foot of space in the pit; the director, composer, and lyricist to go over arrangements and revisions; the general manager and contractor to discuss instrument rentals; or the company manager and producer to talk about performing at a promotional event. Meetings of the creative and music teams alone are just as frequent, if not more so, than production meetings, in preproduction and moving forward.

Music directors bear witness to extremes of interpersonal coordination in a production meeting room. Producers, directors, choreographers, writers, managers, designers, musicians—all want equal time, and all want their needs attended to first. Extroverts mingle with sheepish brainiacs, and all are stressed because their work is soon to be viewed by a lot of people paying a lot of money, or because their college production has only three performances and their friends and relatives are coming to the first two and their favorite professor to the third, or because the entertainment division of marketing at IBM or Intel is hoping to impress the CFO with its yearly industrial show. Somehow, all these passionate and enthusiastic individuals usually manage to harmonize their shared yet divergent agendas and personalities.

When rehearsal time is short, such as in a single-song presentation, in an industrial, or in a stock theater with quick turnarounds, advance communication is even more essential. Long summer-stock workdays that start off running with nonstop rehearsal and orchestration, and continue into evening performances, often end with late-night production meetings.

Scheduling is always a hot topic of discussion. Performers and staff must attend music, dance, staging, and acting rehearsals, as well as wardrobe fittings, hair stylings, sound checks, and sometimes specialized training of some kind (fighting, flying, magic, quick costume changes), and somehow the production team must allot enough time for all of it. At the same time, music must be arranged, sets and costumes built, lights and speakers hung, and all in such a way that all the elements are synchronized. And all within union rules, or after-school hours, or whatever immutable restrictions are imposed; every production faces some scheduling obstacle. Because of its difficulty and importance, scheduling has the potential to incite heated debates, with all departments vying for time. In preproduction, the production team, led by the production manager and/or stage manager, draw up a definitive final master schedule . . . which from then on is perpetually amended. In large commercial productions with extended rehearsal periods, music directors attend meetings devoted entirely to scheduling daily or even twice daily during rehearsal to reassess rehearsal progress and revise the schedule accordingly for the next day, or days. With these constant adjustments, it is helpful for all creative personnel to remain very flexible and cooperative, though in reality stubbornness is the norm, when everyone, quite naturally, prioritizes his or her own needs.

Reprinted here in Figure 8.1 is a glimpse of a particularly crowded production schedule. It is a day in the life of rehearsal of a Disney production of *The Lion King* in Holland. According to the schedule, at 11:15 AM there are, simultaneously, three music rehearsals, two staging rehearsals, three puppet rehearsals, a hair appointment, physical therapy, and language lessons. Performers are moved from room to room like, well . . . like puppets. Creative staff members are in two places at once. And that's only till 12:30; this entire table represents only what happens before lunch. Organizing this pileup of events into a workable routine is an art form in itself.

THE LION KING

THURSDAY February 5, 2004 — Rehearsal

	Staging, Dance, Music					Mirror Work	Fittings				Physio	Phonetics	Kids	
	STAGING Room 14 Steven, Jan-Erik	DANCE Room 21 Marey, Leonora	MUSIC 1 Room 10 Colin, Maurice	MUSIC 2 Room 16 Clem, Maurice	Mini- MUSIC Room 6 Colin, Maurice	PUPPETS Room 17 Louis	PUPPETS Room 17 Louis, Anne, Ingrid	PUPPETS Room 17 Paragon	HAIR MAKEUP Room 7 Carole, Olga	WARDROBE Room 7 Monique	PHYSIO Room 18 Eline	PHONETICS Room 20 Femke, Bob	KIDS ROOM Room 3 Simone, Herma	
11:00a	Blocking Act 2 ⇩	11:00a-11:15a FULL CAST *Warm Up*												11:00
11:15a	11:15a-1:00p Nomvula Dlamini Etienne Poeder	11:15a-1:00p ALL MALE DANCERS *except* Eldridge Labinjo	11:15a-1:00p Laus Steenbecke	11:15a-12:15p Hein vd Heijden	11:15a-12:15p Carolina Dijkhuizen *Vocal with Margot*	11:15a-12:30p Marcel Jonker Marc Lauwrys	11:15a-12:00n Clayton Peroti *Puppet Fitting*		11:15a-1:00p Tamzi Duarte Desi van Kessel Karima Lemghari Nomsa Mahlale Naomi Reingoud		11:15a-12:15p Mondli Makhubo	11:15a-1:00p Azola Dlamini Silindile Lukozi	11:15a-12:30p Marcel Jonker Marc Lauwrys	11:15
12:00n				*Music*		*Tim & Pumbaa Mirror Work in Studio 3*					*Physio Evaluation*	Sakumjzi Mbele	*Timon & Pumbaa Mirror Work*	12:00
12:30p	*Tamitizo / He Lives In You*	*Ground Row*	*Morning Report*	12:15p-1:00p ALL MALE SINGERS *Music*	12:15p-1:00p Mark Fleischmann *Vocal with Margot*				*Make Up Fitting*		12:15p-1:00p Jeane Guimarães *Physio Evaulation*	Yandiswa Quwe *Phonetics*		12:30
1:00p	1:00p-2:00p Tijl Dauwe Carolina Dijkhuizen Nomvula Dlamini Howard van Dodemont Marcel Jonker Marc Lauwrys Erik-Jan Lens Jeroen Phaff *Who's Monkey?*	1:00p-3:00p Laus Steenbecke	1:00p-3:00p FULL ENSEMBLE		1:00p-2:00p Kenneth Herdigein *Vocal with Margot*	1:00p-2:00p Hein vd Heijden *Mirror Work in Studio 3*			1:00p-2:00p Peggy Sandaal *Shenzi Make Up Fitting*			1:00p-2:00p Mark Fleischmann Etienne Poeder *Phonetics*	1:00p-2:00p Hein vd Heijden *Mirror Work*	1:00p
1:30p														1:30p
2:00p	2:00p-3:00p Tijl Dauwe Carolina Dijkhuizen Howard van Dodemont Marcel Jonker Marc Lauwrys Erik-Jan Lens Jeroen Phaff Etienne Poeder *Simba Confronts Scar* ("Nala, Simba" > "Oink")	*Morning Report Can't Wait*	*Music*						2:00p-3:00p Mark Fleischmann Jerrel Houtsnee *Ed, Banzai Make Up Fitting*			2:00p-3:00p Kenneth Herdigein *Phonetics*	2:00p-3:00p ORCHESTRA AUDITIONS	2:00p
2:30p														2:30p
3:00p						3:00p-4:00p								3:00p

FIGURE 8.1 A busy rehearsal day at *The Lion King*. (Reprinted by permission. ©2004 Walt Disney Theatricals.)

Early in preproduction, usually right after a show is cast and rehearsal dates are finalized, music directors formulate a breakdown of how much time they will need with each performer or group on each musical number, and give their estimates to the stage manager. The stage manager combines the wish lists of all departments, compiles a schedule, then checks it with each department head for any adjustments, and again for final approval, and the schedule is set. For the moment. The process repeats as needed, which is ceaselessly.

When calculating rehearsal time, you as music director cannot assume that all performers in all productions go through the same learning processes. Everyone learns in a different way and at a different speed, and you must take this and other variables into account when scheduling. In each production the rehearsal period will differ, as will the performer's knowledge of the material when joining the production. Any music teaching you can do beforehand will be advantageous once rehearsals begin. As the precedents would foretell, the only rule in scheduling is that there is no rule. You can, however, make educated guesses. You propose to the stage manager an ideal estimate of time needed, accounting for all the variables. You will often end up with less time than you ask for, so aim high with liberal estimates. In educational or amateur productions in which voices might not be as mature and musical skills not as advanced, you will want to ask for still more time. In the next chapter, "The Music: Assessment and Analysis," I will offer specific guidelines for rehearsal estimates.

Music directors do not book rehearsal space for cast or orchestra, but can certainly express their preferences for either, and should double-check that rehearsal spaces are adequately equipped for their needs. An improper setup can wreak havoc on a rehearsal, even something so simple as a piano with a broken key. Important considerations when choosing rooms are their size, acoustics, location, comfort, ease of access (for instruments and equipment), and amenities (photocopying, rest rooms, lunch) within easy reach. More detailed discussions of how to physically set up the cast for rehearsal and the orchestra for performance follow in chapter 16, "Orchestras and Orchestrations," and chapter 18, "From the Studio to the Stage," but you begin planning your layouts in preproduction. You diagram or otherwise design a preliminary pit configuration and a choral seating configuration, and communicate them to the stage manager, technical director, sound designer, props department, or anyone else involved in setting them up or constructing them.

It is helpful in most situations for you to devise a few basic charts, such as schedules, contact sheets, and music plots, or keep checklists, either large-scale or detailed, formal or personal, to keep track of momentary and permanent information both. There are many project-management computer applications available; I usually make checklists by hand in journal form in notebooks and devise tables for tracking the music and rehearsal in simple word processing or spreadsheet tables on the computer. As long as every item is adequately covered and presented in a format that is manageable and shareable, nothing fancy is necessary.

Specifically, the documents I usually make are a contact sheet just for music and music-related personnel; a master music calendar and other sub-calendars for singers, orchestra, rehearsal musicians, and other staff (calendars are now easy to share over the Internet); a plot of the music rehearsal progress (counting how often each number has been rehearsed); and a plot of the music preparation by arrangers, orchestrators, and copyists (tracking the music from its delivery to the arrangers through receipt from the copyist and delivery to the necessary performers). Sometimes I break down the rehearsal and music preparation plots into different documents for different phases of the production. Figure 8.2 is but one example.

Casting

The popularized image of celebrity judges behind a table discharging flippant thumbs up or down bears little resemblance to an audition for a Broadway show, even less so from the music director's point of view.[1] In reality (real reality, not reality-show reality), auditions are the creative team's opportunity to match performers with a production. Auditioning a performer for the stage is not a judgment; rather, it is an assessment of a performer's suitability for a production and a part. (This assessment assumes competence; obviously someone auditioning for a singing role who cannot sing at all will be judged inadequate.)

In most auditions, you can appraise the overall quality of a voice within a few moments. In a little more time, you can also get a good sense of a performer's acting ability, musicianship, stage presence, range of talents, and attitude. Judging someone's specific rightness for a part in a production or a role in a musical takes more work and more time, and usually happens over the course of one or more callbacks, sometimes many. Still, you should fully investigate performers' abilities and possibilities in auditions, looking for whatever might be helpful to the music and the production. Certain performers might not seem right at first, yet their talents might be worth exploring further. For example, no ballerinas are needed for your current *Grease*, but you might as well find out if the dancers sing well; you never know where you might find a good Sandy understudy or a singing ballet dancer for another show.

There are several things music directors are seeking when casting. Some are subjective, such as an appealing vocal timbre (the tonal quality) or suitability for a role. They also look for versatile singers who are good actors and have an effective sound over a wide range, a good sense of pitch, good rhythm, and good dynamic capabilities. Musical knowledge in a singer is certainly a very desirable attribute, but not a necessity, and not presumptive. (Oh, how music directors wish that more singers could read music. . . .)

Some performers may have what a production requires, but it is evident only under the proper direction. At musical auditions, music directors (and directors and

---

1. On *American Idol*, the music director writes the arrangements and rehearses the band, while a team of vocal coaches works with the singers and suggests material and arrangements.

THE AENEID–MUSIC PLOT

Songs by Duncan Shiek; Music direction and arrangements, Joseph Church; Kay Matschullat, Director

NUMBER	PAGE	SCORE #	REH.	ARR.	ACTOR(S)	COMMENTS	STATUS
I. FIRE							
LEAVE, LEAVE	4	1.	✓	1/2	BHAV+ALL	Cut 16 mm. for Creusa speech, add sweep	Need 20 mins. w / cast
TRANSITION	7	1A.	✓		n/a	(Leave, Leave playout)	
TRANSITION	12	1B.	✓	✓	n/a		
DO NOT FALL	13	2.	✓	✓	CREUSA		key still undecided
II. WATER							
WATER OPENING	14	2A.	✓		n/a		time underscore in reh.
HAWAIIAN MUSIC	17	3.		✓	n/a	bring uke from home!	
BOAT MUSIC	27	3B.	✓	✓	n/a	look for better patch w/less pitch	
ROPE UNDERSCORE	27	3C.			n/a		
THE STORM	29	4.	✓	✓	BHAV, AENEAS, ALL	Wilson please bring thunder machine	put Aeneas into number
III. EARTH							
DAYS GO BY	43	6.	✓	✓	CREUSA, AENEAS		n.b. no Score #5
LISTEN WELL NOW	54	7	✓	✓	SIBYL	redo guitar part–downstrokes	Needs to work w/her rehearsal tape!

FIGURE 8.2 Part of the music plot for a workshop of *The Aeneid*.

casting directors) can suggest musical or dramatic adjustments to auditioners' performance, to determine if they are directable, and capable of delivering the desired performance. In some cases, an auditioner will undergo a satisfying transformation after spontaneous coaching, but impressive as it may seem, the improvement may not be as reliable a measure of rightness as the inherent qualities he or she brings into the room. In other words, temporary adjustments made in an audition situation will not necessarily be reflected in future performance. The opinions of the casting directors, with their knowledge of the backgrounds and work experience of many performers active in the profession, are highly valuable in determining how meaningful audition adjustments are, and if a performer is directable are over time.

Before auditions begin, the casting director consults with the music director (and of course the director) to determine what types and ranges of voices are needed, to find out if there are performers the music director imagines in certain roles or would like to audition, or if the music director is aware of any performers of whom the casting director is not (this last scenario is unusual: casting directors know almost everyone, but a music director might think outside the box). The music director (and again, of course, the director) briefs the casting director on the kinds of musical selections desirable for a production's auditions.

Music directors are often asked to provide a written breakdown of the vocal requirements of the roles to be cast, as shown in Figure 8.3.

Casting starts out by drawing from a wide reservoir of performers, and gradually reduces the options to a final few. The music director and the rest of the creative team do not usually attend the large Equity-required "cattle call" or "open call" auditions (no appointment necessary). There, casting directors see masses of hopefuls, identify any outstanding possibilities, and schedule private auditions with them. (There is a provision in the Actors' Equity bylaws that requires a music director to be at certain open calls, but because the actors' union cannot dictate a music director's responsibilities, you can send an assistant in your place, who should be paid for the job.) The creative team jointly auditions, by appointment, performers submitted by agents and managers and the most promising candidates from the open calls.

In auditions by appointment, auditioners sing one or more longer selections, demonstrating contrasts in tempo or mood, and a music director has a chance to explore their abilities more deeply. Like stage performance, auditions and audition material must be believable, and sincere in their emotion, even in the obviously artificial and miniaturized confines of an audition. If you see something in the performer you like but that you feel the song selection obscures, ask for a different song, or suggest one. Quick vocal exercises can help to test range, as can transposing audition songs or sections of them. Music directors provide to all auditioners who are being seriously considered for a role some sheet music and/or demo recordings from the production (the auditioners may already have the music, or know it), and are available to coach them when possible or necessary. Music directors often prepare sheet music from the production to be

---

Breakdown of ensemble vocal parts* (cont'd.)

Men:

Man #1 (*Lewis*): Specialist, Reporter, others.
Bass, low E (not a strict requirement) to F# above middle C; also covers Hawker **[note: in national touring company, man #1 and man #8 are combined as one role].** Lots of offstage singing.

Man #2 (*Flynn*): Judge, Kevin's father, others.
Bass, low E (not a strict requirement) to F# above middle C; good character voice with lots of offstage singing; also covers Uncle Ernie.

Man #3 (*Morgan*): Lover, Harmonica player, others.
High rock tenor (D below middle C to tenor high C); style very important; harmonica (or the musicianship to learn it) desirable.

Man #4 (*Arnold*): Lout, others.
Primarily a dance role, but must be a strong bass or baritone (low E if possible, otherwise C below middle C to F# above middle C); must have strong falsetto for solo in "Tommy, Can You Hear Me?"

Man #5 (*Kehr*): 1st Pinball Lad, Lout.
High rock tenor (D below middle C to tenor high D); style very important; needs abilities both to rock out and to blend; currently covers Tommy and Cousin Kevin.

Man #6 (*Hoff*): 2nd Pinball Lad, Lout.
Baritone (C below middle C to G above middle C), character voice ok, style important.

Man #7 (*Dobie*): Drooling lout, others.
High baritone (C below middle C to G above middle C); strong dancing/singing role; currently 2nd cover for Capt. Walker.

Man #8 (*McElroy*): Officer #1, Lout, Hawker, others.
Sings both bass and tenor (should be comfortable from C below middle C to A above middle C), needs wide vocal range, strong falsetto or mix. **[note: in national touring company, man #8 and man #1 are combined in one role.]**

Man #9 (*Warmen*): Officer #2, Lout, others.
Very high tenor, F below middle C to tenor high D; high tessitura and constant singing throughout; also covers Capt. Walker.

Man #10 (*Buell*): Minister, Mr. Simpson, others.
Tenor or high baritone (C below middle C to tenor high B), character voice ok, some solos; also 2nd cover for Uncle Ernie.

FIGURE 8.3 Excerpt from the male ensemble casting breakdown for *Tommy* on Broadway.

used specifically in auditions, versions that feature in compact form the most musically salient portions of the production's stage roles. The music director supplies copies to the casting director to distribute to the performers. With most music now copied digitally, it is simple enough to produce audition material, and to have it ready in multiple keys.

Auditions are mostly held in rehearsal studios; you should avoid those with excessively live acoustics. There really is a table behind which the casting director and creative team sit, just like on TV, and a piano that you should position so as not to drown out the singers.

A very important person in the audition room is the audition pianist. Audition piano is like music direction in miniature. From a piece of sheet music and a few spoken directions from a singer he or she has just met, an accompanist realizes for the singer a nearly full-blown performance. It is no wonder that many audition pianists go on to be music directors (for me, audition piano was the inroad to at least two excellent jobs). The best audition pianists sightread very well and transpose well, and the very best have a music library full of songs at their fingertips, so that impromptu requests and experimentation during auditions are a ready option. Good audition players also follow singers with great sensitivity. They do everything they can to make sure that the singer sounds as good, and as correct, as possible, even if the singer is neither good nor correct. A bad audition pianist can demolish a casting session. It seems obvious enough how, so I won't bother explaining; just be careful not to hire one.

Casting directors will usually consult the music director before hiring audition pianists. As music director you should not, as a rule, play auditions yourself, because in casting sessions your ears need to be those of an audience member, not an accompanist. You may choose at times to accompany music from the production in auditions, as you will be the eventual accompanist in performance, and you can test out your relationship with the singer. It is also acceptable for you to move over to the piano at any time during auditions, for any reason, such as a desire to play for a certain auditioner, or to play a certain song, or to take over for a stumbling pianist, as long as your actions do not detract from the individual audition or the audition process.

Always insist on live accompaniment when casting a production with live music. When singers audition with prerecorded accompaniment, as some now habitually do (especially in Los Angeles), it is impossible to evaluate their ability to collaborate with live musicians. Time permitting, an auditioner can sing both to his or her accustomed backing tracks and with the accompanist.

For dance auditions, the main responsibilities of the music director are to provide the choreographer and the dance department with the music they will use at the audition, to make sure that the musicians (or sound system) playing that music are in place exactly as the choreographer desires, and to conduct or oversee the musical performance at the dance audition, exactly as the choreographer desires.

Dancers who are auditioning for singing roles usually sing a short and safe musical selection (small range, few sustained tones), but good dancers who cannot sing well at all are often cast regardless of their singing ability, and music directors make do. Since interest in theater performance as a profession and educational opportunities in the field have increased, there are fewer stage performers who cannot sing at all (or who sing well but do not dance at all) than there once were; the competition is just too intense.

The whole of the creative team is doing in auditions what the music director is doing. Each member is looking for the candidates who will serve everyone's needs, yet each is biased toward candidates who will best serve his or her own needs. In making decisions, the team's discussions about the auditioners are frank and exhaustive. Quite often the choice is clear, and easily agreed upon by all. Less often the decision might come down to one or two or three people, all of whom have different but attractive attributes, and the discussion continues over dinner, and beyond. Sometimes the casting process continues indefinitely, until someone that everyone can agree upon has been uncovered. Unavailability of a suitable cast has scuttled many a production.

Other than in productions made up entirely of music (concerts and such), music directors mostly accede to casting those who satisfy the primary production needs rather than those who are musically proficient. The ability of a principal performer to embody a song in a way that convinces and fascinates the audience is a far more valuable asset than note-perfect musical ability or twelve years of voice and music lessons with the leading tenor at the Met. Acting or movement can be just as important for a singing performer in a stage show, and a unique, imperfect voice might prove a more interesting musical choice. (Would you have preferred that Fred Astaire or Gene Kelly not sing? Or Cher, or Charo, or Elaine Strich?)

For an ensemble member, vocal ability and musicianship are probably more overriding concerns, but again not necessarily decisively so. Most productions have fixed numbers of ensemble members to cast, plus understudies and swings (cast members who perform only when needed, and cover several roles), all of whom might need to sing, act, dance, or all three. At auditions, the negotiations (or sometimes hostilities) among drama, dance, and music departments to balance the numbers of actors, singers and dancers can be impassioned. Common ground may be found in performers with sufficient ability in all areas to satisfy all parties, the aforementioned triple threats, but more typically physical abilities prevail over musical skill. This is further evidence that stage music and music directors are in the director's sphere, and the onstage vision takes precedence. Informed directors and choreographers will not ignore musical ability when casting; they want good singers, too. They may, however, make casting choices that present unusual problems for the music director, mostly non-singers in singing roles and singers with the wrong range for existing music. I have found that as I gained a reputation as a veteran in the profession, I was increasingly deferred to in musical auditions by casting directors and directors both.

Take notes at all auditions, enough to remember the specifics of each interesting auditioner. You will most likely see numerous people, and it can be difficult later to recall every one, especially in detail. Numeric rating systems and other shorthands are good alternatives to perturbing the performers by scribbling or typing constantly as they sing; performers who are sticking their necks out for a job deserve the attention of those auditioning them. When auditions are over, you can entrust your notes to the casting director, who will archive them and treat them with confidentiality, and keep them available to refer to later on.

In the digital age, some auditions have been digitized as well. Besides, or in lieu of, a live audition, a performer might sing on a recording, or on a YouTube video, or maybe live but remotely from another location. I recommend that all performers be auditioned in person for a live stage show. The presence a performer has when in the room with an audience can be very different from what is apparent on a recording; also, recordings can be edited and doctored.

As noted, casting can become a lengthy process when many individuals and combinations are considered and given due time over the course of several callbacks. The cruciality of casting to a production's success justifies the extreme care and time investment. As the casting process nears its end, the casting director comes away with a hiring list, as well as backup plans, taking into account a wide array of possible outcomes of the job offers. ("If we can sign Ms. X, then we don't need as strong a dancer in track 4, and she can also understudy. But that other show is offering her more money, so if she takes that job we'll have to find a new understudy *and* an extra dancer, split her track, and lose one alto.") After offers are made, there are usually several more rounds of casting to fill in the holes left by the contracting process, and casting continues throughout the run of a show.

For music directors, casting is not separately compensated, as protracted as it often is, except under whatever preproduction fees they might have negotiated. (Audition pianists are paid hourly, and there are union scales, though they are not always strictly observed.)

Determining the Orchestration: Three Scenarios

The dissension of recent years over the size of stage orchestras is, in my opinion, pointless. From an enlightened point of view one can see that the important criteria are qualitative rather than quantitative. To determine the correct size of an accompanimental ensemble, the music director and production team factor in the content of the music, the physical and financial nature of the production, its unique artistic vision, and the audience's expectation. To illustrate, I'll examine the process of determining instrumentation at four levels of accompanimental and production complexity.

Scenario 1: Voice and Piano, or Maybe More

The plainest act of music direction is accompanying a soloist on a single song. For example, a singer approaches a pianist with a piece of sheet music; we'll say it's George and Ira Gershwin's "The Man I Love." She is performing at a black tie affair, the anniversary party for a wealthy CEO and his wife of 25 years, and "The Man I Love" is their favorite song. There will be a grand piano at the site. The singer is receiving $1500 for the brief appearance (she's not a big star, so that's good pay) and will give $500 of that to you, the music director, for the performance and a quick rehearsal a few days before. She wonders if she should hire a bassist, too.

As you would in a more elaborate professional situation, you, as music director, share your insights with the producer, who in this case is the singer herself, and perhaps with the client, the loving couple (the backers, or executive producers). There is a clear argument for a bassist being unnecessary: there is only one song, with a broad tempo and slow chord shifts that fare just fine with piano alone, especially a grand piano with a meaty low end. You could argue the other side, that this is a classy event, the singer is being paid very well, and the song would sound even better with sustained *arco* (bowed) bass notes. The "producer" can afford a bassist, and a good bassist would jump at the quick work for decent pay (perhaps $250). A music director, under certain circumstances (owing the singer a favor, wanting to secure future work), might even consider reducing his or her own fee to accommodate the extra instrumentalist.

Is the price worth the outcome? The singer-producer considers other production expenses, such as her gown, hair, and makeup, and transportation to and from the job. This is a production with only one familiar, simple song, so minimal rehearsal time is required. Orchestrations, such as they are, incur only nominal cost, if any, as several sheet music arrangements are available free or inexpensively.[2] You remind the singer-producer that there must be room enough for a double bass in the performing area. If the clients do express a preference, that will become the deciding factor, as they are the executive producers of the event. If they say, "We want our song to sound as lush and romantic as possible," then maybe the bass is a good idea. But if all they care about is the song being sung to them intimately in their living room, then piano alone is probably enough.

In this simple example the interplay between music and business is apparent in microcosm. A slight modification of this model will significantly increase the number of tasks and the complexity of balancing them.

Scenario 2: Small Ensembles

With more personnel and more musical material come new complications. I'll propose that the same CEO has earned a multimillion-dollar bonus from his firm, and has retired from corporate life. He's always had a hankering to be in show business, and in his newfound free time he has bought a 400-seat theater in Florida and is producing musicals there. He has an idea for a show: an hour-long presentation of the music of his other favorite composer, Cole Porter, updated for a modern audience. He would love if someday the show were to move to Broadway, but that is not his immediate goal. He has engaged a director-choreographer, and he loved your work at the party, so he wants your help in creating the score. He wants his revue to take "an edgy, ultra-hip approach" using "mash-ups" of Porter songs redone in styles "on the charts" today. He wants it "sexy" and "kinetic" and "eclectic." He's proposing a cast of twelve: six mainly singers and six mainly dancers. He wants the band on stage, because he likes seeing the musicians in action.[3]

---

2. This music is not in the public domain, but one-off performances at a private venue like the one in this scenario do not customarily pay royalties or licensing fees, as do venues monitored by licensing agencies.

3. The exact form or content of the show is irrelevant. I am assuming that this and every stage show are sincere attempts at meaningful, high-quality entertainment. I have chosen a revue, and this particular idea for a revue,

Because he is a novice producer, and because he is enlisting your help in realizing the show, he consults you on how to best apportion his musical dollar, and leaves it up to you to decide the orchestral forces. This is by no means the norm, but when entering a project at this conceptual juncture, you may be able to institute, and enforce over time if the show continues, the appropriate musical approaches and accompanimental configuration(s), and may advise on the budget. When given this power, act responsibly. Make concessions and adaptations when necessary, especially as the show develops, to stay within budget. Workshop productions, for example, will customarily use smaller musical ensembles, as might regional tryouts. Because the producer's pockets are deep, and he is artistically driven, the budget in this scenario may be abnormally indulgent; still, you should carefully balance frugal choices and more luxurious ones, for the short- and long-term health of the show. If a less willing producer predetermines the instrumentation, your opinion matters little or not at all, and though under the right circumstances you might offer advice, it might not be heeded.

You, the director, and the producer begin the creative work by identifying and selecting musical material in an assortment of vocal groupings, moods, tempos, and rhythmic feels. You favor music and musical choices that are manageable for the medium-sized physical production and the available talent. There are many pertinent questions. For instance, how true to modern pop styles does the creative team want the updating to be? (Greater authenticity is usually more expensive.) What instrumentation do the creative approach and musical material require to be believable? Should you incorporate electronic instruments? Is this production an approximation of what will later be an expanded version of the piece, or is this a definitive production? What ideas that the director has for the visual and physical element have a bearing on the music; for example, if the band is to be onstage, where onstage will it be, and what role, if any, do the band members have in the action? If the show is intended for further life, will the producer agree to pay higher salaries to the same number of musicians or more in a Broadway production?

A modern pop-rock band, a neutral starting point for this production, is not large. The basic unit consists only of one or two guitars, bass, and drums (or drum machine), and maybe a keyboard (piano, organ, or synthesizer) or possibly two. Stage orchestrations typically supplement this basic configuration with "horns" (the pop music term for trumpets, trombones, and saxes in a section), strings (usually just violins, but sometimes cellos and violas), and percussion of various kinds. Recorded popular music, meanwhile, tends toward broader but more temporary strokes, using a multitude of striking orchestral and electronic effects that enhance a recording but are difficult to reproduce

---

because it is easy to explain in a few words, and because it involves a bold musical choice. It may not be the most original or compelling idea for a show, but it will serve the purpose of exemplifying a limited but multifaceted musical production. (We're working with widgets here; if I had the world's greatest idea for a show, I would not squander it on a textbook example.) A show like this one is not at all uncommon; in 1999 I contributed a few orchestrations to an ill-fated Broadway revue entitled *The Gershwins' Fascinatin' Rhythm*.

in live performance. To achieve the producer's ideal of an authentic modern pop sound, you would apparently need either a large ensemble or a large sample library. For a stage production, where the onstage performance element will be the focus, you can employ clever approximation and still achieve musical authenticity. You can forsake some of the more extreme features of what would be on a recording, which are hard to accomplish live and may also be superfluous in a theatrical context. The music can and should make a strong stylistic statement, but need not make it in exhaustively vivid detail, and can stay in line with the limitations of a first production.[4]

Start with, along with the rhythm section, a small contingent of horns, maybe trumpet, one trombone, and one saxophone (alto or tenor or both). Add one more of each instrument for a larger and more versatile sound. An additional percussionist would add a wide range of color and fortify the rhythmic element. One or two additional keyboards would be useful, if they are well programmed and amplified.

That's probably as far as you'll need to go here in Florida. You will most likely snub the strings at this point, and maybe forever, unless the string component is conceived as particularly extensive or idiomatic. (For what I am about to say, may all string players please forgive me; I am trying to exemplify prudence, not envision a perfect music world, which would always have real string players, even if they played nothing but whole notes, or ten notes, the entire evening.) In popular music, audiences are already used to hearing string parts emulated by synthesizers, so counterfeit strings are certainly justifiable, especially in a start-up production. Eventually, if a show in this style uses string players, they will be in a larger section, which also supports their omission at this early stage. (When you do use a single string player in a pop ensemble, a cello is often as good a choice as a violin; it is loud and strong and fits in well with the brawny overall timbres of rock. Electric violins and cellos, too, have remarkable capabilities when played well, and they are becoming more common, though to my knowledge there has been only one in a Broadway pit, for the musical *Side Show*.)

There will be room to expand the orchestra if a show continues to grow and its commercial outlook is positive. If the show moves to Broadway and really would sound better with a big violin section, that is the time to put up a fight for musical integrity, and justifiably. In truth, a few extra musicians do not necessarily cost an undue amount, especially compared to the outlandish costs of some other production values and personnel. But one reason producers are reluctant to produce cutting-edge, intellectually challenging work is that the financial risk is too great. Let music directors encourage them by making start-up productions more cost efficient.

---

4. I learned this the hard way myself in doing a revue of period rock music. I tried to precisely reproduce arrangements from the original recordings, but found myself instead fighting to find room for some unique effect or another in the orchestration or the sound mix, and often when I would finally bring it out, the director would ask me to cut it because it didn't work with something on stage.

Scenario 3: Orchestra Reductions

As noted in Part 1, "Music Direction: A Job Description," many Broadway, touring, and regional revivals have recently been presented in scaled-down versions. Some of the cost cutting of today is, from a musical standpoint, indefensible. Most music directors will not condone these cutbacks, but they do want to work, and will always try to make the music its best regardless of the circumstances. How do you accomplish this? The answer depends on the nature and intent of the reduction.

In one scenario your assignment might be to drastically reduce an existing orchestration, while "making it sound just like the original." In such cases, approach the reduction by concentrating on the overall sound of the music, on how the listener will hear it. Look for solutions and shortcuts that essentially deceive the audience's ears into thinking they are hearing the fuller ensemble. Reduced sections and synthesizers may be the inevitable solutions. On the other hand, if you are hired to stylistically overhaul an existing work, as in the Cole Porter example, fabricate an integral version in the new style, not a replica but a reinterpretation. Use the original material as a starting point, and then tailor its sound, embodied in the arrangements, to the new production, to its look, its feel, and its cast.

Let's say you are hired to revamp a production of *Sweeney Todd*, a show whose grand orchestration and vocal style seem inseparable from its musical and dramatic content, for a cast of fifteen and an orchestra of five, as opposed to the thirty and twenty-six of the original. You are to select the five instruments and rewrite the vocal arrangements for the severely downsized company. (Farfetched as this may seem, it is a surprisingly typical request; it sounds a bit like a nonunion tour.) The density and dynamic range of the large ensemble will suffer no matter what you do, but perhaps you can preserve some of the timbre. A keyboardist could play both piano and organ (and a few other instruments, such as harp or xylophone, presumably on synthesizer), along with a trombonist (who perhaps doubles on another brass instrument), a clarinetist-flutist, a cellist, and a double bassist. Two pianos (or keyboards) and a bass with one reed doubler and percussion would also be a sensible choice. Choose instruments with wide ranges of register, color, and volume so that some of the original orchestral detail might be transferred in. Of course, if you are so inclined, you can simply synthesize the accompaniment.

Reducing the vocal arrangement to uphold the larger choral sound is also a challenge, but a less formidable one. The choral sound does not dissipate as quickly when reduced in size; voices are the only instruments in a chorus (unique though each voice is), whereas an orchestra has many different instruments. The difference between sixteen voices and thirty-five is audible, but not as audible as the difference between orchestras of five and twenty-five. Simply assign fewer people to each choral part, and omit some vocal doublings or inner lines. The dynamics can still have a wide range, and most, if not all, of the written notes can survive. The biggest problem in a reduced *Sweeney* vocal arrangement might be that principals will have to double in the ensemble for there to be any sort of chorus at all.

If the production were conceived instead as a stylized, popularized *Sweeney*, with a deliberately modernized sound, still with the same size limitations, you might prefer to use one or two keyboards, one or two guitars, bass, and drums, and replace all the choral harmonies with unison singing, or arrange melodies with backup vocals, and scrap the choral homophony (music in which the vocal lines move in rhythmic alignment with one another). Here the style is the musical determinant, and as music director, you have the job of inventing a customized ensemble that effectively communicates it.

Music directors whose primary concern is the success of the music both on stage and in context of production release themselves from false righteousness about numbers, and represent both artistic integrity and fiscal restraint. Music directors who work from these principles will be sustaining the music, supporting any production they are involved in, acting responsibly toward all divisions of their creative corporations (at whatever level), and thereby furthering their careers.

9

The Music
Assessment and Analysis

A music director's first encounter with a new score may be as exciting as unwrapping a present on Christmas morning, or it may recall the apprehension of turning back the front cover of a massive textbook on the first day of class. Thrilling or daunting, new music is what musicians live for and thrive upon. The initial meeting triggers a kaleidoscope of feelings and thought processes. Music directors, in their multiple capacities, view their new discoveries in at least two primary frames of mind.

Musicians reflexively assess large-scale musical structures and gauge their parts in them. This organizational impulse immediately has you, as music director, estimating what you will have to do to enact what you hear or see. You project yourself into your eventual state of professional involvement and compare your sensibilities and capabilities to the nature and demands of the music. It is how you are able to instantaneously classify a simplistic piece as manageable, and with no hesitation decide that it needs little preparation for performance. The challenges of a long, involved work are also immediately tangible, and when you meet them, as you might with the bulky textbook, you may decide to defer your learning until you have sufficient time to devote to it, and you begin organizing that time.

The opposing, creative state of mind is not so much a conscious feeling but an absence of feeling, a state of rapture, or submersion. As you hear or see the music for the first time, it takes over as the operative force, and you are nearly passive in the experience. This capitulation is not unlike composers losing themselves in creating a new piece, or singers channeling feelings through their voices on stage. In performance you may have a corresponding experience. Some music you meet for the first time may require more than one listening to fully appreciate; indeed, some of the best music is difficult at first to apprehend, because it is new to the ear (just ask the critics who lambasted Beethoven's Fifth and Stravinsky's *The Rite of Spring*).

Learning and Practicing Scores

When preparing any piece of music for performance, all musicians, including music directors, strive for the highest level of technical command and intellectual grasp. Music from the stage literature, despite its predilection toward derivative musical content, can be difficult to play or conduct well. It is often very detailed and richly textured, and can be very specific. One of the most challenging jobs for a music director can be approximating the full orchestral sound of a score at a piano, especially if the music was not written with the piano in mind.

Most of the time, you will have the chance to learn a score for yourself before teaching it to others and leading its performance, but in some situations, you will not. If mastery of the score is the basis for a music director's work, this latter circumstance presents obvious problems. Sometimes you'll have to learn a score learn very quickly, and sometime you'll have to fake it. For this reason and others, most music directors are excellent sightreaders.

No matter how much practice time you have before rehearsal, you can only fully master the music once you get to rehearsal. A score is only fully realized in rehearsal, and so is your interpretation of it. The repetition that goes on in rehearsal cements your cognitive and physical processes of performing the music in context. A show score thoroughly occupies a music director's brain and the hands during an immersive, intensive rehearsal period; the score's pervasiveness alone assures its absorption, and near permanence in the memory. The relationship between musician and music is deepened and ingrained over time. Once a piece has taken hold inside of a musician it is to some extent never lost. (Other music directors and I can still play from memory, and are still haunted by musical "ear worms" from show scores that we worked on ten or twenty or more years ago.) Memorization might happen over time without effort, and is a tremendous asset for a stage conductor or pianist; venerable Broadway maestro Paul Gemignani will conduct only from memory.[1] I find that if a show rehearses for more than a few weeks, I usually have the score memorized by opening night. Because I am not a facile memorizer by nature, I can conclude only that this is a result of the working process. It is apropos that music directors may mark up their scores considerably when practicing (fingerings, cautions, verbal remarks) and in rehearsal (direction and conducting notes such as cues and dynamics), but their performance scores tend to be very clean, with only the most important markings.

How to perfect music at the piano is up to you. Each musician approaches his or her practice discipline uniquely, and there are far better advisors than I on technical matters. Besides which, I hate practicing. I have always hated practicing, especially in childhood. I loved music but I was too impatient to achieve the sort of absolute dexterity

---

1. Robin Pogrebin, "Elevating the Broadway Pit: A Legendary Conductor Shapes Musicals with His Baton," *New York Times*, 19 April 2000, http://www.nytimes.com/2000/04/19/theater/elevating-the-broadway-pit-a-legendary-conductor-shapes-musicals-with-his-baton.html/.

I coveted. Even now, I practice only when I need to perform publicly (I do play for fun), and then I become very pedantic: I separate hands, turn the metronome down to half tempo, and slowly work my way back up. And I also do scales and arpeggios... but only when I must, to stay in shape. I discourage such indolence in others.

I will put forth, however, three important considerations for music directors practicing or getting ready to practice in preparation for a stage production. First is that you may have to reconstruct, decipher, or arrange a written stage score, as well as learn to play it. The condition of some written stage scores can impede the learning process, so allow time for these extra steps. Second is that rehearsal accompaniment should always be of the highest technical and musical order. Learning a score at the piano on the job is sometimes unavoidable, but whenever possible, pianistic (or other accompanimental) perfection should be the norm. As much as you as music director might want to do the playing yourself, there is no harm—indeed, there are many advantages—in assigning the job to someone who plays it better. Third, if rehearsal accompanying duties are to be shared, all accompanists should interpret the score consistently so that those dependent on the rehearsal accompaniment hear the same thing regardless of who is at the piano.

How to prepare to conduct a score is also discretionary. From the time I began conducting, I have used the same method: I read through, sing, or play at the piano each orchestral and/or choral part, one at a time, from beginning to end. (By "beginning to end" I mean a song, a movement, or perhaps an entire show or large segment thereof.) Sometimes I transcribe parts from a recording; this practice gives me even greater familiarity, but of course takes longer. Mine is a time-consuming method, and perhaps overkill, but it has served me well, and I have gotten speedier at it over the years, with the help of digital media. (In college, I carelessly but unwittingly vandalized the music library's precious hardbound copies of Brahms and Beethoven symphonies with my unrelenting page turning and pencil marks in the margins.) It is certainly not the only way to learn a score.

As I go through individual parts, I make notes, written or mental. I learn who plays where, and with whom. If an instrument has been at rest for an extended time, I mark in my score to cue the player upon re-entering (like many conductors, I use blue for cues and red for dynamics and articulations—some reverse the colors). As I become familiar with one part, I sometimes add on others. For example, once I know the bass and tenor parts of a choral SATB arrangement, I may go back and play them together. Or if they parallel each other for long passages, I may study them at the same time. I would do the same with saxophones or other woodwind sections, first and second violins, and similar combinations. I was frustrated when I started conducting musical theater works, and discovered that most full printed orchestrations are not readily available from publishers, only piano reductions with orchestral cues. For these shows I obtain perusal orchestral parts and listen through with score in hand, marking cues in my piano-vocal reduction.

Though at one time I did concentrate quite hard on mastering the physical motions of conducting, I seldom rehearse them anymore, unless the music is very involved or its metrical or rhythmic content is very unusual. Once I comprehend a piece of music in analytical detail, my arms and hands mostly respond accordingly. I practice the thought process more than the technique, which for me leads to technical clarity and communication. I may be the exception in this profile; I gather from years of teaching conducting that to most people, musical aptitude comes more quickly than it does to me, but the gestures of conducting are a greater challenge.

Preparing Scores for Rehearsal

In the Introduction, I defined the term "score" as the music belonging to a show or production. It does not necessarily denote a printed document. Because there are so many types of music for the stage, and so many possible steps in its composition and production, the condition of a score when it reaches the music director can deviate widely. Still, almost every stage production has some type of *written* score. Multipurpose piano-vocal, piano-conductor, or piano-vocal-conductor scores (often abbreviated by musicians to "PV," "PC," or "PVC") are the most common form of rehearsal and reference document. These are written scores with vocal parts and comprehensive yet (mostly) playable piano reductions of the orchestration (whatever orchestration there is, that is, or will eventually be written). These scores communicate the music to the music director, musicians, and stage performers in rehearsal, and all who depend on it for their functions in the production, such as directors and stage managers. Some music is inherently difficult to write down (improvised music, for example), and the essence of some genres is not easily captured in writing (such as pop and rock, which can demand performers' stylizing). Some scores, however meticulously notated they may be, are disregarded in performance. Usually, though, once complete, the written score is an informational axis, acting as a reference book, a road map, and sometimes a bible.

Music directors work on stage productions with existing music and with new music. Within these two categories, there are subheadings, such as new shows with existing music, new shows with new music, new shows with existing but extensively revised music, old shows with new music, and shows with both new and existing music. Random samplings of Broadway seasons bear out the equilibrium among these types.[2]

The most overriding issue in readying an existing score is determining how and how much of it will require changing for the production. These determinations, as noted,

---

2. Of the twenty-four musicals gracing the boards in the 2013 half of the 2012–2013 Broadway season, for example, six were revivals (*Annie, Chicago, Evita, Pippin, Pump Boys and Dinettes,* and *The Mystery of Edwin Drood*), six were transfers from film or television (*Cinderella, Kinky Boots, Mary Poppins, Newsies, Once,* and *The Lion King*), five were jukebox musicals or book musicals developed from the catalog of a composer or style (*Jersey Boys, Mamma Mia, Motown: The Musical, Nice Work If You Can Get It,* and *Rock of Ages*), six were original book musicals (*Hands on a Hardbody, Matilda, Phantom of the Opera, Spiderman, The Book of Mormon,* and *Wicked*), and one was a concert (*Barry Manilow on Broadway*). In about half of these productions, the music director or music team played an active role in creating or revising the music, its arrangements or orchestrations. In about an equal number, the music director or music team was connected to the project in its very early phases.

will most likely be tied to a director's or producer's overall vision, and only in certain situations will music directors will be involved in the conceptual process. Large-scale changes to an existing score can include reordering or interpolating songs, writing new orchestrations, adapting songs to a change in the story or to a different character, or customizing music to a featured performer. Depending on the scope of the work, music directors might take on whatever tasks they are assigned alone, or organize a team effort.

During preproduction, you, the composer, the director, the choreographer (if there is one), and usually some members of the music team meet, formally and informally, to ready a rehearsal score. By the time their participation in rehearsals begins, all performers will need copies of what they are learning to sing or play. Arrangers will need reference music. Stage managers, when they are doing the photocopying and distributing, need the music in advance, and will keep permanent music archives, though perhaps not as thorough as yours. As production moves forward, you either complete the written score or supervise its completion, or for preexisting music notate alterations in the score (and parts).

At the outset of rehearsal, as music director you usually need some portion of the score on paper, unless the show's music is prerecorded, or in a situation in which creating the music is part of the rehearsal process. Because singing is customarily the first thing rehearsed (see Part 4, "Rehearsal 1: Singers and the Stage"), music directors often give priority to organizing, arranging, and notating vocal parts. It is not just a caution to make sure that vocal parts have correct and updated lyrics; it is a necessity. I can attest to the futility of rehearsal without them; an entire music rehearsal can be lost to dictating words to a group.

Rented musical materials usually come in three parts. First is a master rehearsal score, in piano-vocal score or piano-conductor form, as previously described. Second are the orchestra parts, occasionally bundled with a full orchestral score (again, scores copied on computer are more likely to include the full score). Also often included are "vocal books," separately printed parts of only the sung material, printed for the convenience of the singers in rehearsal (fewer page turns and no confusing accompaniments). If stored synthesizer patches or a proprietary synthesized version of a show is available, it can also be bundled with the scores and parts. Many "classic" musicals that were originally copied by hand are now in digital form (scores and orchestrations both), and are thereby far easier to manipulate, and the remaining hand-copied scores are mostly legible, if at times recondite. Materials from the major publishing houses are now mostly in reasonably performable condition.

Some existing written stage scores, however, are in disarray. They are confusing, nonspecific, and, in a few cases, unreadable. There are any number of explanations. Production restraints might have led to hasty copying of a score at the time it was created, or quality control over the music might have been brushed aside for more urgent issues. A music director or copyist preparing the score for an earlier production might simply have never finished the job. Or perhaps no one ever bothered to notate a score properly because everyone played and sang the show from memory. Scores that predate computer copying are obviously much more prone to illegibility, and any mistakes that appeared in a handwritten version may well have been transferred into the digitized update. On occasion I have recopied into computer notation large portions of older scores, because doing so was only a slightly greater time commitment than clearly marking the changes in the existing hieroglyphic manuscripts.

In published scores you might find details and discrepancies that result from their connection to the production at the time of publication and printing, and not because they belong to the composition or arrangement. For example, the music director of an original Broadway production might have demanded that a certain *sforzando* (a strong accent) be especially powerful to accompany a pronounced lighting shift. The published score and parts show a *ffff* marking (indicating extreme loudness) and huge accent signs, but those markings were the exaggerations, there to alert the players and their subs to the important cue; a simple *sfz* or *sffz* would have been sufficient.[3] Another whole passage could have been marked just as loud because it was a transition played over a noisy scene shift, but compositionally it was intended as *mezzo forte* (moderately loud). This phenomenon is apparent in orchestration, too. For instance, orchestrators will write melodies into instrumental parts to double singers whose pitch or volume would benefit from the support, but the doubling is not the composer's intention; it merely helped a singer's intonation in the production for which that orchestration was written.

It can be tricky to filter out spurious information, especially when you cannot interview the original orchestrator or copyist or music director. You might never know if older piano-vocal scores provided by publishers were what was on the conductor's stand on opening night of the original production, or if they are revised or re-orchestrated versions, perhaps an anonymous attempt to tidy up an existing one. Certain shows are offered only in their revival versions, and not in original form. Furthermore, any changes in the original production that were made after the music had gone to print may not have made it into the score, so even an original production may not be accurately represented.[4]

Times have changed. Nowadays music directors, orchestrators, and copyists are very conscientious about perfecting written music, even when not directly compensated for all the revisions. Rental materials for newer shows exhibit this by being completely legible and nearly errorless (it is nearly impossible to get every detail of a score perfect in every way). Of course, computerized notation has made this ideal much more possible.

---

3. A marking of this kind appears on a cymbal crash in the first measure of the score of the stage version of *Peter Pan*. It represents an attempt to terrify the rowdy children in the orchestra seats into silence.

4. Back when music was copied by hand, it was first inked onto what were called "skins," or onion-skin paper, which was then photocopied to vellum for the orchestra parts. Any changes made in rehearsal might not appear on the printed music because it was reproduced from the skins. Hand-copied music was rarely revised after opening night.

File sharing and portable data formats have made procuring existing versions of single songs and many scores nearly effortless. Digitized sheet music of countless titles are available at low or no cost. Lesser-known and more complex songs excerpted from stage musicals are also available, often condensed or simplified, from online sources and in vocal anthologies and so-called vocal-selections books.[5] Perusal and reference piano-vocal scores are available in libraries and music shops and online (some are unauthorized). Nevertheless, whenever a show is produced in any venue that performs publicly and charges admission (and some that don't), its written materials—scripts and music—must be leased from an outfit such as Music Theater International, Tams-Witmark, or Samuel French, and a royalty paid for their performance. Some shows exist in multiple printed editions, which makes sense, given that scores are production-specific. The more often a show has been revived, the more likely that there will be several notated versions of it. With some exploration, a resourceful music director in the information age can probably unearth every conceivable notated version, printed or digital, of every work of stage music.[6] At the Broadway level and by repetition, revivals of these shows net their publishers significant incomes.

The main distinction of a new show with new music is that some portion of the musical creation runs concurrently with preproduction and rehearsal, rather than preceding them. The composer is more likely to be on site, and will likely be involved in all musical decisions, changes, arrangements, and additional material. Probably he or she will entrust some portion of both creating and decision making to you as music director and to your music team, and only some composers take on the task of generating the final rehearsal score. On the other hand, not all new scores undergo complete overhauls between composition and workshop and opening night. Many have been lovingly incubated before they are developed or presented to the public. And even if a score has not gone through any exploratory or developmental steps, some diligent composers will still deliver a complete version that calls for only minimal modifications in production (usually these are more legitimate or sung-through scores).

For a new show, providing a notated score is ultimately the responsibility of the music director, though obviously the composer or arrangers may have already made one by the time a music director is hired. It is especially important in rehearsal, and when a production is reproduced into secondary production, or when a new show is published

---

5. Vocal-selections books are collections of the most popular songs from stage musicals, published with simplified arrangements, without a full score's references to specific stage actions, and at reduced cost. They are the offspring of the tradition of playing one's favorite popular tunes on the living room spinet or Hammond organ (some of the older vocal selections books are also available for organ, and some for guitar) as a way of re-experiencing at home the joy of the music one has heard on a recording or in performance. This tradition, of course, was in an era that predated running down to the record store to buy a 45, or later streaming or downloading the song in an instant.

6. By providing this information, in no way do I intend to condone the piracy that has allowed every significant musical theater score from every major rental company to be scanned and freely exchanged over the Internet.

and printed. Eventually, if a show makes it into a licensing catalogue, the written score a music director creates or oversees will likely become the published version, the one that will be rented to the repertory companies by the publisher, the authentic written record of the music and its intent. Of course, once a written score has been "finalized," each new production might well alter it in some fashion.

Transcribing

Creating a written score often involves transcribing. Transcribing, the act of making a transcription, or "takedown," refers to writing down music from an aural source, a recording or performance. In music class, students "take dictation"; dictation in its many forms is an invaluable ear-training tool. Transcribing a score for a stage work is dictation on a highly glorified scale, and involves qualitative choices of how the music should be heard and notated, and how a performer will interpret the notation.

In some transcriptions music directors seek pinpoint accuracy, hoping to capture a recording or performance by putting every note, rest, and expression in place. In most cases, there is no need for such finality or formality. Most valuable in a transcription are the elements that truly characterize a musical work. For performers, referring to the original source is often as helpful as your notational exhaustiveness. A transcription may just be a starting point.

Let's say that at his party our wealthy CEO instead wants to hear Cole Porter's "I Get a Kick out of You," as sung by Frank Sinatra on *Songs for Young Lovers*—he insists on that version. Without recommending that he hire the Frank Sinatra, Jr. Orchestra, you will probably not bother precisely transcribing the arrangement for this one-off affair. Rather, you'll look for a good Frank sound-alike, and do a takedown that captures the essence of the recording, for the musicians that you have budgeted for and that fit in the performing space.

At its other extreme, transcription reaches its apex of detail and attention to authenticity in Broadway musicals such as *Jersey Boys* and *Motown*. The transcribers in these bio-shows work toward genuine reproduction, and plumb the original recordings for the minutiae to achieve it. The career value for music directors of such conscientious transcription became obvious when the arrangers—or transcribers—of these shows were nominated for Tony awards for their orchestrations.

Here are some tips and shortcuts for creating a rehearsal score and for transcribing.

Work from a template of staves (homemade templates usually serve you better than those from a library) that sets up the attributes of the full score and each staff (their print layout and size can wait). As you do individual transcriptions and arrangements, save these templates for use in later projects (this practice works in both hand and computer copying).

First, enter any large-scale, score-wide items, such as key changes, meter changes, or tempo markings. Put in markers (such as rehearsal letters, lyrics, and formal indications like "verse" or "interlude") early on, as landmarks (as soon as you have entered the notes, or even before). Making an outline and filling it in is more efficient than working linearly.

Next, enter the notes and their modifiers. This part of the operation is fast, and faster still if you determine beforehand what will be repeated in any way elsewhere in the score. Enter that material only once, with all its detail—such as articulations, dynamics, expressive markings, spacing, chords, and lyrics—and copy or paste it elsewhere. Adjust the pasted segments as necessary. This procedure is crucial to transcription and notation rapidity when working on the computer. Making changes or deleting redundancies is always more efficient than entering material from scratch, because so much information needs to be entered, and in the right order. From Figure 9.1, a four-bar passage of the George Siravo orchestration of "I Get a Kick out of You," large chunks of the score can be copied, pasted, and adjusted.

FIGURE 9.1 "I Get a Kick out of You," Cole Porter, orchestrated by George Siravo, mm. 18–21 and 88–91.

Determine in advance your notational approach, especially how specific you plan to be, and follow it consistently. The manner in which you transcribe the music suggests or indicates certain performance practices. Written chord changes, for instance, can imply a loose interpretation of the written notes, even when you write them above specific notes. Therefore, when including chords, make sure to specify how much freedom is desired. When transcribing chord changes you need write them only throughout one

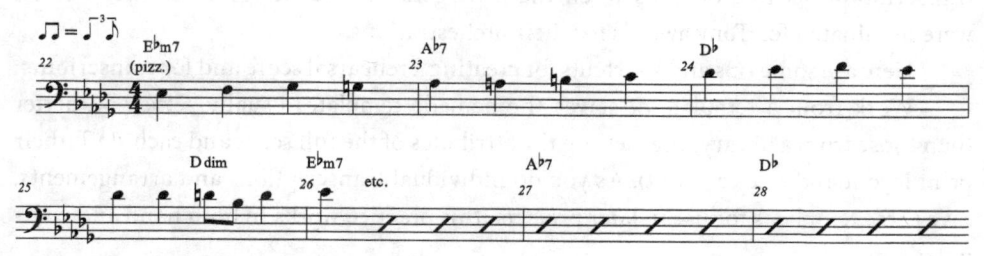

FIGURE 9.2 "I Get a Kick out of You," bass.

FIGURE 9.3 "I Get a Kick out of You," drums.

part, then copy them to other parts as needed. Figures 9.2 and 9.3 balance exactness with shorthand.

In a difficult transcription, take care of less complicated passages first. They will provide clues to material that is harder to hear and transcribe, and you can then add further detail with reference to what you have so far ascertained.

As discussed earlier, recreating a sound's essence is often paramount to recreating the sound exactly. When transcribing, seek out and write down the musical elements

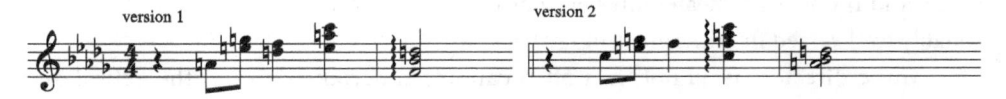

FIGURE 9.4 "I Get a Kick out of You," piano fills.

that best capture this essence. There are already variables affecting the sound, such as transposition and instrumentation. Figures 9.4 and 9.5, two versions of a piano fill, are very similar in sound. When a particular musician plays these notes on a particular instrument—no two players or pianos sound exactly alike—they will take on acoustic properties beyond the notes on the page. Therefore, these versions are virtually interchangeable, and open to further revision by the player, who will also want to make the music "sound better" (musicians will often take it upon themselves to alter a part so that it meets their satisfaction). Violin parts voiced a certain way in an orchestration might work better for a piano-vocal score in a more playable configuration, though something may be lost in translation. In Figure 9.5, reduction sacrifices the contrary motion seen

FIGURE 9.5 "I Get a Kick out of You," violins.

in the top two lines of the original (the top line descends, while the second ascends), but making it pianistic adds a new expressive element:

Practical Analysis for Music Direction

Professional music directors, indeed, all professional musicians, are collectors. They delight in trivia, dates, lists, rosters, who-played-with-whoms in whch show, on what song and which album, and with what orchestra. Most of them cherish their understanding of the mechanics of music as well: how it operates, how it should be performed, how it should be recorded, and all the details that bring it to life. The musicology and music theory one might have slogged through in school might have seemed dry and tedious, but in application for a working musician it is diverting and enriching. Music directors also take pride in broadening their musical scholarship over time, and cram on a specific topic when a job calls for it. (You should have seen me boning up on African music and Indonesian theater after presenting myself at my *Lion King* interview as reasonably well versed in ethnomusicology.)

Music directors need not, and often cannot, undertake rigorous theoretical and historical analyses of every piece they work on, but they do need to discover and address whatever in the music is germane to a production, and comprehensive knowledge is advantageous. What follows is a musical analysis in the context of a hypothetical academic performance. Probably only the most obsessively scholarly of music directors would approach most jobs, particularly this sort of job, with the analytic breadth of the upcoming examination. I have selected a short but relatively rich and "classical" (as well as "classic") work of stage music and a work situation that open up several relevant lines of inquiry. The analytical methodology is informal but multifaceted, examining the work historically, theoretically, and empirically.

A university has hired you as music director for its musical theater club's performance of "Make Our Garden Grow," from *Candide*, music by Leonard Bernstein and lyrics by Richard Wilbur, at the June graduation ceremony. You will have two rehearsals, a sound check, and the performance, and you will accompany at the piano. It is an apt choice for a graduation song, because of its subject matter (making a new start after extended trials); its hymn-like, earnest sound; and its accessible musical sophistication, all very appropriate for an audience of college baccalaureates and their proud families. The song works well out of its dramatic context. It is a plainly lovely piece of music that tugs at the heartstrings, and sounds elegant and ceremonious even when put forth with less than absolute assurance (as may be true with college singers).

In an event such as this, at which music is not the primary focus, the song's history and performance authenticity are probably of little concern to the audience. In a concert or musical theater setting they would be more significant. Still, under any circumstances, examining the history and historical context of any piece is a worthwhile analytical step, and a good first step.

The checkered past of the satirical musical *Candide* is well documented. Its secure place in the repertoire probably owes as much to the involvement of luminaries Leonard Bernstein and Hal Prince as it does to the piece itself. Despite several different first-class productions, none has apparently been to the satisfaction of the entire creative team, and no one version is considered definitive. The original 1956 Broadway production was a famous flop, running only seventy-six performances and opening to tepid critical response. Prince's madcap 1973 Broadway revival was the most commercially successful production and critically the best received.[7] The score is serious, colorful, and beloved, but the show has had trouble finding its stage legs. Its genre is confounding. Is it an operetta? A musical? *Candide* falls somewhere in between, with some moments driven by the music, others by the text. It is long and twisty and sometimes vague, and despite the glorious score, it wobbles under a linear and threadbare structure.

There are several editions of the piano-vocal score. (We'll put aside the orchestration for this piano performance.) Music director John Mauceri worked with Bernstein in 1989 to shape what is now known as the "Scottish Opera" version. I work from that edition now, because in its foreword it claims to represent "the composer's final intentions regarding *Candide*,"[8] and because it's the one that happens to be on my bookshelf. A survey confirms that the choice is arbitrary for this concert presentation. One of the handful of songs that has survived intact in every major *Candide* publication is "Make Our Garden Grow," and the arrangements in all versions are very close. (It was transposed down a whole step in a 1999 revision.) If you had been hired to conduct the full musical in performance at the Library of Congress or Lincoln Center, you would probably be more assiduous in your research on source materials.

To understand the significance of the song and its text, one needs to know the story. Here is as succinct a synopsis as I can manufacture.

Based on the 1759 Voltaire novel, *Candide*, the musical, follows the tale of its title character, the illegitimate nephew in a noble family. The family is financially ruined, and Candide is cast out into a cruel and unforgiving world. On a long journey of survival, he and his cohorts, among them Dr. Pangloss, his lifelong mentor, and Cunegonde, the object of his affection, are subjected to various horrific, random injustices and physical and moral tortures. All the while they retain their devotion to Pangloss's philosophy that everything happens for the best in this "best of all possible worlds." Having survived riches-to-rags humiliations, debilitating injuries, deathly experiences, and crises of faith, the principal characters eventually all come to rest in the same place. There they

---

7. To my generation, the 1973 "Chelsea version" revival was an introduction to the piece, one in keeping with the theatrical freedom and outlandishness of that era, and of the outrageous, circuitous story. Director Harold Prince, with the help of scenic designer Eugene Lee, staged a lively production with performance spaces distributed around the theater, using the disparate stages and the distance between them to evoke the myriad locales of the story.

8. Leonard Bernstein, *Candide*, Boosey & Hawkes, 1989 (originally published 1955), distributed by Hal Leonard, Milwaukee, WI.

collectively renounce their idealism and replace it with pragmatism; they conclude that if one immerses oneself in daily life, then philosophizing becomes irrelevant. This is the argument behind "Make Our Garden Grow."

The musical interest of "Make Our Garden Grow" lies in three main areas: its mild but ear-catching tonal and modal idiosyncrasies, its clever key structure, and its highly distinctive (one could say unforgettable) melodic contour, a series of soaring pickup gestures that float gracefully downward in three- and four-note, mostly stepwise descents.

All these features are related to text and context. As in all good theater songs, the content, sound, and form of the music stem from the textual content. The song's anthemic character derives from its location at the conclusion of the story. All that is left at the end of the twisting saga is a plot of land and a promise to press on, and the music beautifully embodies the plainness and irony of this truth. The song's stolid sentimentality is partly sincere (the relief one feels after surviving disaster and returning to normalcy) and partly cynical (if the music did not have such a strong sense of finality, given the rest of the story, one might expect an army to enter mid-song and bloodily slaughter the singing company).

The song's form is an eighteen-measure AA'BA"[9] played in full three times, plus an instrumental introduction and coda, and, connecting the larger sections, brief (but significant) interludes that recall the introduction. Candide sings the first AA'BA" alone. Cunegonde enters the second time around, partly in unison and partly in harmony with Candide. In the third AA'BA", all the principal players sing the first two A's. The full company then joins in for the final B and A" in an astounding *a cappella* break (see Figure 13.3 in chapter 13, "Ensemble Vocal Rehearsals") before the accompaniment reenters to bring the musical to its conclusion. Only in the A and A' sections do the lyrics differ; all the B' and A" sections have the same lyric: "We'll build our house and chop our wood/And make our garden grow/And make our garden grow."

Throughout the piece, there is a slight quirk in the tonality, manifest in some indecisiveness in the seventh degree of the scale. In mm. 12–13 and again in mm. 20–21 a

FIGURE 9.6A "Make Our Garden Grow," mm. 7–8.

---

9. An AABA form is perhaps the most common basic theatrical song form ("My Funny Valentine," "On the Street Where You Live"), and is also common in popular song ("Yesterday"). There are several other common song forms, among them ABAC, AAA..., and "verse-chorus" forms (ABAB, ABCABC, or ABABCAB). It is a standard practice in theatrical music to vary, break, and otherwise manipulate all songs forms.

FIGURE 9.6B "Make Our Garden Grow," mm. 20–21.

lowered seventh and a traditional leading tone are juxtaposed in adjacent phrases (and adjacent measures), shown in Figures 9.6A and 9.6B.

This disagreement evokes a vague but perceptible "cross-relation," a term used in Renaissance counterpoint to describe a diagonal coincidence of chromatically contradictory notes in different voices, such as a major and minor third, or, as here, a leading tone and a lowered-seventh scale degree. This "clash" seems more than mere coincidence. The musical style of the show (its libretto, too) is infused with a sense of antiquity and innocence, and epitomized by this musical cross-relation and the folk-like quasi-modal chord progression. The conflicting notes, falling as they do within adjacent statements of the title lyric, might also be Bernstein's device, a sonic effect indicating the singers' subtextual ambivalence toward their fate.

The key structure of the song is notable. The introduction begins in C over a pedal G; the opening melodic phrase confirms the initial tonal center. In its second statement this melody continues on to an ambiguous A, still over the pedal G. The subsequent phrase perpetuates the ambiguity. The A holds on while the melody continues upward to a B; the G pedal is then released and then replaced with another B. This dyad suggests the dominant seventh of E, if indeed the pedal B is a dominant pedal as was the G in the phrases

FIGURE 9.7 "Make Our Garden Grow," introduction.

before (there is no D#, no third, to confirm it, but the sound is right). The suspicion proves correct, and the sung melody of the first verse sets off in E major. See Figure 9.7.

The piece remains in E the first time through the AA′BA″, then the first interlude (mm. 23–26) modulates in exactly the same way as the introduction did, to a new tonic of A-flat (equivalent to G-sharp) major. If the same thing were to happen in the next interlude (mm. 45–46) and final AA′BA″, then the symmetrical modulations by major thirds would return the tonality to C major, and that is indeed what happens. (Is there a religious undertone to this trinity, three sections going around by major thirds, an octave divided evenly into three parts? Or does the equal division refer to the socialism of the show's conclusion? Given the composer, neither is unthinkable.) In the coda, the melody from the introduction and interludes recurs, and it seems as if the music might modulate yet again. But this time the pedal G persists, with the A and B sustaining above it, and the unsteady cluster is joined by a *pianissimo* F in the bass. After a *fermata* (pause), a loud solo cymbal crash announces a unison statement of the opening motive, *fortissimo* and accented. The motive gets a brief canonic treatment (the strictest form of contrapuntal imitation), and then the final cadence (conclusion to a phrase) ensues by way of three crashing, emphatic G minor seventh chords. (The leading tone confusion is back, and so is the hint of medieval modality.) The coda pushes its tonal boundary, but

FIGURE 9.8 "Make Our Garden Grow," coda.

never leaves C major. After several twists, the song has come to a resolute end, as have the characters. See Figure 9.8.

The melody is notable for its soaring, lyrical beginning and earthbound, noncommittal conclusion. The upward leaps in the penultimate phrase of each verse (mm.18–20, 39–41, and 58–60, "We'll build our house and chop our wood/And make our garden grow...") cannot help sounding optimistic. In contrast, the subsequent closing phrases ("...And make our garden grow") are nearly static, and perhaps equivocal.

The number delivers its final blow in spoken text, Pangloss's very loaded and pointed question posed during the fermata at m. 87, at the very point where the listener expects the modulation to occur. "Any questions?" he asks. Of course, there are questions; the music and drama both brim with ambiguity. Yet the characters resolve that questioning will from now on be secondary to honest labor and mundane existence. To reflect this certitude, there is no modulation. The piece is staying in C major, and there shall be no more musical doubt.

This analysis discloses significance in the key structure, the connection of text to melody and form, and the logic of the innuendo in the sound. In rehearsal, you can explain your observations and conclusions to the group and explore how they apply; this is music direction, at a scholarly level, and in academia, it is especially appropriate.

How does the analysis affect your interpretation? You do not back off from the cross-relations; rather, make sure they are heard. You coach the singers on an appropriate vocal approach. Have them avoid overusing vibrato as an expressive quality (although legitimate singers have been wobbling their way through this piece for years). Show them that although the notes at the end of each verse do not in fact grow, as the lyric would have them do, they can characterize the irony of the phrase with musical articulation (in this case, *sostenuto*—in a sustained or prolonged manner). Point out to them that the primary motive resumes in the accompaniment under the final cadence of each verse, another level of irony. How long is the fermata at measure 67? Long enough to give the audience a moment to apprehend the several levels of textual meaning, but not so long that the moment becomes ponderous. You might quantify it by listening to the performer's delivery of the line, determining how many beats the line takes to deliver (two?), and how many beats you want to wait after the line for the crash (two? three?). You may want to consider a contingency in case the audience laughs or otherwise reacts to the line. Investigate the *sfffz* marking at measure 64—could it be an instance of exaggerated notation that is a vestige of an earlier production, or is it a compositional assertion of the dominant pedal in the final tonal area of C? A more thorough analysis would entail checking other printed versions, and the percussion parts, to confirm the consistency of the marking.

Moderately rigorous analysis has revealed important dramatic, structural, and tonal features of the piece. Will such intellectual exercise make a difference in how you rehearse and perform? Yes, probably, if not always, then sometimes, and some effects will be subtle, while others are sweeping.

Analysis is beneficial to music directors even when there is no immediate or apparent application of its results. As the representative, curator, and primary custodian of a stage score, you strive for an exhaustive understanding of the music and its operations. You are a production's musical authority, and your absolute comprehension of the score empowers you in these duties. As your career continues and you examine many works, your understanding will deepen, and your analytical facility will improve, and your insight into music will become ever more useful to all productions that employ you.

10

Arranging for Music Directors

Music directors apply what they discover through musical, textual, and historical analysis to the arranging process. In a manner similar to composers writing music, they examine and manipulate what they have so far invented as a means of generating new material. The same forces drive both composing and arranging, among them motive, melody, harmony, tension and resolution, and constancy and contrast, as well as who will be performing and attending the performance, and in what setting. This chapter will discuss planning and imagining an arrangement and delineate some possible approaches and techniques.

Arranging means constructing or reconstructing music into a new or altered form or type of music. The term also denotes the adaptation of music to a specific purpose, such as arranging for voices, orchestra, dance, woodwind ensemble, *a cappella* group, marching band, or for a certain performer or stage act. I have done arrangements for occasions as diverse as the opening of a Disney theme park and a state-championship figure-skating program, and for ensembles as dissimilar as a traditional Korean orchestra and a Californian thrash-rock band. Revising the structure of songs or musical numbers also falls under the heading of arranging; "routining" is another term for this aspect of the craft. Arranging does not always entail specifying every note to be performed, and sometimes it happens only at a conceptual level.

In any composition some form of arrangement is inherent, in some more than others. An arrangement can be viewed as part of the composition. Ravel's String Quartet is not music arranged for string quartet; rather, it is a composition for string quartet, yet a string quartet is its arrangement. A pianist can also play its notes at the piano (some of them, anyway), in a piano arrangement. I suppose a dry melody, a series of notes played without expression or direction, is devoid of arrangement, but does that melody even qualify as a composition? The fine line between composition and arrangement is again visible. Musicians often just use the shorthand term "writing" for either of these activities because the work so often straddles the boundaries that separate them. When arranging as a music director, you bridge any gap that might exist between composition and a production.

Among the different arrangers the Broadway theater employs, it celebrates (and grants a Tony to) orchestrators in particular, I think, because instrumental arranging is a bit more tangible and audible to a listener than other forms of arranging. (That was the apparent outcome of the 1994 union music directors' committee effort—orchestrators, don't forget to thank the committee next time you accept your Tony!)

It is imperative in the current musical environment for music directors to regard arranging from a modernistic, technological point of view, because so many new technologies are available and in use, and because music directors shoulder part of the responsibility for leading stage music toward a productive creative future. Traditional Broadway arranging formulas remained undisturbed for some time, but as in popular music, the scope of arranging possibilities and the range of sounds have blossomed in recent years. Broadway, as always lagging a step behind, has yet to fully commit to the transformation, but it seems only a matter of time, and there have been excursions into this new ground. The gradual digitization of orchestras is one harbinger of the change. Nonetheless, there have been very few productions that have pushed Broadway sound into the eclectic and vivacious sonic mainstream (*War Horse* did this with its onstage incidental music and prerecorded score, and pop musicals like *Mamma Mia!* and *Bring It On* have flirted with the style and technology). Regardless of their tastes or desires, arrangers for stage productions still limit their vocabulary and their forces to what producers dictate, what directors envision, and what a production's budget allows.

A music direction job might or might not entail contributing arrangements, but you'll usually end up doing some writing for every show (regardless of whether it was in your contractual job description), even something as minor as penciling in an introduction or ending. From those small tasks, the arranging work grows: transcribing the composer's demos; writing lead sheets (melody, lyrics, and chords on a single staff); arranging and notating the piano part for the rehearsal score; arranging or composing the scene change music; transposing a song and rearranging its feel; reducing a large orchestration for a promotional event or talk show appearance; creating the dance arrangements, the vocal arrangements, and the orchestration, or maybe all of the preceding. (Here again I remind you to make sure you are paid for your work—you might need to bill producers who are unaccustomed to compensating music directors for arranging.) When working on an original project, you may be the one who develops the musical arrangements into what will later become the definitive score.

Every so often a music director spearheads a major musical reconstruction of an existing stage work. Common cases are in academic theater, and in some professional outfits that concentrate on the music and its authentic or interesting treatment in production, among them the Encores! series at City Center or the York Theater's Musicals in Mufti, both in New York. But for the most part, the commercial musical theater is a creative empire ruled by eminent stage directors, writers, and choreographers whose conceptualizations are the impetus for much of the musical arranging work done for the stage (Twyla Tharp comes to mind). Music directors take care of the many nuts-and-bolts tasks of realizing the material musically, but most often they fit into a director's interpretation, vision, or revision. They aspire to a status at which their creative colleagues will consult them on how the music should be handled.

The examples and principles of arranging I offer here may not be applicable to every situation, and certainly they are not intended to be systematic; rather, they form a list of what you might expect. Enter into each situation with an open mind.

Starting an Arrangement: Approaches and Rightness

As music director, when do you arrange? Sometimes the need for arrangements will be obvious, such as when the score of a show is made up merely of lead sheets, or when the director asks you to make a certain musical moment—a song, dance, or transition, for instance—sound a certain way. (Some scores need no new arrangements; either the composer or an arranger on an earlier production has already done them.) From there you assess the task at hand. Is it large or small? Is it familiar or new? How long will it take, and is the time frame manageable? Do you want to do the job yourself, or delegate it? If you do hand it off, it is still your responsibility to properly connect anyone you designate with the production and with his or her creative collaborators, and see that he or she delivers the work on time.

The foremost arranging question is, "Why?" The many facets of production—most important, the overall vision—hold the answers. Next, "How?" You examine the music. What can be done with it? What are its structure and its syntax? What is its tonality? What is its style? What are its feel, its sound, and its texture? Is the melody manipulable, and can it bear elaboration? What about the harmony, meter, or rhythm, or the phrase lengths, or the structure?

Accompanimental stage arrangements are clever, but not excessively complex. Vocal arrangements tend to be simpler yet than orchestrations, but most stage orchestrations are not highly elaborate, except when they stand alone, not accompanying voices. If they are too complex under vocal parts, they run the risk of detracting from, rather than sustaining, the stage content. Ideally, audiences should be unaware that there is an arrangement; they should only hear music, music relevant to what is going on onstage. In your arranging you support (or contradict, if you are being satiric, ironic or comedic) the time, the place, the mood, the character, or a specific event, an activity, or an emotion on stage. Your musical intent need not be too obvious; you should respect and trust the audience enough not to spoon-feed it information through music. Writing that is "over the top" (exaggeratedly "on the nose") becomes broadly, and perhaps unintentionally, comical.

Most stage arrangement conceptions stick to the basics. If there is something happy on stage, the arrangement is happy. If the story is set in Europe in 1700, the music is arranged in a Baroque style. But there can be multiple levels of meaning. A happy stage moment with subdued or dissonant music can reveal, or foreshadow, that an emotion other than happiness that is in play. Arrangements can shift as the story progresses to perpetuate subtext, and modify it. Arrangements are key players in drama or storytelling. The marvelous *Spring Awakening* uses indie rock arrangements as a metaphor for curious, rebellious youth (inherent in the composer's style, but the instrumentation and vocal and instrumental arrangements deepened and reinforced it). Andrew Lloyd Webber's *Phantom of the Opera* uses quasi-classical and pop-electronica arrangements whose combination is appropriately anachronistic for a classic story remade to appeal to a mass audience. Webber's arrangements are also masterful in their peaks and valleys; the score takes the audience on a thrill ride of suspense, romance, spectacle, and danger.

Three recent Broadway shows are interesting examples of rightness in conceiving arrangements. All three are based on songs by well-known contemporary rock-pop icons, and each features its music very proudly and prominently in the staging.

American Idiot originated in recorded form as a "concept" album, recorded "rock opera" in the tradition of The Who's *Tommy* and *Quadrophenia* and Pink Floyd's *The Wall*. For the Broadway score, an onstage duplicate of Green Day's band played the music from the album. The Broadway orchestration added a small string section and an expanded keyboard part. The strings and keyboard were part of the vision of the Broadway stage version from the outset, and not there to satisfy the union orchestra minimum at the theater. (The show received an exemption from the minimum number of musicians required by the union in the St. James Theater under the Special Situations clause.) Adding musicians, however, seemed entirely unnecessary (something that I myself have been guilty of, as you'll see). When the full band was playing, the strings and keyboard were barely audible from the house. The strings offered alternative colors for the few quiet passages in the music, a choice that was somewhat effective, but most of the time both strings and keyboard were wallpaper-like padding for the acoustic rock songs, which did not work nearly as well. The sustained strings and synthesizer pads weakened the hard-edged sound palate with an inappropriately syrupy timbre, a musical platitude in any context but especially so on Broadway stages, where platitudes abound. The added instrumentalists were a very un-Green Day–like musical choice, and inconsistent with the counterculture tone of the music and the onstage drama. The presence of an unneeded conductor-keyboard player (not the music director–supervisor) planted downstage left of center was intrusive. Because the score was largely played to click tracks, and rock music does not really require a conductor to keep it together, click or no click, the conductor's presence further detracted from the seditious spirit of the piece.

The hit jukebox musical *Rock of Ages* presents its 1980s pop-rock standards in versions very faithful to their original recordings. Its small onstage band (two guitars, bass, drums, and keyboard) is roughly the same size and makeup as most of the bands that originally performed the material. The creative team mashed up some songs and interpolated out-of-tempo introductions to others, and here and there slightly rewrote a lyric to fit the story, but for the most part the musical material is easily recognizable in the way listeners first heard it. The melodies and harmonies, texture, timbre, and basic instrumentation are virtually unchanged. In style, the show is a model of consistency and authenticity, and to these qualities it owes a great part of its success. *Rock of Ages* is devoutly faithful to all things 1980s in every story and design element, including its music and music direction. It helps that the show never takes itself too seriously. It is a self-conscious spoof that delights in its imitative bent, musically and otherwise, as do, judging by the show's financial windfall, the audiences. The music director wisely trusted the power and familiarity of its songs in their original state and original sound.

The score of the another hugely successful jukebox musical, *Jersey Boys* (a jukebox musical with a serious, biographical plot), also does not stray far from the original sound of the hits it was built on, the catalogue of Frankie Valli and the Four Seasons. Years of robust ticket sales for the show are evidence of the enduring popularity of that band's music among baby boomers, as well as of the high quality of the musical. This music director had only to shine up the old songs, transcribe and codify their arrangements (which were quite solid to begin with), make the distinctively bright vocals even crisper, and get it all in better tune. The effect is almost like a remixed, remastered version of the old recordings, with the tempos a bit brighter. Combined with a superb sound design, the musical has an effect on the audience members that is immediately palpable; it is as if they are hearing their favorite songs sounding the same, but better than ever. Furthermore, the surrounding story is well told and moves in excellent coordination with the music, each enhancing the other.

These evaluations suggest that less is more when it comes to stage arranging, especially when the existing music is strongly rooted in a time and style. The same holds true for the "Great American Songbook." The contemporary artists (Rod Stewart, Harry Connick, Jr., and others) succeed by interpreting these standards with great reverence to their original styles, without trying to improve on what is already excellent, and giving an audience what it hopes to hear. Here are two further examples:

When *Tommy* moved from the La Jolla Playhouse to Broadway in 1993, the producers, director, composer, and music team were forced to augment our orchestra to satisfy the large St. James Theatre orchestra minimum (it was twenty-four at the time; the lower minimums were not yet in place). Reluctantly we brought in a string quartet, a second French horn, a percussionist, and the orchestra understudies and walkers I mentioned in chapter 1, "Music Direction Today and Yesterday." The extra musicians had little positive effect. They only complicated the sound palette, crowded the pit, confused the musical style, and cost the producers unnecessary money. We would have been far better off by leaving the original La Jolla band intact, as the Dodgers (the producers), Des McAnuff, Pete Townshend, and I all agreed.[1]

In 2004 I wrote, with librettist Stuart Ross and director Gabriel Barre, a modernization of Gilbert and Sullivan's *The Gondoliers* for the Roundabout Theater in

---

1. The original La Jolla band consisted of two guitars, bass, drums, three keyboards, and French horn. Pete Townshend was fascinated with and the orchestral possibilities of *Tommy*, which was, at the time, one way that orchestrator Steve Margoshes and I justified our choices.

New York. The workshops of the show attracted wonderful performing talent (such as Neil Patrick Harris, Mary Testa, Christian Boyle, and Hunter Foster), the comedy was sharp-edged, the story an enjoyable G & S romp, and the music inventively and idiomatically arranged in all sorts of danceable and quirky pop styles, with colorful instrumentation. The score melded wonderfully with the boisterous stage action. (Apologies for reviewing my own work so favorably; it really was good work but, as is about to become evident, work with no future.) Audiences at the readings received the project with unanimous praise. Soon, though, interest in the project waned, as it did over time in *Hot Mikado* (a similar undertaking) and a rocked-out Mozart show in France, and various Broadway-pop crossover projects such as *The Rock Tenor* and *Rocktopia*, all of which have shown great potential, but have all ultimately struggled or fizzled in finding long-term profitability. The workshops were the end of the line for *The Gondoliers*, as promising and musically hip as it may have been.

The reason is now clearer to me. These transfers of style or intent are by nature artificial. (A 1981 modernized *Pirates of Penzance* did quite well at the box office, and a revival is currently in the works; I suspect its original success was spurred by its marquee full of star names in the leading roles.) The arrangement choices made for *Tommy* and *The Gondoliers* and *American Idiot* were made as much for their own sake as they were to enhance the productions. (Similarly, transfers of classic tales such as *A Tale of Two Cities* and *Jekyll and Hyde* to the musical stage have little staying power, because there's no vital reason to set those stories to pop music, except, perhaps, to feature a star and make a profit.)

Believability is the utmost benchmark. As music director you will often find that believability is inherent in the composition, and that you will best achieve a convincing, emotional, and meaningful performance through authentically enacting a score rather than rearranging it. This is not an absolute, of course; you must consider the job situation, the performers, and the audience. Audiences in European cities such as Hamburg and Rotterdam wholeheartedly embrace the classic novel adaptations, but American audiences have not shown them the same affection. If you are a music director of a stage extravaganza in Las Vegas, you might want to put on a very shiny new coat of paint on those old standards before presenting them to a modern-day crowd.

On the other hand, just because an arranging concept may be of uncertain or limited appeal, or even artistic feasibility, does not mean that you should not pursue it. It is entirely possible to create new arrangements of existing work that equal or surpass their source material. The William Elliott arrangements of both the 1981 *Pirates* and our *Gondoliers* score are engaging to listen to, and the comedy and music worked well together on stage. The ingenious dance arrangements in *Newsies* elevate an already lively score to high entertainment.

Technical Fundamentals of Arranging

In the arranging process there are several categories of technical operations.

Distribution, Registration, and Voicing

If a composer gives you as music director a stack of lead sheets with chords and melody and calls it the score of the show, you have quite a few decisions to make before performing the music in public. If you wanted to demonstrate to a layperson what arranging is, this would be a good circumstance in which to do it.

The melody is usually where you start; this is the *cantus firmus* (literally, fixed song, or the primary melody). Melody and words are the prime communicators or storytellers in stage production, and are therefore the musical epicenter. Who is, or should be, singing or playing a line of melody? Where in the singer's or instrument's range should it fall? If there is another line (counterpoint) or a chord (harmony) that goes with the melody, such as in an ensemble vocal piece or, more apt to this study, an accompaniment, to what voice(s) or instrument(s) do you assign it? The answer? The ones that are right for the composition and production. A Bob Dylan song in concert with rhythm guitar. An ABBA musical with multiple keyboards and drum machines. "Seventy-Six Trombones" with . . . you get the idea (and you won't need seventy-six).

Once you have assigned a line or chord, how should it be played? If it is not the melody, what is its connection with the melody? Is the line or chord one part of a homophony, or does it move independently? Questions such as these will determine how expressive it should be, and in what way. If an accompaniment is chordal, you give the chords details, such as duration and articulation, with specific purpose. You might treat them rhythmically in a pattern or arpeggiate them (sound the notes of a chord in succession, rather than simultaneously), either in a preset pattern or perhaps at the player's discretion. A line can either coincide with the melody or move against it contrapuntally. Each accompanying chord, or line, may be only one of many, and you coordinate them into a whole that best supports the melody and the meaning it carries. In some cases you arrange the melody in response to an accompaniment.

You can place lines in different octaves, or registers, and voice chords in various ways. The vertical placement of the factors of a chord, its voicing, can dramatically alter the chord's sound and the meaning of what it accompanies. What part(s) of the frequency spectrum, high or low, do you want your arrangement to occupy? What are the appropriate choices of voicing and instrumentation for a certain musical style? Is the melodic line (usually a vocal line) high or low, and is it in a strong vocal register? How does it change through the piece? See Figure 10.1 for the very different sound and implications of the voicings of the same chord played on the instruments specified.

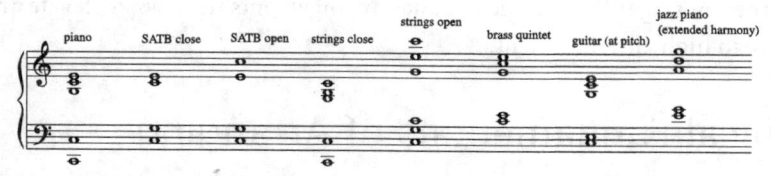

FIGURE 10.1 Various voicings of a C-major chord.

Dynamics and Articulation

Part of arranging is indicating dynamics and articulations to notes, on their own and relative to others. Loud or soft, harsh or gentle, detached or connected: these are the extremes, but in between lies a universe of possible ways that size (dynamics) and shape (articulation) interact. These two interconnected values give personality to music. Any of the chords in Figure 10.1 will sound entirely different on the same instrument if played at different volume levels and with different ways of striking, holding, and ending a tone. Because your intent is to capture the mood and flavor of what the music is accompanying, dynamics and articulations are among your most powerful and versatile tools.

Be specific and consistent in notating dynamics and articulation. The dynamics you indicate must make sense in relation to one another, and have context as well, particularly in the way they progress from one to the other (for example, make sure your crescendo has a start and an end point). Dynamics imply changing states of energy as well as constant energy, and music, as a temporal art form, is in a constant state of change (even when it is unchanging). In a long stage score, think of dynamics as production-wide, as well as specific to each number. In a small show in a black box theater, the overall dynamic range is narrower and lower than in an arena. Articulation symbols may be specific to context or genre, and open to interpretation. Develop a consistent language for each score, and, if need be, include a written key or guide that explains your symbolic terminology. Subsequent chapters will frequently revisit these essential musical elements.

Key

A composition's original key (the one in which the composer wrote it) carries little weight in stage production. Keys are more than just flexible on stage; they are also purposefully flexed. Rises and falls in keys, modulations dramatic or subtle, sudden shifts from major to minor—these are among arranging's materials. An explicit example of manipulating keys is a folk song that gradually moves up a half step with each verse as the drama heightens (Jimmy Dean and Roy Acuff's "Big Bad John" is one). You have almost complete freedom as an arranger to formulate key structures that suit the needs of the performers, the storytelling, and the production.

Certain works of music are tied to certain keys, especially works of classical music and "classic" popular music. Indeed, listeners may know when they hear a song in a key other than its original. Certain keys are also idiomatic to certain works, certain voices, and certain instruments, again mostly in classical music, but also in popular music, such as with guitar power chords and open tunings. When choosing a key for a song that is best for the singer and best for the show, you might check to see if a song was originally in a certain key for a reason. Sometimes a nearby or acoustically related key sounds closer to the original (D-flat instead of D, B minor instead of E minor), if that is a consideration.

The choice of key has the greatest practical effect on voices and orchestration, as a transposition of an existing vocal arrangement or orchestration might put some voices or instruments out of range or into a register with a different timbre. As a rule, you should decide the key of a musical number before the arrangements are completed. Small key revisions are easiest, but can still be complicated for some singers and for some instruments such as harp, guitar, and some woodwinds and brass. (Because some woodwind and brass are transposing instruments, that is, are based on keys other than C, changing keys and instruments both entail changes in key signatures. For example, on an alto saxophone, changing from A-flat major to A major changes the key signature from one flat to six sharps.)

Feel and Style

Almost all musical material in stage productions has some rhythmic element, and the majority has a strong rhythmic element. As with its key, a song's rhythmic underpinning and progression, its "feel," may be associated with a certain writer or artist, or a particular style. Some rhythmic feels are inseparable from the composition. "The Greatest Love of All" will probably always remain a pop ballad. Would you give the dainty threads of *The Nutcracker*'s Sugarplum fairy a country backbeat? (Please, no.) Yet jazz and theater standards, songs originally written for the radio or the stage, are rhythmically and to a lesser extent melodically reinterpreted as a matter of habit. Though the Sinatra or the Tony Bennett or the Nat King Cole version of a standard may be the best known, it is only one in a multitude. As a music director, part of your work will involve giving a new feel to—that is, arranging the feel of—material from the standard musical repertoire.

Feel and style are interconnected. The feel of a song is closely related to dramatic or thematic context, location, historical period, a story told in its lyrics, or its general character and mood, all of which are also determinants or elements of style. Stage music often resembles "programme" music, that is, referential or pictorial music. Much music for musical theater alludes directly to stylistic values of the stage content. There are the gentle two-beats of "Cain't Say No" and "Surrey with the Fringe on Top" and other songs from the wide-open frontiers of *Oklahoma!*, the staccato, pointillistic motives of *Sunday on the Park with George,* and the minor-key laments of *Fiddler on the Roof.* There are the episodic grooves that form an extended rock story song like Meat Loaf and Jim Steinman's "Paradise by the Dashboard Light," Billy Joel's "Scenes from an Italian Restaurant," or Stevie Wonder's "Living for the City." It would be hard to justify in an arrangement changing the style of any of these musical-dramatic masterpieces.

Style allows performers and listeners to contextualize music in history and in human and musical experience. Different styles call for different performance practices. Researching performance practice in contemporary music has been immeasurably easier since people began recording music. Musical style and vocal style are your prime concerns as music director and arranger. How authentically or deliberately inauthentically are you interpreting an existing work? As in all arranging choices, the overall vision of the production and the qualities of the performers involved will be your guide.

Tempo

Tempo is connected to feel. Tempo decisions and tempo management are usually only a small part of arranging, because only when music is performed is its tempo actually in effect. There are tempos that are quantifiable and those that are nebulous, those that are subtly shaded and those that are rigid, but tempo will always to some extent be a subjective matter. Arrangers do not as often decide tempo as they are given a tempo by the music director, choreographer, or director. Tempo will be a huge object of attention of a music director's life later on in production, but is less a focus in the arranging process.

Structure

The structure of musical numbers gives logical, perceptible shape to storytelling and emotional content. It also includes the beginnings and endings and the climaxes and lulls that lie between. When arranging songs not written specifically for a production, you often alter their structure. You might extend, truncate, interpolate, reorder, combine, or otherwise manipulate structural components into new forms. On a smaller scale, often because of what is happening on stage, you might have to perform smaller operations, such as inserting measures between phrases to accommodate dialogue or a set change, suddenly dropping out the time in an *allegro*, switching temporarily to an alternate meter, or dividing alternating phrases of a song between two singers with completely different ranges. There is great skill in doing these sorts of things without upsetting the essence of music, or better yet, by enlivening it.

Notating Arrangements

Music directors create or organize any written arrangements so that they are ready for use in production, and if the job calls for it, so that they may be reproduced in future productions. The crucial part of writing out any arrangement of any kind is clarity of communication. A written arrangement exists so that players and singers can apprehend a great deal in a short time, just by reading the music, so your work must be meticulous and can be time consuming. Notwithstanding the ease of quality notation in the computer age, there is haphazard, nonspecific notation everywhere, and it can easily lead to inefficient rehearsal and poor performance. All elements of arranging deserve notational attention and accuracy.

When entering an arrangement into a computer file, you can arrange and notate simultaneously. Copying is now to some extent an ongoing process. There will be several steps remaining before the final printed product (scores and parts), but readying the material in digital form for a copyist (perhaps you) to copy is part of the job of modern arranging. There are still writers who work by hand, in which case a copyist will transfer their output to computer notation, and there are other arrangers who do not write down their arrangements at all, in which case someone will probably have to transcribe and copy them. Not all arrangements need to be written down to be effective, and some arrangements are written in various musical shorthands. Rudimentary or makeshift parts are referred to as "charts" (as shown in Figure 10.2). Arrangements improvised by the accompanimental unit are sometimes called "head" arrangements.

FIGURE 10.2 A thorough band chart for an excerpt from "Ghostbusters."

Arranging for Voices

All musicians sing, or can sing, at least sort of. The fundamentals of putting a voice to a melody are instinctive to most practicing musicians, even those with little or no theoretical or technical training, and even for instrumentalists without vocal inclinations. At times, arranging vocals doesn't even feel like a skill. Someone sings a melody; someone else harmonizes with it or sings another line against it. If a line doesn't fit in a singer's voice, you try another key, change the notes, or swap singers. Whatever you conceived in advance that doesn't work on a voice can be readily modified later. Vocal arranging in stage contexts, however, does have special conditions and concerns.

With most new theatrical scores music directors have some part in devising and notating the vocal arrangement for rehearsal and for publication later on. In each production the music director makes adjustments to existing vocal arrangements to suit the cast. Not all vocal arrangements are written; some are learned by ear. Some are hard to represent in writing, such as those that involve improvisation or are highly stylized. Like a score or script, vocal arrangements are incomplete on paper; only when sung are they fully realized. You cannot complete an arrangement until you know who will be singing it, and where and how it will be performed. You will need to know the exact numbers of performers, their vocal ranges, their vocal types, and their musical abilities, and account for the performance venue, the production values, and the sound reinforcement. You finalize the work in rehearsal.

For a vocal arranger, the act of creating music and then hearing it performed by talented singers is endlessly satisfying (the same holds true with orchestrators and their orchestrations), and music directors take great pride in their vocal arranging. Yet vocal arranging is a rather loose designation. A riff improvised by a singer is a vocal arrangement. Choosing the singer(s) who will be singing a line that a score merely indicates as "Solo" or "Ensemble" is vocal arranging. Harmonizing a vocal line is vocal arranging. (Again, the line between composing and arranging blurs.) A choice of vocal style is also in a sense vocal arrangement, even though it may not be visible in notation. Many people might contribute vocal arrangements during production: the composer, the music director, the singers, the director or the choreographer, even the producer watching from a folding chair ("That girl on the left really should have a solo line or two . . .").

Like any other musical element, above all, vocal arrangements serve the story or theme. The exception is when a production is presentational, where there is little or no story to tell and the act of singing is the focus, for example, in an *a cappella* group. Vocal arrangements also assist the performer: what specifics of a sung line will sound best on a certain performer or group of performers? The goal is always believability: what will make the performance sound most convincing?

Matching a melody to a voice is highly specific, highly personal, and quite possibly the make or break of a song or a production. In a sense, casting, that is, whom you assign to a certain vocal part, makes some of the vocal arranging decisions for you. Liza Minnelli essentially wrote the best-known vocal arrangement of the songs she sang in *Cabaret* by performing her role definitively in the film, as did Robert Preston in *The Music Man*. No one can sing the Beatles like the Beatles, as the middling novelty Broadway Beatles tribute shows (*Beatlemania* and *Rain*) and the dearth of hit Beatles covers demonstrate.

There are many music directors who sing quite well, but to be a good vocal arranger you need not be a singer yourself. You should, however, have a strong grasp of vocal technique and of the voice as a musical instrument and a means of stage communication. My master's-degree minor in voice and years of singing in choirs and bands have obviously done no good; I still have a nasal, unpleasant singing voice. I have, however, studied, experienced, and understood well how the vocal mechanism operates, and I can imitate and demonstrate effectively with my voice. The voice is always there for you as a rehearsal instrument; you never have to take it out of its case or lug it to the job, and even when you're not very good at it, like me, it's useful. When you're arranging for voices, try them out on your own.

As do all tasks of music direction, vocal arranging ranges from very simple to very complex, and the pool of stylistic and technical possibilities you draw from is very wide. All the practices of group singing of the last hundred or more years comprise the modern stage music vocal vocabulary. Among them are the early blues of the deep South and later Kansas City and Chicago, the operetta choruses of that same era, the patter of

Gilbert and Sullivan, the close harmonies of 1940s swing, the traditions of doo-wop and other "street" harmonies, gospel, Motown, funk, hard rock, soft rock, medium rock, girl groups, boy bands, and now rap, hip-hop, and world music.

Traditional regulations of harmony and counterpoint have limited relevance in stage vocal arrangements, but knowing the rules is helpful nonetheless. Many writers who write vocal arrangements are not schooled musicians, but have great facility with voices and how best to use and combine them. Music and vocal arrangements for the stage heavily emphasize melody, which communicates text. Unison group singing prevails because it is straightforward and reliably audible. When counterpoint does come into play, vocal arrangers carefully balance melody and countermelody to direct listeners' ears toward where they should be listening to make sense of what is happening. Harmonizing a melody should never obscure a melody or its text, unless that is the desired effect. Uncomplicated harmonies are often preferable, and are the most common choice in stage vocals. In the entire three hours and twenty minutes of the epic *Les Misérables*, despite choruses of students, beggars, prisoners, prostitutes, revolutionaries, ghosts, and more, there are but three brief passages of three-part harmony and two of four-plus-part harmony, a total of about thirty-two measures. As a rule, unless there is a good reason to elaborate on a group melody, it is best left in unison.

As vocal arranger you factor in any stage action connected with the singing, and when possible coordinate the two. Among your concerns are stage placement (who is where on stage), lighting and scenery, and, most importantly, choreography: if everyone singing on stage is physically exerted, a complicated vocal arrangement might not be feasible. Meredith Willson's *The Music Man* is unequaled in using vocal arranging as part of the staging and story, with its barbershop quartets, its shared song motives that combined in medleys ("Goodnight, My Someone" and "Seventy-Six Trombones"), its vocal crossovers ("Pick-A-Little/Good Night, Ladies"), and its spoken-sung arguments ("Rock Island," "If You Don't Mind My Sayin' So").

The following are descriptions of several examples of excellent vocal arrangements for the stage. Besides being musically convincing and interesting, they are each driven by storytelling, and their musical styles are firmly rooted in the stage content.

First is the iconic group vocal from the opening of *A Chorus Line*. In this example, the vocal arrangement, accompaniment, text, composition, style, and story all operate in artful alignment.[2] The composer, Marvin Hamlisch, provided only the solo melodic lines; most of the vocal arrangement was written by *A Chorus Line*'s music director, Donald Pippin.[3]

---

2. The orchestration melds a rock sound, using a rhythm section typical of the era (electric piano, electric bass, electric guitar, and drums), with a "show tune" sound (adding three trumpeters, three trombonists and four multi-reed players for color and punctuation).

3. Donald Pippin, phone interview, 5 May 2010.

ARRANGING FOR MUSIC DIRECTORS | 167

The passage reflects the intense desire, even desperation, of the characters for success ("God, I hope I get it . . ."). The melody, as shown in Figure 10.3,

FIGURE 10.3 "I Hope I Get It," from *A Chorus Line,* mm. 81–86.

changes from completely conversational, to overtly lyrical (Figure 10.4):

FIGURE 10.4 "I Hope I Get It," mm. 94–97.

The first melody requires little elaboration from a vocal arrangement; the result would be not conversational, but musical. The melody is purposefully composed to be anti-melodic. The tonality and harmony of its accompaniment are similarly less musical and more like the rumblings of a crowd, or a street in the Broadway theater district. The later lyrical line is a solo, and stands out from the rest in its warm consonance, a brilliant contrast made possible by the timing of the phrase's appearance—an interruption of a group crescendo (an example of routining to effect a dramatic shift)—and by its striking key change (an example of manipulating keys for emotional impact).

As the tense atmosphere and the characters' desires mount, a simple counterpoint forms with one voice sustaining alternately under another (mm. 84–85, Figure 10.3). After a brief return to unison at mm. 86–87, there is one more measure of simple call-and-response imitation, then a burst of three-part harmony, shown in Figure 10.5 (actually six-part harmony, because each part is doubled at the octave by male and female voices) at mm. 89–90. A sudden rest (or, more accurately, a brief "stop-time" episode) in the accompaniment leaves the voices temporarily unaccompanied.

FIGURE 10.5 "I Hope I Get It," mm. 89–94.

These phrases reach one temporary climax within a greater build, and harmonizing them creates both a perfect release of the tension and a sharp contrast to the counterpoint and unison immediately preceding (as well as a twist on the text). By using a triadic and parallel harmonization, the arranger equalized the lines to form a group melody, or three parallel melodies, any of which could be construed as the primary melody without loss of focus or communication. (On the original cast recording of the show only the highest written line is sung, or mixed, with any power; the other lines disappear into the texture.) The text of this homophonically harmonized phrase ("Look at all the people/At all the people") insinuates both the collective fear and the competition in the group. The stark parallel triads are a perfect arranging choice to underscore this duality.

Immediately following, at measure 91, there is a *subito piano* (suddenly quiet), and two voices begin a wiry harmony, the lower voice a simple rising minor scale against the melodic upper voice (that the upper voice is the melody is quite clear). The effect is stark and hollow, and beautifully echoes the surging desire of the singers. The mostly dissonant dyads formed by the two lines add to the tension. So does the now higher register of the lead line, which embodies the characters' hushed apprehension, and against it the low-register counter line creeping ominously upward. This two-part counterpoint (really four-part, as again, the high and low lines are doubled at the octave) builds in volume as the voicings become closer together (adjacent, rather than widespread, tones within the chord) and squeeze the sound as in a classical *stringendo*. At its peak the arrangement abruptly yields to the *dolce* female solo.

While it is true that all vocal arranging for the stage is text driven, there is ample room for musical style and technique to show through, even when a theatrical essence remains preeminent. The opening sequence of *The Sound of Music* is a gentle musical exposition of the setting and an introduction to the leading characters. It takes place in a nunnery; from off stage female voices sing in unison with chant-like solemnity from a theatricalized liturgy (Figure 10.6A). The style of the vocal arrangement establishes the characters' environment, and their piousness (setting and character). The change from the starkness of the unison to the richness of the harmony of the subsequent hymn, "Rex Admirabilis" (Figure 10.6B), a selection from the matins, or morning service; the writers did their homework), evokes the abbey's warm inclusiveness, and a foreshadowing in music of the eventual climax and resolution of the story. (These arrangements were also written by Trude Rittman.)

FIGURES 10.6 Excerpt from (A) "Mono Chant," and (B) "Alleluia" from the "Praeludium" of *The Sound of Music*.

Like the classical stylizing in *The Sound of Music*, popular vocal arranging styles are a natural fit in shows with pop culture settings. Large production numbers such as "The Rhythm of Life" from *Sweet Charity*, "Sensation" from *Tommy*, and "$96,000" from *In The Heights* all draw upon vocal styles of their period. "The Rhythm of Life" recalls The Swingle Singers and other similar classical/pop crossover groups, "Sensation" nods to the Beach Boys and other vocal rock bands, and "$96,000" borrows heavily from hip-hop, rhythm and blues, reggaeton, and techno-pop vocalists. All those songs are also routined for the stage in multi-themed, episodic forms with carefully calculated rises and falls, nowhere with greater calculation than in the vocal arranging.

Another fine example is the expository number from *Little Shop of Horrors*, "Skid Row." As composer Alan Menken's music director Michael Kosarin points out, Menken conceives his melodies in his own voice, and leaves it up to the music director and performers to "translate those melodies to the voices of the characters, in terms of range, details of pitch and rhythm, style, and above all, dramatic purpose."[4] There are many singing characters in "Skid Row," in part the concoction of Howard Ashman, who was the lyricist, bookwriter, and director of the musical. Both Ashman and Menken were quite familiar with doo-wop grooves and sounds, as was music director and vocal arranger Robert Billig, and Ashman contributed significantly to melodic rhythms and musical authenticity.[5]

Beginning with the freely belted first phrases ("Alarm goes off at seven/And you start uptown"), and continuing as the tempo kicks in, the disparity between the lighthearted music and the anxiety of the words is quite apparent. The "girl group" harmonies and call-and response melodies of the first two choruses do not just swiftly orient the audience into the era, but also highlight the ambiguity. In a simple yet masterful choice of vocal assignment and registration, each chorus begins with a bass wino who pops out from under a pile of garbage or emerges from an alleyway. He sings a solo pickup phrase that propels the music forward and simultaneously epitomizes the neighborhood's downtrodden existence and the dark humor of the libretto.

The vocal arrangement is perfectly in line with the style and storytelling. Not just in this song, but throughout the show, the pieces fit together so well that an audience forgets that it is watching a play adapted from a grade B horror film about a man-eating plant from outer space that begins its conquest of Earth in a decrepit flower shop on Skid Row, told with early 1960s-style pop songs, and instead begins to care deeply about the characters.

Because vocal arranging is so innately musical and universal, to offer instruction in it seems presumptuous. But the peculiarities of vocal arranging for the stage warrant the following few guidelines.

It is safe to say that melody in stage music occupies middle registers of the voice more often than it does its extremes, though the high ends of both male or female ranges are obviously used for expression and climax. Most of the time, however, stage melody, with its mainly conversational tone, and also much popular music, which tends to be universally singable and memorable, are found in speechlike, unstrained ranges. Other obvious exceptions include rock songs sung by stratospheric tenors, legit stage scores with high soprano and tenor parts, and, rarely, low bass and contralto parts. Singers generate the most amplitude

---

4. Michael Kosarin, in-person interview, 6 May 2011.
5. I had the rare privilege of watching Ashman and Menken at work, composing a revised "Mushnik & Son" for the *Little Shop* national tour.

in the middle and higher registers of their voices. (Amplitude is not to be confused with volume; amplitude is a measurement of the amount of air displaced; it is also referred to as the ability of a sound to "carry." Volume is a measure of perceived sound, the result of amplitude.) High baritones and second tenors (the range of most male stage singers) carry the farthest from about C below middle C to the A above. Females "belt" in an approximate range from several steps below middle C to the C an octave higher, or much higher still. Many male stage performers have remarkable high notes and powerful falsettos that vocal arrangers love to exploit (and not just for the sake of impressiveness; Billy Porter's award-winning performance in *Kinky Boots* on Broadway is exemplary). Extreme high notes written for females in ensembles are less common, though they do occur at the ends of numbers and in occasional *obbligati*, or prominent, essential counterlines ("Seasons of Love," for instance), and the high end of a female belt register is constantly pushed by writers and singers alike.

I reiterate that unison singing and lines doubled at the octave comprise most stage ensemble vocals. Lead voice parts convey the story through melody, and therefore deserve the focus. Unison singing leaves no doubt of the lead or melody. Registers an octave apart become almost equivalent; singers in ensemble can freely switch octaves in a melodic line without loss of melodic connection. A baritone can start a phrase, a soprano continue it, and two tenors in harmony reach the cadence as if they all shared a *tessitura* (the high and low ends of a singer's range and the range of a melody).

When adding harmony or counterpoint to a lead line, always uphold the primacy of the lead (unless you are writing purposefully harmonized lines). Don't rely on a sound operator to enhance the right parts at the right time; rather, pre-balance the arrangement by putting the right vocal lines on the right singers in the right groupings. Close harmonic voicings usually take precedence over open ones; the latter are more the stuff of classical choral composition. Two voice parts on a lead line in octaves and a third voice on a secondary unison line creates depth without losing the lead. A fourth voice can usefully double one of the existing lines (the counter line may be doubled at the octave) rather than completing the triad. Seldom will four voices form an extended harmony, unless the style calls for it (such as in vocal jazz, or the *Sound of Music* excerpt, Figure 10.6B). It is extremely common to double a two- or even three-part voicing in male and female or high and low divisions. Because of all the resulting parallelisms, the doubling gives an effect closer to unison than does a wider SATB-like voicing, as in the *Chorus Line* example (Figure 10.5).

Before putting a countermelody whose lyrics need to be independently understood against an existing melody, present it by itself first. Voices in canon or imitation can are possible ("Perpetual Anticipation" from *A Little Night Music*, for example, or "Money" from *Cabaret*) as long as the interweaving is not so complex that the text is lost. Call and response, too, works well on stage ("Blow, Gabriel, Blow" from *Anything Goes* or "Summer Nights" from *Grease*), as it is inherently dialogic.

Here is a short, simple vocal phrase arranged in several ways for a combination of male and female voices. It is a fragment of another iconic theater melody, Stephen

Sondheim's "Being Alive," from the musical *Company*. Its range is typically modest; even at the song's melodic and emotional peak, it reaches only an octave above its lowest note. The melody is quintessential Sondheim, consisting of the repetition and permutation of a small motive, or cell. The first and third phrases are palindromic, a motive looking at itself in the mirror. There are also typical Sondheim parallelisms in the lyric ("*Somebody* hold me too close/*Somebody* hurt me too deep," for instance). For each treatment I have provided a brief explanation and rationale, but in performance their effectiveness will be borne out only by performers interpreting them.

Figure 10.7A is the basic version, in octaves, which may be transposed to any key,

FIGURE 10.7A Excerpt from melody of "Being Alive" from *Company*, arranged in octaves.

and here it is again in Figure 10.7B, in unison. The key is now limited to one in which both men and women can sing the same pitch without undue strain.

FIGURE 10.7B Excerpt from melody of "Being Alive," in unison.

In the next two versions the melody is harmonized. In Figure 10.7C, the female voice leads. The secondary male line has slightly less motion, and the lead line is in a higher register. Depending on dramatic context, the harmony might suggest either concordance or divergence of feeling. The second harmonization, Figure 10.7D, typifies the doubled three-part male and female splits often heard in stage harmonizing. It is hard to imagine such rich voicings in anything but a warm, hopeful setting.

FIGURE 10.7C Excerpt from melody of "Being Alive," in two-part harmony.

FIGURE 10.7D Excerpt from melody of "Being Alive," in multi-part harmony.

To create imitative counterpoint, the secondary line in Figure 10.7E inspired a slight melodic modification, but the palindromic shape of the melody remains. Counterpoint can, depending again on context, signify discussion, agreement, or disagreement, among other things, and allows characters to share related material with slight differences at different times.

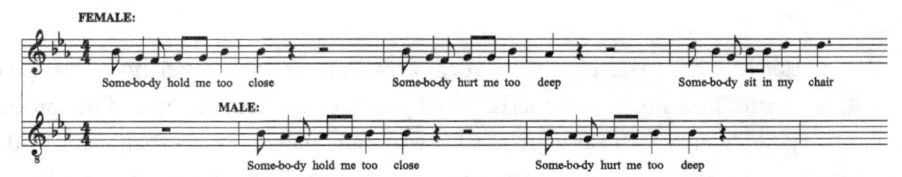

FIGURE 10.7E Excerpt from melody of "Being Alive," in imitation.

In Figure 10.7F, vocal arranging spills over into routining, with a sudden modulation by common tone (the B in the melody) between the second and third phrases. There would very likely be an action or event on stage that coincides with such a prominent tonal shift.

FIGURE 10.7F Excerpt from melody of "Being Alive," with a modulation.

Quite often, simple, homophonic "background" or "backup" vocals support the melody, as in Figure 10.7G. This is idiomatic to pop styles, perhaps not right for the urbane and cynical *Company*, but it could sound lovely out of context, if the production should call for loveliness of sound.

FIGURE 10.7G Excerpt from melody of "Being Alive," with background vocals.

Figure 10.7H is more pure musical elaboration than anything inspired by an occurrence on stage. Vocal arrangers seeking variety and color in their work are sometimes more openly gestural, and explore combinations of techniques such as those herein:

FIGURE 10.7H Excerpt from melody of "Being Alive," using multiple vocal arranging styles.

No matter how well you plan your vocal arrangement, no matter how clearly you notate it, no matter how much you cherish what you have created, realities of the production will very likely encroach on your ideal. Rehearsals inevitably yield change. In dramatic musicals, the writers, director, and/or creative team jointly assign the solo lines of an ensemble vocal arrangement, and often change their minds. (If solos have not been assigned by the time I reach music rehearsal, I usually take the safe road and teach everything to the whole group—the politics of choosing soloists are too treacherous.) If a production undergoes major revision, vocal arrangements may be among the first things revised: it is far quicker to relearn music than it is to rechoreograph a number or redesign a set. Vocal arrangements are rarely the scapegoat for an ailing show, but any kind of overhaul is possible when a production is in trouble. There are many reasons you might have to rewrite a vocal arrangement, among them, story revisions, restaging, and reaasigned vocal parts.

From these accounts it is evident why music directors often choose to handle vocal arranging duties personally and do not assign someone else to the job. Vocal arrangements lie so close to the heart of a show and its production that it would seem almost irresponsible for a music director to let them out of his or her sight.

Arranging for Movement

Music directors might feel less responsible for dance music, because in writing for dancers and the choreography, they are not writing for people directly under their tutelage, as they are for singers. Because of this reason, and for reasons discussed earlier, music teams often consign separate dance arrangers. In any case, as music director you have the dance arrangements within your jurisdiction.

Good stage choreography has a storytelling function similar to text and music. Music accompanies dance as it does words, with aesthetic purpose, by capturing or otherwise treating the emotion and meaning of the movement in sound, abstractly and referentially. Dance supports the story. Music supports the dance *and* the story. Dance arrangers use material from the score and variations thereof (as well as some original music) to portray and at times expand upon events that are expressed choreographically (as in the "dream" ballets "Somewhere" from *West Side Story* and "Out of My Dreams" from *Oklahoma!*).

The gradients between blocking and movement and dance in a stage production are very fine, and the generalized term "dance" is manifest on stage in a wide assortment of ways. The terms "staging," "movement," and "dance" freely intermingle, despite some specific connotation to each. There is movement that happens on cue or in rhythm that is really just an exaggeration of natural movement (*West Side Story* again, and the gangs' transition from walking to dancing in the "Prologue"). There are stage musicals made up entirely of dance with music (*Contact, Movin' Out*). There is dance within songs, while people are singing ("De-Lovely" and "All through the Night" from *Anything Goes*). There are dance breaks, when singing or speaking ceases and dance music takes over, sometimes for a full-length ballet (*On Your Toes*) or long tap-dancing sequences (*42nd Street*). There is movement worked into scenes as a dramatic element ("Razzle Dazzle" from *Chicago*, "You Can't Stop the Beat" from *Hairspray*). There are danced transitions, danced entrances and exits, and source dance, that is, dance within the context of the story (for example, a couple dancing at a supper club while having a conversation). Something that needs expression through characteristic movement, something for which dance is the ideal expression, or the only possible expression, is usually where a dance begins. Dance is very comfortable on performing stages, but dance without music is even more naked than a movie without music.

In Broadway-style shows, it seems presumptive that every production have movement of some kind, and somehow even shows that do not require it manage to work it in. Besides dance that is integral to stage action, music directors might also work with dance that is purely presentational. This sort of dance arranging is common in revues, concerts, early musical theater works, and dance competitions. Virtuosity, athleticism, extravagance, or some other aesthetic enticement can suffice as a dance's reason for being. In this realm, music directors are more likely to work with choreographers who know before rehearsals exactly what they want to choreograph and what they expect from the music.

In most repertoire musicals, dance arrangements come with the published score. (Sometimes the choreography, too, is notated or otherwise documented, and in some shows using the original choreography is mandatory.) If there is no real disagreement on how the music should be arranged or performed, your task as music director will be to see to its proper and accurate rendition and, if necessary, restoration or modernization. You can enjoy rehearsing and performing some wonderfully vital and virtuosic pieces of music, such as "Marian the Librarian" or "Shipoopi" in *The Music Man*, the danced fantasies in *The Pajama Game, Damn Yankees,* or *Finian's Rainbow,* or the mind-boggling breaks of *Bring in 'Da Noise, Bring In 'Da Funk*.

The process of creating new dance arrangements naturally varies widely. The routes that the choreography takes to get to the stage can be very complicated, and the music is in tow. Each choreographer has his or her own means of creating movement and putting it on the dancers and the stage. As with vocal arranging, the dance music for a production may begin in preproduction but isn't fleshed out until in rehearsal. Choreography depends on dancers to complete the creative process, as song does singers, but more so. (I can play all the parts of a vocal arrangement on a piano, but there is no such approximation of dancing.)

In preproduction, the director, choreographer, music director, and dance arranger discuss the dance needs of a production and the music that accompanies it, or review existing music. A choreographer might already have devised choreography, and your job is to fit the music to it. When there is new choreography, the choreographer and a few dancers or an assistant choreographer might get together with the music director and possibly some instrumentalists in a studio to try out ideas. Music that begins as an improvisation in preproduction meetings or dance rehearsal often becomes the final dance arrangement. As mentioned earlier, many choreographers use "dummy" music as they develop a dance, and some will presume that the eventual dance arrangement will have the exact structure and feel of their mock-up.

A dance may be indicated in a script, as in the following particularly descriptive example, and the music crafted around it, as was the music for Figure 10.8, a single, dense paragraph of stage directions.[6]

Adjustments to music to fit a dance are common, even constant. They may be on a large scale, such as a choreographer wanting an entire section of music repeated, or a recurring syncopation to be moved over by one beat. On a small scale, a four-bar musical phrase might have to become five bars, or a choreographer may insist on an accent in an unusual place. Though problematic, any of these changes can make for interesting arranging possibilities, and a creative resource for the writing. Under the right circumstances, you might suggest slight adjustments to the choreographer's musical expectations or to the choreography for the sake of musical sense, but don't expect compliance.

Whereas dance arrangements conform mostly to the choreography, the music itself can display a bold sound palette: dynamic, coloristic, rhythmic, and often flamboyant, with the same "staginess" as the stage. Dance music "takes stage" along with

---

Everyone is dancing. VANESSA and JOSE. USNAVI and YOLANDA. BENNY and CLUB GIRL. NINA finds another guy to dance with and spins by BENNY. BENNY is pissed. USNAVI swoops in and takes VANESSA out of JOSE'S hands and dances with her. JOSE, without missing a beat, slides back in and VANESSA back, mid-turn. To add insult to injury, he grabs YOLANDA, and is now dipping and spinning them both on the dance floor. During this impressive display, USNAVI and a very drunk BENNY slide in and each grab a girl, leaving JOSE dancing alone. JOSE, angry, starts to tap USNAVI on the shoulder. Without missing a beat, BENNY hauls and punches JOSE across the face. More and more instruments add to the mix. The dancing gets intense, crazy. It is a whirlwind of movement, a release of stress, when suddenly:

THE POWER GOES OUT IN WASHINGTON HEIGHTS.

FIGURE 10.8 *In The Heights* script excerpt; end of the "Club scene" into the "Blackout."

---

6. See the original cast recording of *In The Heights*.

choreography (though of course it would never steal the spotlight). Dance arrangers and choreographers might want to connect notable dance moments with equally striking musical gestures, such as hits and runs and flourishes. Each kick, should they so desire, can have a cymbal crash, each pelvic thrust a flam on a tom-tom, each leap a trumpet fall-off or harp *glissando*. This sort of referential arranging can be as hackneyed as the dance moves it sometimes accompanies, but its persistence in modern music attests to its continued audience appeal.

Dance arrangement further obscures the lines separating composers, arrangers, and orchestrators. Melody, tonality, phrase length, counterpoint, expression, and form are among the materials that dance arrangers use to connect dance music to stage action. Led by the content of the dance and the production, and unavoidably by their musical knowledge, taste, and proclivities, they think and write as composers do,

FIGURE 10.9 Arranger David Chase's dance music for the 1996 Broadway revival of *A Funny Thing Happened on the Way to the Forum* and the 2013 Broadway production of *Cinderella*.

Continued

FIGURE 10.9 Continued

transforming ideas into meaningful sound. They look for interesting contrast, color, shape, and dynamics. The only difference is that dance arrangers work primarily with existing themes and arrange them to suit the choreography (composers, too, work with existing material, their own and sometimes others').

Dance arrangers notate in their sketches dance counts and highlights of the choreography that the choreographer and dancers refer to in rehearsal. They and the dance team may devise shorthands and nicknames for certain sections. Music directors later transfer the most relevant indications to the rehearsal and conducting scores (Figures 10.9A and 10.9B). Such markers are indispensable both for outlining and creating the dance music, and as a rehearsal convenience.

Production meetings are under way; the cast and music team are in place; the schedule has been set and emailed. You have the score and you're readying it for production. The pace heightens, the pressure mounts, the time already seems short, and the butterflies start fluttering. Soon you will be sharing your excitement and anxiety with a company full of excited, anxious colleagues, where the action really heats up, in rehearsal.

PART IV

Rehearsals 1

Singers and the Stage

11

Overview of Rehearsal Process

In rehearsal, music directors share their knowledge of a score by teaching and explaining it to others, mostly in words at first and later in gestures, from a rehearsal podium or behind the piano. The director directs the whole production, and as music director you direct the music. Rehearsal is seldom a topic of aesthetic inquiry, because it is not part of an audience's experience of a performance, unless the performance's faults are so obvious that the audience questions the performers' and directors' competence or preparation, and can no longer suspend its disbelief. To a study of music direction, analyzing the process of rehearsing is essential, as rehearsal is essential to music direction.

Everyone loves the first day of rehearsal. In rehearsal studios everywhere, optimistic artists overjoyed to have employment gather on the first morning of a new production over bagels, fresh fruit, and gourmet coffee to share in the unveiling of a new masterpiece, to rejoice in the birth of a new addition. At colleges and camps and community centers, people from all walks of life assemble with a positive common purpose, one that brings them joy, or acceptance, or escape, or just some close new friends. It is the first day of school. Even though I go to school as a member of the faculty, on the first day I choose very carefully what I am going to wear, and I always bring along note paper, a few sharpened pencils, and a snack. It is a rejuvenating moment, bubbling with anticipation and apprehension. Putting on a show may be stressful, but it is also fun. And rehearsing, to those who truly appreciate the work, may be more fun even than performing.

Like music direction, rehearsal will dissolve into the shadows in performance. When audience members view a show and it is well performed, they do not think about the process that led to that performance. They pretend that the performance is, for the duration of their viewing, acceptably real to them.

Rehearsal belongs almost exclusively to its participants. There is no shroud of secrecy; still, most professional stage show rehearsals are closed to visitors, to protect the sanctuary of the environment and prevent premature exposure of the work. In large commercial shows, dress rehearsals are opened up by invitation to the production's financiers, as well as selected friends and family members of the company. One of the most exciting moments in a producer's or investor's theatrical life is when he or she views a show in the final phases of rehearsal.

In the rehearsal room, the performing company—the music director and director, the cast and the musicians and the stage managers—are able to ply their trades in the safety and company of peers. Mistakes are not just acceptable but welcome. They help the team to learn, improve, and generate new ideas. Everyone in rehearsal laughs at everyone else's jokes, and at others' foibles as well, because everyone still keeps a sense of humor about oneself. (This may not be the rule once performances begin.) Everyone feeds off everyone else's energy, and shares in the individual and collective highs and lows, remaining united in progress and in confusion.

But that's only sometimes. Other rehearsal periods are mad scrambles of worried operatives trying to do more than is humanly possible in the time they have. Tempers flare, egos inflate and deflate, and everyone is hopelessly behind schedule and red eyed with exhaustion. It seems as if the road ahead is all potholes, and that the destination is nowhere in sight.

Miraculously, many of these chaotic states eventually become organized. Sometimes, with the help of competent participants, things come together at the last conceivable moment. And other times, a production goes in front of an audience before it is ready. An entire evening may be spent in a state of panic, with cast, musicians, and crew just barely holding the proceedings and themselves together, doing their damnedest with what they know, and faking the rest. Those who have been through this ordeal will tell you that the majority of the time, the people in the audience are unaware of any problem. And when they are, they don't necessarily dwell on it. They are complicit in understanding the monumental effort unfolding before them, and they tolerate tiny errors or a small measure of unpreparedness. Obviously, I do not mean to imply that a haphazard approach to rehearsals is good enough, or a good idea. Regardless of any spirit of forgiveness on the audience's part, the quality of rehearsal can very much affect the quality of performance.

Rehearsals are as crucial to a production as its performance, and the two parts are inextricable. Productive rehearsals (usually) result in superior performances, and performances that are unrehearsed or underrehearsed can be shaky, or worse. Certain approaches work better in certain rehearsal situations than others. Rehearsal efficiency is always essential, but you cannot force the wrong rehearsal style on the wrong group of people and production. Furthermore, effective rehearsals require the cooperation of those you are rehearsing, something your work can inspire in them. It is up to you to assess each production and your place in it to find the best approach to rehearsing it.

In short, a Broadway show rehearsal period goes something like the following. (The sequence of rehearsal events is not immutable, and some productions customize their schedules to their needs.)

Each rehearsal week is six days, eight or nine hours a day (including breaks), with extra hours tacked on as performances draw near. The first day of rehearsal starts with information exchange, such as introductions, paperwork, scheduling, and design presentations. Then there is often a reading, usually around a table, of whatever written material that is ready to be read, and the music is sung or otherwise presented however it can be presented, in various states of polish.

The first few days of rehearsal, up to a week, are usually devoted mostly to music, but also to dance, costume fittings, special skills, and early dramatic discussions or staging sessions. In the second and third weeks, the dramatic work deepens and the production is fully physicalized, that is, the performers rehearse their scenes (musical and nonmusical scenes both), learning blocking, staging, and dancing, usually scene by scene, in a predetermined order. Performers review their singing mostly on their feet, but there are also music reviews along the way. At all rehearsals, except for pure character and dialogue sessions, there is an accompanist, quite often the music director and if not, someone he or she designates (with the approval of the director or choreographer). Most performers try to memorize their material quickly, as scores and scripts are unwieldy in rehearsal, though of course performers will always keep them handy for writing notes and cues and such, and some performers memorize more slowly.

Usually around the fourth week of rehearsal, the staff and performers begin to put the show together. Performance conditions in the rehearsal room increasingly resemble the real thing. Music directors conduct these rehearsals as they would a performance, or lead from the piano. They may designate some rehearsal conducting to an associate or assistant conductor. The run-throughs culminate in dress rehearsals, which approximate full performance conditions, but without most technical elements.

The show then moves from its rehearsal space to its performing venue. As the performers find their way around the stage and parade their costumes, technicians focus the lights and test the microphones, and you as music director can take in the view from your podium. You acclimate yourself to the space and its layout, its assets and shortcomings, how you will hear the sound around you, and what your connection to the stage and to the audience will be. Technical rehearsals move into final dress rehearsals, this time with all production values in full force, but with all material still subject to change.

Shorter rehearsal periods than those of the Broadway model have their time similarly apportioned, but in miniature. Stock and repertory theaters are particularly expert in accomplishing five or more weeks' worth of work in a matter of days, and their employees earn nothing close to a Broadway paycheck.

In Part 3, "Preproduction," I discussed preproduction vocal rehearsal estimates that music directors give stage managers for scheduling. Here is a rough formula of what you might request, though of course without context it cannot be definitive. These are idealized estimates, only realistic in a full-length rehearsal period.

For music that is entirely unfamiliar to an individual actor or a small group of actors, a musical number of average length (between three and five minutes) takes about an hour to learn—that is, to learn the notes and rhythms, and the words and music together, and get at least a preliminary grasp on the details. Longer or more elaborate numbers obviously take more time, shorter or lighter numbers less. Groups that are more musically proficient learn faster. If music has been partially learned in advance, the estimates can be cut down. For music that performers have learned fully before rehearsal, only enough time is needed to ensure that all is current and performance-ready, but it can't hurt to request a full rehearsal anyway. In some cases, performers need or want no rehearsal, and in others, there is no time for it.

When rehearsing music a second time (in a separate session) for more intensive work, you should schedule a similar amount of time. Rehearsals later in the process can be somewhat shorter.

With a larger group of performers in a chorus, especially when part singing is involved, expand these time frames liberally. A first round of rehearsals on a single musical number of average length with multiple vocal parts will take a minimum of ninety minutes, more safely two hours or more, again depending on the skills of the singers and the degree of difficulty of music. Five minutes of unison singing of a repeated melody can be learned in ten minutes, but there are many levels of complexity between that and a Gilbert and Sullivan finale. You should from the outset schedule at least one follow-up rehearsal on each ensemble number (subsequent rehearsals can be shorter, as they do not involve teaching notes), as singers tend not to absorb fully their ensemble musical material in a single rehearsal. You can use scheduling as your ammunition to combat this tendency. Try to reserve time for follow-ups from the outset, as later in the process, rehearsal opportunities will become scarce.

Do not overlook shorter numbers and reprises of numbers when scheduling. They can be as tricky to learn as full pieces. Reprises may differ from their originals only in their vocal arrangement or some other inconspicuous way, and a performer must recall the subtle differences between nearly identical passages in different contexts. For this and other reasons, you should also consider carefully the order in which you rehearse the numbers in a production, because learning certain segments will hasten the learning and retention of others, and thereby necessitate fewer follow-up rehearsals. For instance, to maximize efficiency, teach first any song with material that is reprised elsewhere in a score.

Another reason to reserve time for follow-up rehearsals, particularly when performers are less musically or vocally reliable, is that once performers begin to focus their energies on staging and tech, the notes you thought they absorbed so completely will evaporate like beads of rehearsal-hall perspiration. Other departments will also inevitably be behind schedule and want to extend their rehearsal time slots, too. A little territoriality early on can sometimes go a long way, but expect a contest to the bitter end.

For orchestral music, the amount of rehearsal time needed again depends on the amount, complexity, and difficulty of the music, and on the skills of the musicians. (Symphony orchestras often have only enough time to read through virtuosic works of great scope once or twice, if at all, before a public performance in front of the most discerning audiences paying top dollar.)

There are always restrictions. In academic and amateur productions, the producers or department heads will probably preset the schedule, and an academic calendar will impose limits upon it. Professional musicians are expensive, especially in groups, so in commercial productions, orchestra rehearsal time is carefully controlled. The upside is that costlier musicians prepare more quickly. The producers and music coordinator of a commercial production usually predetermine the orchestra rehearsal schedule on the basis of the budget and the scope of the score, in consultation with the music director. Broadway and similar orchestral units traditionally have between three and five three-hour sessions to rehearse the score for a show. If an orchestration is new, the first or first two of these rehearsals may be devoted entirely to reading it through, correcting errors, and making revisions. The orchestra also has other opportunities to rehearse, such as dress rehearsals and a *Sitzprobe* (literally, "sitting rehearsal," an unstaged sing-through; see chapter 18, "From the Studio to the Stage," in Part 5). For less experienced musicians, I would recommend at least double these amounts of time.

Sectional orchestral rehearsals can be very helpful in learning aids and great time and money savers, especially when a score features a certain orchestral section. A show, for instance, in a contemporary pop style played by a rhythm section and only a few orchestral instruments needs minimal time with its orchestral contingent. Brass sectionals in a big-band score can tighten and tune the section before they join the rest. String sectionals can be used to work out such issues as bowings and *divisi* (divisions into separate parts, usually on one line), so that time will not be misspent in larger rehearsals. When multiple electronic keyboards play together, keyboard sectionals allow synthesizer programmers to check their work in the same manner as orchestrators do at the first orchestra reading, and to balance the electronic components among themselves before they are balanced with acoustic instruments. Sometimes the music director delegates the task of leading a sectional to an associate or assistant conductor or a principal player from the section. Another very useful practice is to schedule a series of rehearsals of increasing forces, leading up to perhaps only one full orchestra session (first rhythm, then add the brass and reeds, and last the strings).

Union bylaws stipulate certain rules in professional rehearsals for the benefit of stage performers and musicians. These rules are worth living by in any production, regardless of its level or budget. Breaks are regular and predictable, five minutes each hour or ten or more every two hours. Lunch hours are generous and their exact times and durations are left up to the stage performers. The workday and workweek allow reasonable time off between rehearsals, and premiums for overtime. Vocal rest is important for performers, as is homework. Rehearsal practices can contribute to a company's morale by providing periods of rest, relaxation, and study that help them work more efficiently to master the material.

Music directors are beyond punctual, and don't always enjoy these considerations. They arrive at rehearsals long before the "hit" or "downbeat" (the scheduled start time), they rarely take breaks, because breaks are when people ask them questions, they order in lunch so they can attend lunchtime meetings and cover staggered rehearsal times, and they hang around afterwards for daily debriefing and planning for tomorrow. (Then they rush home and enter into the written score the revisions from the day's rehearsal and distribute them to the necessary parties.)

The custom of beginning production rehearsal processes with music rehearsal puts the music director in a unique position. You may be the first to introduce the performers to the world of the show. You are the representative of the production and the score, and as always the advocate of the stage vision. Your manner and expertise in these rehearsals sets a tone for the remainder of the proceedings. In this period, you can gain, or lose, the trust of the directors and performers, and cement your position on the podium as a responsible trustee of the production. Go into rehearsal comprehending the material thoroughly, and remain faithful to the director's vision from the outset. Be focused, fast, articulate, confident, and strong, as well as flexible, encouraging, kind, and humble. The delicate balance of these qualities may be difficult to maintain, but maintaining it is rewarding and expedient in rehearsal and beyond.

The best way to examine the specific operations of rehearsals is be in case studies. Over the next chapters we'll observe in action the different skills and thought processes music directors apply in different kinds of rehearsal.

12

Individual Vocal Rehearsals

Coaching a Singer

Coaching music is not the same as teaching it. Teaching is a technical process, the goal of which is technically correct performance. Chapter 13, "Ensemble Vocal Rehearsals," will discuss some effective and efficient ways of teaching basic notes, rhythms, and musical values. Coaching may entail teaching, but goes deeper, dealing with meaning, emotion, history, style, and other aspects of music and text. The music director's purpose in coaching a singer is to encourage those values that make the singer most convincing in performance, most effective in the production, and most musical. Usually the best way to realize all three goals is to approach them in conjunction with one another, though this strategy is not always possible, and not always necessary. Sometimes all that the singer has time for in rehearsal is a basic education in the musical material. When the object of the performance is merely to deliver a song convincingly, without delving into its dramatic purpose, there is more rehearsing and less coaching; that is, you run through the music rather than breaking it down.

What follows are descriptions of coaching sessions with solo singers in simple stage rehearsal contexts. They presume that the singer does want, and the production does require, the music director's full range of coaching skills. Also presumptive is that the music director is able to positively effect the performance, and that there are no major obstacles, such as a singer who cannot sing. In actual coaching, only some fraction of the information in these examples would most likely be imparted, but for study purposes, it's better to be thorough. This level of rehearsal detail would be most common in rehearsals for Broadway and regional shows with longer rehearsal periods, in new works in development, and in academic productions.

For musical examples I have selected two musical theater songs in two distinct styles. First is "Sometimes a Day Goes By," by composer John Kander and lyricist Fred Ebb, from the 1981 musical *Woman of the Year*, based on the 1942 film of the same name.

I propose as a test job situation a fictional Kander and Ebb concert; there has already been one successful Kander and Ebb revue Off-Broadway, *The World Goes 'Round* (1991), and a Broadway-bound version of another compilation is reportedly in the works at the time of this writing. This scenario will demonstrate a song coached on its own terms, rather than within a wider dramatic context. The other song is "Easy to Be Hard," from the musical *Hair* (1967), music by Galt MacDermot and lyrics by Gerome Ragni and James Rado. Many of the songs from *Hair* are musical vignettes rather than complete songs; "Easy to Be Hard" is something of an exception, a story-driven, full-blown emotional statement in a blues-rock yet theatrical sound[1]. Quite successful and controversial in its initial incarnation, *Hair* has inspired a resurgence in interest in recent years, its critically acclaimed 2009 revival enjoying formidable runs on Broadway and the West End.[2] For this example, we'll assume any high-quality professional repertory production of the full musical.

I will break down rehearsals into the most important issues covered in them, and view the music from each of these aspects. I will reuse this methodology later with group vocal, dance, dramatic, and instrumental rehearsals, and new musical examples.

Rehearsal Process and Conduct

Most coaching sessions involving a music director and singer are very friendly, frank, and efficient. As noted, sometimes the director or composer will attend. A director might lead the rehearsal—it is his or her prerogative to do so—and if the composer and/or lyricist are present, their contributions to the coaching take precedence. No matter who runs the rehearsal, as music director you keep track of the work, and keep the work on track. You will be the performer's companion in performance, and therefore should remain active in rehearsal even when not taking the lead, but as accompanist and translator of the director's or composer's wishes into performance terms. At rehearsals for the majority of musicals from the repertory, the composer is not present. In the case of the musical *Hair*, not only was the composer present for the rehearsals of both the original Broadway production and some of its Broadway and touring revivals, but he was also the music director of the original production.[3]

Coaching sessions tend to begin with pleasantries—isn't-it-great-that-we-got-this-gig's, did-you-ever-work-with-so-and-so's, have-you-seen's—and not just for the sake of small talk; these exchanges are the basis for a musical coalition. Singers and music directors find common ground in their backgrounds and tastes; they explore

---

1. Galt MacDermot used the word "bluesy" to describe the song in our interviews.

2. The redux of appeal is possibly attributable to a favorable demographic convergence: the baby boom generation were, as of 2009, in their fifties and sixties, and it is those age groups who traditionally spend the most money on theater tickets.

3. In our interview MacDermot expressed that he believed only he could properly handle the job on the original *Hair*.

means of articulating their thoughts that they will use in rehearsal. Often they share the experience of that first encounter with the music, the rapturous and pragmatic sides both, and any conclusions about the work they may have drawn then or since. The most effective rehearsals unfold naturally and uniquely.

Rehearsal time permitting, and when it the situation calls for it, coaching includes in-depth analysis of the musical material. Obviously you would not give a lecture on the score of the *The King and I* to Yul Brynner, but you would be well advised to explain the historical significance of *Hair* to a singer born a generation after the original production opened, and who thinks "Easy to Be Hard" is a song about treating erectile dysfunction.

A coaching usually sets off with a complete reading of the song (or more than one, depending on difficulty and familiarity). A speak-through of the text is another good starting point, even before the singer sings; directors, naturally, find great value in this practice. A speak-through can be out of rhythm, in rhythm, or some combination; in many songs there will be only minor differences between spoken and sung rhythms. This exercise not only engenders familiarity and comfort with the text, but also helps reveal the dramatic meaning of the song and its expression in rhythm and melody. You and the singer apply to the music the dramatic values found in treating the words as a monologue in a way that convincingly connects the two elements, by manipulating the emphasis, dynamic, phrasing, diction, timbre, or any other musical value that is useful.

If the first readings went well, and even if they didn't, your initial encouragement is always welcome. Praise need not be empty; you can always find something to appreciate. It is a signal to the singer that he or she can rely on your unconditional support. During the first reading, you will also most likely identify certain issues in the singer's performance (and your own) that you want to work on. But criticism too early in the process can make a performer nervous. Focus first on reinforcing positive qualities and on practicing technical elements, and slowly mete out more specific advice. Once a singer has had a chance to evaluate his or her own performance, he or she will be more open to adjustments and improvements. Of course, if the performer raises an issue first, then the door is open.

In a professional production, and many nonprofessional ones, you can assume that performers bring with them at least serviceable skills and experience; courtesy is the norm. When giving criticism, always distinguish between the performer and the performance. The way you give a note should be about the music and to the singer's treatment of it, and never a derogation of the singer's abilities. In academic settings, the rules may be different, but it is still important for music directors to think of themselves as helpers or mentors rather than superiors, although teacher-student relations may countermand this attitude.

Express your comments in a way that enables improvement rather than risks discouragement. For example, if a singer is sliding from below, or "scooping," into vocal entrances, telling him or her, "I think the beginnings of the phrases would be stronger if you begin them firmly on the middle of the pitch" is better than, "Don't slide into the beginning of every phrase, because it sounds whiny." Say to a singer who is interpreting a pop song too legitimately (that is, classically, or operatically), "Don't give up your great sense of pitch and rhythm, but you can get a more accurate sense of style with less vibrato, and by making the melodies more conversational, and a little less legato." (This scenario is not uncommon.) Strategizing to correct a singer's intonation is preferable to pointing out that he or she is off key.

Most productions allow for only one or two coaching sessions on each number with individual performers, so use the time as you scheduled it, and review the material whenever possible, and whenever the singer requests it. Once performers have attained a higher level of technical, dramatic, and stylistic mastery, music rehearsals turn to refinement and repetition. Problems that need more time to correct will no doubt surface, and you can prescribe additional rehearsals once you have identified them.

Background, Analysis, and Style

"Sometimes a Day Goes By" is a song typical of its writers in its simplistic yet subtly sophisticated tone. Yet in this song, Kander eschews the vaudevillian musical pastiche[4] often associated with the songwriting duo, and displays the influence of soft-rock artists of the time and the concurrent appearance on the theater scene of more pop-oriented composers such as Stephen Schwartz and Andrew Lloyd Webber. It has been covered by, among others, Placido Domingo, and was beautifully arranged into a duet-medley by music director David Loud and arranger David Krane for *The World Goes 'Round*.[5]

Although this fictional performance of "Sometimes a Day Goes By" stands alone, whenever you excerpt a song from a dramatic musical, its original context deserves inspection. Lyrics that appear generic may be contextual, and make complete sense only when viewed within the show as a whole. At the same time, a song's original context should never weigh down its performance when it stands alone. In our fictional concert the audience does not expect a portrayal of the character from *Woman of the Year*; they are very likely unaware that the song is from a musical.

In *Woman of the Year*, "Sometimes a Day Goes By" is sung by the leading male character, Sam Craig. It appears in the second act as his "eleven o'clock number," a song sung by a primary character late in a musical, at the moment when his or her story reaches its denouement, or the character has a life-changing realization, or undertakes a plot-changing action. In its original dramatic context, Sam, the singer, is quite nonplussed by the sway of his amorous feelings; normally he is far more hard-nosed,

---

4. A pastiche is an imitation, or parody, of an existing style. In *Cabaret*, for example, Kander and Ebb successfully evoked the sound of the musical's time and place (pre–World War II Berlin), and have used a similar pastiche in several shows, such as *Chicago* and *Steel Pier*.

5. "Sometimes a Day Goes By" is what is referred to as a "liftable" theater song. Producers of new musicals are always on the lookout for liftable songs, songs that can be popularized outside the show, because the sales from ancillary use of the material can be as profitable as the production itself.

and not likely to be disarmed by romance. Knowing this about Sam at that moment in the show reveals a greater depth to the lyric and suggests possible specific acting and musical choices. "Sometimes a Day Goes By" is a touching and heartfelt piece, but also rather plain and not necessarily character specific; it becomes so only in context of the story. It need not rely on context or character to communicate. It epitomizes Kander and Ebb's ability to captivate their audience through sincerity of tone, with beautifully linked words and melody. A sweet love song such as this that treats its emotion so unsentimentally is a paragon. It allows the singer room to create a realistic world for the song and the audience members room to fill in their own sentimental connection.

The song is in a brief AA'BA'B' form, the B' section equivalent to a coda. The three A sections differ only at their cadences. The melody is also simple. The A section starts with a two-bar phrase, subsequently repeated with a slight variation. The melody begins with repeated notes (as many theater songs do, using repeated notes as a device to smooth the transition from speech to song) beginning on the second beat of the measure (syncopating a melodic entrance usually reads as more realistic than entering on a downbeat), then continuing upward stepwise. The most notable feature of the melody is the upward leap leading to the cadences, where the melody diverges strikingly from its conversational single-note and stepwise quality. The harmonic vocabulary of the piece is unsurprising, essentially a series of chord progressions surrounding the tonic in basic "turnarounds" (ii-V-I, or supertonic-dominant-tonic chord progressions[6]). Only the secondary dominant at the end of the second A suggests any excursion from the tonic, but the harmony returns immediately to two consecutive turnarounds in the original tonic.

The piano part arpeggiates the accompanying harmonies in a soft eighth-note pulse. Its slowly rolling eighth notes seem to emulate a guitar pattern, which is consistent with the style and era. Their slight metrical offsetting makes the feel of the accompaniment a bit unsettled. In contrast with the rather stolid and regular melodic rhythm, it forms a counterpoint that drives the song forward in understatedly urgent two-bar phrases.

The recurring theme in this brief analysis is simplicity. As music director you infer from your findings that the performer need not encumber his interpretation with unnecessarily pronounced or outward emotion, and you reinforce these values in coaching sessions, and in the accompaniment. (This conclusion will be reinforced with a look at the text; the acting choices translate to musical approaches.) The singer should not slide dramatically up and down the signature leaps, but rather treat them with diffidence. He should sing the rhythms mostly as written, to clarify the rhythmic interaction of melody and accompaniment and the simple form and melodic development; in those features

---

6. Clearly audible examples of ii-V-I progressions would include the jazz student workhorse "Autumn Leaves," or in the bridge of the Beatles' "Yesterday," the chord progression under the words "I don't know, she wouldn't say," or "now I long for yesterday."

lies the musical interest. The folk-like style argues for a smooth, measured vocal timbre, unburdened with vocal intensity, but musically clean and honest (even Domingo does his best to tone it down).

Originally produced in 1967, *Hair* was representative of its generation's culture and controversies and, in some ways, of its popular music.[7] Usually categorized as a "rock" musical, it draws as much from the theatrical well as it does from its alleged genre. It is an inordinately commercially successful example of the so-called experimental theater movement of the 1960s that paralleled the forays of music and other art forms into the avant-garde, the exotic, the improvisatory, the drug-induced. *Hair*'s music, not really rock, is more aptly described as an amalgam of several pop, rock, rhythm and blues, and bouncy show-tune styles. *Hair* has several story lines, but more than a story-driven musical, it is a cultural immersion.

As in the previous example, "Easy to Be Hard" is specific to its show context but also can work by itself. Most songs in *Hair* stop the action to zoom in or comment on or lampoon a certain character or topic relevant to the large-scale themes of the show (racism, war, the sexual revolution). This song is a traditional rhythm ballad, and part of the storytelling, one of only a few such moments in the musical. The singer, Sheila, is an upper-middle class college student with a burning social conscience. She is not insincere, but she is naive, and her politics are not her foremost reason for running with the "Tribe," the antiestablishment group of friends whose adventures are recounted in the musical. Sheila has strong feelings for Berger (the main propagandist among the hippies), and makes him a T-shirt as a gift. In his arrogance he tears it to pieces, and "Easy to Be Hard" is her response.

As music director you take into account the tone and function of the other songs in the show. Even a dramatic song such as "Easy to Be Hard" needs the same light touch you give to the smaller, comedic numbers. If the performance is too emotive, too boldly melodically expressive when the other songs are not, it will appear melodramatic and out of place, and the character of Sheila will not be as believable or likable. Because of the natural soulfulness of the melody, the singer can rein in her emotion, for the melody and words by themselves will carry much of the burden.[8] This direction holds whether the performance is in or out of show context. It is supported by an understanding of the text, as will shortly be evident, and through musical analysis, with which I will again try to be very succinct.

The form is a simple AABABA'. The last A differs only in that it has a brief codetta that repeats the last two phrases of the A. The melodic structure is just as straightforward.

---

7. I have never worked on a production of *Hair*, but I have seen many, and I know the show and the score well. In 1967 I was nine years old; the original cast album of *Hair* was the second LP I ever bought.

8. This approach is borne out in the original 1967 cast recording, in which Lynn Kellogg sings the song with great control but remarkable feeling, never overstating her argument. Caissie Levy's performance in the 2009 revival was not quite as restrained, but still controlled and not over the top, and certainly in line with the funky, jam-session quality of the accompaniment.

It begins with a stepwise melodic phrase, the first note of which is sustained for a half note (and all except one set with the interrogative "How?"), its most pronounced feature. The phrase repeats, and is then interrupted by the title phrase, whose long note is instead at the end of the phrase. This second phrase is then itself repeated almost exactly (with different words), and reaches a full cadence. The bridge (B section) melody is more grooving and a more powerful melodic statement, also presented twice, then a third time up a step. A fourth phrase begins as did the third, but it descends and wanes, leading back to the A.

The harmonic progressions are primarily in Mixolydian mode, though at the end of each A section a conventional dominant seventh chord and diatonic leading tone do coincide with the more prominently displayed flatted seventh at the beginning of each A. (This juxtaposition does not have the effect of a cross-relation as it did in "Make Our Garden Grow," though the modality again evokes an innocent, primitive musical character. Here it seems more to have to do with the blues.) The B section appears to portend a modulation, but the upsurge dies out, and the music returns defeatedly to the A section.

More uncertain than the tonal content, however, is how that content is to be arranged, sung, and played. The piano-vocal score and written orchestration bear only faint resemblance to the sound of the song as recorded and generally heard in performance. With so much left up to the imagination, a singer might gratuitously decorate the melody or emote too vigorously. Although rhythm-and-blues-based vocal improvisation was indeed characteristic of the music of the time and to some degree the intent of the composer, the understated melody of "Easy to Be Hard" does not bear heavy improvisation well. In a full production of *Hair*, any such strong stylization of the song would need to be part of the director's vision, and would thus be the starting point of your coaching session. (Whether you agree with such a stylistic approach or not, as music director you are professionally bound to pursue it.) Ideally, in any production of the show, the music director, director, and singer will agree on a temperate deployment of embellishments and variations, always with honesty in characterization and storytelling.

If there is disagreement over how much liberty can be taken, you can find compromises that assuage the singer while respecting the music. For instance, in a simple tune like "Easy to Be Hard," you might encourage her to improvise in places where the melody is at rest. There is a full bar of silence available at the end of each A section that can be filled. In fact, in both Broadway recordings, in the measure preceding the second statement of the bridge the singer adds a tastefully improvised connecting phrase. You probably won't have to teach riffs and other improvisations to a vocal performer; he or she will devise and present them, or just sing them, and might ask your advice or approval. If you feel comfortable doing so, you can suggest slight alterations, or a lick that the singer hadn't thought of, or you might sing some of your ideas for the singer to copy.

Key

One of the first coaching decisions is a song's key. As discussed in chapter 10, "Arranging for Music Directors," there are several influences on key selection, but foremost among them is what is best for the singer. In principle, any key is acceptable, whichever the singer feels comfortable in, and shows his or her voice most effectively and convincingly.[9] In a complete work composed for the stage, the key of one song may rest in part on larger the key structure of the score. The score of *Hair*, although it is an amalgam of songs as much as a score conceived from beginning to end, contains song sequences that are tied together by key, for instance, the last measure of "Donna" is identical to the first measure of "Hashish," so the two songs overlap. If one is transposed, the other may need to be transposed proportionately or to some other key that makes sense in the transition. As a rule, when a show is performed in its entirety, transposing beyond a small interval is unnecessary, because casting is done partly on the basis of vocal range. Often, however, transposition is mandatory, for any number of reasons, perhaps due to reassigning a song or part of a song to a different singer, or casting. Sometimes you will want to defer the choice of a key, and experiment as you rehearse, but when there are arrangements to be written, you must set deadlines for your decision.

"Sometimes a Day Goes By" owes its very manageable one-octave range to the nature of the character who originally sang it, who as noted was not inherently musical or lyrical. (As also noted, many songs in the musical theater repertoire have a small range because they are sung by performers adept at acting but perhaps less so at singing.) Therefore, in "Sometimes a Day Goes By," you should probably keep the highest notes out of a showy range to reflect the unassuming tone. On the other hand, if the singer is a vocal virtuoso like Placido Domingo, someone who not only wants to show off his or her glory notes but also deserves to, you might choose a key that places the higher notes of the first phrase of the B section and the coda in most spectacular area of the singer's range. With only a one-octave range, there would be several options.

In the original Broadway production, "Easy to Be Hard" was in the published key of F major; in the 2009 revival it was up a semitone. Here again the song's written range is only an octave. But singers often move the two phrases at the end of the A sections of the song (see Figure 12.3) down an octave from the written music, which increases the range downward; that has become an accepted performance practice for the song.[10] If the singer observes this practice, then the range is relatively wide, an octave plus a perfect fifth.

---

9. Music directors should be facile transposers. The best way to learn to transpose well differs for each musician. Translating written chord changes to Roman numerals or functional harmonies can work, as can absorbing music by ear, then playing it back by ear in the new key, or perhaps using an imaginary clef substitution. The best way to learn the skill if it does not come easily, as it often does not, is by constant, long-term repetition.

10. An exception is the original London cast, which featured a very folk-song like version of the song in which the singer, Annabel Leventon, would switch between octaves in the two phrases. It was not a "bluesy" interpretation, and according to Galt MacDermot, it was more the vocal style he had envisioned for the song.

The term *tessitura*, as explained in chapter 10, "Arranging for Music Directors," refers both to the high and low ends of a singer's range and to the range of a song. In coaching sessions you hear how a song sits in an individual's voice in different keys. Where in the *tessitura* does the melody live most of the time, and when it does go to its extremes? What is the key's relevance to the storytelling, character, and style? What, if anything, is happening textually and musically that supports or coincides with the extremes?

Typically, a human voice will be softer on lower notes and more forceful at the middle and high ends, until the highs become so high that the vocal apparatus is no longer functional, and the sound dissipates (such as in falsetto). What key will make the soft sound in the low phrases of "Easy to Be Hard" sufficiently audible? Will the strength of the voice in its higher register align with the musical and dramatic content when the melody is higher, in the bridge? One cannot simply generalize that for altos, such-and-such is the best key, while for sopranos, this-and-that is better. Each vocalist possesses a unique instrument. As written, the pitches in the B section sit high in a typical female singer's "chest" or "belt" range, and seem designed to indicate a heightened emotional state. In choosing a key you enable the singer to, or dissuade her from, exploiting her full vocal force at this point in the song.

Tempo

Tempo, though to some degree quantifiable, is malleable, and preexisting written tempo indications are often neither reliable nor useful. What is your starting tempo in rehearsal? You or the singer might have an idea of what a customary tempo might be, through your acquaintance with the music or from a marking in the written score, but there will be many variables.

There are tempo precedents for songs from the repertoire, and you can begin there. As accompanist to a singer, you determine tempo by what suits the singer best, as you do with the key. You can specify suitability as that which affords the greatest breath and pitch control and the most effortless and honest communication of text and characterization. Quite often, a tempo simply "feels right" to all parties. (Music director: "Did that tempo feel okay?" Singer: "Yeah, perfect. Maybe a hair faster at the matinees.")

Eventually, however, you will need consistency. But how can you quantify what is subjective and elusive? Follow the clues. The tempo markings in the various editions of "Sometimes a Day Goes By" are not very informative, but the eighth-note motor rhythm (Figure 12.1A) is.

One can surmise from the cross-beaming two-bar patterns an intentional forward motion, but do the tempo marking "Flowingly, with expression" (Figure 12.1B) and "Faster - Flowing" (Figure 12.1C) suggests that the tempo is not steady? Looking ahead, you can see a clearly indicated *ritardando* (becoming slower) at the end of each A section. This tempo marking supports there being little, if any, variation in tempo up to that point. The historical period of the song also provides a hint; its feel exhibits the folk-rock influence in the theater music of the time, and in that style, tempos are customarily fixed.

FIGURE 12.1 Three printed versions of "Sometimes a Day Goes By": from (A) *Woman of the Year*, (B) *The World Goes 'Round*, and (C) the single sheet.

How fast should the eighth notes go? Breath control influences tempo, such as in the second half of the A section. The singer should sing the phrase "When I don't think of her" in one breath, for at least three reasons. First is to observe the two + two + four phrase structure. Second, the only other place to easily take a breath is after "I," and a breath there would break up the important upward leap. Third, breaking up the melodic phrase would likewise fragment the clarity of the lyric. Therefore, the eighth-note pulse should be rapid enough to easily allow this long phrase ("When I don't think of her") in one breath.

The seemingly offhanded lyrics are most poignant when delivered at an easy, natural pace. The audience must believe the character's aloofness, and be touched by his adoration. Too slow a tempo would elongate the words unnaturally, and too pregnant a pause at the end of the A section would be an undesirably pensive interruption of the flow. You might quantify this metronomically with a marking of a quarter note equal to 144, which would be sufficiently flowing, but not hurried. "Hurried" might begin at about 156. (Domingo's version clocks in a broad quarter = 122, but he has wicked good breath control.)

How much should you slow down at the A section cadences? Again the terminology on the printed music is not trustworthy; such terms as *ritardando* and *rallentando* in show music rarely denote the subtleties of their literal meanings; *rallentando* usually just means a greater decrease in tempo than *ritardando*.[11] In this case, the slowdowns should again not be so great as to defeat a naturalistic delivery of the lyric.

As you better understand such subtleties, and as you rehearse, you are better able to "set" a tempo. You can propose boundaries for the tempo of "Easy to Be Hard" on the basis of the unspecific "Moderate 4" marking in the score, and on performance tradition, but anything you decide will be subjective and temporary. For answers, you look to dramatic effect, the effective declamation of the lyric, the feel, and the singer's comfort level. To me, a metronome marking of quarter note = 96 borders on "fast," while a metronome marking less than quarter note = 76 feels "slow." The original cast recording clocks in between 92 and 94; the 2009 revival is considerably more leisurely, between 80 and 82. The original cast recording was an uncomplicated, innocent reading of the song. The later version modernizes the sound with a deep musical "pocket" (implying solidity and palpability to the feel) and a far more virtuosic and improvisational approach, vocally and instrumentally. To accommodate these changes, the metronome marking had to be more generous.

Another important influence on the tempo of "Easy to Be Hard" is the melody and text of the B section ("Especially people . . ."). There, Sheila attacks her antagonist's hypocrisy while at the same time revealing her own, and exposing her youth and vulnerability. When the song is believably sung, the audience easily forgives Sheila's duplicity, and she gets their sympathy. The verbal attack is already musically heightened, in its register, modality, style, and insistent melody. If the tempo is too slow, this emotional sweep can come off as self-indulgent and overbearing (regardless of whether the melody is embellished upon). If the tempo is too fast, the result might be unwanted fervor, or overzealousness. A fast tempo might also make the singer's emotional turnaround in the third and fourth lines appear too hasty. The correct tempo seems to be a middle ground, one that is literally moderate, in the middle, as the score indicates.

---

11. In fact, *ritardando, rallentando, ritenuto, allargando,* and other terms for slowing down all have specific connotations. Their differences are largely ignored by stage musicians.

In a solo vocal rehearsal, use a metronome only very judiciously, only as a reference tool, or to practice with if a click track will be used in performance. A metronome can also ensure that all rehearsal musicians are playing at the same metronome markings. Otherwise, in a solo session it is usually too much of a distraction.

Vocal Technique

Singers accept advice from music directors on their vocal production to varying degrees. If you do offer counsel on vocal technique, make sure you know what you are talking about, and do not thrust upon a singer vocal philosophies, well grounded or not, that he or she is not prepared to accept. The voice can be a fragile instrument, as can a singer's ego. When working with a stage performer unaccustomed to singing (such as a student or a dancer), or when a singer asks for your technical assistance, offer it freely.

Here are a few methods that I have found universally productive, or at least benign, for singers having problems in three technical areas.

Pitch (Intonation): If a singer sings consistently off-key, there's little you can do, except to make sure that singer is not hired. If a few pitches are consistently out of tune, the reason is probably either a technical issue with the singer's voice on those notes, or a problem with the way the singer is hearing pitch. To eliminate the first possibility, transpose the song. See how it sounds in keys both nearby and far off. If the singer's ear turns out to be the problem, try working the individual notes and intervals in exercises on different vowels. Have the singer tune pitches while sustaining voiced consonants, such "v" and "z." Have the singer slide up and down until the pitches are in tune, and concentrate on hearing the difference. Try tuning the voice with instruments (not just piano) and with other voices (your own, for starters, if you sing in tune). Tuning forks and electronic tuners, and the software versions of them, are portable, so the singer can practice at home. (It would not surprise me if there were soon an autotune device for live stage singing.)

Breath control: In coaching sessions you and the singer plan or confirm the phrasing and breathing in a song. Most choices are obvious, based on the meaning of and punctuations in the lyrics or how long the singer can sing without breathing, but some warrant discussion. For example, should the singer breathe between the last two phrases of the B section of "Easy to Be Hard" (Figure 12.2)?

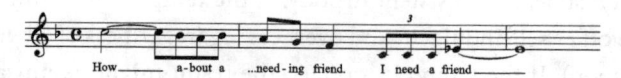

FIGURE 12.2 Excerpt from "Easy to Be Hard," from *Hair*.

These are clearly two different phrases of text and two separate musical thoughts, but the textual phrases unite in the wordplay and repetition of "... needing friend" and "... need a friend." The melodic register drops to show plaintiveness; a breath that is running out might enhance this impression; thus you can argue that no breath should be taken, or conversely contend that a breath is needed to separate the thoughts, and because the phrase is indeed long.

Vowel sound, placement, and diction: Vowel and consonant sounds should sound natural when sung on stage, that is, natural to the person or character singing them. Voice students are taught "pure" vowel sounds ("ah," "ee," "oo," and so on) and diphthongs (combinations of pure vowel sounds), which are useful concepts even in advanced vocal performance. Slight adjustments to them can produce the full spectrum of vowel sounds. Vowels that are too pure, however, cease to sound natural. When coaching, you can purify or adjust a vowel so that it is both healthy and appropriate in sound. Begin with natural phonetics and move toward purity, not the other way around.

With "placement," a singer moves a vowel sound to a different part of his or her vocal apparatus—the mouth, nose, throat, or chest. Placing a tone differently changes its sound to the hearer and how it feels to the singer. When working with diction, you and the singer can apply placement either to achieve expression or for vocal comfort.

I prefer to focus on consonants rather than vowels when coaching for the stage. Consonants articulate and define both melody and text and, when combined with correct breathing, promote excellent vocal technique in any musical style. The manner in which a singer pronounces a consonant is a musical value called diction. Singing from consonant to consonant, as opposed to from vowel to vowel, ensures impeccable diction, and relieves the mental and physical pressure from the act of sustaining a tone (the vowel). It also more clearly shapes the lyrics. Breath control also becomes easier. Therefore, the singer's attention can be, as it should be, on the meaning of the text. This approach is equally effective with trained and untrained singers.

Accompanying and the Accompaniment

Music directors for the stage follow the singers (and dancers) they accompany, but do not constantly attend to each nuance of singers' vocal lines and breathing, as classical accompanists do (stage music in a classical style is an obvious exception). In a manner of speaking, the singers in most stage productions follow the accompaniment as much as the accompanist follows the singers; most stage accompaniments are autonomous. Still, the notion of "following" is manifest in several ways in music direction, and a music director's adherence to what happens on stage is paramount, if not absolute.

There is "following" that is planned for, and that which is not. The first variety includes music that is purposefully out of tempo or in a flexible tempo.[12] In coaching sessions you rehearse the give and take between accompaniment and voice, and in performance you listen to singers as you conduct, and keep the accompaniment with them. You can also plan to be unplanned, that is, plan to improvise or take liberties in performance. If a singer decides to enter at will, you hold, or vamp, until he or she is ready. If a singer wants to speed up a tempo, you speed up. If a singer misses a beat or more, you jump to wherever the singer

---

12. Terms indicating free or flexible tempos are often confused in commercial stage performance. *Rubato*, which belongs only to slow tempos, is by definition a balanced give and take of time: one phrase is hurried, and to balance it, another is held back. *A piacere* and *ad lib.* are interchangeable; both indicate complete freedom of tempo, literally at one's pleasure or liberty. *Colla voce* literally means "with the voice"; that is, the vocalist determines the tempo. "Recitative" implies no measured time at all, and "accompanied recitative" is a combination of free tempo and short stretches of measured time.

ends up (as unnoticeably as you can). If the audience is so entranced by a song that you have to repeat the chorus endlessly, or sing the song again as an encore, so be it.

As a rule, an accompaniment's volume level should never exceed the singer's, unless the score dictates otherwise. Perhaps in the spaces between the singer's melodic phrases, the accompaniment might rise to the singer's level, but not so noticeably that the contrast is obvious, and diverts attention from the singer. If the melody of "Sometimes a Day Goes By" never rises above a *mezzo forte*, neither should the accompaniment. In modern production, achieving a balance often falls to sound designers, but as music director you preset a balance in your accompaniment, and communicate the correct balance to the sound department to enhance as needed.

The different published versions of "Sometimes a Day Goes By" (Figures 12.1A–C) provide enough information, and enough consistent information, to decide on a piano accompaniment, and to imagine an orchestration. The piano-conductor score for "Easy to Be Hard" does not; it is minimally and confusingly notated. The composer merely sketched a rehearsal score, and later an anonymous person of the publisher's designation transcribed the sketch for publication. According to MacDermot, because the original performing troupe rehearsing *Hair* in its early stages were musically very inexperienced, and because the musicians and singers always took liberties in performance, he saw no need to notate the music accurately or update it constantly. He was content just to have the music ready for rehearsal.[13]

What appears in the piano-vocal score is, from the bottom up (Figure 12.3), in the lower voice of the left hand an approximation of the electric bass line from the orchestration (the bass part is fully written out but often interpreted freely), and in an upper left-hand voice, clarinet cues from the orchestration (measure 7). The right-hand rhythm appears as four quarter notes per bar throughout the song. There are no chord symbols, so one might presume that the written chord voicings should be interpreted literally, but that is not the case. Also on the treble piano staff, in a line above the repeated quarter notes, is the complete vocal melody. Because singers traditionally treat the melody with freedom, a written melody cue is not very useful, and is not generally played as part of the orchestration. (The original transcriber might have intended the vocal cue as optional support, in keeping with practice of the time, and of vocal selections books.) The top staff contains the vocal melody and the lyrics.

FIGURE 12.3 "Easy to Be Hard," Piano-vocal score, mm. 3–7.

13. Galt MacDermot, telephone interview, 8 June 2012.

The orchestra parts differ completely in content. The keyboard part consists merely of chord symbols and slashes indicating very basic rhythms. The guitar part is chord symbols and all quarter note slashes, with no specific rhythms. The drums parts are merely structural charts.

Clearly, the accompanimental arrangement of "Easy to Be Hard" is a wide-open issue. In the latest Broadway revival, the musicians referenced recorded versions, especially the original 1967 cast recording, and were advised by the composer in rehearsal.[14] As in the original production, the band as a group formulated the arrangement. (MacDermot receives credit as orchestrator or arranger in all Broadway versions.) The motor of the groove in the major cast recordings, alongside the bass, drums, and percussion, is the electric guitar. It keeps the same pattern through much of the song, percussive stabs on beat two and the offbeats of beats three and four. The piano-vocal score does not indicate this rhythm in any way, nor does the orchestration. The 2009 version (under music director Rob Fisher, who did not conduct or play in the all-star band) is quite different and modernized, but the rhythm guitar part remains very similar.

There are a few possible approaches to playing any song at the piano: (1) read the music as written (not always a wise choice, but a common one), (2) rearrange it to sound like the orchestration, or (3) rearrange it in a pianistic fashion that might or might not resemble the orchestration, but still captures the feel and provides effective accompaniment. If you choose to emulate the "orchestration" of "Easy to Be Hard," you can make the left hand suggestive of the bass as written in the bass part, but with a few small additions to enhance in the same manner as a bassist might. With your right hand you can play the customary rhythm guitar part. In this revision (Figure 12.4) I have added chord symbols, suggesting some freedom in the voicings.

FIGURE 12.4 "Easy to Be Hard" mm. 3–7, revised and arranged for piano, with attention to reproducing the instrumentation.

During vocal coaching, you can experiment with the possibilities of an unspecified accompanimental arrangement such as this. The singer and director may express a preference as well. Let's say they want the song to be "warmer": use the same pattern but sustain the guitar chords. They want it "sexier": slow down the tempo and add a few more syncopations, but soften the accents slightly. Or maybe "angrier": try a pattern of

---

14. Andrew Schwartz, telephone and email interviews, 9 June 2012 and 7 July 2012.

repeated eighth notes in the right hand, but keep the accents where they were. A more pianistic version might replace the guitar stabs with longer notes in the right hand, or perhaps a gentle quarter-note pulse with occasional lightly syncopated variations, as in Figure 12.5.

FIGURE 12.5 "Easy to Be Hard" mm. 3–7, re-revised and arranged for piano, with attention to idiomatic pianism.

In both of these revisions, the left hand serves not only to stand in for the bass, but also helps the overall continuity of the rhythm, functioning as a drum kit does, to provide pulse and connective material (fills) between melodic phrases.

In rehearsal, to assist a singer with a melody, you might play it loudly ("plunk it out") while simplifying the rest of the arrangement. You can also slow tempos down, repeat sections at will, or break the music into more manageable and learning-friendly sections. Any of these manipulations of the accompaniment can facilitate the singer's learning process. Be creative and flexible, and work according to the individual singer's and production's needs.

Text and Singing

Musical numbers in a show present or represent dramatic or pictorial moments. Text and its relation to the music that it is set to are the mainstays of composition and performance for the stage, and therefore are at the center of coaching. As music director you guide the singer in rehearsal toward creating a believable character or story by using text and music together.

There are so many ways one can utter (and sing) a word, a phrase, or a sentence, and one's manner of utterance alters meaning completely. Depending on intonation, articulation, or punctuation, a simple interjection such as "hey" can range from seductive to spiteful, from pitiful to joyous. The way one emphasizes and de-emphasizes words within phrases is just as potent. To shade meaning, one can bring out the words that one especially wants heard, or obfuscate them by mumbling. One can create characterization through speech. A very simple example is an accent. What would Miss Adelaide in *Guys and Dolls* be without her signature New Yawk-isms? Much of her humor, and much of the humor in the show, lies in linguistic mannerisms. The mere articulation of a consonant can be transformative. "Love" is a word probably sung as frequently as any other. Music magnifies in this word what is only somewhat onomatopoeic in speech. Extending the "l" or the "v" can make it sexy. A long, breathy vowel sound can be adjusted toward "ah" and have the same effect. A guttural "l" or an explosive "v" can suggest animalistic feeling, or perhaps anger or disdain.

Style comes through text as well. Modes of speech, dialects, vernacular, lingo, and many linguistic idiosyncrasies are the hallmarks of stage songs. There are hooks, puns, poems, reminiscences, elegies, tirades, and gags that, along with the music, delineate the era, the location, the identity of the singer, and why he or she is singing. There is text just for its own sake, too, such as "Supercalifragilisticexpialidocious," or simple vowel sounds such as "ah" or "ooh," that can be perfectly communicative on their own nonsensical terms.

Within each lyrical phrase are "value" words, those that carry more significance than others. One focus of coaching is determining how much and what sort of value a singer gives such words. In our first example, the first and third words are arguably the most important: "*Sometimes* a *day* goes by," and in the next phrase, the redundant "*whole entire*." They connote the singer's frustration with his feelings. He expresses this with dynamic, duration, articulation, or any number of other ways, and probably a combination of more than one. He can firmly but not sharply accent each syllable, with an insistent dynamic, and hold each note its full duration, if not slightly longer. When a song is well written, the value words and musical events that support them will already coincide, and your coaching involves pointing out the coincidences.

The first note of the first two phrases of "Easy to Be Hard," as written, falls on the downbeat, its pitch unstably perched on the major ninth of a modal harmony. The composer and lyricist have coordinated these musical and lyrical elements to intensify the singer's questioning ("How . . .?"). In performance practice the first note is often delayed to the second beat, but my observation holds true with either interpretation.[15] In comparison to the first lines, the music for the title line (the third and fourth phrases) is less exceptional and more relaxed. The sarcastic play on words in the title is ironically underscored by music that reaches a familiar and gentle diatonic cadence. As music director you advise dynamic and emotional restraint in delivering the strident opening note of the first phrases and the pointed turn of phrase of the last two, allowing the melody and lyric to do their work: the emotional interpretation is already suggested in the melodic shape. In rehearsal, you take the singer through the analytical thought process that informs a choice such as this one.

Acting and Singing

The realism of text and the abstraction of music meet halfway in stage songs. Words become poetry, not always sophisticated or profound, sometimes just mundane or

---

15. There are many reasons for the performance variations in this phrase. First is the notion that a syncopated vocal entrance sounds more natural. Another is that the phrase is repeated so often in the song, and the actor will want to make a variety of acting choices. Still another is that the frequent repetition of the rhythm can become musically monotonous, the initial distinctiveness of the melody becoming less striking with each new statement.

amusing, and music becomes more descriptive, and stylized, the lyric's partner. (Note the simple timelessness of lyric and music combinations such as "Hey, Look Me Over" or "I Could Have Danced All Night.") Performers, with the guidance of directors and music directors, look for truth in song performance. Most performers are naturally convincing; that is their talent, and in coaching sessions you and the singer explore different routes to believability within a production and practice to gain the assurance that upholds it.

Presentational performance, on the other side of the coin, may have genuine feeling, as do the *American Idol* singers, but it is unorganized, and often misdirected into pure showiness. Nonetheless, presentational performance can be very affecting, and convincing. When the Beatles sang "She loves you, yeah, yeah, yeah . . ./And with a love like that/You know you should be glad," we *believed* them. (And they were so cute!)

Performers must often sustain believability, specific or generalized, over an unnatural amount of time, particularly in stage song. A thought or feeling that in reality occurs quickly may be protracted in a musical setting. One might call it slow-motion acting, keeping a single action or idea alive and truthful over an artificially extended period. Prolonged believability of a single, simple emotion can be achieved only through a performer's commitment of his or her own inner life to a particular song; in other words, he or she must in some way *act* the song.

Some performers employ acting methods, while others have a mystifying ability to simply put a song across with confident convincingness. One cannot know at what level of specificity a Barbra Streisand or a Diana Krall or a Hugh Jackman is thinking while performing, but the power of their emotional force is undeniable. John and Paul didn't know it, but just by being so convincingly in the moment, they were acting. When Domingo performs "Sometimes a Day Goes By," he eschews small acting beats for expansive, sustained emotional states. He transforms his feeling into a style in which the beauty of the note supersedes the meaning of the text. This contradictorily makes the song more believable—believable, that is, for Placido Domingo.

There are traditional approaches to acting a song that you can apply as a music director. Most are derived from the work of acting teachers Lee Strasberg, Stella Adler and Sanford Meisner, all of whose methods originate in the work of Konstantin Stanislavski, the acknowledged founder of modern, realistic acting study. These strategies, all similar and all malleable for different forms of stage singing, form the argot of coaching from amateur theater to the Broadway stage. This is not a book on acting for the musical theater, but any music director would be well advised to research this topic in greater depth. In case you do not, a paragraph here.

In rehearsal you and the singer (and director, perhaps) examine a song both in its entirety and as a series of moments. You break a song down into "objective," "intention," and "action" (or "actions"). The objective of a song is what the character wants from the song. An intention is an expression of purpose, the reason for singing the song at that moment. Actions are the means by which a character accomplishes an intention. Actors use multiple actions in a song to accomplish the intention and answer to the objective. The actor makes choices of objective, intention, and actions by analyzing the character, then drawing on his or her own experience and emotional life and extrapolating the truth of those feelings to the fictional situation. As music director you share in the actor's process and help translate his or her experience into musical truthfulness. Coaching sessions often involve applying specific actions to phrases or sections of songs, a process that suggests or demands musical values that clarify those actions. When a series of actions form a sensible whole, the singer is believable, and the audience members perceive a quasi-reality, what they take to be a rational thought process taking place over musical time. Specific actions are particularly helpful musically, as they give variety and color to musical values, forming a musically active inner life that parallels (or otherwise relates with) the inner life of the character and the drama. Actions are not to be confused with "activities," which are simply things that a character does (washing the dishes, knitting a sweater) that are not necessarily related to the dramatic moment.

You can also simplify this concept, and instruct it more directly, in terms of why, what, and how. Why is the singer singing, especially why at this moment? What does he or she want, and how is he or she going to get it? These are the overriding questions. Questions of who and to whom are important, too: who is the singer, and to whom is he or she singing? The answers are usually implicit in the story, when there is one. If not, finding answers to these questions is also part of coaching. As a rule, a singer should always sing to someone, even an imaginary someone: stage singing and stage songs are communicative by nature, and are most effective when directed and focused at a responsive listener, and not into the ether.

I should include a caution here that coaching sessions involving highly emotional acting choices can at times bring up intense states of feeling, made more palpable by the music. As music director you must always treat performers with great sensitivity. They are in touch with their own deep feelings, some painful, some joyous, and when singing in rehearsal they may be releasing them for the first time. Eventually in performance they will rein in these feelings, but in rehearsal singers might feel them outwardly, provided that they are comfortable with the music director as a trusted friend as well as a mentor.

In "Sometimes a Day Goes By" the objective of the character, what he wants, what he is struggling with, his conflict, is the woman he cannot get off his mind. The actor can play the intention in two ways: wanting her back, or wanting to forget her. Both have interesting results. His actions include complaining, justifying, pleading, hiding his feelings, or anything that feels right in the progression of the song and the scene it outlines. Because the lyric covers very little ground dramatically, metaphorically or otherwise, it is completely acceptable for the actor to apply choices unrelated to the lyric, and use the lyric only as superficial text above his own more meaningful subtext. Similarly, the music is only subtly expressive, and cannot be manipulated to intensify emotions that do not warrant intensifying. Other than generalizing the emotion and acting in slow motion (as Domingo does), personalizing the song to the singer is the best way to achieve believability.

Sheila's objective in "Easy to Be Hard" is to be loved. Her intention is get her boyfriend back. She directs her musical tirade at Berger, still on stage with her. She can begin by scorning Berger with mock bemusement ("How can people be so heartless/How can people be so cruel") that darkens into sarcasm ("Easy to be hard/Easy to be cold"). This translates to music with a moderately soft and unchanging dynamic and not a great deal of emphasis. The singer can extend first syllable of "*Ea*-sy" to reinforce the sarcastic subtext. The character can then become be more accusative ("How can people have no feelings"), then lay on the guilt ("How can they ignore their friends"). The vocal and instrumental accents fortify, and the dynamic increases. Or instead, she might ask for pity, and withdraw slightly. To achieve that effect, a softer dynamic would again be in order, as well as perhaps a bit of hesitancy to the rhythmic pacing of the melody. In the bridge, with the words "Especially people who care about strangers/Who care about evil and social injustice," she holds forth with rhetoric, and reminds Berger of his professed beliefs. As a result the eighth notes that begin the bridge melody ("Especially people . . .") should be sharply and rhythmically articulated, and "care about strangers" should be equally emphatic, but sustained rather than accented. These melodic values in turn dictate a more forceful accompaniment.

Any acting coaching you do as music director is subject to the director's approval, but your understanding of the director's vision should be such that your coaching is entirely in line with it, and consequently the director should trust your work. When coaching acting values without the director present, you should make clear to the performers that the director may later make adjustments to the choices you make in music rehearsals.

You can use some of the rehearsal practices and techniques described above in rehearsals with a few soloists singing together in a small ensemble. As groups get larger, though, performers' interactions may begin to override the cooperative one-on-one discussions that typify individual coaching. As music director you will need to strike a new balance between leadership and collaboration.

13

Ensemble Vocal Rehearsals

The gregarious personality of a single stage performer can be irrepressible in rehearsal. Multiply that by many, and you have an ensemble vocal rehearsal. The music director, or whoever is teaching the music, must assume some sort of leadership role, often a strong one. Remember your high school choral director raising his voice, slamming his fists on the keyboard, constantly exasperated? It was because he was trying to wrangle a herd of boisterous, unruly teenagers amped up on singing and the pleasure of one another's company. It may not be all that different for a music director rehearsing a cast. Principal performers, too, must also sometimes sing in the chorus. Some may consider learning ensemble parts drudgery, because they'd rather be singing their solos. It is also safe to say that some professional singer-actors are (to music directors' dismay) no more musically proficient than college or even high school students, so you will very likely invest the same teaching time and effort, regardless of the performance echelon.

But that's just the downside. The payoff for all involved, for you, and for all who listen, is a marvelous musical experience. When all those vocal lines come together, when all the singers have memorized their parts, when they're all really thinking together about the same musical ideas, really investing in the words, when the spirit is strong, then the glorious sound of ten, or twenty, or forty voices singing together is without compare.

Though choral rehearsals may get rowdy, the camaraderie is part of the fun. There's no cause for you to be an authoritarian, but discipline is essential to the mastery of a multifaceted work of music—not only rehearsal discipline, but also vocal discipline, dramatic discipline, and discipline of executing several levels of artistry simultaneously. As music director you are a model of discipline rather than a disciplinarian.

As you engage in personnel management and full-score management, your level of preparation must follow in kind. You must comprehend not just the whole of a piece, but also everyone's part in it, as well as or better than any individual.

Ensemble Rehearsal Process

Smart preproduction planning and thorough score preparation go a long way, but more important in the end is the unwavering commitment of every individual member to the ensemble, something you can instill as a director but not enact in performance. Because much ensemble vocal music for the stage is a collection of solos rather than a choral work, each individual part must be strong. Motivational speeches early on and throughout the process can imprint a sense of pride in the vocals, as in "We're going to be the hottest singing group ever to hit the stage," or "The true power of this show is in the sound you make as a group," or "Let each of us commit from now until the final performance to sing every note every day with pride, energy, and musicality." The worth of these resolutions will multiply as rehearsals continue and the ensemble's attention is pulled away by everything except the music, such as the dance, their costumes, their hair, and the lighting.

An important rehearsal decision will be whether to accompany yourself or only conduct. Some music directors are not facile pianists, or simply prefer working with an accompanist. I like to play for my own rehearsals early on, but I am an experienced accompanist. I bring in other accompanists at later stages of rehearsal, especially if in performance I will be conducting and not playing. When rehearsing with a separate accompanist, especially when teaching music, I get bogged down in communicating to the accompanist such points as where we're starting, which part or parts we're working on, whether I want the accompanist to play along, and whether I want him or her to play parts or the accompaniment. When I play for myself I can make these decisions and enact them without having to tell someone else, thus saving time and keeping a constant focus on the work. Yet there are shortcomings to accompanying oneself, the greatest of which is probably that it hampers your ability to shape the music gesturally as a choral conductor typically does. But rarely in stage performance is such specific control possible from the podium. One could therefore argue that in rehearsal such conducting is entirely unnecessary or, conversely, argue that rehearsal is your only chance to have such control of the sound, so you should take advantage of it. My approach satisfies both arguments.

Whether accompanying yourself in rehearsal or not, establish clear procedural conventions early on. For example, always announce your starting point with the same phrasing ("high and middle women alone from measure 17," or "all men from letter A," or "everyone from the top"), so there is no confusion or delay. Efficiency is always a virtue. Work through passages of similar size in similarly methodical fashion (for example, in an SATB arrangement, one verse or chorus at a time, parts alone from top to bottom, then men together, then women together, then all together). Eventually the singers will recognize and sync with your rehearsal patterns, and anticipate your next step. Keep the process moving, but not so rapidly as to leave the singers catching up or catching their breath. Do not proceed too far into a number without going back to review what has already been learned. Vocal memory can go cold fast. And do not stay with one pattern for too long; change things up periodically to keep everyone's attention.

Seating in rehearsal should facilitate contact, that is, hearing one another's voices and seeing one another's faces. Once performers leave the rehearsal room, this contact will be a luxury, so take advantage of the opportunity. Circles and semicircles are always good formations, with rows no deeper than two or three, depending on the size of the group. Keep every singer close to you. The farther away a singer is and the more people are between you and a singer, the harder it is for you to get and retain his or her attention. I segregate sections only for the first rehearsal or two. After that, I like to mix them up, for instance, putting people together who will be together on stage, putting opposing parts next to one another to challenge the performers' ears, and putting weaker singers next to stronger ones.

Always insist on a real piano for vocal rehearsals, never an electronic keyboard. The piano offers richness of tone and harmonics that an amplified keyboard cannot, and that are essential for accompanying singers. Yet as a rule in rehearsal, the voice is a better demonstrator of a vocal line than a piano. The piano is essentially a percussion instrument; it allows one to hear notes clearly but is otherwise unlike the voice. A piano can be useful in the learning process (it attacks hard and plays multiple notes very well), but your voice is a powerful rehearsal implement. Use it whenever you can, and always sing when it's the best way to communicate a musical idea, such as a vocal technique or an exact interpretive phrasing. You can play parts once or twice on the piano, so that the singers can clearly hear the pitch and rhythm, then go *a cappella*. Don't be vocally shy; even an unattractive voice (like mine) is very useful for demonstration and education. Rehearsing *a cappella* is useful in several ways, including weaning the singers from the pitch and rhythmic support of the accompaniment, and so that you can conduct with two hands from behind the piano.

Some music directors delegate teaching the basics of a score to an associate music director or accompanist, and join in later to do detail work, or as a conductor. Whereas you may not want to be hampered by tasks that can be menial and are undoubtedly time consuming, I believe that there are great benefits to teaching the music yourself. For one thing, your absence from early rehearsals undermines the importance of the musical fundamentals: because you are handing their preparation to a subordinate, you are suggesting to the group that the notes are purely technical. They are technical, but the handling of those technicalities is what makes up a performance, and defines the music direction. Initial ensemble rehearsals are also an excellent opportunity for a music director to connect with the performers, initiating a relationship that will continue into performance. If anything, I believe the opposite scenario to be preferable, in which the music director does the initial teaching and a delegate handles subsequent rehearsals for practicing and drilling. If the music director will not be the eventual conductor of the performance, it is more acceptable to assign teaching to an associate.

Before rehearsals begin, identify musical themes that recur in a score, teach them *en masse* to all who will eventually be singing them, and break them down later. This approach can save time, and keeps large parts of the group continually involved in rehearsal. You should also rehearse any extensive solo lines that are part of a larger vocal arrangement outside of ensemble rehearsal, when the soloist has more leisure and privacy. (We'll add here two musical examples from the contemporary literature: "Blackout" from *In The Heights*, the show's ambitious and modernistic Act I finale, and "What Is This Feeling?" from *Wicked*, a more traditional pop-rock number.) In the highly episodic "Blackout," for efficiency, you can first teach the ensemble all the "Oh no" sections, then move to all the "Powerless" sections, and finally to all the "Look at the fireworks" sections. For "What Is This Feeling?" you would schedule separate rehearsals for the Galinda and Elphaba parts, which can require more attention that the rather easily learnable choral parts. A joint rehearsal for the soloists and ensemble can be brief. In "Make Our Garden Grow" there is little change in the melody; the main theme can and should be learned and refined collectively. Your biggest challenge will be coordinating the climactic *a cappella* section. In "Blackout" and "Make Our Garden Grow," almost all the principals have solos as well as parts in the ensemble singing. This will amount to rehearsing in four segments: the ensemble (no principals), the principals (each one alone, also rehearsing his or her ensemble parts), a principal put-together, and a longer ensemble-principal put-together.

Classically trained music directors working on a stage production should not expect, nor do they require, the rigor of a classical choir, unless the music is classical in style. The reality is that the majority of ensemble vocal rehearsal time for a stage production is spent teaching and mastering the notes and other basic musical elements. Furthermore, music teaching has to be slowed down to the slowest learner's pace, because eventually everyone must achieve mastery. (Slower learners can be tutored separately, but rehearsal time is always very dear.)

With sufficient rehearsal time, you can start ensemble rehearsals with some discussion and analysis of the music, the story, the style, and the production. (Open discussion is good, but don't let it get out of hand—stay on the subject, and not on the cast's résumés or anecdotes or their favorite flavor of throat lozenge.) As you do with the conversations of a coaching, you and the group get accustomed to one another through shared musical experience. Then, again, as in an individual rehearsal, a reading of the full number or of the text without music (better in rhythm for a group) is a good way to familiarize the group with the music and the task at hand. You and whichever performers already know the music can shepherd those who do not. A very rough performance is fine at first, and anyone can sing any part. Next, if there is a primary theme, as in "Make Our Garden Grow," the entire group can sing it and work with it in unison. Some choral directors like doing this on a neutral syllable, so that the text does not interfere with tonal comprehension and vocal production. For most stage music I would say that this step is tangential, as the text so strongly influences the musical values. When rehearsing piece in a legitimate style, however, such as "Make Our Garden Grow," using "la" or "ooh" in place of the words while learning the notes could be a valuable technique.

Another introductory method, advocated by choral director Wilhelm Ehmann,[1] is to have the ensemble improvise a vocal arrangement on the primary theme. This approach can be hugely informative when you are building a vocal arrangement from scratch in rehearsal, or you are customizing it to the group. You can also use this method to familiarize yourself with the musical and vocal abilities of the ensemble members. Obviously something like this would more likely happen in a developmental or academic production, when rehearsal time is generous (there was a lot of this method in *Lion King*).

The process of teaching and mastering the notes is usually rather direct and dry, but you can keep it fun, brisk, and lively. Always stop or slow down to offer additional help, even if it interrupts the flow. You may find, for instance, that the men take five passes at a part to get it right, while the women sightread perfectly the first time through. Be patient with the men, and don't ignore the women for too long.

The following are some techniques and tips for teaching notes. The main purpose of these or any other systems is to cement the musical material into singers' minds and memories. Because stage performers will be adding on to what they learn during rehearsals, musically and extramusically (staging, for instance, and much, much more), they will be better equipped to retain what they learn if they have rigorously rehearsed the music early in the process.

- Work on short sections, no more than perhaps thirty seconds or sixteen bars of music.
- Play the parts one at a time at the piano with the singers listening only. Don't let them sing along or record yet—if they want to record the entire rehearsal, that's fine, but the starting and stopping of recorders can be disruptive.
- Next, do the same while the singers record the music for later review.
- Before you begin, make sure everyone's recording device is cued up and ready to go, and that everyone is quiet.
- Don't bother with recording sections that are too long; they won't be useful to the singer yet. Later in the rehearsal you can record full passes of each part.
- Discourage all conversation until every part in the passage has been heard and recorded. Everyone will focus on those measures, and hear everyone else's part.

---

1. Wilhelm Ehmann, *Choral Directing*, Minneapolis: Augsburg, 1968, pp. 186–87.

- At first, play the parts in their actual registers. However, parts that sit high or low on the piano are better heard and recorded in a middle register, so play them there, too.
- After all parts are recorded, work each part through one at a time, perhaps with everyone singing everyone else's part. Do so until the parts can be done without the assistance of your voice or the piano.
- Gradually assemble the parts until the passage is correct in its entirety. You can deal with persistent errors by breaking down and slowing down the music and drilling the offending portion until corrected. Take it note to note if necessary, and slowly bring it up to speed.
- Begin teaching musical values beyond pitch and rhythm while still hammering out the notes at the piano. Dynamics, articulations, breaths, intonation, vocal production, and especially text should be part of the learning process from the outset, except with the most inexperienced singers.

Unless the accompaniment is helpful to the sung parts, do not introduce it fully until the notes are learned; except in early read-throughs, it will be a distraction. At first you can double parts at the piano to help with intonation and rhythm. Listen for what need helps, and when, and play along selectively, but wean the singers from your help as early as you can. Bring in the accompaniment bit by bit, first those elements that will help, and then, gradually and selectively, those that might confuse them. If a piece or a section of a piece is to be performed *a cappella*, rehearse as much as you can without accompaniment.

Unlike in an individual rehearsal, with groups it is acceptable to give criticism and correction more openly. Of course, you should still be respectful, but in group rehearsal there is safety in numbers, and an atmosphere of collective self-effacement. Feelings are not as easily hurt, as long as commentary is restricted exclusively to the music, and is never personal (if it is personal, feelings will be even more hurt, because they were hurt in front of others). If there is any unavoidable rehearsal dispute among ensemble members or between you and a member of the ensemble, resolve it after and outside of the rehearsal.

After the lengthy endeavor of mastering the notes and details of an ensemble vocal piece, subsequent rehearsals concentrate on review and repetition. Consistency of ensemble singing and retention of what was learned in rehearsal are not, unfortunately, hallmarks of stage ensembles—there are simply too many variables and obstacles, and sometimes the music gives way. At different points in every vocal rehearsal process, it will seem that everything that was rehearsed has been forgotten or ignored, and it appears that you'll have to go back and start all over. In the rehearsal room you may have the group sounding like a crack singing outfit, but the real test will be in reproducing this vocal energy and precision on stage in performance. You can introduce in vocal rehearsals any stage movement or other extramusical elements (the longer music rehearsals go on, the more information on staging you will have), and have the ensemble mark them as they sing. You can help the singers associate musical events with choreographic and story elements as part of their preparation, an exercise that will solidify the musical performance beyond rehearsal and better integrate the music and stage action.

Choral Techniques for the Stage

As before, let's now itemize the primary musical and textual values that you will rehearse with groups of singers. Although the overlapping among these values makes them difficult to distinguish, separating them assists their clear demonstration as part of a rehearsal process. You can rehearse any one element in isolation, but its interaction with others might matter more. Ensemble diction, for example, depends on articulation, and both are connected to vocal technique. Expressive values such as staccato, legato, *diminuendo, dolce,* and many more deepen musical and textual meaning. Vocal production has timbre, which is a determinant of story, character, and style.

Dynamics and Articulation

Singers enact dynamics and articulation through vocal techniques, mostly the use of air and the body parts that make up a vocal apparatus, and motivate them with a dramatic rationale.

There is little information in the piano-vocal score of "What Is This Feeling" about dynamics or articulation (Figure 13.1), other than a few accents written in the accompaniment. The charm and humor and the changing vocal textures seem the writers' main concerns.

FIGURE 13.1 "What Is This Feeling," from *Wicked*, mm. 61–67.

The number is an accessible charm song, almost a throwaway, built around the one gentle gag of singing about reciprocal abhorrence in a very upbeat, major-key setting. The vocal arrangement and orchestration build steadily to the end, so the song may be acceptably sung with little more than an observance of that crescendo and a clear delivery of the text, which translates to an appropriately dry delivery of the joke. The melodic lines come out moderately loudly in volume because of their moderately high vocal range, and because they are preceded by a duet section, to which several more voices have now been added. The tight harmony in a strong vocal range also enforces this moderately loud dynamic.

You might add some dynamic interpretation, as long as your choices are relevant and motivated. You could easily and appropriately distribute the melodic phrases, the actually sung lines of dialogue, among a few soloists or smaller groups. You might vary the dynamic line to line. You could make one phrase *sotto voce*, in a stage whisper, as if telling a secret (so that Elphaba doesn't hear?), or insert a *subito piano* (suddenly soft) on the fourth beat of m. 64 for the same reason, and follow it with a crescendo into Galinda's entrance. It might be tempting to articulate the single, sustained word "good" with a *fortepiano* (loud, then immediately soft) attack and a crescendo to the cutoff, but only as accompaniment to some stage action, perhaps a movement, would it make sense.

The written score for "Blackout" contains more specific information. The *forte* dynamic is again implicit because so many voices come together at this moment for the first homophonic choral statement in the song (Figure 13.2).

FIGURE 13.2 "Blackout," from *In The Heights*, mm. 83–90.

The accents (>) in mm. 83–84 musically tighten and dramatically vitalize the irony of the group vocal statement (admiring a fireworks display during a power outage), reinforce the clarity of the diction, and outline the clave rhythm that is an organizing feature throughout the show and an echo of the opening of the act here in its final moments. The *tenuto* markings in mm. 88–89 (the line under the last notes of each measure in the bottom two staves) are a notational shorthand indicating that the singers should re-articulate the notes (without benefit of a new syllable).

Measure 54 of "Make Our Garden Grow," the first bar of the song's unaccompanied climactic section (Figure 13.3), is marked with a crescendo into *forte* (only in the ensemble parts, but it is implicit throughout). In rehearsal, however, a moderately strong volume, no greater than *forte*, is preferable. It will be more forgiving to the voice, considering the high *tessitura*, and will permit the singers to better hear themselves and one another, and their collective intonation. Tenors may sing their A's in a mix or falsetto. Gradually work the dynamics up to eventual performance levels. Having the group hold back in rehearsal will also counteract any tendency to treat this section as a contest of who can sing the most loudly, or with the widest vibrato.

FIGURE 13.3 Excerpt from "Make Our Garden Grow," mm. 53–57.

Breathing and Phrasing

Breath is the origin of vocal sound, and breath control is among the primary concerns of stage singers, or should be. I noted earlier that amplitude, the displacement of air, the dispelling of breath, is what takes a sound off the stage to a listener's ear (that, along with microphones and a sound system). In rehearsal you outline the group's breathing patterns, based on the text, the music, and the need for sufficient air to produce the necessary amplitude. (Singing softly can require greater breath control than singing loudly, because when one sings softly, the consonants, which use more air, do more of the work of carrying the sound.) The lyrics and their punctuation (printed or implied) will be the strongest indications of where to breathe, and musical phrasing will resolve any remaining indecision. You'll probably spend more rehearsal time on long phrases and where, if anywhere, within them to breathe, and on breathing for dramatic rather than technical or musical purposes (singers might breathe for textual clarity without needing to breathe, and therefore will adopt unnatural breathing patterns).

In "What Is This Feeling?" in the middle of the phrase "How do you stand it?/I don't think I could" (mm. 63–64), the question mark would suggest, and the lyric would gain from, breathing there. But a quick breath, given the fast tempo and eighth-note rhythm, would probably sound forced and do more harm than good. Instead, have the group accent the first "I" in the second half of the lyric to delineate the punctuation. In the long phrase that follows ("She's a terror . . . you're a martyr"), you will have to remind the group to conserve breath early on so that the end of the phrase remains strong. Or, as I suggested before, you might break the long phrase into smaller groupings or solos that rejoin for the last line (see Figure 13.1).

The long notes seen in Figure 13.2 in mm. 87–88 and continuing through 89 in "Blackout" are difficult for the actors to sustain, largely because they are executing elaborate staging (in the semidarkness) while singing. Prepare the group accordingly, with proper support, posture, breath conservation, and consistent vowel sounds, and again, by marking the movement in rehearsal. The specific articulations and re-articulations of the notes at mm. 88 and 89 are helpful to vocal production, for they reenergize the tone in the middle of its span. (The articulations also offer opportunities to recalibrate pitch.)

In "Make Our Garden Grow" (Figure 13.3), mm. 53–55 alone are enough to exhaust a good portion of a singer's natural breath capacity, and you can help the chorus through the soaring lines. Even in a setting that is sung legato (in a smooth, flowing manner, without breaks between notes) like this one, emphasizing the consonants helps the chorus conserve and control breath. Encourage the group to *feel* the consonants, to "taste" them, or "chew" on them, to give them specific, contextual articulation. It is while a consonant is enunciated that singers can best feel their vocal mechanisms at work. A consonant gives singers the feeling of tightening the muscles of the chest around the air in the lungs, releasing the air more slowly and efficiently, as if gradually letting the air out of a balloon. A strong consonant at the end of a phrase impels a strong intake of air, the breath, for the next phrase. Working with this technique has the added advantage of enforcing clear diction as an inherent part of the performance. In this particular musical passage, breath conservation and cleverly placed catch breaths are both useful tools for an effective reading.

Vocal Production and Technique

For most ensemble stage music, the only technical vocal coaching you will offer as music director is to help singers through the vocal requirements of the production, and help them be most believable. Consistency of tone and perfection of blend are not the objective of a stage ensemble (unless the style demands it), though of course good singing technique is vital. I don't usually do warm-ups with stage ensembles, unless the rehearsal is very early in the day (voices always need a little extra limbering in the morning) or the music I am about to rehearse will somehow improve from technical exercise. Group warm-ups can indeed promote healthy singing, but technique will be part of the music rehearsal anyway, so it need not consume precious rehearsal time on its own. The exception is working with less experienced singers who are still learning vocal technique, as in an academic setting, where a music director might be a vocal pedagogue. There is no harm at all in warming up an ensemble or an individual should you choose to, especially if the singers are physically not ready to sing. Some directors ask music directors to warm up the performers, so I try always to be prepared to, and to do so in a way relevant to the material. Many professional singers would not go to a vocal rehearsal without being ready to sing, but a surprising number do.

Try to make whatever warm-ups you do relevant to the music of the production. To begin your "Make Our Garden Grow" rehearsal (especially with untrained voices, as in the graduation ceremony), for example, you might devise exercises for the group by using legato leaps of fourths, fifths, and octaves, or with scales that pause on or hold the first and fifth degrees of the scale. Use different syllables to see how the pitches feel with different vowel sounds. This technique would certainly help the singers' intonation in negotiating the tricky melodic contours of the song, and introduce the issues of breath control they will face.

Regardless of the extent of your focus on correct vocal technique, as music director you should always do your best to encourage it, with the understanding that in a stage ensemble every singer's technique may be different, and at a different level. You should also treat performers' voices, which are easily fatigued by hectic rehearsal schedules, with proper care and caution. When voices are tired, mark the music, speak it, or call off the singing and talk about the music and lyrics instead.

When possible, translate vocal technique into musical terms. For example, encourage the ensemble to treat breaths as musical notes, and to give them due attention. Have them breathe on a musical count, and either associate it with a physical action or make the breath its own physical action. The breath can itself have character, and that character can be a healthy inhalation. You can treat the re-articulations of the sustained tones in "Blackout" technically, as diaphragmatic compressions, and as reactions to the exploding fireworks (as if they were oohs and ahs).

It is a good rule of thumb to have the ensemble make a crescendo on all long, sustained notes, even where it is not indicated, and continue each swell to a strong cutoff. The gratuitously applied crescendo on the held note in m. 62 of "What Is This Feeling?" that I mentioned in "Dynamics and Articulation," (see Figure 13.1), if not overdone, will result not in an unwanted vocal effect but merely in sustenance of tone. The same is true of the long notes of "Blackout" (Figure 13.2). A crescendo will not be apparent unless exaggerated; it will read only as a strong sustain. With no crescendo, it can sound to a listener as if a tone was decaying.

Intonation

Intonation in group stage singing need not always be as precise as in classical music or with a solo singer. Quite often the communicative effect of singing *en masse* supersedes the need for precise tuning. Of course, you will want an ensemble singing a traditional choral piece such as "You'll Never Walk Alone" to be on key, and as a rule, out-of-tune singing in an ensemble is undesirable. If there is an offending voice in your ensemble, you can hide it in the vocal arrangement, and make sure it is always on an easy part, and doubled by a better singer. If need be, ask the director to place the singer on stage nearby someone singing the same part(s). As a last resort, have the singer sing only where his or her tuning is not problematic, or have the sound operator turn the singer down in the mix.

In group rehearsals, as with individuals, there are several ways you can help singers adjust their pitch. You can use any of the techniques for soloists mentioned in chapter 12, "Individual Vocal Rehearsals." You can change vowel sounds, change the placement of the tone, or simply slide notes up and down and practice hearing them in and out of tune. You can in some ways "trick" singers' ears and minds. One contrivance that I find quite effective is to have singers think of downward melodic motion in very small increments and upward motion in large ones. This prevents flatting as notes rise and overshooting as they fall. It might be a very useful means of keeping the breathless singers in tune in the "Blackout" segment, both for the upward leap of a fourth, and for the descending, sustained scales.

In "What Is This Feeling?" the chorus sings through a key change at mm. 66–67 (Figure 13.1). So that the tuning holds through the modulation, in rehearsal slow the jumpy melody way down, down to one note at a time, and drill it. Have the group hold adjacent pitches and work the intervals between them, or break the melody into tiny pieces and drill them, forward and backward. Have one group hold the first pitch while another group moves to the second pitch and holds, and tune the interval. You might temporarily replace the text with a vowel sound or syllable to focus on pitch.

Because of the wide leaps and high *tessitura* in the "Make Our Garden Grow" *a cappella* break, tuning may well become an issue. Leaps are harder to tune in the voice than steps, because leaps may involve changing vocal registers (chest voice, head voice, mixed voice, falsetto). The root and fifth of a chord are especially noticeable when off-key because of their natural acoustic consonance. Making matters more difficult in this piece, the transparent two-part vocal arrangement, doubled in octaves, will clearly expose any questionable intonation. In rehearsal, as well as painstakingly drilling the pitches at the piano, you can apply vocal technique (working the voices on the melody through different registers) and basic ear training (working on hearing and singing intervals) to achieve better intonation.

Text and Diction

As noted in "Dynamics and Articulation," diction in singing refers to the enunciation of words. Words and their component parts must be easy for an audience to understand, for without them the storytelling cannot properly function. (Sometimes the audience will already know the words, but that is beside the point.) Diction is enhanced by musical articulation, and connected to the meaning of the text and to the intentions and actions of the performers.

Diction is also a key part of vocal production. There is enunciation both in consonants and vowels, but consonants define and characterize more than do vowels. As I suggested in "Breathing and Phrasing," you can use diction, particularly consonants, to ensure good vocal production and to effect clear and meaningful communication of the text, in groups as well as with individuals. Diction is also related to, and assists with, rhythmic accuracy. An entrance or cutoff that is together allows meaning to come through, but to blur the beginning or end of a word distracts the audience members and unsuspends their disbelief. Instead of following the story as they should, they note the imprecision or try to figure out what someone said.

Diction is not for diction's sake; as an inexperienced music director I suffered from not understanding this doctrine. In a summer stock theater where I worked, I was so tyrannical about it that my opening-night good-luck cards from three ensemble members had only one large word on it, "DICTION!!!" Since then I have learned that diction is only as good as the meaning behind it, and that diction elucidates meaning, and has no meaning on its own. When possible, associate diction events with physical and dramatic events to further secure them in the singers' minds.

If in "What Is This Feeling?" the chorus were to enunciate with too much formality and precision, it would be untrue to character; the singers are flippant juveniles. Nonetheless, you must ensure that their words are clear enough to hear. (Later in the song you will have to contend with making a fabricated word ("disgusticified") intelligible to the audience.) Togetherness on consonants is more important than forcefulness and is one reason that some music directors employ the choral device of having only one singer vocalize a final consonant in place of the group. I reject this technique outright because it is so obviously an artifice, and forces singers into doing something unnatural (omitting a final consonant).

The rapid-fire words in the "Blackout" excerpt (Figure 13.2), on the other hand, deserve very strong, precise enunciation in spite of the characters singing them, who are not necessarily precise enunciators. Imprecision would throw the already rhythmic nervousness of the song into chaos. What is notable about the segment in the figure is that the many characters singing, each of whom with his or her own story thread, suddenly unite in a dramatic climax. Their unity makes the point of the scene (and contains the song's primary hook). Therefore, although the characters are very individualistic, in rehearsal you precisely match the group vowel sound and the timing of the consonants in "fly" and "sky" for clarity and energy. Remind the chorus of that in a diphthong (in this instance "y" = "ah + ee"), they sustain the first, open part of the sound, and treat the second, tighter vowel almost as a final consonant, leaving it for the end of the tone. (One can also gradually shift between the two vowel sounds of a diphthong, but should do so only for extreme effect.)

In rehearsal you might have the chorus speak the words of these two fast-paced songs in rhythm. The singers will discover that the value words in the lyric coincide very well with the musical stresses, metric and syncopated, and that words of greater value tend to fall on notes of longer duration. This natural prosody absolves singers from having to think about creating emphases where they do not fall. The opposite is true with the words of "Make Our Garden Grow" (Figure 13.3), which are sustained and slowed to an unnatural pace, allowable by the more classical style. Moreover, at the musical climax one finds a rather insignificant syllable ("*nei*-ther" at m. 54). The clarity and scansion of the words are perhaps less at issue than the musicality of the lines, again, as long as the words are intelligible. Furthermore, all the words in m. 53 through the end of the example have been sung earlier. The consonants should be precise but not overemphasized, because so many voices are threading through and crossing over one another. Help the chorus match their vowels, but perhaps not so exactly that the blend resembles a church choir. Slight imperfections and individualities will probably not hamper the performance, and might contribute to its believability. These are delicate stylistic and technical balances for a group to strike, and a situation in which a leader—a music director—who has a clear vision and who can lucidly articulate and project that vision on the ensemble makes all the difference.

Acting and Characterization

Stage performers singing in groups have character, and conviction, just as do principals and soloists. They are engaged with the material or the audience, even if they merely believe in the words they are singing, without thinking about them or acting them too profoundly. In a good stage musical, everywhere the audience looks, even on the periphery, every inhabitant of the stage seems alive. One person out of character or uncommitted to his or her actions can shatter the illusion. In ensemble vocal rehearsal, you explain the objective and intention of the material, and help make that purpose evident in the music. You will, however, eschew most specific acting beats in favor of dramatic content on a more general scale, applicable to many people at once.

In "What Is This Feeling?" a bright, rhythmically animated approach will point up the student ensemble's exuberant antagonism, while performers retain their individual qualities. Other dramatic choices may be less obvious. If the *In The Heights* company sings "Look at the fireworks fly/Light up the night sky," reacting with pure joy to the spectacle, it will not be as interesting or powerful as their singing the words with apprehension: why are there fireworks, and could their light help me find my way home, or to whomever or wherever I am seeking in the darkness? As the long notes sustain (and crescendo), the undercurrent of agitation will intensify the articulations and the sustain, and give subtext to the obvious. "Make Our Garden Grow" requires walking the line between the slow-motion acting style of opera and a more realistic musical theater approach. The objective of the characters is to find peace, safety, and happiness. Their intention in the song is to start a new, simpler life. In this song (and in a university setting) applying specific actions might be productive. First, the group confesses ("We're neither pure nor wise nor good . . ."), then communes with their neighbors ("We'll build our house . . ."). This shift in action has both musical and dramatic effect, as well as a positive vocal influence: it motivates the characters' accord, encourages rhythmic togetherness in the final homophonic section, and at the same time wards off an excessively operatic vocal approach.

Movement

When feasible, at some point during ensemble vocal rehearsals, you should connect any staging or choreography that performers have learned in other rehearsals with the singing. Rehearsing music and movement together informs and enhances each element, and helps the performers retain what they have learned musically. Associate specific movements and their meanings with specific musical events and their meanings; the writers and arrangers will also have done this in advance.

You can also use movement as a means of learning and mastering music, with eurhythmic exercises. You can the have group clap melodic rhythms instead of singing them ("Blackout," "What Is This Feeling?"), and once the clapping is tightly coordinated, add the pitches and gradually eliminate the clapping. The percussiveness and short note values of clapping will immediately expose any imprecisions and physicalize their correction. Working with movement is also entertaining, and helps to maintain the ensemble's interest during rehearsals.

Choral Conducting for the Stage

Some techniques of conducting singers differ from those of conducting instrumentalists, the topic of Part 5, but there are also similarities. Classical choral conductors pay particular heed to the vocal demands of a work, such as diction, articulation, and of course breathing, and do not always feel the need to keep strict time, but stage performers require music directors to keep time; that is among their primary functions. Music directors attend to the stage and orchestra equally.

As a vocal conductor you should always breathe for, and along with, the chorus, visibly, and if you like, audibly. It's perfectly okay to open your mouth wide and inhale loudly—your back is usually to the audience, who are not watching you, anyway. This approach is fine when you're conducting orchestras, too, as many instruments of the orchestra require breath, and in a way, there is a "breath" before every musical phrase. Breath is the most natural and fundamental form of physical and musical preparation for action, and thus falls in with notions of believability of stage performance, as well as with good vocal production.

In the "What Is This Feeling?" excerpt (Figure 13.1), the chorus will be cramming a mouthful of words into a strict rhythm. Your gestures, with their precision, anticipation, and your specific comprehension of the text, can help, especially in rehearsal, when you have the group's undivided attention. In your rehearsal conducting, you may decide to abandon beat patterns in favor of a particular detail you want to exaggerate, or if a section has trouble with a certain passage, you attend directly to those singers to specify and bolster their effort. In the call and response "Look at the fireworks" phrases (mm. 83–84 of "Blackout," Figure 13.2), instead of a conducting a four-beat or dictating the eighth notes, you can conduct only the accented notes (which form the syncopated half of the clave rhythm): "*Look* at the *fire-works* (fly)," with one hand to one chorus, the other to the other band. You might also mouth the words clearly, in rehearsal and performance both, as a reminder that there are important syllables between the accents.

In the "Make Our Garden Grow" *a cappella* section (Figure 13.3), you will want to train your conducting on vocal support that carries the singers through the demanding vocal lines. Your posture should be that of a singer with lungs full, chest high, shoulders back, scapulae together. Your arms should stay at sternum level or above, shoulder width, the lower half of your body stationary to further indicate support, with your hands, wrists, forearms, and torso leading your motions. Your patterns will resemble a classical conductor's, pulling the somber tempo along with viscosity and vocal support in your motions.

Certain groups may be more or less responsive to certain teaching and coaching methods, and as music director, you must, as always, remain completely adaptable. For example, increasingly often in recent Broadway shows, music directors work with children (*Matilda, The Lion King, Shrek, Annie*), who require additional vocal attention and learning time and whose voices music directors assume some responsibility for early in their lives and careers.[2] View each challenge as a chance to widen your musical scope and add to your skill set.

---

2. *Matilda* has a separate music director just for the children, the marvelous Deborah Abramson, and *The Lion King* runs training programs for young Simbas and Nalas.

14

Rehearsals with Directors and Choreographers

Musical theater productions typically rehearse in numerous spaces, small rooms for coaching, larger ones for ensembles, and dance studios with mirrors and barres. The "main room" earns its name by being where the stage director is in residence, and where the emerging production takes shape. The music director and stage manager also camp in the main room. This is company headquarters of Broadway show rehearsals, the point of convergence where the creative team and performers intermingle to coordinate their specialized, individualized efforts.

At the beginning of every new rehearsal period, music directors stake a strategic claim in the main room to an area sanctioned by the stage manager, usually near the piano. I am partial to a corner, with easy access to the rest of the room and to an exit, working AC outlets, and good light. I establish a musical outpost by setting up necessities like one large and one small table for the computers and printers and printouts, seating, a portable cabinet with filing space, office supplies, and recycling bins. In this space I can accompany, arrange, consult, or do paperwork, or I can jump out to work with others, give a note, or retreat. If there is a separate rehearsal podium in the center of the room, I make sure there is an unobstructed travel lane between there and the music "office."

Staging and Dramatic Rehearsals

The main rehearsal room hosts many activities. Staging rehearsals involve the physical placement and movement of people on stage, while dramatic rehearsals deal with textual and emotional content of the material and the performance. One of these two kinds of rehearsal may precede the other, or they may happen concurrently. Almost invariably a musician is behind the piano, either the music director or a rehearsal pianist. Though these rehearsals are the realm of the director, choreographers may have a large part in, or even supplant, directors in blocking and staging a musical show, and almost always have something to do with determining and rehearsing the traffic patterns of the people on stage. Logically, there are many fine stage directors who also choreograph, or choreographers who also direct (among them Bob Fosse, Tommy Tune, Rob Marshall, and Susan Stroman). As music director, you should have an allegiance to the choreographer in these situations as wholehearted as it is to the director.

Your role in staging and dramatic rehearsals will change with the nature of the show and the production, and with what's being covered in them. You should be able to adapt with relative ease to the approach and the pace of these rehearsals. Some directors' methods may be a bit unorthodox, and all are quite different from one another, but you will be a follower more than a leader, observing, accompanying, and deciding how to best fit the music into the director's process and vision. It is natural for a musician at these rehearsals to become disengaged as the actors and director prattle on about details of character or what shade of makeup looks best in the light, but these rehearsals are your chance to gain a deeper understanding of the onstage work and of what occupies the director's and the performers' minds, so that you may more confidently support them.

"Blocking" is the process of placing and moving the performers around the stage in a semblance of real movement, informed and motivated by the story or content of the drama and music.[1] Directors and choreographers block shows by vastly diverse means, and different productions call for vastly divergent styles and staging techniques. Some directors enter rehearsal with a fully formed vision of the staging, while others encourage the performers to follow their natural impulses, and in rehearsal help them to shape their ideas into coherent performances.

When blocking a song or musical scene, many directors want no musical accompaniment, preferring to work with the text "dry," although the singers may sing *a cappella*. Regardless, a music representative should always be in attendance. Staging rehearsals start out stop and go, moment to moment. At first, your involvement as accompanist is mostly secondary, unless your help is solicited. As the material accelerates gradually to performance speed, you can become more industrious and assume a greater voice and presence. A music director interjecting musical comments too soon might rightly be viewed as intrusive; it's usually better to wait until the performers are more comfortable with the staging. If a director's or choreographer's work directly touches on something relevant to the work you have done in music rehearsal, then your direct involvement is probably welcome, if not obligatory, provided you do not interrupt the workflow. If what the director or choreographer brings up corresponds with something you have rehearsed, you may reinforce it. If what the director directs is in conflict with something you have coached, first discuss the variance privately

---

1. The term "blocking" derives from the practice of moving blocks, representing actors, around a model stage.

with the director alone (not with the performers), outside of rehearsal, before arguing or adjusting.

In staging a show from the repertoire you might make alterations to a score at the director's request, or suggest them yourself. For example, if an actor has nothing to do on stage during a musical interlude, you might shorten or cut the interlude. If an accented movement is part of the blocking of a song, you might add an accent in the music as a response to it. You might want to change the introduction or put a new ending on a song to support a change of mood in a musical number. In the right rehearsal situation, you can experiment with musical values like tempo and sometimes key and arrangements as you accompany—again, as long as your musical explorations do not interfere with the rehearsal process.

In a new musical or a heavily revised existing musical, the score and script will be more flexible still. Arrangements, keys, introductions, and endings may still be undecided, and underscoring and transitions yet unwritten. In rehearsal, with the writers (when on site) and the director, you pin down how each musical moment will unfold, particularly the cueing (see chapter 15, "Adapting Music to the Production"). You and the creative team will have discussed many of the choices in preproduction, and you make new ones both independently and in collaboration on the spot in rehearsal. If you incorporate a musical idea on your own—for instance, if you try a slightly different cue that you feel certain will improve a transition—you will probably hear about it only if the leader of the rehearsal does not like it.

In a developmental production, the material you begin with may still be far from complete. More than accompanying in dramatic and staging rehearsals, the majority of your effort could be spent on rewriting or deconstructing and reconstructing the score, as discarding and introducing musical material is a daily exercise. As the chief accompanist in the main room, you need to stay on top of all changes (and communicate them to other accompanists) so that the writers and director can always hear the approximation of a completed state.

In a special event, or a production that has only informal staging, such as a benefit, sing-off, or awards show, a music director often takes a more active part in any staging rehearsals there might be, sometimes because they are the only rehearsals (some numbers may have been pre-staged or pre-rehearsed offsite). He or she, along with the stage manager and perhaps a technical director, might run the rehearsal. If dance or movement is a major part of a special event, the choreographer will very likely lead the way. In a cabaret or concert rehearsal, the performer(s) will often be on the front lines of rehearsal, and neither a music director nor a stage director nor a stage manager will take the lead unless requested.

At an elementary level of staging rehearsals there are calisthenics and warm-ups and theater games and the like. Many academic and nonprofessional dramatic rehearsals will begin this way, and professionals, too, might warm up or do some sort of exercise or theater game in rehearsal, especially if there is something unconventional about the material or the performance requirements (flying or stage combat, for example). As music director you may be asked to improvise an accompaniment for or take part in a warm-up exercise. Sometimes the director and performers begin by discussing character or analyzing the drama, and don't need rehearsal accompaniment at all. Music directors are still often invited to these rehearsals, or volunteer to observe them.

Again, because the music is not the priority in staging and dramatic rehearsals, many music directors assign rehearsal pianists or associates to them. This is fine, as long as communication is perpetually available for when changes are needed. You don't want to find yourself at a run-through tripping over a measure in three-quarter (3/4) time that had been inserted into a long section in four-quarter (4/4) time a week ago because the rehearsal pianist rightfully went along with the director, who staged it that way without consulting you, and neither the director nor the pianist told you about the dropped quarter note. Be proactive in staying updated, and devise a system by which all rehearsal musicians can share modifications and questions instantaneously.

Whether you choose to accompany or designate an accompanist to dramatic and staging rehearsals, and when and if you decide to only conduct, is mostly up to you, but you must assess what will work best for each production. The director will tacitly approve your decision, or ask for a certain rehearsal configuration: he or she may ask you to conduct all rehearsals from the podium with a certain accompanist at the piano. You, the director, and the producers together determine when and if to bring in other rehearsal musicians. By the time rehearsals reach their later phases, your rehearsal accompaniment and accompanimental configuration should closely resemble what the performers will hear in performance. If you will be conducting in performance from a podium or from behind the piano, do the same in rehearsal, and if you will not be conducting in performance, conduct in rehearsal only very sparingly.

A fully polished musical accompaniment is not essential during earlier phases of staging and dramatic rehearsals, though it will be very shortly, when putting the show together. Rather, your objectives at first are to capture the spirit of the proceedings and support the work of your collaborators. You might want to begin by lending gentle support to performers still learning their music, doubling and bringing out their melodies in the accompaniment. You might want to first establish grooves and introduce the details later on. Still, accompaniments should not be fumbled. If you haven't had time to practice a score, or if the music is very difficult, hire a more prepared or facile pianist, or in rehearsal play a simplified and clean version until you are able to deliver a fully accurate reading.

When production time is tighter, as it is in stock companies, the pace is attenuated, and you will incorporate the full accompaniment sooner. Methodical work is a luxury, and learning scores in advance in preparation for a long repertory season is highly advisable. Directors and choreographers stage large sections at once, rough out onstage and backstage traffic, and have little time for fine tuning. In these situations, too, you can support the performers' musical efforts, in your accompanying and by giving notes judiciously in rehearsal, as long as you do not impede the director or choreographer's breakneck velocity.

The rehearsal convention is for the music director or accompanist to await the director's or choreographer's word to begin playing, until the accompanist is directed to take over this protocol at will. A rhythm usually develops, as it does in other rehearsals, that regulates when and how much accompaniment is desired, and how much attention can be paid at what moment to the state of the musical performance.

Rehearsals in the main room progress to increasingly large segments until the whole of a show has been assembled. It is an arduous period because you and the performers are repeatedly expending sustained physical and mental energy in pursuit of perfection. But the stamina you build up will pay off. It is also the time when as music director you solidify your place as a prime executor of the performance. Absolute technical accuracy and consistency in the accompaniment will become the norm in later phases of dramatic and staging rehearsals, as the score dissolves into the work as a whole.

Movement and Dance Rehearsals

The dance rehearsal process usually casts music directors in a supporting role, primarily as accompanists to the movement, unless they are writing dance arrangements. Most music directors assign an assistant or a rehearsal pianist to movement rehearsals. Like their musical or blocking counterparts, dance rehearsals involve substantial time learning and drilling technical elements. In movement, there are also extensive warm-ups, technical work, and stringent repetition. The musical element can be unexciting. One might picture a stereotypically craggy demoiselle at the piano in a ballet class, scanning for the ballet master's count-in over a pair of half-glasses and past her *New York Times*, and pounding out squarely rhythmic dances such as *Ländler* and gavottes in pedantic tempos. She is inconsolably grouchy because she plays the same pieces *ad nauseum*, and she is lucky to get so much as a thank you from the dancers or choreographer.

A good dance rehearsal pianist is sensitive to the format and pace of movement rehearsals and the rehearsal styles of each choreographer (or whoever from the dance department is running the rehearsal, perhaps an associate choreographer or dance captain). He or she can sense when accompaniment is needed or wanted and when it is not, when to play softly and when to play out, when to relax the tempo and when to bring it up to speed. Some musicians are more fluent in the silent language of choreography than others, sometimes through a relationship that develops with a dancer or choreographer over time or a particular shared stylistic sensibility. As in dramatic and staging rehearsals, choreographers will cue the accompanist, sometimes verbally, sometimes with signals, sometimes with only the movement itself. Other times they and the music director or accompanist will jointly set the pace as they go, tacitly or through discussion. Occasionally, a music director or accompanist will lead, counting off tempos and determining where to start and stop. When things are working right, the accompaniment just flows with the rehearsal current.

It is ultimately up to you as music director to make sure that one of these scenarios, or another that is equally effective, is in operation at all dance rehearsals. As in dramatic rehearsals, choreographers might request changes to the music in rehearsal. And again, you must be in communication with all rehearsal musicians to make or approve changes, or empower them to make decisions in your stead, and insist that they relay any changes back to you.

Dance rehearsal accompanists will sometimes be expected to improvise or play without written music. For instance, the choreographer may want to hear a general rhythmic pattern or a certain song for a warm-up or other exercise, or might want to try out ideas in a certain style in an exploratory dance jam session. The latter case is an example of spontaneous dance arranging, not unlike the preproduction dance-music experimentations discussed earlier, and, as noted earlier, many dance arrangements are indeed created in rehearsal. The element of spontaneity is important to dance, both in its creation and later in its place on stage, and is a consequence of dance's proximity to natural movement. Dance, unlike music, is a form of expression that appears as part of everyday life. We do not break out into song on the street when we're joyful (most of us, anyway), but we might very well jump up and down or skip around a bit.

Requests that choreographers make of the musical representative in a movement rehearsal might seem unmusical at times. They could ask you to make a tempo alteration that goes against the groove, or to repeat a phrase whose repetition would upset a musical structure, or to place an accent in a musically awkward place (witness the drum part for *Tommy*, with its un-Who-like downbeat cymbal crashes, there by dint of the choreographer's insistence on highlighting leg kicks, much to the music team's chagrin). As I have recommended before, you can either try to view these obstacles as musical inspiration, an opportunity to make something better out of what was already musically right, or simply don't let them bother you, because what matters most is what works on stage. If you assume that any musical detail a choreographer insists upon is in the best interest of the production, then it is always in the production's best interest for you to make it work, even if you consider it musically wrong. Your opinion may be better kept to yourself, though not always. (The orchestrator and I protested fervently the *Tommy* accents, but in the end we had no choice but to concede; despite the director's sympathy with our cause, he did not overrule the choreographer.)

As another example of the oblique relationship between dance and music, choreographers frequently organize and rehearse their work into groups of eight counts, or "eights," that together form larger units ("Let's take it from fifth count of the third eight of the traveling section in the double-time tap break!"). Yet the groupings do not always align with phrases of music. If need be, you can adapt the music to suit the dance, either by restructuring it or by changing the way it is notated. Most of the time, though, you can just ignore, or embrace, any discrepancies. The counts exist only for convenience and collective reference, and have little effect on the performance except to assist in its rehearsal.

In chapter 12, "Individual Vocal Rehearsals," I recommended against the use of metronomes in vocal rehearsals. In dance rehearsals, on the other hand, a metronome is indispensable. Without a metronome, the commotion over tempo in dance rehearsals can be unbearable. Even with the metronome, the discussion of tempo correctness may not abate, but it will help.

At times during a dance rehearsal you might be able to inject musical directions or corrections, although your comments will more often than not fall on the deaf ears of a dancer concentrating on a physical task. There are, however, a few ways you can improve on the music during these rehearsals. Bring out on the piano vocal lines for singers who are struggling. Don't ever refuse a performer who sneaks over to the piano to ask for a quick run-through of his or her part. Try to persuade the choreographer and the whole dance department to reinforce musical values as a part of their teaching process. Once you see a number on its feet, adjust the vocal arrangements so that the staging is not in the way of effective singing, and vice versa. Give the most challenging vocal parts to the least active performers. Add offstage singers for support. (Offstage singing can sound artificial, but with so much of onstage vocal sound now just as "piped in," this issue is moot.)

When you are working in the director's and choreographer's rehearsal rooms, the trust that you engender by respecting and sustaining the vision of those who are mounting the production on stage will benefit you throughout the production and beyond. In future collaborations with these directors and choreographers and performers, and by reputation, your voice will be better heard and your contributions solicited and taken more seriously. For now, though, the job is still incomplete. There are holes in the score and the show yet to be filled in.

15

Adapting Music to the Production

Before rehearsals for an original musical begin, the writers and creative team formulate the components of a production—its songs, scenes, dances, transitions, whatever it might contain—into a meaningful order, according to large-scale and moment-to-moment rationales. During rehearsal there is additional assembly, and alterations to existing material that range from small tweaks to complete overhauls. Directors and music directors work out any cues that have not been predetermined, mostly during staging and dramatic rehearsals but also in music and dance rehearsals. In a revue or concert, musical numbers likewise have logical sequence and calculated detail in the way that they begin and end, and progress from one to the next. In a repertory musical, the material is pre-ordered, but still subject to change if permissible.

Believability is again the overriding criterion when assimilating music into a stage show, or altering music already there. Believability does not require that an audience literally believes everything on stage to be real; rather, the audience should accept whatever reality that the production intends to project. The audience never questions why to "Be Italian" (*Nine*) one must growl and gyrate suggestively, or why a crowd of dress-alikes are singing backup vocals and busting a move alongside Michael Jackson. These things just make sense, on their own theatrical terms. The audience's belief, in the form of applause, is what revives Tinkerbell in *Peter Pan*. Correspondingly, audiences should not be aware of the musical mechanics behind their experience, only the experience itself. Music directors, in coaching performers and manipulating musical and textual material to make them believable, and by keeping their manipulation disguised, help to allay the audience's cognizance that what is unfolding before them is illusory.

As in their other tasks, music directors' involvement in adapting a score to a production differs from job to job. Some writers or directors take complete charge of all such matters, and unless their determinations feel tremendously ill advised to any

Cueing

The term "cue" has many definitions, as either noun or verb, depending on context. When music directors speak of a cue they are usually referring to one of two things. First, any concurrence of events that takes place in performance is a cue. It can be any meeting of, say, dialogue and music, staging and music, some technical aspect of the production and music, or even multiple musical events within the score. The term is also applied to dramatic and design elements. An actor gets a cue to make an entrance. Lighting and sound events are known as light and sound "cues." The verb "to cue" denotes the act of indicating that point of concurrence. A conductor cues an instrumental or vocal entrance, or takes a cue from the stage. Second, "cue" is a term for a distinct section of music: any piece of music of any length might be referred to as a cue. Each separately numbered piece of music in a score is one cue, and there are cues within cues.

In a series of musical numbers, the point at which you begin one musical number in relation to another just completed is also a cue, as is the moment at which you bring in underscoring. The point in a line of dialogue at which you start the accompaniment to a song (so that the actor on stage can make a smooth transition from speech to song) is another cue, called the "cue line" or "cue word." The timing of your initial upbeat that begins the opening number of a show is a cue, often an important one. Some initial downbeats or cueing sequences are more important than others. Precise timing of the opening sequence of cues in *The Lion King*—the famous initial vocal outburst, the lights, the sunrise, the chorus, the entrance of the giraffes—is hugely important to the technical execution of the director's perfectionist vision of a massive stage picture, as it is in the opening moments of many musical shows.

The cues that you and others devise and the way you execute them influence believability in all stage contexts. We can generalize that if music has a strong dramatic presence in a show, such as in a traditional musical, the cueing must be exceptionally sensitive and seamless, and it likely will be more a part of the composition. Cueing in dramatic musicals is especially crucial because it addresses the innate incompatibility of music and drama. These uncomfortable cohabitants meet at the point of a cue, so you must treat their collision, so to speak, with particular care. In a production in which music functions independently of a dramatic element, as in a concert or revue, the cueing will have more to do with entertainment value and energy, and as music director you will probably be more involved in determining how it works. There are many rationales behind good cueing, but only viewing a work in rehearsal and performance will validate the rightness of a cue.

The ground between song and speech is well trodden in the musical theater literature. Because of the difficulty of switching convincingly between spoken word and music (or dance), writers have deeply plumbed the middle ground for believable in-between states. In addition, the musical stage accommodates performers who have believable rather than beautiful singing voices. Though they may comfortably toe the line between speech and melody, the audience must still accept the fact that their speaking voices spontaneously metamorphose into melodic instruments. The most artfully written examples are in dramatic musicals that make the transition without audiences being aware of the change. Many writers employ as a bridge some form of accompanied recitative, such as this well-known Figure 15.1.

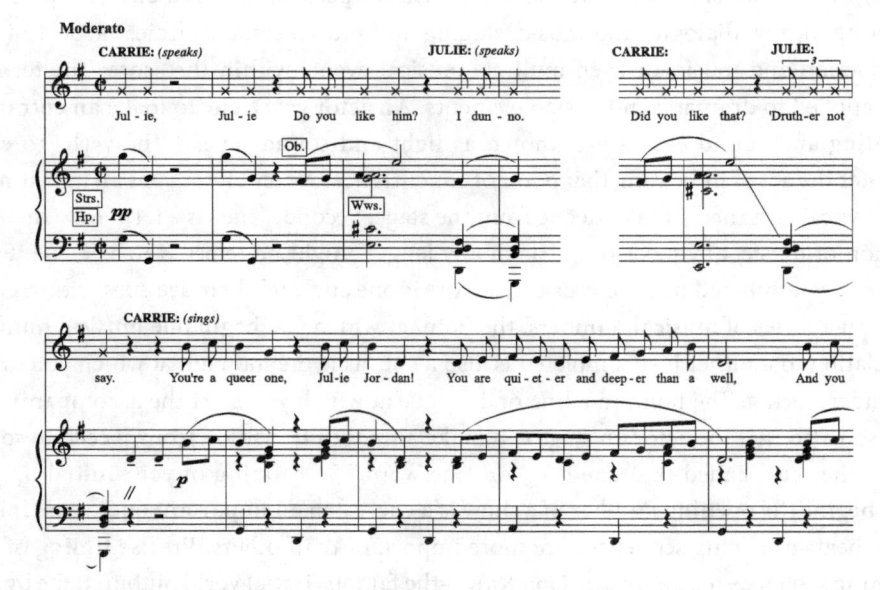

FIGURE 15.1 Musical scene from *Carousel*, Richard Rodgers and Oscar Hammerstein II.

In Figure 15.2, the shift from realism to lyricism is so cleverly executed that the audience members do not see that the writer is laying bare the process for them to see (this reprint from the piano-vocal score uses beautifully demonstrative graphic notation).

When devising a cue into a song, quite often your intent is to mask the musical entrance. Look at any text that precedes the song, and the way the actor delivers it, and look at the first few lines of the lyric. Perhaps you can find a value word in the dialogue to associate with the start of the music, or a small stage event, such as the opening of a door, a spotlight coming on, or just the turn of a performer's head. Music coinciding with one word can have a very different effect from what it does when coinciding with another. Trial and error and back and forth between the director and music director in rehearsal are the norm. ("Let's try the music one sentence earlier. No, two words earlier but stronger. Now two beats later, and softer." And so forth.) Sometimes you adjust the music, or the director might alter the stage dialogue or action. A musical solution that seems clumsy at first, such as a three- or five-bar introduction to a song or no introduction at all, is without reproach if the timing on stage feels right, that is, if the cueing is

HAROLD: What am I hearing?

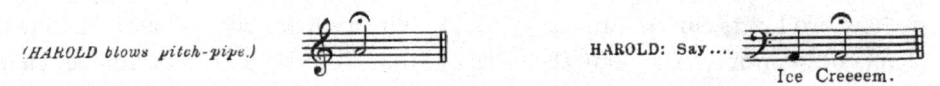

(HAROLD blows pitch-pipe.)

HAROLD: Say.... Ice Creeeem.

OLIN: Ice Cream.. but I don't sing, young man, if that's what you're ......
HAROLD: All right, talk then. (Speaks in low pitch.) Down here!
OLIN: Ice Cream.
HAROLD: Talk slow!

OLIN: Ice Creeeem.

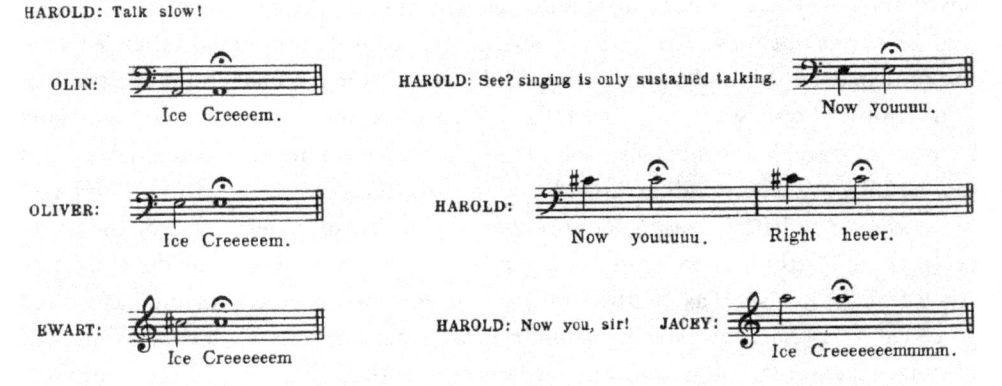

HAROLD: See? singing is only sustained talking.

Now youuuu.

OLIVER: Ice Creeeeem.

HAROLD: Now youuuuu. Right heeer.

EWART: Ice Creeeeeem

HAROLD: Now you, sir! JACEY: Ice Creeeeeemmmm.

HAROLD: Ladies, from now on you'll never see one of those men without the other three.

FIGURE 15.2 Cue into "Sincere," *The Music Man*, Meredith Willson.

believable. The music always remains pliable, even if it was perfectly balanced as composed or notated.

Not all cues are inconspicuous, nor are they meant to be. Some take center stage, such as the bell tones in musical comedies like *Spamalot* or *The Producers* that come from nowhere to herald the beginning of a song (that overworked gag invariably gets a laugh). Although a music cue may not need to be unobtrusive, you may still have to experiment in rehearsal to figure out how best to make it work. New factors will influence your determination, such as timing, technical elements, or the demands of a star performer ("Honey, when you hear me say my name, you *hit it!*").

Many cues are related not to speech, but to movement or visual events. As with speech, writers and directors manipulate these elements to affect the audience's reactions. Physical action and visual events are often in intermediary states of realism. A repetitive motor activity, for example, might regularize and rhythmically modulate into the groove of a song. Strolling down the street can turn into a soft shoe. In the charming "Ugg-A-Wugg" from *Peter Pan*, ritualistic hand percussion grows into a production number. Sound effects often transform into a rhythmic pattern as well, such as cash registers ("Checkers") and a factory assembly line ("Millwork") whose noise patterns underpin two songs from the musical *Working*, and the Rock Island train of the opening of *The Music Man*. (*The Music Man* is something of a textbook on cueing and musical theater construction.)

Cues are not just at the beginnings of songs. There are internal cues, small and large. Music cues can coordinate with or highlight any noteworthy aspect of stage content, such as a lighting effect, a change of scenery, or an emotional shift. You can cue an accent in movement or dance to the music, or vice versa, either directly (a cymbal swell as two lovers run toward each other) or satirically (a flute trill as a dancing elephant does a pirouette). To indicate passage of time, you might use a distant key change and a simultaneous shift in texture. You might cue a timpani *glissando* to a performer's pratfall, or add a grand pause as the stage freezes. Indeed, certain cues are inconspicuous by their very obviousness; their presence folds into the pseudo-reality.

The ends of songs are tremendously important in the impression they leave on the audience. For example, how long should you hold the big final chord of a production number? You'll want to hold it long enough to let the audience's need to applaud become unbearable, but not a moment longer, lest the tension fizzle before the ovation erupts. Like any cues, endings may be composed, they may be part of an arrangement, they may be part of a cueing sequence you devise in rehearsal, or they may be any combination. There are strongly stated endings and understated ones. Some come from stock, such as "buttons" (final staccato notes, usually in the bass, often preceded by a *fermata*), "stingers" (big buttons, often in octaves and open or wide voicings), fade-outs, and false endings. Many sync with stage actions, quite commonly with lighting shifts, especially blackouts, scene shifts, exits, and physical poses. Some evolve through exploration and mutual agreement among the creative participants, some are part of the technical plot, and some happen in real time in performance, by your reading the audience, such as when you are accompanying a solo performer.

As well as endings, the space between numbers is also crucial (see the following section, "Underscoring, Transitions, and Incidental Music"). In revues and concerts with little or no dialogue, how one piece follows another influences the ongoing energy of the performance, and so the transitions may be no less calculated than they are in a musical play. A long pause between numbers dissipates energy; after an up-tempo song and before a ballad, therefore, you take a longer break. Songs often "segue" from one to another, meaning that there is a brief pause (no more than a few seconds) in between. Moving from one number to the next as if the two were contiguous, called "*attacca*," allows you to defeat applause between numbers (sometimes audience members will applaud no matter how hard you try to stop them). In written show scores you will see the terms "direct segue" and "segue as one," which you can interpret either as equivalent to *attacca* or as a very tight segue; the usage is muddled. For an "applause segue," wait for the peak of the applause for one number (or some other preset point in the applause), then begin the next. When deciding the number-to-number motion of the show, also consider the large-scale pace of the show. Shows have ups and downs, tension and resolution, builds and climaxes and letdowns. Taken all together, they must entertain and emotionally connect with an audience.

In rehearsal you plan and practice the timings of cues, but when conducting you follow and adjust to the performers even if they miss or ignore what was rehearsed. Some stage performers listen actively to the music under them, and some modify their performances to correlate with the music and your cueing. Others remain deliberately unaware of any accompaniment or underscoring, or might not be able hear it well. As music director, you make it work either way.

You'll plan most of the technical cueing—cueing that is related to the physical production rather than to the text or staging or music—with the stage manager and director, and often with a technical director or designer. Many cueing sequences cannot be fully realized and quantified until technical rehearsals are underway, or even until you are in front of an audience, as both technology and audience reactions are significant variables. You can approximate technical cues for practice purposes in rehearsal, such as "synchronizing" a lighting fade with a musical *diminuendo* (a drastic descrescendo, or softening) on a stage manager's count during a run-through.

Though audience members might not outwardly recognize a defective music cue, their experience will nonetheless suffer. I recently attended a new Broadway musical whose pace was deadly slow. Its structure alternated song and scene with torturous regularity. A series of three-chord ballads made up the majority of the awkward and soporific score, and each had a four-bar introduction. Each introduction started *after* a cue line, the last spoken line before singing, and so in each song the singers were forced to wait through their introduction before singing, with no activity to occupy them while the seemingly interminable four bars went by. A simple adjustment of dovetailing musical introductions under preceding lines of dialogue would have tempered the audience members' impatience, which mounted steadily and increasingly posed a threat to the show's already threadbare believability.

Underscoring, Transitions, and Incidental Music

Incidental music refers to those parts of a stage score that are somehow secondary in function. This category includes underscoring, transitional music, overtures and other showpieces, and source music (which is often a sound cue rather than a music cue). Like all other forms of stage arrangement, incidental music may be a part of the composition or may be created during production. How and when dialogue needs or benefits from underscoring is a subjective matter, and has broad implications for a show. Music directors often compose or arrange incidental music, for new shows and existing ones, or alter existing incidental material, guided, as always, by the larger vision of the production.

The writer(s) or the director usually determines the type and placement of dialogue underscoring. Music that plays under dialogue is mostly kept very low in the mix; nevertheless, it has a profound impact on a story and its emotional content. A movie without its musical soundtrack seems denuded, and movies without music (such as Hitchcock's *The Birds*) are notable for its exclusion. Movies, though, have the advantage of being able to balance musical scoring with spoken dialogue. They also feature carefully recorded background noise, which mixes with (and often drowns out) the score and dialogue. Music on stage, by contrast, is conspicuous by its mere presence. For an illustration, consider the orchestra at the Oscars interrupting a long-winded acceptance speech. Regardless, many stage plays and musicals use music under scenes, though most scenes communicate more believably without it. More commonplace is music under action, such as dance, and whenever there is no dialogue. Music on stage (and in movies, too) can also replace dialogue and take part in the storytelling, as with a *Leitmotif*—a phrase of music that has a direct association with a character, object, or idea—or in a ballet (as described in chapters 5, "Choreographers," and chapter 10, "Arranging for the Movement"), as well as, of course, in melody and song. (Sung material can qualify as incidental music, if it is far enough in the background.)

Though it is impossible for stage incidental music to go entirely unnoticed as it is in the cinema, it is possible to prevent its intrusion at the wrong moments, both in composing and performing it. As a rule, underscoring is best kept to a minimum, and minimal in sound and texture. Very high and low registers work well, as long as the material is not too active. Sustained tones and chords can be effective, too. Single notes, usually long tones, and short, uncomplicated, repetitive percussive patterns are other good options.

Sneaking in under dialogue, this example of stylized, tasteful, and effective underscoring from *West Side Story* starts with a simple counterpoint that restates the introductory melody from "Maria" (see Figure 15.3A), heard in full moments earlier (note the slurring in the third and fourth measures that reflects the lyric),

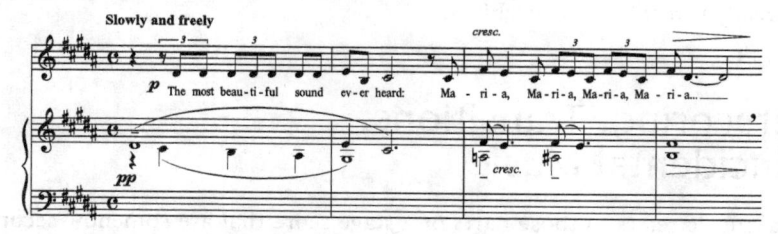

FIGURE 15.3A Top of "Maria," from *West Side Story*.

against a softly descending, then ascending counter line (see Figure 15.3B), Because the material is now familiar to the listener, it requires little attention, and the two lines in a single register take up very little sonic space. It is also of dramatic value, in that it connects the listener to an underlying and unresolved emotion.

FIGURE 15.3B Balcony scene from *West Side Story*.

The presence of music at the beginning of this scene opens the door for continuous music throughout, and for increasingly expressive music. A new and crucial *Leitmotif* is first introduced later in this underscoring (m. 112 in the piano-vocal score)[1], the "Somewhere" theme that will recur at the climax of the play. The emotional referents in the underscoring are part of the musical-dramatic composition, as is the cueing of dialogue throughout this extended underscore.

As with dance or vocal arrangements, your governing principle is to use underscoring only when it will genuinely enhance the storytelling or thematic content. If there is no need for music under, do not put it there. Trying to beautify a moment or make a feeling more profound with music can seem overwrought on stage. The lyricism of *West Side Story* and its connection with the seminally romantic balcony scene of *Romeo and Juliet* permit a musical approach that might be indulgent in other settings.

In a classic musical such as this one, you would be understandably reluctant to make changes to the underscoring, so usually the stage performers will adapt, as will you and the director. Because pop composers are so much more a part of today's musical theater scene, music directors have many more opportunities to create incidental music, and many pop composers are happy to entrust the work to someone they believe will have a keener sense of how it should be done.

Figure 15.4 is from a workshop of an original musical, *Havana* (music by Frank Wildhorn; the show has not gone beyond its developmental productions). On this job the composer and director would tell the music director (me) what themes they wanted in the incidental music, describe the feeling they wanted the music to have, then leave me to write the arrangement, and either approve my work or send me back to the drawing board. This piece underscored a melancholy, romantic farewell scene (the scene, and the music, were cut before the show was presented publicly).

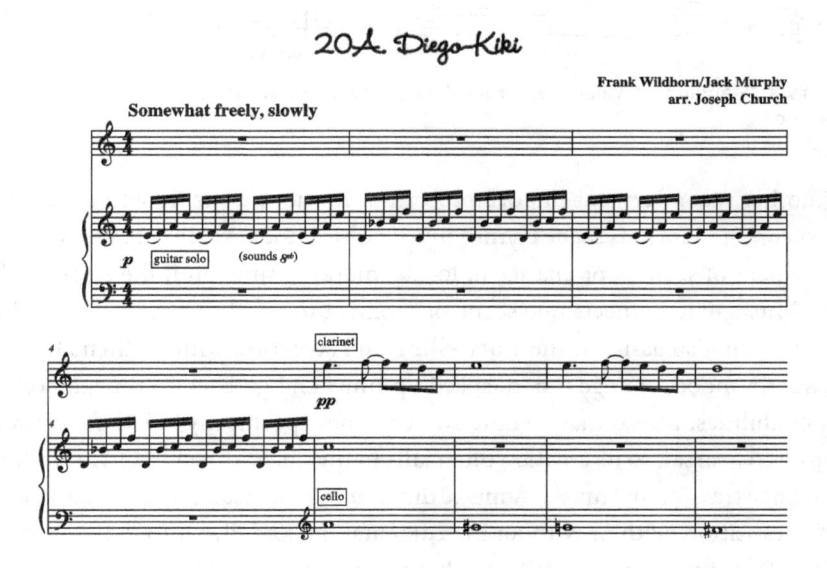

FIGURE 15.4 Underscoring from the musical *Havana*. (Property of author.)

1. Leonard Bernstein and Stephen Sondheim, *West Side Story*, vocal score, New York: G. Schirmer, Inc. and Chappell & Co., Inc. 1959.

In a very different mood, Figure 15.5 is the music under a shocking, graphic murder of a beloved character. The selection is from the musical *Faust*, by Randy Newman. On this job the composer gave me free rein in writing dozens of incidental music cues of all kinds, jokey, dramatic, and highly referential, and encouraged me to make unorthodox choices. (The plastic fork used on the piano strings for the stabbing was, surreptitiously, sitting on the piano in a container of fruit salad, one of my preferred rehearsal snacks.)

FIGURE 15.5 "Stabbing of Valentine," from Randy Newman's *Faust*. (Reprinted by permission of Alfred Music.)

Another secondary but important form of music is transitional music. Probably the most common form is scene change music, which does exactly what it says: it covers the movement of scenery or change of locale, marking time until the stage action can resume. Music that connects one scene or moment to another helps to set pacing and mood, and can also assist in the storytelling and structure with its thematic usage. It can maintain mood, change mood, speed up time, and go back in time, among many other possibilities. Music that a composer does not specifically create for a transition develops in rehearsal, so its creation often falls to the music director. Orchestrators, too, often arrange transitional music. A music director in rehearsal might sketch a piano version of a transition, with or without instrumentation, and give it to the orchestrator to complete. Transitional music walks the boundary between incidental music and music in the foreground. Yet in many older productions, transitions are merely hurriedly written arrangements of songs from the show. The reason is not lack of care but lack of time.

Computer software has raised the bar on transitional music, as orchestration and copying turnaround times are no longer vindication for sketchy work.

There are several types of transitions you may work with. "Playouts" are partial reprises, sung or instrumental, of a number that was just sung, and usually follow quickly after the applause begins, in a tight applause segue. You can speed up or slow down the tempo of a playout from its forerunner to affect the energy of the transition. "Playoffs" are similar; they use a portion of the music just heard to cover an exit, to literally play while the actors go off stage. Again, this music usually starts on the heels of the number just ended. Some numbers or scenes are followed by reprises of themes from elsewhere in the show, often rearranged to reflect a change in the story or the proceedings. There are also crossovers and "traveling" music, both of which accompany the movement of a person or group who for some reason move, or "travel," from one place on stage to another. If a crossover happens downstage of a concealed set change going on behind it, it is called an "in one" transition.[2] You usually keep transitional music as brief as the stage action allows. Most scene changes move as fast as they can, and the music helps move the show forward.

Overtures, Bows, and Exit Music

Overtures showcase the music and the orchestra, but also give an audience a chance to settle into their seats. Tarnished though they may be by chatter, ringtones, candy wrappers, and latecomers, overtures are a rare chance for an orchestra to be heard on their own, and for a music director to take a bow. Overtures, though, are now largely relics, belonging only to classic musicals. The production conceit by which they existed, a preview of salable tunes from the score, is somewhat obsolete. Now the music of any show is immediately available to audience members before or after they attend the show—on iTunes, YouTube, subscription radio—and the music needs no preview to be sold. The CD is hawked in the aisles at intermission. Indeed, the music the audience has heard in advance may be the reason the theatergoers bought tickets. Pre-show announcements asking audiences to silence their electronic devices signal the start of the show, so an overture is not needed to calm the house. Furthermore, the orchestra that an overture was meant to feature may be three synthesizers, bass, and drums, and no matter its size, it is heard through a sound system. It doesn't make sense for an offstage orchestra to play a showpiece.

Overtures (and entr'actes, the parallel form that occurs before the second or third act of a musical) traditionally take one of two arranging approaches. They either present a collection of themes from the show, either music to the story or songs expected to be most popular, or they are original pieces with themes not necessarily found elsewhere in

---

2. Some entire scenes are "in one." The term derives from the numbered entrances from the wings to the stage; the entrance farthest downstage is numbered one, and downstage of that is where an "in one" scene takes place.

the show, but that set the scene or introduce the drama. Examples of this "tableaux" element are the "Carousel Waltz" and "Runyonland" from *Guys and Dolls*. Overtures are and were commonly arranged by a music director and orchestrated by an orchestrator, but there have been many variations on this formula. Many orchestrators do both, as do many music directors. Composers seldom write their own overtures, with some notable exceptions (*Candide*).

Overtures may be mostly defunct, but their opposites, music for bows and the audience exit, live on. This music is sometimes casually arranged—bows music is likely to be obscured by cheering no matter how much it is amplified—but other times it can be a showcase for the skills of the band or the orchestrator. The bows and exit music are probably among the last arrangements written for a show (because they are likely the least crucial to a show's ultimate success), which also explains their sometimes offhanded quality. Musical themes for bows are compiled much as they are in an overture, highlighting featured melodies, and sometimes attaching character-related music to certain characters' bows. Writing music for the curtain call can be an enjoyable routining task for a music director. The time it takes each performer or group of performers to bow will often determine the shapes and durations of phrases in the music. A director or choreographer might also contribute ideas to the order and presentation of themes in the bows music.

Exit music, or "walkout" music, is music that plays as the audience leaves the theater. It can highlight members of the orchestra with improvised solos; some orchestrations for exit music are just chord charts organized around one or two themes that the band jams on. The informality reflects the relaxation of the theater experience in its closing moments. Music directors will have more say in determining which themes to use than they do with bows, but still the director might state a preference, or dictate a choice. When assembling themes for exit music, remember that it will be last music the audience hears, and will leave some sort of impression. The choice should be made with regard to the audience's experience of the show. Right to the last note, as music director you keep in mind the vision of the entire production.

PART V

Rehearsals 2

Musicians, Technicians, and the Venue

16

Orchestras and Orchestration

Music directors rehearse with the musicians who make up the band, or orchestra, or whatever an accompanimental unit consists of, toward the end of a production rehearsal period. Instrumentalists make a late entrance for a variety of reasons, for example, they have the least material to learn, in performance they usually read from printed music, and they are already quite skilled at their instruments. Onstage performers are skilled, too, of course, but their effort is more production-specific than the musicians', and unlike musicians, they must memorize lines, sing, act, dance, change clothes, and be in full view of the audience. Musicians can learn their parts faster, sometimes so quickly that they barely need rehearsing at all.

As in every aspect of music directors' work, the organization and instruction that they provide to orchestras depends on what the musicians and the production require. Some orchestras not only need very little rehearsal, but also very little conducting. A music director makes his or her greatest mark on an accompaniment in rehearsal by working with the musicians to realize, standardize, and perfect their contribution to the whole. This is not to say that music directors do not influence the music while conducting in performance, but in performance they obviously cannot stop to make suggestions or corrections. In addition, the written score and orchestration contain much relevant musical and performance information; thus accurate, communicative notation is invaluable.

Organizing the Musicians

General information on contracting a group of musicians was a topic of chapter 6, "The Music Team," but because every production is a different undertaking, the challenges lie in the specifics. For one thing, a Broadway pit orchestra is not at all the same as an orchestra for a local or community theater, or a college show, nor is the process of rehearsing the musicians. The divide is mostly between professional (or practicing amateurs, most of whom are semiprofessional) and nonprofessional musicians. Professional musicians anywhere in the United States (and Canada, Europe, and Asia, too), almost all of whom belong to the union and perform with at least some regularity, can reliably deliver a creditable or better performance of virtually any piece of written music within a few tries.

You (and the contractor) will presumably seek out musicians whom you know, by experience, reputation, or audition, to be capable of playing the music for your show. You consider not only their musical skills but also their ability to work artistically and professionally in a group, a skill that, as noted, is just as crucial. If a musician does prove musically incompetent or otherwise unsatisfactory after hiring, most union locals will support you in replacing him or her, but only within the first few days of rehearsal. Once a musician becomes identified with the part he or she is playing, the union, supportive of the music director in an obviously errant hiring situation, will turn about and protect that musician's right to his or her job so fervently and litigiously that many organizations would rather tolerate the rotten apple than try to remove it from the barrel.

Orchestra contracting procedures and conditions are quite different when salaries are lower or the pool of musicians is limited or unknown. For example, at a stock theater in a rural area, the local musical talent may vary, and you might want to complement a group with ringers. Or, at a university, the students and faculty of the music department lean strongly toward serious music, but you are the music director of a hard rock science fiction musical.

You must accept that you cannot get an ideal sound from an imperfect orchestra, or work miracles of contracting. You can only do your best with what you have, and above all, accompany the stage in the same spirit and with the same absolute support that you would in a lavishly funded entertainment. Apportion rehearsal time according to the needs of each particular group. If you know that the guitarist and drummer don't read, schedule private sessions before ensemble rehearsals to work them through their parts, and insist that their parts be memorized. Mark the music so that a non-music reader can at least follow the routines and know, for instance, where to start and stop, where to play loudly and softly, and where they are playing solo. If need be, reduce a player's part to a minimum, and cover as much as you can on piano or synthesizer, or distribute it to other instruments. There are many ways you can customize an orchestration to suit a group that you know in advance will be understaffed or imbalanced, including using the simplified or synthesized versions that publishers offer. Remember, too, that when a seat does not demand top dollar, or a production is more for fun or fulfillment than for profit, your collaborators' and the audience's expectations may be lower, and you may well exceed those expectations by merely delivering a solid performance and making the process musically fruitful and enjoyable for all.

The contractor and producer will help in scheduling rehearsals, securing space, finding gear, and contacting all personnel involved to ensure their appearance in the right place at the right time (in an amateur production these duties may fall to you). Most orchestra rehearsals involve more than the musicians. Power and amplification must be working. Everyone will need room to play and a way to hear, see, and communicate with you and other musicians. Music must be on the music stands (professional pit orchestras pay a small stipend to a librarian, a member of the orchestra, to take charge of the printed orchestra parts). The sound designer or operator will probably attend, as will technicians who oversee amplification, electrics, and lighting. In a new show, the orchestrator and copyist will be there to make changes. In later rehearsals, certain performers or the producer, director, or choreographer might drop by. (Earlier rehearsals are better left to the musicians alone, and you can ask that a rehearsal be closed if you think privacy is important to the process.)

Orchestra rehearsal will often overlap with the final phases of cast rehearsal, and you will have to attend both (you can anticipate putting in very long hours). Make yourself as accessible as you can to the musicians, as they will always have questions. The classical custom of a conductor materializing on the podium precisely at the rehearsal start time does not belong in stage music direction; music directors have no star mystique or special privileges.

Guidelines for orchestra rehearsal scheduling are generally based on professional conventions, but of course, larger professional groups are more costly, in personnel, equipment, and space. You can rehearse an amateur orchestra as much as you need to, schedule permitting. Assuming your orchestra is at least somewhat musically adept, you will need about thirty minutes to rehearse a piece of music in full, perhaps more for one complex or newly written, considerably less for something easy or familiar. Typically, fully musicalized, full-length shows have between one and two dozen musical numbers of about five or more minutes' duration, plus interstitial material. The size of the orchestra makes only a slight difference in time allotment; a larger group has more variables, but the music is the same. Three-hour rehearsal sessions are the norm, including within that time about twenty minutes of breaks. (Breaks are useful not only for rest but for catching up. You or the contractor should monitor breaks so that twenty minutes do not turn into forty.) By this formula, rehearsing twenty-four musical numbers would require twenty-four half hour segments, or four three-hour rehearsals. That schedule would allow you to work on each number only once. The quantities of music and the constraints of time can be daunting. Rehearsals sometimes run overtime; four hours is about the most one can expect the musicians' concentration to last, and overtime for professional musicians costs extra, at a premium. Also factor in the time it takes to prepare each separate number for rehearsing. Does the reed player have the right instruments ready and tuned? Are the keyboard patches in the correct order? Do the strings agree on the bowings?

FIGURE 16.1 Music director Charlie Alterman enjoying orchestra rehearsal for the 2013 revival of *Pippin* on Broadway. (*Credit:* Photo by Steve Singer.)

Again, smart planning can save time. Group into the same rehearsal session similar pieces with similar instrumentation. Prioritize: schedule more time for the long, complex selections, and leave the simpler ones, such as transitions, for last. If the score needs the musicians to realize it (e.g., when working from lead sheets), schedule time for that as well; improvisation takes time to coordinate. At first, do only basic readings, and later, if time permits, go back and refine what you might have only superficially covered. Use sectionals wisely, and hold off the participation of secondary or auxiliary sections; don't waste their time or the production's money by having them sit and wait while others work. You will have some time during dress rehearsals and the *Sitzprobe* (see the next section, "The Orchestra: Sections and Setup") to do additional orchestral refinements, but by then your attention will be on many things, not just the instrumental performance. Figure 16.1 shows a music director at work in orchestra rehearsal.

The Orchestra: Sections and Setup

The positioning of an orchestra in rehearsal should reflect the way its members will later see the conductor and hear one another in performance. The configuration is especially important if the instrumentalists will be playing with little or no amplification. On the other hand, if in the pit they will be monitoring through headphones and adjusting their own mixes, it matters less where they sit in rehearsal. However, they do need to see you.

Video monitoring is not essential in rehearsal, even if it will be used in performance, but musicians should always have a clear view of the conductor.

The following is a description of different sections of the orchestra, with suggestions for their setups in rehearsal and performance.[1]

Rhythm Sections: Keyboards, Drums, Bass, and Guitar

Stage accompaniment is very often piano-centric. The piano is a great generalizer: it can carry the load of several instruments. It can play rhythmically and expressively, simply or virtuosically, and is an ideal rehearsal tool. Its revered traditions in art song as the singer's companion have persisted to the present, and many a stage performance is accompanied by piano alone, or with the piano as the primary instrument. Nightclubs, workshops, amateur and stock shows, and children's shows all typically perform with a solo piano or a small ensemble based around a piano, and there is a pianist at work in virtually every coaching session and ensemble vocal rehearsal.

The piano has evolved electronically, and now a myriad of piano sounds are available sampled and synthesized, either built into a keyboard or by connection to a keyboard controller. Many electronic keyboards have eighty-eight weighted keys, making them somewhat piano-like to play (without all the expressive capabilities of a real piano, of course), and they are certainly less expensive to own and maintain. Many venues that used to own pianos now have a keyboard instead. A real piano is far preferable for performance, especially on its own; a piano patch coming through an amplifier can never have the presence of the real thing. When only an electronic instrument is available, do not settle for anything less than an eighty-eight key weighted keyboard, and try to put the instrument through a house sound system and not a freestanding amplifier. Make sure any electronic keyboard is working properly before you start a gig, because you never know what condition the last player left it in, or if he or she rewrote the patch list. Also inspect any real piano to be used in a production; pianos vary widely in sound quality, playability, and wear and tear. For performance, they should be tuned daily or several times a week.

Keyboards can form an orchestral section of their own, especially in modern orchestrations using more than one. Keyboards in stage accompaniments are used in four main ways: as rhythm section instruments (pianos, electric pianos, and plectral keyboards such as clavichords and harpsichords and clavinets), as color instruments (organ, celeste, or classic synthesizer sounds such as Moogs, Mellotrons, and synth brass), as emulators of non-keyboard instruments, and as generators of sound effects and loops. Many orchestrations with multiple keyboard parts distribute the workload along these lines. An electronic keyboard part can take time to decipher and perfect. Before and during rehearsal, you, the programmer, and the keyboardists map the

---

1. There is a comprehensive guide to traditional orchestra setups at http://andrewhugill.com/manuals/seating.html.

FIGURE 16.2 Synthesizer programmer Randy Cohen at work on Broadway's *If/Then*. (*Credit:* Photo by Taylor Williams)

sounds (put them in performance order), tweak them, and learn to play them idiomatically (Figure 16.2).

Position rhythm section keyboard players or acoustic pianos near the podium (or the equivalent, which may itself be a keyboard), along with the rest of the rhythm section. A keyboard player or pianist directly under the podium is common, but there it takes up the space where an acoustic instrument (violin, most likely) might be most easily audible. Nevertheless, keeping the core of the rhythm section together and near the conductor is sensible even when the sound is not live; the physical proximity helps the players play more tightly. You might also want to position coloristic keyboard instruments near the rhythm section, as their functions may well overlap or coincide, but their positioning is less crucial. Even less so is where to place auxiliary, emulating keyboards, and to save space you can tuck them into a low-ceilinged corner of a pit. Their output will usually go directly into the sound board and mix with the real instruments, if any. If the keyboard part is augmenting a certain section, you might seat the player near that section, but in my experience, the real players do not pay much attention to their electronic "support," live or on an audio monitor. An electronic keyboard rig at its most basic, a keyboard on a stand with a music stand and a bench, does not take up much space. Any additional equipment, however, and there usually is more, will increase the footprint considerably, and a minimum six-foot square is a safer bet. A piano needs room for . . . well, a piano. Figure 16.3 lists the space needs of orchestral instruments.

Instrument/Setup	Equipment	Space
Minimal keyboard rig	Keyboard (on stand), music stand, bench	> 5' × 4'
Larger keyboard rig	Keyboard (on stand), music stand, bench, amplifier, monitor mixer, etc.	> 6' × 5'
Piano (upright)	Piano, bench	6' × 4.5'
Piano (baby grand)	Piano, bench	6' × 6'
Piano (grand)	Piano, bench	Varies, > 6' × 7'
Accordion	Accordion, chair, music stand, stand mic (optional)	4' × 3'
Small drum kit	Kick, snare, 1-3 tom-toms, hi-hat, ride and crash cymbals, stool, music stand(s)	5' circle
Large drum kit	Above kit plus extras	> 6' circle, expanding elliptically
Percussion	Varies	Varies
Bass (upright)	Bass, music stand, stool (optional), stand mic (optional)	4' circle
Bass (electric)	Bass, music stand, amplifier, chair or stool	4' × 3' minimum
Bass (both)	Upright and electric basses, music stand, amplifier, chair or stool	6' × 4' minimum (with space for upright and stand for electric when not being played)
Guitar (any)	Guitar, music stand, amplifier, chair or stool, stand mic (optional)	4' × 3' minimum
Guitars (multiple)	Same, plus guitar stands and multiple amplifiers (optional)	> 6' × 5'
Woodwinds (except saxes) and Trumpets, solo	Instrument, chair, music stand, stand mic (optional)	> 3' circle, plus space for mutes and accessories
Trombone, Bass Trombone, Tuba solo	Instrument, chair, music stand, stand mic (optional)	5' × 3' (room in front for slide on trombone), plus space for mutes and accessories
Woodwinds and Brass, multiple	Instruments, chair, music stand, stand mic(s) (optional), instrument stands	Varies, > 5' × 4'
Violin, Viola, solo	Instrument, chair, music stand	4' × 3'
Cello, solo	Instrument, chair, music stand, stand mic (optional)	5' × 3' (room in front)
Violin, Viola, stand of 2	Instruments, chair, one music stand	6' × 3' (two across)
Cello, stand of 2	Instruments, chair, one music stand	6' × 5' (two across)
Harp	Instrument, chair, music stand, stand mic (optional)	5' × 3' (room in front)

FIGURE 16.3 Chart of space requirements for orchestral instruments.

Also worth mentioning, as it appears in several well-known stage scores, is the accordion. Several music directors I know play the accordion, and the skill has made them more employable. The instrument has a beautiful, evocative tone, and the most expert players generate sounds that are soothing, thrilling, or magical. It can also be quite a loud instrument, and is usually amplified just with a microphone in front of the instrument, if at all. As often as not in modern performance, keyboards emulate accordion sounds, but in doing so relinquish many of the accordion's idiomatic possibilities.

Drummers are usually the loudest players in the orchestra, they occupy the most space, and their role in the accompaniment is central, so their position is crucial to your floor plan. When a score is rhythmic and the drum set drives the beat, I prefer to place the drummer directly in front of me, for ease of communication between the orchestra's two primary timekeepers. Ideally I also like to be able to orally communicate with drummers, for emergency purposes and to make real-time adjustments. But many drummers are now encased in plexiglass, for several reasons: to isolate their sound, as protection for the rest of the orchestra, as a volume limiter for the audience, and so that the drum kit can be mixed at the board, as in a recording studio. I prefer a booth with an open front or, at very least, a microphone feed to the drummer. I do not believe that full isolation of any instrument is necessary or desirable for a live sound design, but my stance is obviously overruled by most new Broadway productions. There are many reasonable and viable approaches to controlling drum volume. Partial isolation and acoustic treatment are very helpful, by the same rationales that designers use for complete isolation.

Some stage drum kits are very elaborate, with all sorts of specialty drums, percussion, and electronic pads. Ethnic or obscure instruments can be unusually shaped and need to be mounted or placed in an unusual way, which can eat up pit space. More traditional or less rhythmically driven shows might have only a small drum kit: kick (bass) drum, snare, hi-hat, one or two tom-toms, a ride cymbal, and maybe a crash or splash cymbal. A smaller kit like this, played at reasonable volumes, may not need acoustic baffling, but larger kits usually will.

Also part of the rhythm section are other percussionists, though their roles may not always be rhythmic. These players include tympanists and mallet players (xylophone, orchestra bells or glockenspiel, marimba, vibraphone), who will also very likely play a great variety of hand and auxiliary percussion, both colorful and rhythmic. Their setups require substantial space as well, especially for tympani and mallets. Most of these instruments played alone are not as loud as a full drum kit, and so do not need muffling (xylophones and glockenspiels cut through everything, but usually on purpose). Often these players are placed far away from the conductor, as in a symphony, at the back or off to the side. Percussionists are accustomed to economizing their space. They use it wisely and creatively, for instance, by stacking instruments, rigging them to the wall or suspending them from the ceiling, and building shelves and cubbies for sticks and mallets. In an orchestra with a large drum set and an extensive percussion battery, the drums and percussion may occupy a majority of the floor space in the pit or playing area.

One cannot undervalue a drummer's part in the success of a musical accompaniment. The best drummers understand this point, and the importance of their connection to the conductor, who they know connects the orchestra to the stage. They listen more closely to, know more about, and care more about what is going on around them than many other orchestral players. Many drummers have become fine conductors and music directors; perhaps the most notable is Paul Gemignani. A player with great time (metronomic accuracy), sensitivity to what others are playing, and the ability to capture a feel or groove whether soft or strong will bring levels of rhythmic interest and energy to a show that reach beyond the sound, into the movement and the spirit. A drummer with poor time and insensitivity to his or her surroundings and colleagues and who can groove only when pounding can lay waste to a score.

The drummer playing in your pit is often part of cast rehearsals as well, again especially when a production in very rhythmic. The drummers in your pit bands deepen their relationships with the creative team, the music, and, of course, the cast. For this reason a choreographer or director might ask that you contract a certain drummer for a show. Unless you have a strong musical reason to object, respect the request.

Almost as influential and just as circumspect are bassists. Most good bassists are superb, sensitive musicians. They hold down the bottom of the harmony and drive the rhythmic pulse, and because of this principal responsibility, they, too, often work as music directors. The bass provides a fundamental pitch that, lying octaves below other instruments, brings out the harmonics of all sonic events above it. The difference in quality between any ensemble with and without a bass is unmistakable; still, eliminating the bass is among producers' favorite cost-cutting suggestions.

Very rarely does a pit have more than one bassist, but many orchestrations have both electric and acoustic, or upright, basses, in one part. Some parts call for more than one electric bass, perhaps a fretless as well as the main instrument. Switching among basses is not simple, and you should account for this requirement in the setup (and orchestration), allotting space for each instrument. Five-string electrics are now the standard; though not all orchestrators write for them, most bassists love the low B string and use the instrument anyway. The low C extension on a double bass is not commonly written for in show orchestrations, and *arco* (bowed) passages are sometimes limited, with the orchestrator's (often faulty) assumption that a great groove bass player may not be as skilled with a bow. Bassists usually read and improvise both very well; many are stylistically well rounded, are equally schooled in popular and classical music, and love to play jazz and rock and other genres as well.

Position the bassist near the drummer, and again their nearness is more consequential when the music is rhythmic. The bassist coordinates constantly with the drummer. In a straight- ahead rock song, for example, the bassist will be locking in with the kick drum, and vice versa. A jazz bassist walking a line on the upright will be listening to the four-beat on the ride cymbal, and the drummer will be grooving to the bassist's constant quarter-note pulse. If the two players can have visual and verbal contact as well as auditory proximity, all the better. Consider carefully how you amplify a bass. Bass sounds that are too diffuse in a live setting do not function as they should acoustically, because their waves are too scattered, and bass sounds that are too small and compressed do not blend well in timbre with live instruments. A mix of direct and live feeds is often best, though the standard on Broadway is to take electric basses direct only. (Obviously acoustic basses always produce some live sound.)

The rhythm section is rounded out by guitar. Guitars, like pianos and keyboards, are good generalists and can cover a great deal of registral and textural ground, as well as sounding quite full by themselves. They are, unlike keyboards, flexible only on their own terms: chords can be voiced only in certain ways, and the timbre is always guitar-like, though different types of guitars, amplification, and effects pedals offer a seemingly endless spectrum of sonic possibilities. Guitarists, too, are versatile musicians, and often work as music directors, especially if a score is guitar based.

Guitars in traditional musicals and in early song standards were often relegated to playing light rhythms that filled out the harmony under a melody. They might occasionally have played a simple line or fill, but mostly just stuck to the offbeats. As Les Paul and others pioneered the electric guitar and its range of sounds after World War II, the guitar began to move forward in the orchestral texture. And when rock, folk, and pop invaded the stage, the maturation of the guitar into a central and versatile feature of the soundscape was complete. Far more frequently, shows had two guitarists instead of one, mimicking rock bands, with one player usually the lead and the other the rhythm guitarist, or with one mostly on electric and the other on acoustic. Acoustic guitars are usually strummed or picked, with a pick or with fingers, for rhythmic underpinning, while electric guitars tend toward hits, stabs, long chords, strummed chords, chorused chords, power chords, lead lines, volume swells, feedback, scrapes, and other effects, with endless possibilities.

Guitarists, like drummers, especially those without classical training, may not always read as fast or as fluently as you might like. Most guitarists like to spend time with their parts before rehearsals begin. Like some drummers, there are some non-reading guitarists who are so dexterous that once they do learn a part that it will have been well worth your effort to bring them up to speed.

Depending on the music, one or two electric guitars, one steel acoustic, and one nylon acoustic comprise a typical modern pit guitar setup for a single player. He or she might double on mandolin, banjo, or twelve-string or steel guitar, among others, and once in a great while on pedal steel (*9 to 5*, the musical), for country or tropical music. The guitarist in *The Lion King* doubles on *m'bira* (better known by its brand name, Kalimba, or generically as a thumb piano); the *In the Heights* guitarist also played *tres* (a Cuban guitar-like instrument with three pairs of strings). Many guitarists are undisguised "gear heads" who collect and want to include in their setups all sorts of vintage and customized equipment, each for its unique properties. The resulting details of sound may not be evident to most listeners, and therefore not necessary for the production. If you have the space, and switching from one instrument to another is uncomplicated, that's fine, but the player's desire to house a museum's worth of guitars should not impair the rehearsal or performance process in any way, nor should it entail unnecessary cost.

The sound of guitars is transmitted from pit or stage to audience in various ways. Electric guitars are often taken both directly and from a mic placed in front of its amplifier. Different pickups on the electric guitar, as well as different guitars, make very different sounds, and the guitarist usually knows best which one to play on and how best to amplify it. Acoustic guitars might also have pickups, built in or external, or have a mic placed close to the guitar's opening, closer to the fretboard.

Together these multi-skilled instrumentalists make up the rhythm section, the nucleus of many stage orchestras, and they are the musicians most in demand as professionals. As a music director you will very likely form affinities and preferences for certain rhythm section players. The reliability and artistry they bring to a production will make your daily rehearsal and performance life immeasurably better. Once rehearsed, they can be nearly autonomous, shortening your agenda and guaranteeing that one main element of the music is always well executed. Rhythm sections contribute creatively by adding thoughtful detail, and sometimes participate in creating the score. They also adjust quickly when things veer from plan: if something goes awry on stage, a good rhythm section will adjust within moments.

Woodwinds and Brass

Brass sections in pit orchestras are usually smallish contingents of trumpets and trombones, with the occasional French horn, tuba, euphonium, cornet, piccolo trumpet, or other specialty horns. Saxophones, clarinets, and flutes are the main wind instruments, with bassoons and oboes making occasional appearances in shows with classically styled music, or in classic shows with their original instrumentation or a faithful re-orchestration. Reed players who double on several instruments now bother far less frequently to learn double reeds. (These instruments often appear on synthesizer patch lists: oboe, English horn, and bassoon are highly expressive solo instruments and are the darlings of orchestrators; all take well to digital sampling.)

Large theater orchestrations, by convention, divide woodwind or "reed" parts by register, on the assumption that players will specialize on either high or low instruments. In a four-reed section, Reed 1 might play flute, piccolo, clarinet, and soprano and alto saxes, while on the other end Reed 4 plays tenor and baritone sax, clarinet and bass clarinet, and bassoon. Players have adapted to the practice, and orchestrators avail themselves of the players' multi-instrumental abilities. (*The Book of Mormon*'s lone reed book has six doubles recognized by the union—in fact there are ten total instruments played—including exotic flute and oboe.) In keeping with modern trends, reed sections are now often downsized, and rare now are the four or five reed parts of the classical musical theater orchestrations or classic pop arrangements. The particular reed combination is dictated by the musical style and sound, as well as the budget.

Brass sections have been shrinking, too, the quintets or larger groups of earlier orchestrations dwindling to one or two of each instrument. French horns are used mostly for their solo timbre, but occasionally there will be a horn section, as in *The Lion King*. Brass players are less likely than reed players to double on other instruments, and when they do, it is usually on instruments in the same family: trumpeters on cornet or flugelhorn, trombonists on the other low brass like euphonium or baritone horn, for example.

Brass players sound best in groups of three, the three instruments able to outline a triad or the essential factors of a jazz chord (the third, seventh, ninth, or beyond) in a close voicing, in which they also sound best. Trumpets form these chords in a treble range, and trombones in a tenor; sometimes when playing together their voicings are duplicated in their respective registers, while other times the voicing spans the whole of the brass section, and can include the reeds as well. Brass often played with mutes on to lower their amplitude and for expressive effect/ Orchestrators understandably love the possibilities of plungers (wah-wahs) and Harmon mutes (with very small openings for a reedy timbre), among others, for their unusual and versatile emotional and stylistic effects. Brass and winds play solos, trombones with sustained tenor lines against a melody, a soulful sax *obbligato*, or a high flute or trumpet descant, a tender clarinet solo, but more often they play together. In ensemble, they execute rhythmic hits and stabs and short licks, and in between melodic phrases might play imitative echoes or independent fills. When the singer is singing, brass and winds keep mostly quiet, except perhaps with sustained chords in a modest register. Brass and winds also take the melodic lead in many dance arrangements, notably in the bold, jazzy ones from the "Golden Age" musicals.

Brass and woodwind sections have, as do most sections, a communal sense of pride in their quality and dependability. Clams (mistakes occurring at the embouchure, where the player's lips meet with and blow into the mouthpiece) are unavoidable, especially on brass instruments, but good players still punish themselves for them (and one another, in fun), as they do for poor intonation, shoddy ensemble playing, or lackluster articulation. They are self-policing, and do not need to be told when they make mistakes. Most brass and wind players sightread brilliantly, and need very little rehearsal. They may not be as cognizant of the entirely of a production as a rhythm section player, but they will be aware of the entirety of the orchestral sound, and their sound relative to others.

The traditional symphonic positioning of winds and brass endures in most pit orchestras, with each section grouped together and the two near each other, toward the back or side. The blaring volume of brass, saxes, and flute and piccolo can be problematic, and sometimes sections are isolated or partially isolated, individually or together, with physical barriers, or placed in a separate room (I recommend against this; see the next section, "Strings"). Microphones for both brass and woodwinds, used as much for balance as for reinforcement, sit a few inches past the opening of the bell, and overhead mics are used as well, for amplifying whole sections.

Strings

It is almost impossible to write about strings in stage music without waxing nostalgic. On Broadway, large string sections are now rare, and smaller production outfits often seem content with strings in a box, that is, played by a keyboardist. The disappearance is in part musically explicable. In Classical and Romantic orchestral music, and in classic or classical stage musicals, strings carry more of the melodic load. Strings in modern stage arrangements play mostly countermelodies, rhythm patterns, and sustained padding. Violins play high sustained string tones in ballads (often with synthesizer support to center the pitch), while cellos play "thumb lines" (mid-register, long-note internal countermelodies that can be played in a piano arrangement with the thumb of either hand). When playing together, strings provide warm triads and extensions thereof, sounding lovely in either wide or close voicings. They execute effects such as fast runs, tremolos, harmonics, and *glissandi*, and add lovely and sometimes daring countermelodies that enhance the simple figures of the singers' tunes. Except for a solo violin, viola, or cello playing expressively, most of these musical functions can be somewhat convincingly imitated by a synthesizer, especially through a sound system.

It does not take a host of string players to get a full string sound, but a few do not a section make. The violin's harmonically rich tone and its deep vibrato blends well only when there are three or more. Two cellos or two violists, on the other hand, can sound like a small section, because of their lower range. Symptoms of string blight are evident in the gradual displacement from stage orchestrations of second violins and violas and multiple cellos. Most now omit violas completely, except as a violin double. It is hard musically to justify excluding the altos from the chorus, but it is understandable to want to make the most out of the forces you have, and violas can be, sad to say, an extravagance. The standard, pre-reduction Broadway orchestra had a typical string complement no fewer than four first violins, three second violins, two violas, and two cellos, or three firsts, two seconds, two violas, and two cellos. But now those numbers are down to between one and four violinists, one perhaps doubling on viola, and one or maybe two cellists.

Often a synthesizer augments whatever live string players there are. The Broadway production of *Sister Act* that I worked on had a moderately large orchestra (nineteen), playing disco music (whose characteristic "Philly" and Hollywood sounds call for busy strings in ample sections) and Rodgers and Hammerstein–like songs and comedic chases (also typically string laden). The show played in a large theater, and had only four (strong and brilliant) violinists and one (strong and brilliant) cellist. This quintet, supported by a well-programmed keyboard kept low in the mix, did manage to approximate the sound of a large section at its source, yet despite an excellent sound design, from the house there was still emptiness to the string timbre. If music directors accept reduction as a reality of modern production, the *Sister Act* solution is possibly an acceptable one. At least in that configuration a large part of the string soundscape remained available and audible.

Strings sit together as a section, and two players on the same instrument usually share a music stand. When one pictures an orchestra, the strings are in front, surrounding the conductor. This is the symphonic blueprint because in classical music the strings so often play the melody, and they are not as loud, even in large numbers, as other sections. Thus in pit orchestras, too, the strings usually sit in front, near the conductor, near the center, near whatever opening in the pit there might be. Their sound is also usually enhanced, individually, with a pickup or close microphone on each instrument, and as a group, with overhead microphones. The violins sit closest to center because they usually play the predominant role in a string section; if a cello were to take this responsibility, the cellist should probably go to the front.

In some modern stage sound designs, violins (and sometimes brass and reeds) are isolated in the same way as a drummer, in a booth, behind some sort of acoustic treatment, or in a separate room. This is fine if no live sound is needed or desired, but a string section piped into a large theater from another location soundscape is hard to make sound as if it were on site, so their very inclusion in the production is put into question. I generally bristle at the notion of placing any orchestra member or section in an entirely different room, as it sets them apart not only physically but in their energy. It is difficult for a player in isolation to connect to the whole, and connection to a whole is the essence and the goal of stage music. Separating sections or individual players is a last resort, when no other space options are viable, and I resist the notion that isolation will improve the sonic output in a live setting. If combining live and amplified sound is problematic, so, obviously, is all live amplification.

Along with violas, another stringed instrument that is nearly extinct in pit orchestras, yet one that appears frequently in stage orchestrations, is the harp. The enchanting idiomatic capabilities of the harp have a natural stage presence. One might compare a swirling harp *glissando* to a stage curtain opening to reveal a magnificent setting. Synthesizer programmers, however, have sampled much of the standard harp vocabulary and made it playable with the mere touch of a key. A keyboardist can emulate the volumes, durations, and attacks of the harp strings, and not bother with pedal switches and other limitations of the real instrument, especially its size. Harps require maintenance and space and incur additional fees for cartage, so they are a prime target when downsizing.[2] The sound of a real harp, like that of real strings, can never be replaced; nonetheless,

---

2. The harp has lived on, thankfully, as a fixture of the longest-running musical in history, *The Fantasticks*, which, shortly after closing following a thirty-plus-year Off-Broadway run, was revived in midtown Manhattan. The orchestration of *The Fantasticks* is a duet of piano and harp.

it is being replaced. Most harpists have pickups for their instruments that feed directly into the sound board for amplification, or a mic can be placed near the strings.

Some orchestras feature exotic or unorthodox or specialty instruments, but the exotica are also increasingly synthesized, for ease of use and maintenance. Orchestras may have unusual setups, which can also be visual elements. The box percussionists in *The Lion King* and the organic folk ensembles of *Once* are two examples from modern mainstream musicals, as would be, of course, an onstage orchestra.

Orchestration: Notation and Parts

The collected parts for each instrument of all the musical numbers in a production are called a "book."[3] Occasionally musicians will play by ear or work from a score, but most orchestra rehearsals begin with books on the stands. In any production, clearly notated and reproduced parts will expedite the rehearsal process, and later the performance. As music director of a new show or a show with a new orchestration, you will have the responsibility of ensuring that all music is written, copied, and printed clearly and usefully for the orchestra.

Limit the changes you make to an existing orchestration during rehearsals. If you are rewriting, or recopying, fix the parts in advance. Dictating changes orally to musicians is a lengthy effort that consumes too great a portion of rehearsal time. When making new parts, take into account the players who will be playing, but most conventions of music preparation already exist for ease of reading. As music director you should understand these conventions. Let's examine orchestration and orchestra parts by revisiting the sections of the orchestra.

Rhythm keyboard parts, unless they are simple charts, can be lengthy, with a grand staff throughout. Many consist of some combination of written notes and rhythmic notation with chord symbols that leave some specifics, such as voicings, up to the player. Keyboard parts for orchestral keyboards, legitimate music, and synthesizers will be more specific. Organ parts might include drawbar settings that refer to standard electric organ registration, such as those on the Hammond line of organs (these settings are in turn derivative of church organ stops). Accordion and harp parts for stage productions will be laid out the same way, on a grand staff, each with its notational idiosyncrasies: the accordion's combined chords, lines, and registration settings, and the harp's pedal configurations and changes.

---

3. Historically, orchestra books have been printed on nine-inch by twelve-inch paper, usually a thicker, woven stock, such as vellum, their color slightly off-white, a creamy eggshell that is easy on the eyes in the dark under a music stand light. With computer copying now so widespread, those standards have lowered, and now parts often appear on everyday, white, home-printed, letter-sized paper that tends to fall off the stand or blow away in the breeze, and glare under a stand light. Still, the convenience compensates for some of the loss of quality. A major disadvantage of vellum and similarly woven papers is that they eventually disintegrate. At long-running shows on Broadway the original parts shred at the corners and eventually turn to lint.

Copyists lay out keyboard parts to avoid awkward page turns, as they do with all parts. In parts for synthesizers that play many different sounds, they leave ample free space for labeling, understanding that players might put in notations or stickers or otherwise highlight their parts to vividly indicate patch changes and volume settings. (Patch-change mistakes are keyboard players' nemeses: nothing is more embarrassing, than, for instance, a quiet solo mistakenly played on a blaring sound.) A synthesizer part should include a patch list in a key, or lexicon, at the upper left of the first page of each number (Figure 16.4). The player needs to know what sounds are about to be played in order to ready for them mentally and physically, and should be able to think of them in groups, the player's "orchestra" for a musical number. In rehearsal he or she should be able to move freely among patches, regardless of if they are mapped in their eventual order. Figures 9.2 and 9.3, from "The Music: Assessment and Analysis," are typical of stage rhythm parts, in that they combine specific notes with suggestions, and are clear in indicating both. As with keyboards, more legitimate styles will have more specific notes written out for both bass and drums, and more modern and pop-oriented scores will have more slashes, rhythms, and chords (drum kit parts do not need chords or key signatures, but they might be included anyway, or there might be a note saying, "Key change!"). Repeat symbols are used in safeties and vamps (see the next chapter, "Instrumental Conducting for the Stage"), but otherwise, repeat signs and *da capo*'s and *dal segno*'s (instructions to play from the top or from a section marked with a sign) are off limits in orchestra books for musicals. Players need to be able to read from beginning to end, because things on a dramatic stage seldom repeat exactly. Concerts, special events, and nightclub shows might have only lead sheets or sketches for the rhythm section, and these parts do use structural shorthands, but other instruments (brass, winds, strings) require specific parts (though they, too, may sometimes include shorthands). Again, readability is paramount, because rehearsal time is short. Percussion parts, like synthesizer parts, should include a listing of instruments, and perhaps a guide to interpreting the notation, such as a diagram of where the different drum set components are notated on the staff.

Guitar parts are mostly on one staff, but sometimes spill over into two, and good copying again leaves room for pencil markings. Instrument choices or modifications (which can be specific, such as "Taylor steel" or "Strat w/50% distort ped.") and amplifier and volume settings (also specific, such as "Fender Twin on overdrive" or "open back 40-watt w/chorus") may appear in a part, and the player might specify them further. Guitarists will also add notations such as amplifier, pedal, and volume settings. Chord symbols routinely replace written notes in guitar parts, often with verbal notations such as "power chords" or "flat picked in eighth notes." There might be a skeleton of a chord voicing or arpeggiation pattern, or one note head indicating the desired top note of a chord with a stem extending past it.

Sometimes music directors and orchestrators work with drummers and guitarists (and bassists and keyboardists at times, too) to create their orchestra books. The

FIGURE 16.4 A well-detailed synthesizer part

highly idiomatic, variable, and personal nature of these instruments makes the players' assistance invaluable, and in truth many arrangers do not know how best to write for these instruments (though they may not admit it—and there are, of course, some music directors and arrangers who play these instruments and/or arrange for them fluently). A drummer or guitarist will know, for example, when to be specific in notation and when shortcuts are acceptable, and can best communicate to others in writing how to play a part. Music directors, arrangers, and producers have not always properly acknowledged, with credit or payment, the contribution of these players to an orchestration and a score, but they should, without fail.

Reed books combine all the instruments each player plays into one book. Instrument switches and key signatures resulting from different transpositions must be indicated with unfailing clarity. Like a synthesist, a reed player doesn't want to be on the wrong instrument or in the wrong key. Brass parts and string books for stage shows look like traditional orchestra parts. If there are multiple trumpets, or trombones, their parts might be combined into one book, usually on two staves but occasionally condensed into one. Only *divisi* string parts share a single staff; that is, violins 1 and 2 (when there are separate violin parts) should each have their own.

Page turns in orchestral parts for stage shows are crucial: unlike in a symphony orchestra, almost all players have stand partners who can turn the page while the other player plays on. Therefore, page turns should best occur at a reasonably large rest, and when a player has no rest, the part should be printed so that it can be opened out on the stand. If the part is too long, it can be divided into shorter sections that can be pulled aside. There is a foolproof method of taping pages of music together in accordion fashion (not the instrument, the shape) that keeps individual pages taped together from falling off a music stand, even a flimsy one or one on a rickety piano shelf.[4] Musicians are primed to enter a new era of reading music in live settings: already an iPad can turn warmly backlit pages of music with the tap of a finger or the click of a footswitch. It seems only a matter of time before the industry goes completely paperless.

The nonmusical information contained in orchestra books for shows is almost as important as the notes and musical markings. At the top of each piece of music there is a score number, by which the piece is referred to as often as by its title, as "big number X."[5] This is a convenience for reordering songs during production, and for creating a hierarchy of musical numbers: full musical numbers get numbers; transitions and interstitial material will have a number appended with a letter. For instance, the playout of big number 14 would be numbered 14A; a transition that follows will be 14B. In rehearsal: "Let's start at the last bar of 14A and play through 14B into the intro of 15, and I'll stop you."

Inside each big number there should be measure numbers and rehearsal letters. Having both is extremely convenient (not all scores have both). Rehearsal letters are attached to structural junctures in the music for easy reference, for starting points, and for outlining rehearsal segments ("Let's work from Rehearsal A through C"), with measure numbers in between. Inserts and changes to show scores can make for some unusual measure numbering and rehearsal lettering; I have seen long inserts all marked within one measure number (The title song of *In the Heights* has mm. 271a–z, then 271aa–zz, 271aaa–zzz, and so on) or subscripts to rehearsal letters (A_1, A_2, etc.). These ordinals can be confusing, but may be unavoidable when changes are extensive. Dividing the score into chunks makes cuts and additions easier in rehearsal.

---

[4] An excellent description of this technique appears in Donald Oliver, *How to Audition for the Musical Theatre*, Lyme, NH: Smith and Kraus, 1995, pp. 64–65.

[5] The term "number," as it refers to a stage act, derives from the numbering of scenes in vaudeville shows.

FIGURE 16.5 Musical supervisor–orchestrator Stephen Brooker and orchestrator Stephen Metcalfe examine the score at orchestra rehearsal for the revised *Les Misérables* (2014). (*Credit:* Photo by Steve Singer.)

Beyond standardized markings, stage productions will have in their orchestra books indications of other matters affecting musical performance. "Safeties" and "vamps" (see next chapter), fermatas long and short, and caesuras (or "railroad tracks," indicating a momentary interruption of the music by silence), sometimes with fermatas over them, are ubiquitous in stage music. Double bar lines delineate the boundaries of larger sections, and they, too, can have fermatas. Lines of dialogue or stage actions often appear in orchestra parts as cues to begin, continue, or stop, though of course the music director will still be doing the cueing, and everything is subject to change.

Conscientiously organizing and understanding the musicians and the music, and setting up rehearsal space with forethought to its functionality, will get orchestra rehearsals off on the right foot. Your knowledge of the orchestration and its notation and your comprehension and mastery of the score will be your resources in efficiently and sensitively solving the issues that emerge in rehearsal. You will be able to address issues and answer questions on both the player's terms and your own. The musicians will trust you equally for your comprehension of the material and for your skills as an overseer, and trust that their contributions are being given their full due, alone and as part of the whole (Figure 16.5).

17

Instrumental Conducting for the Stage

Conducting is the act, sometimes the art, of conveying to a group of musicians the realization of a piece of music, through physical gestures, knowledge, and attitude. This terse definition suggests the different qualities a conductor possesses: good communication skills, mastery of conducting techniques, clarity of motion, absolute comprehension of a musical score, and performing experience. At least historically, compelling orchestral leadership and conducting abilities have carried more weight and are more exalted than choral direction, or at least symphonic conductors have achieved eminence far more often than choral conductors.

For a stage music director to aspire to the conducting styles of the great symphonic *maestri* is admirable, but unnecessary. Conducting for the stage is mostly utilitarian and rarely ostentatious; its audible outcome supersedes any visually manifest expressiveness. (As usual, there are exceptions: when I conducted Radio City's Christmas Show, the producers prompted me to be a little flashy.) Aspiring to and pursuing the musical abilities and conducting technique of a great symphonic conductor is another matter. The great variety of music alone that music directors handle calls for musicianship of the highest order. Stage music may not be as challenging as some "serious" music (some is), but as experienced musicians know, simple music can be just as hard to play well. In simpler music, flaws are easier to detect, and there is beauty in simplicity that can be brought out only with very deft and tasteful handling.

Good conducting for a stage production is manifest in both rehearsal and performance. In rehearsal a music director evaluates and practices a score with a group, refining its many musical and nonmusical elements. In performance he or she reminds the players and singers of the values learned in rehearsal, while coordinating the various performing and technical elements of the production.

If I may be permitted to express here what other conducting texts might not: conducting is fun. Lots of fun. Ever since I first tried it, it's been one of my favorite things to do. There is nothing quite like raising the baton, bringing it down, and hearing an orchestra respond with . . . music! Richly textured, orchestral music. It's a similar thrill playing with a smaller band, counting off, and letting it rip. Whereas working with singers and the creative staff may occupy the majority of a music director's time on a production, my interviews with music directors showed near unanimity in their preference for rehearsing the instrumentalists, and I concur. Whether conducting or playing or both, the exhilaration of making music with other players is without compare. (Is it not every aspiring music director's secret fantasy to conduct a rousing symphony or rock out with a band?)

Conducting, as a purely physical activity of moving one's arms in a given pattern, is not terribly difficult, the evidence being the profusion of technically clumsy conductors steadily employed, the deserving butts of conductor jokes and objects of the disdain of orchestra musicians. Conducting, that is, the gestural aspect of it, is a bit like dancing, in that some people simply look awkward doing it and others don't. A conductor's time and musicality can be impeccable, yet somehow these abilities do not always translate into fluid physical motions. Music may sound and operate better when the conductor is technically clear and even better if he or she is graceful, but some productions manage just fine with a less facile or agile conductor, as long as his or her knowledge of the score and rehearsal skills is strong, and there are good musicians playing and good singers singing. Even some greatly revered symphonic conductors never look entirely comfortable on the podium.

To be a good conductor on every level, on the other hand, is very hard indeed, because of the requisite combination of intellectual depth, physical grace, communication skills, and personality. It's a short list of people who excel in all areas. In my youth I idolized Georg Solti, Herbert von Karajan, Seiji Ozawa, André Previn, and of course Leonard Bernstein, for their mind-boggling musical command and overpowering charisma. In their movements were embodied every nuance of the music, a seemingly preternatural facility sprung from passion and talent, ripened and perfected through decades of hard work and experience. The argument for good technique is that the goal of all conductors is to channel the music freely through their bodies. The music itself, not their (or anyone's) technique, is the entire focus when performing. To accomplish this, they must have a technique of such a high order that it disappears into the music.

My many fine conducting mentors all emphasized the same two essential guidelines for good conducting, both very apt for music directors: *clarity* and *purpose*, with efficient gestures. An accompaniment exists to support and enhance, and must do so with unerring accuracy and consistency. Superfluous conducting gestures are just that; they serve no purpose when conducting as an accompanist to a larger entertainment. These precepts are further supported when music directors are also playing, and by necessity conducting with limited use of their hands. Conducting as a music director means giving only what is needed, to the performers and to the music. For stage conductors the interest lies in attaining precision and capturing the character of the music. In truth, there are many instances when they need not conduct at all, if they can achieve their goal without it. In saying this I do not mean to condone the deadpan, detached, purely metronomic approach taken by many stage conductors. They certainly are inconspicuous, a desirable trait, but their lack of expression severely shortchanges the music.

I leave the reader's education in the standardized gestures and beat patterns of conductors to great conducting tracts such as those offered by Max Rudolf, Elizabeth Green, and Rudolf von Laban, among others.[1] Theirs are the preeminent guidelines for conducting technique, and the physical language they teach is universally understandable to ensemble musicians. The focus here is how to apply those techniques to the stage.

Rehearsal Process

Unlike in ensemble vocal rehearsals, in orchestra or band rehearsals you won't usually need to devise strategies to maximize absorption of information. Instrumentalists do not have to be taught music, unless the players are very unskilled or inexperienced, as in some community or academic productions. They are far more likely than stage performers to be self-sufficient and self-correcting in learning and in retaining what they have learned. Most professional musicians prefer the forced efficiency of abbreviated orchestra rehearsal periods. Pit players may not be as invested in the totality of a production as you and your creative teammates are. Most have other gigs and, as mentioned, are late invitees to the process. Once they arrive, however, and whenever they are there, you can count on their absolute focus on and enthusiasm for the task at hand, and in the unlikely event that it is absent, you can demand it.

Unifying the sound—getting the instrumentalists to play together tightly as a sonic unit—is the challenge of most orchestral rehearsals. Music directors may appreciate the efficiency of working with instrumentalists as compared to singers, but it can be considerably more difficult to blend an orchestra, with its variegated timbres, than it is a chorus, and more difficult yet when players are of different skill levels or different stylistic leanings. Along with the very short rehearsal times customarily given orchestras, these conditions require that music directors be especially clear, efficient, and communicative in their conducting and rehearsal techniques.

Instrumentalists look to the music director–conductor for confident, uncomplicated leadership. Most can already play the notes and play them musically, and they listen to the others playing with them for good ensemble. They view the music director as their advisor, their adjudicator, their timekeeper, and their liaison with the stage. What constitutes confident, uncomplicated orchestra rehearsal leadership depends on

---

1. See the bibliography for references to these texts.

the group. With expert professionals, it might be as simple as getting everyone to sit down and turn to number "X," bringing the group to "attention" (a gesture indicating readiness for playing), starting and stopping the music, and offering useful and constructively phrased advice along the way, particularly when things go wrong. If you so desire, you can open up rehearsals to the full participation of the musicians, but in a larger group, you run the risk of slowing rehearsal down significantly. This approach works best with informal, smaller groups made up of people with whom you collaborate often, or when a score or orchestration is new, or when the band is playing head arrangements. Unless you specify otherwise, musicians will defer all leadership duties to you.

Acquaint yourself with the musicians you are working with and rehearse according to their tendencies. A student orchestra will obviously warrant a slower pace and more instruction, and you might even simplify your conducting style for even greater clarity. A professional group with whom you share mutual trust and respect will render your job largely custodial. Very importantly, if the musicians in an orchestra are more musically skilled or experienced than you, allow them a greater voice in shaping the music, so long as their suggestions do not interfere with the whole of the production or the rehearsal process. I have seen several rookie music directors suffer the scorn of their bands by feigning musical prowess only accessible to those who have paid the dues of many more years in the profession.

To begin a rehearsal, you might offer a few words of introduction. An overall direction and a sense of what is happening on stage will inform the playing, and give the orchestra a frame of reference, stylistic or otherwise, that is musically illuminating and saves time in the long run. "Welcome, ladies and gentlemen. This is a lost Gershwin song from 1927 in a bright march tempo. It's sung by the leading man with a full choral arrangement kicking in at letter C. Let's try to capture the energetically innocent spirit of the period as we read it down." "This song has a guitar-driven groove, so everyone please listen to the strumming on the acoustic as your guide." "The composer wrote this ballad as an ironic memorial to his beloved yet domineering mother. Let's be aware of the sentimentality, and the ambiguity of feeling." "Play all notes marked staccato extremely short, and all written accents very sharp, and dig into the dissonances; they express the character's anger." "Please interpret all note lengths with extreme precision. Cutoffs exactly as written. I've instructed the chorus to be precise, and so must we." "We all know this tune and have played it dozens of times, but let's try to bring some freshness to it. Feel free to improvise a *tiny* bit if the urge moves you." Your speech should include a synopsis of any story being told on stage, and the place a musical number has in the show. You can sing vocal melodies along with the orchestra as they rehearse (or invite singers to orchestra rehearsals). As you rehearse the accompaniment, consider how your conducting relates to the stage. Orchestra rehearsal is your chance to view the accompaniment in isolation, under a microscope, before your attention is drawn elsewhere.

How to begin a rehearsal is up to you. Stepping up to the podium and starting the music involve a combination of formality and pragmatism. Your leadership calls for confidence and command, but in truth you are just one of many fine musicians getting down to work. For a first reading, you can simply count in and go; conduct or count off a full bar or two in tempo (if there is a tempo). Later you can decide and communicate to the group how you will start the number in performance: with a single upbeat, with a longer count or preparation, using a click track count-in, or from a stage cue. Eventually you should have the musicians write into their music (if they have not already done so) the events or dialogue that cue each number, as well as a warning line or cue a few seconds earlier, and what the conductor's preparation at the start of the number will be.

From there, you can continue until the music breaks down or something goes wrong. An uninterrupted first reading helps everyone get his or her bearings, even if it is imperfect. Muddle through at least until a major section break, and then go back and work problem spots. With proficient musicians and a clean, well-notated orchestration, it is quite possible that you will get all the way through a number, and need give only slight corrections before any subsequent readings. By beginning rehearsals with simpler, more familiar sections of the show, and by identifying and prioritizing material that recurs in the score, you can help the orchestra can settle in and get comfortable playing as a group. As in chorus rehearsals, make sure that no group of musicians goes unattended for too long, lest they lose their concentration.

Like all performers, instrumentalists enjoy their work and approach it with professionalism, energy, and humor. Positive attitudes and mutual enjoyment undeniably enhance the quality of the output. As you would with any professional colleague, frame your criticism of an instrumentalist's playing constructively and in a way that does not call into question the player's ability (even if it is questionable). Most orchestra players have thicker skins than stage performers, yet they, too, take pride in their craft, and presumably work hard at it, and can be wounded by a pointed phrase, unintentional though it might be. Some measure of directness is certainly acceptable, and you need not couch your critiques in platitudes, but you should deliver them with due regard for the recipient. Most simple corrections are unnecessary, because musicians know and freely admit to their mistakes. Usually, you will need to speak up only when you want a musician to play something differently. Phrase your comment in terms of how you want something played, rather than describing what the player did wrong or not to your liking. Diane Wittry's excellent *Beyond the Baton* offers many fine suggestions for good communication with orchestra members. Among the most important to keep in mind is that "... anything you say to a player or section is heard by the entire orchestra. Try to build up the orchestra with your comments, not tear them down. An effective rehearser can motivate an orchestra to play well beyond the individual talents of its members."[2]

---

2. Diane Wittry, *Beyond the Baton,* New York: Oxford University Press, 2007, p. 186.

Hours pass very quickly in orchestra sessions. The paucity of rehearsal time glares in evidence as two readings of a six-minute number occupy a half hour, once you have fixed the articulations in the brass parts, given the reed player a few moments to transpose the oboe part for clarinet, and tried three different string pads to see which blends best with the live string quartet. Breaks in orchestra rehearsals may seem like an inconvenience when you have so much to do and are fully engrossed in the work, and in many rehearsals the musicians keep working through breaks. The musicians' union standardizes rehearsal breaks, in a configuration similar to Equity's, approximately fifty-five minutes on five minutes off, or an hour and twenty minutes on, ten to twenty minutes off. At the beginning of the session, you (or the contractor) might take a straw poll to agree on the breaks for the upcoming session, and plan accordingly.

Music directors might be surprised when players leave their music on the stand at the end of an orchestra rehearsal. Why would they not take it home overnight to work on? In commercial productions, musicians are not permitted to take the music with them, so if they do want to practice, they have to make a photocopy. But music unpracticed following an instrumental rehearsal is not a symptom of orchestral indifference. Rather, it is a hallmark of musicians' competence, an assurance that they will responsibly perform to the best of their abilities what you have directed. Twenty minutes before an orchestra rehearsal you might very well find the musicians in their seats, going through what they did yesterday, warming up, practicing passages that give them trouble, marking their books, checking their intonation, and practicing with other musicians. (Drummer to bassist: "Hey, before everyone else gets here do you want to play through that part with all the unison syncopations? That alternating 6/8 and 7/8 really tripped me up.") After rehearsal ends, the band will often continue working and discussing; the boundaries of orchestra rehearsal are not always well defined. Musicians continually think about whatever music they are working on, going over it in their minds, and keeping it in their hands and bodies. Once they thoroughly absorb and master a piece, their ownership of it will be decisive, even proprietary.

Conducting Styles

Traditional orchestral conducting, consistent with what is taught in the textbooks and conservatory courses and used by symphonic conductors for the last century, is the foundation for conducting as a music director, but there are many possible conducting styles you might make use of. It is not always necessary, desirable, or possible to enforce the strict directives of classical conducting.

To determine how you should conduct a musical show, ask yourself what music and what performers you will be leading. An orchestra of thirty classically trained musicians playing in the pit of *My Fair Lady* or *Evita* or at a concert featuring Audra

MacDonald will appreciate, and the music will benefit from, good traditional conducting technique. Music just as serious but smaller in forces would be overwhelmed by grand gestures, though the complexity of the music demands from its leader equivalent skill and clarity. A larger orchestra playing a groove-driven pop score such as *Starlight Express* or *Hairspray* may not need traditional beat patterns. Indeed, if there are click tracks guarding the time, the conductor's timekeeping may be rendered unnecessary. (If you do conduct along with a click track, make sure your gestures are precisely in time; otherwise restrict your movements and have the orchestra follow the click.) Still, the conductors of both *Starlight Express* and *Hairspray* on Broadway used traditional beat patterns and conducting styles, and the tradition continues, at *Wicked*, *Phantom*, and elsewhere, regardless of the presence of clicks.

A smaller rhythm-section-based band obviously needs less conducting, and more likely you will be behind the piano or some other instrument. A jazz band or big-band musical style, quite common in stage productions, also does not require classical gestures. Jazz bandleaders mostly just count off the tempo at the top, then lightly keep time throughout, with occasional cues, mostly structural, to keep everyone on the chart. You cannot be this casual in a stage show, as you are responsible for too many elements, particularly tempo changes, but you need not conduct brassy, rhythmic charts in as detailed a fashion you would, say, *Porgy and Bess*. A rock band does not need, nor will the members necessarily follow, a conductor. (A group such as Metallica may hire a conductor for an arena concert to link the jobbed-in strings with the band, but that conductor is not the music director of the show.)

All that a trio in a club act really needs from you as conductor is the tempo, which the musicians will probably know as well as you do, and indications of where the chord changes fall in any out-of-tempo sections. Count-offs, head nods, isolated gestures, and your verbal directions comprise the entirety of the "conducting." The same holds true with you at the piano and only one side musician, such as a cellist, bassist, or guitarist, whom you lead only when necessary, and who might know the score (almost) as well as you. In these small groupings, you are still the indisputable leader (aptly, "leader" is a term used to refer to the conductor of a club date band), but your leadership, at least in performance, will be subtle. You lead as much with your playing as you do by conducting, and as a player, you both lead and follow; in other words, while leading, you are also playing in an ensemble.

A pickup group at a benefit concert may be sightreading, or scrambling to hold together hastily scribbled arrangements and underrehearsed numbers. In this sort of rehearsal situation, and at the first reading of a new score, devote your conducting to assisting the musicians in enacting the written (or unwritten) notes. Give frequent cues for instrumental entrances. Make your beat patterns, especially downbeats, very lucid, because orchestra members will be counting. Exaggerate dynamic indications and articulations, and do the same with tempo shifts. Don't be afraid to be verbal; if need be, raise your voice over the music. Most important is to disseminate the essential information quickly and get through everything once, giving the players some measure of security later in performance.

Your conducting approach may also change completely within a production. A hybrid orchestra, one capable of different groupings (as in *The Lion King*), will require different conducting styles at different times. Furthermore, when the singers on stage need your attention, your conducting will always favor them over the accompaniment. Whatever conducting method works is acceptable, provided that it functions with musical integrity and is devoted to impeccably accompanying what is happening and meaningful on stage.

Visibility and the "Field"

Regardless of how you conduct a number, or a production, your conducting must be not only clear but also clearly visible to those needing to see it. You assure sight lines when seating the orchestra (see "The Orchestra: Sections and Setup" in the previous chapter, "Orchestras and Orchestration," and the next chapter, "From the Studio to the Stage") and constructing your podium or conducting area. When conducting, you centralize your gestures into a confined but movable area, so that an observer's eye may easily apprehend it. My term for this area is a conducting "field." Imagine a rectangular plane facing you, like a flat screen television but of variable dimensions and proportions, that floats or moves wherever you place it and can rotate on its vertical and horizontal axes. The field is not unlike conductor Max Rudolf's grids[3] on which he delineates his beat patterns, but a field is mobile in three dimensions. It acts as a surface on which you draw or place your gestures. A logically positioned field allows all players access at a glance to all information you are communicating. The invisible boundaries help to organize your gestures and keep them easily visible.

A video camera on the conductor and a video monitor help to define, and confine, the field, but the camera is a double-edged sword, as it restricts where you can place the field, and its image is two-dimensional. If you are conducting into a camera, a wider-angle lens allows your field to shift position somewhat and increase and decrease in size. Place the camera so its view corresponds to where you naturally place your field most of the time.

Baton, Head, and Hands

Articulate conducting with no hands is entirely feasible. Sometimes you will be able to conduct only with your head, such as when you are playing. Your head, unlike your hand or a baton (or "stick"), has no center. It is a slightly elongated sphere, not a long object

---

3. Max Rudolph. *The Grammar of Conducting: A Comprehensive Guide to Baton Technique and Interpretation*, New York, Schirmer Books, 1995, pp. 8, 10, ff.

coming to a point. Fortunately, your head contains your face, which has many moving parts and communicates detail quite well. Your head moves, your mouth moves, and so do your eyebrows, lips, and cheeks. Facial expressions are powerful conducting gestures.

Your shoulders, chest, posture, and breathing also fulfill the functions of your hands or a baton, as do the sound of your instrument and your voice. If musicians can see your hands as you play, they may follow them as well as your conducting gestures. Therefore, make absolutely certain that your playing is in line with your conducting. In other words, play as if you were conducting yourself. Far too many playing conductors play as if they were not following the conductor properly.

Is there value to using a baton to conduct stage productions? Not when playing, obviously; it is too awkward to pick it up and put it down whenever your hands are free. The original purpose of a baton was to provide an unmissable view of the conductor's beat to a very large ensemble, some of whom (in a symphony orchestra, or a concert or marching band) were far away. The lights in many pits and on many podiums are dim, to keep light from spilling on to the stage, and the bright shaft of a baton can be a beacon. (Radio City showmanship returns here with its famous lighted baton, infamous to us conductors who had to wield the old tendonitis-inducing five-pound version.) On the other hand, unless an orchestra has difficulty seeing the conductor, a baton might be seen as mere pretension at legitimacy. Music directors and tech staffs make a special effort to ensure the conductor's visibility—thus the recent trend toward video monitoring. The choice is largely situation dependent, and somewhat dependent on the comfort of each music director. If you are more communicative with a baton, or without one, and using one or not using one fits with the musical needs of a production, then so be it.[4] A few symphonic conductors eschew batons, as do most choral conductors, preferring the expressiveness of the bare hand. You may choose to use a baton for certain pieces and not for others.

Some music directors use the tip of their index fingers in place of a baton. Although a pointed finger does share some qualities with a stick, I find it restrictive and, if not used cautiously, overbearing. I prefer an inverted, slightly concave hand position with the thumb slightly separated, and perhaps the pinky as well. In this position, from the player's point of view, the tip of the middle finger becomes the baton tip, and all the other fingers point to the tip of the middle finger, with some symmetry. This hand position is also very malleable; you can rotate your wrist in any direction to indicate dynamics and other values and return to the "inverted cup" as a home base (Figure 17.1).

As long as your hand position is not in constant flux, which might be confusing, you can vary it. You can use the inverted cup, separate your fingers to connect to individuals, pump your fist for a *pesante* (meaning heavily, or forcefully), undulate your

---

4. It seems almost unworthy of mention, but it does happen, so I will relegate it to a footnote: on the same grounds, if you do use a baton, always hold it in your right hand, even if you are left handed. The reversed beat patterns resulting from leading with the left hand are confusing to an orchestra.

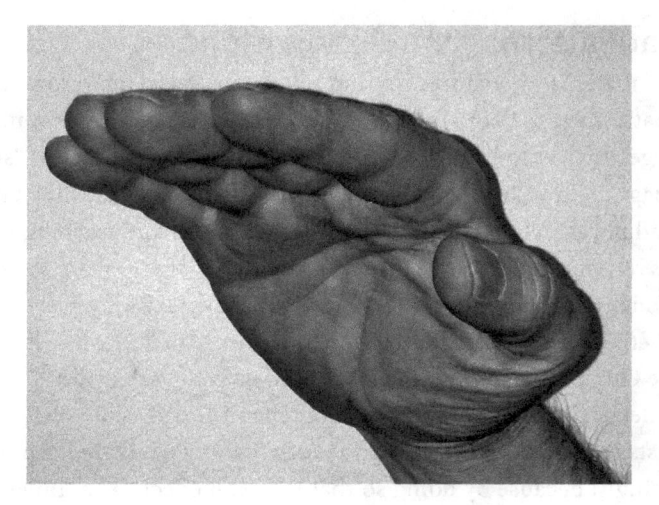

FIGURE 17.1 The "inverted cup." (*Credit:* Photograph by Susan Aquila.)

wrists for legato, beat time with your fingertips for an extreme *pianissimo*, or use any position that sensibly communicates its musical intent.

Conducting Techniques

One can break down the technical elements of conducting for stage productions into specific actions and thought processes that fall under the following widely overlapping rubrics:

- Meter, beat patterns, and subdivisions
- Preparatory beats and cutoffs (beginnings and endings)
- Rests and holds
- Safeties and vamps
- Free tempos, recitative, and following singers
- Tempo and tempo changes
- Feels, grooves, and syncopations
- Dynamics and articulations
- Cues and the stage

The last entry on the list is what initiates, motivates, and regulates all that a music director undertakes, artistically and professionally. As in chapter 13, "Ensemble Vocal Rehearsals," we'll now examine each technical element of conducting stage bands in action, and in the context of musical numbers in a production. In orchestra rehearsal, you can describe your conducting issues and techniques to the players. Though your gestures may be entirely lucid, there is no harm in narrating their intentions to those following them, so that you and the orchestra are thinking as one.

Meter, Beat Patterns, and Subdivisions

The purpose of meter is to organize rhythm and move music forward in time. The purpose of beat patterns is to visually organize meter and its progression in a vocabulary and syntax of gestures with somewhat specific meanings. A conductor "speaks" in this gestural language to an orchestra. Beat patterns in stage conducting likewise bring order to the beats and phrases, and facilitate counting measures and tracking meter changes. Yet repetitious rehearsal and performance, as well as the often square structures of stage music, can render counting moot, except in early rehearsals of a piece or in a limited engagement. Let's look at beat pattern usage in three distinct musical styles and genres.

In "Make Our Garden Grow" the meter and its changes are almost imperceptible. Rather than metrical structure, listeners apprehend broad, slow phrase lengths. The instrumentalists, on the other hand, particularly in rehearsal, are keeping track of the meter, interestingly, because by doing so that they can effect the seamlessness, the disappearance of bar lines. As the conductor leading this effort, you beat the meter with clarity and continuity, and some gravity, but not angularity.

You will very likely conduct "Sometimes a Day Goes By" from the piano with both hands playing, so any beat pattern will be less apparent, but you still interpret the meter. Should you conduct in two or in four? As the analysis in Part 3, "Preproduction," showed, the piece moves in two-bar phrases. Whether in two or in four, you undercut the second downbeat to help elide the two measures. The meter is marked 4/4 in all three published versions, but to conduct all four beats in the measure seems insistent, and a cut-time, or 2/2 beat pattern, would more readily disguise the second downbeat. Besides, with only your head available for time beating, you would have to do quite a bit of bobbing about to beat a four pattern in the tempo range set earlier. Beating half notes gently with the head, up and down in a semblance of a pattern, is therefore the best conducting approach. You might "think" the quarter-note pulse under the half-note motions, and that pulse might be slightly manifest in your physicality. As the piece becomes more familiar to the players, you can reduce your movements. Once you do, reintroducing them at any time enjoins the orchestra to pay attention, such as the slowing at the ends of the A sections.

"Easy to Be Hard" does not change tempo, except at the end. As noted in chapter 12, "Individual Vocal Rehearsals," when conducting this number you will probably be seated at the piano, and no beat patterns are necessary. No one is counting measures; the players are guided by their understanding of the groove and the song form, and their place in them, not by the conductor's beats. The groove, rather than the mechanics of the forward motion, i.e., the meter, is what you work to improve in rehearsal. Everyone is already thinking (or more accurately, *not* thinking) in four-beat groupings and longer phrases, so for a conductor to beat constant time would be fruitless. Should the time rush or drag or the time become uneven, again, your resuming conducting indicates that you want to restore the groove or the tempo.

Articulate beat patterns boil down your metrical direction into a universally legible and respected format. The shape and quality of your patterns depend on feel, articulation, style, and other influences. A legato beat pattern, for example, in which smoothly curved lines move from beat to beat, or from ictus to ictus (the "ictus" is the precise point in the pattern at which the beat occurs, often marked by a "click," a small but sharp gestural emphasis), works only for legato, and would not properly demonstrate the character of a bouncy, staccato rhythm. A staccato or *marcato* pattern stops on, sharply bounces off, or forcibly marks each ictus. Staccato patterns are generally smaller, as the insistence of the clicks prohibits extremes of motion. The rhythmic nature of much of the stage music literature makes staccato patterns probably the most common.

There are many reasons to conduct most of "What Is This Feeling?" in a traditional, clearly defined four-beat staccato pattern. The rhythmic portion of the song's accompaniment consists almost entirely of rhythmic pulses, syncopations, and punctuations; there is also some recitative. Often there is space between the punctuations, as in a "stop-time" feel (a term borrowed from tap-dance arrangements). A beat pattern helps the orchestra keep track of the orientation of these "hits," or accents, as they occur at different points within the meter. After repeated rehearsal or performance, continually indicating these events may seem unnecessary, but it is not: it continues to enliven each performance. Furthermore, the instrumental and vocal groups of *Wicked* are sizable, and beat patterns are customary for large ensembles, and essential in the recitative sections (see the section "Free Tempo, Recitative, and Following Singers"). A definitive beat pattern, by mere virtue of its formalism, supports the collective precision of the stage and orchestra. Exacting gestures appropriately demand accuracy and concentration from the performers. The orchestra's togetherness enhances the musical and dramatic power, of the punctuations and of all other elements.

When conducting "Belle," the opening song of Alan Menken and Howard Ashman's charming, lush score for *Beauty and the Beast*, a clear two-beat pattern makes sense for the feel of the music, and not because the pattern is somehow impeccable or incontrovertible, though it is appropriate for the moderately large, legitimate orchestra. In leading a piece such as this, you might feel at times like a metronome, but in some sense, the music requires metronome-like timekeeping. Its rhythmic doggedness should not flag for quite a long stretch—five-plus minutes—and your consistently energetic and explicit conducting will sustain the effort.

Persistence, not necessarily a beat pattern, is also crucial when conducting energetic rock numbers. "Time Warp" is perhaps the best-known song from *The Rocky Horror Show*, an audience favorite and stock and academic theater warhorse. When you are not playing piano and your hands are free to conduct, beat patterns are convenient, but hardly mandatory. The piece begins with an eighth-note electric guitar rock-boogie groove (Figure 17.2). Nine bars later, the drums and bass enter, stop time, and eight bars after that, the rest of the band, including the piano, joins in full groove. Conduct the solo guitar for a few measures at least, while you are still able, to set the feel and tempo.

Cue the bass and drums by beating time with your right hand and using your left hand alone to show the stop-time hits. When the groove kicks in and your hands move to the keyboard, feel free to head-bang the quarter notes for a few measures and periodically throughout. Once the tempo has caught on, however, let the band members play; they are the ones driving the music, and you have shown them the way. If the exuberance flags at any moment, resume conducting with hand or head to restore it. Keep the groove going in your mind, body, and piano playing to maintain the vigor over the length of the song.

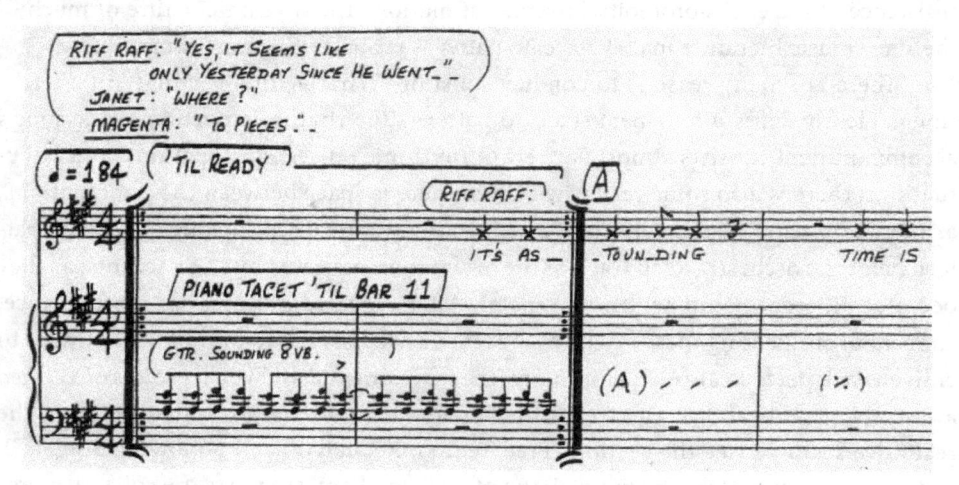

FIGURE 17.2 Top of "Time Warp," from *The Rocky Horror Show*.

None of the examples up to now has had a defining rhythmic triple feel, and songs in a lilting three have a prominent place in the stage literature. For conductors they present the interesting issue of choosing between a three pattern and a one pattern, that is, conducting three subdivisions of a triple-note value, or a single beat, usually a dotted half or dotted quarter, as in a bright waltz. Alternating between three and one, depending on the phrase, is often the best approach. Beat patterns containing triple subdivisions are rounder in shape, less sharp cornered than their duple counterparts. (The reasoning behind this perception seems empirical; threes, sixes, nines, and so on simply suggest to most people a curvilinear shape, whereas twos and fours seem somehow squarer.) The following examples, "Oh, What a Beautiful Morning" from *Oklahoma!* and "Breathe" from *In The Heights*, show how your choice of pattern is musically motivated, and has an impact on the stage.

Both songs begin in a moderately slow three. Both have colorfully stylized introductions preceding the singer's entrance: the fluttering winds in the cornfields of "Oh What a Beautiful Morning" (Figure 17.3) and the flute, nylon string guitar, and voices of the 'hood in "Breathe" (Figure 17.4). In both, the lead singer enters singing sentimentally about his or her locale, and his or her place within it (in musical theater terms these are "identity" songs: "There's a bright golden haze on the meadow . . ." and "This is my street/I smile for the faces/I've known all my life . . ." are theatrical lyrics that define character). Both orchestral accompaniments are light at first.

INSTRUMENTAL CONDUCTING FOR THE STAGE | 275

FIGURE 17.3 Top of "Oh, What a Beautiful Morning," from *Oklahoma!*.

FIGURE 17.4 Excerpt from "Breathe," from *In The Heights*.

After a short verse ending with a *ritardando* (see Figure 17.5), "Oh, What a Beautiful Morning" explodes into its familiar chorus, its tempo a bit faster and its mood (and lyric) now more celebratory than descriptive. Your beat pattern accordingly shifts from a small three to a sweeping one, upholding the jubilant spirit while characterizing the feel, and keeping the time, as seen in Figures 17.5 and 17.7.[5]

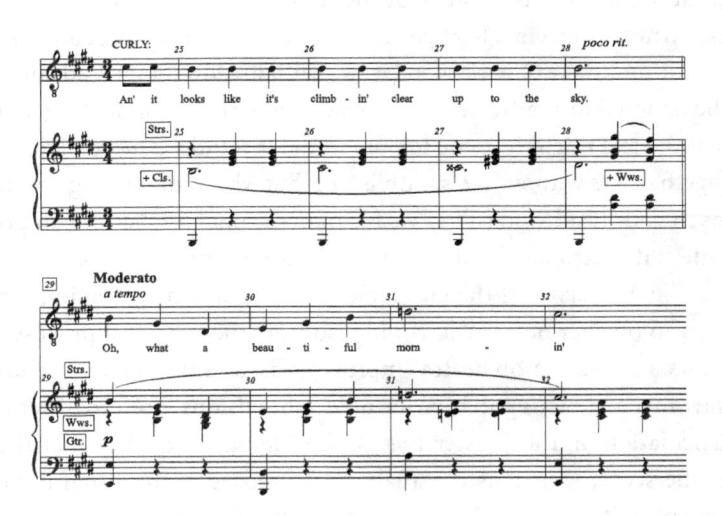

FIGURE 17.5 "Oh, What a Beautiful Morning," mm. 25–32.

"Breathe" holds back its lyrical outburst for a longer time, and the shift from three into one is more subtle, and more discretionary. The words of the first verse deal with

---

5. Technically, the second verse and chorus of the stage version would be a more accurate example, as the first verse of that version is *a cappella*, but I think I've made my point.

the conflict the singer faces. She ends her verse reminding herself to relax, "just breathe," and the background voices from the introduction return, their harmoniousness now more pointed in light of the singer's predicament. Gradually, during this choral interlude, the music, and your beat pattern, transform from three into one, supporting the lyricism. When the lead vocal returns, it has a more conversational tone, and your conducting continues accordingly in one, not interrupting, as it were, the conversation. You explain these sorts of dramatic connections to the instrumentalists in rehearsal; they inform the accompanimental interpretation.

In "Belle," you similarly cross the lines of subdivision, but in duple time. In the bridge of the song, Belle rhapsodizes ("Oh, isn't this amazing/It's my fav'rite part . . ."), and the march-like cut time accordingly shifts to a soaring, more sustained feel. You break the two-beat pattern and conduct this passage in one, beating the whole note. In this written score, the change is specified in writing as "L'istesso—in one," but such notations are not the norm. (The careful, beautiful arranging and meticulous notation of the *Beauty and the Beast* music is typical of Alan Menken's scores, in this case with the help of the outstanding music team of David Friedman, Michael Kosarin, Glen Kelly, and Danny Troob.)

Subdivisions are readily associated with slowing of tempo, when you might subdivide a beat to keep the orchestra together during a deceleration. Your subdivisions progress from slight to emphatic, increasing in resistance and size as the tempo decreases. Keep subdivisions within the confines of your beat pattern, and place and articulate them so they cannot be confused with the primary ictuses. You can physically execute subdivisions at the wrist, the forearm, or the shoulder, or with your whole body. Slight "hitches," or extra motions in a beat pattern, suggest an underlying subdivided pulse.

In conducting "Make Our Garden Grow," with its slow tempo and compelling text, you might be tempted to subdivide into quarters rather than conducting half notes. The danger is that the feel might become too plodding. It is indeed more difficult to achieve rhythmic togetherness without the subdivisions, but while conducting you can keep the subdivisions in your head, and subtly visible in occasional hitches. If you properly connect your internal metronome with your physical movements, the internal pulse will be evident to the musicians. If the ensemble is having difficulty staying together, then you can resort to quarter notes. You could also start the rehearsal process by showing the inner beats and, as the orchestra improves, discontinue them. The forceful coda certainly warrants conducting in quarter-note subdivisions, both to effect the strongly accented articulation and to bolster the *"Molto Maestoso"* quality that the composer indicates in the score, which, as the analysis showed, is in meaningful contrast with earlier statements of the theme. Figure 17.6 outlines the conducting.

In "Sometimes a Day Goes By," the end of each A section slows down. To accomplish the deceleration as a playing conductor, whether conducting in two or in four, stretch your existing beats, that is, broaden your head movements and suspend them slightly at their apogee, to imitate the broadening of the tempo and, assuming you are conducting in two, temporarily subdivide the last bar or half-bar of the phrase into quarter notes. You can use a four pattern for the subdivided two, moving your head

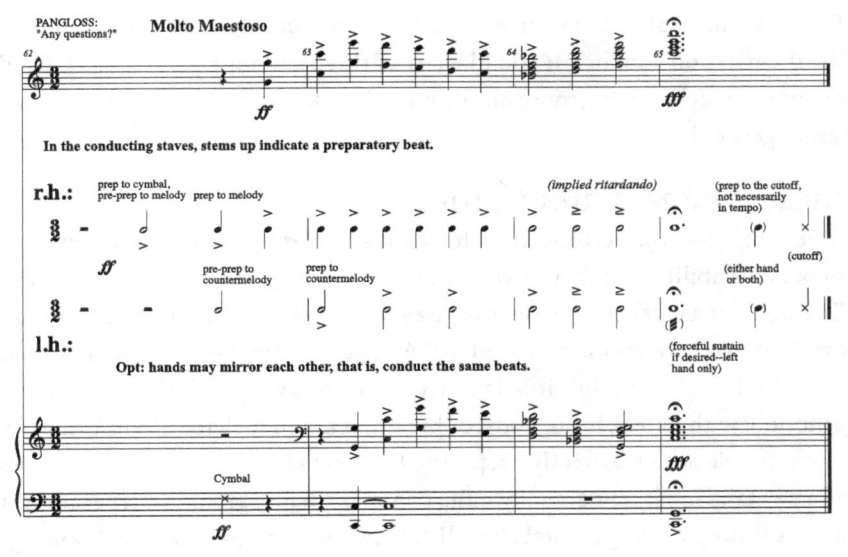

FIGURE 17.6 "Make Our Garden Grow," coda, with conducting annotations.

laterally as well as vertically, or subdivide your up-and-down two pattern with neighboring ictuses.

The "*poco rit.*" marking at the ends of the verses of "Oh What a Beautiful Morning" is deceptive; the convention is to begin slowing down a measure or two earlier, and it is not *poco* at all; it is more of *molto ritenuto* (a sudden holding back of the tempo), with the last beat of the last measure of the phrase held as a fermata. You would not subdivide the quarter note in this instance, as the quarter is already a subdivision of sorts, and there is no motion between the beats. Moreover, at that moment the tension builds precisely because of the deceleration and the hold, and any secondary subdivision would defuse it. You will, however, give two beat threes in the last measure before the chorus, the first one to hold beat three, and the second to prepare the next measure. This is, in effect, a subdivision. Figure 17.7 shows the conducting beats.

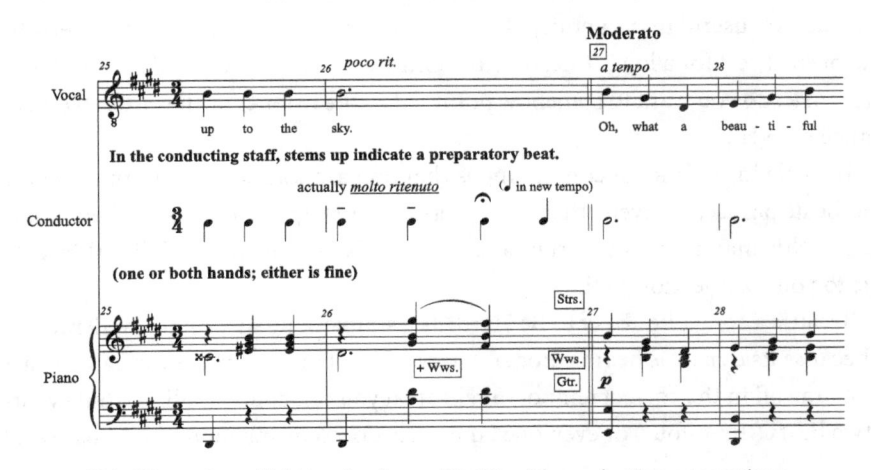

FIGURE 17.7 "Oh, What a Beautiful Morning," mm. 25–32, with conducting annotations.

Early in rehearsal, make your beat patterns and subdivisions more academic, and describe them as you conduct, if you like ("two, three and four . . . and . . ."). Gradually adjust your approach, relying more on the musicians to implement the material and less on flagrant gesticulation.

Preparatory Beats and Cutoffs

Unlike beating time, the gestures used to begin and end music are such a strong determinant of believability that their precise execution must persist into performance.

The beat (or beats) the conductor gives to set music in motion is called a "preparatory beat," or "preparation," or "prep." A "one-two-three-four" count-off, a loudly vocalized "And . . . ," an audible inhalation, an upward swing of the baton, or any preparatory motion, with hands, head, body, or breath, is a sign replete with information. The apparently simple act of correctly preparing (or "prepping") a group musical entrance with all its details in place is actually quite complex. Before giving a preparation, a conductor goes through a long mental checklist. How many preparatory beats am I giving? Who will be playing? Does everyone know where we are starting? How will the players respond to my gesture? What is the tempo, the feel, the style? What are the dynamics, and the articulations? What is the feeling or meaning behind the music? The conductor then communicates a pronouncement of all of these elements, and more, with a gesture indicating, incontrovertibly, that everyone will enter . . . precisely . . . and in character . . . *here*.

Preparatory beats are not limited, of course, to the beginnings of pieces. They are in constant play; conductors are always preparing their fellow performers for the next event. The difference at the beginning of a piece is (usually) that the preparatory beat or beats indicate a certain tempo. Nonetheless, it is not always necessary, or possible, for preparatory beats to be in the tempo of the passage that they prepare (several examples follow).

In a way, all preps are also cues. The primary purposes of preparatory beats are to cue entrances and to forecast musical events. As rehearsals progress, you can decide which cues are useful in perpetuity. The two criteria are the needs of the player—has he or she been at rest for a long time, or is the entrance somehow difficult?—and the needs of the music: do you want to somehow point out to the listener or the ensemble a certain entrance or event?

The rule in traditional conducting is that preparations are always in the character of the beat, phrase, or event that they prepare. In stage production, where character abounds, this maxim no less essential, and extends beyond your relationship with the music to your connection to the stage.

Because a song like "Easy to Be Hard" is a simple song in a single moderate tempo, and because its dynamic begins moderately, your preparation at the top can consist of a plain count-off in the correct tempo. In rehearsal you can count a full bar, but eventually just two beats (three-four) or even one (and) may do; counting more than a bar would be excessive, even at first. Just as important is that you count off in the feel of the song, that is, in a way that captures the mood, character, and groove. You wouldn't want to shout or otherwise overemphasize the count, or for that matter underemphasize it, but you do want it firmly in the pocket and emotionally connected to the stage from the outset.

Starting "Time Warp" involves intense yet contained energy (see Figure 17.2). Although the dynamic may be subdued at the top to allow for a build later on, you can render in your opening count-off the irrepressible verve that lies underneath. In this fast tempo, a two-bar count-off will be helpful at first—"One-two [two half notes], (a-)one-two-three-four!"). Make your preparatory beat to the bass and drums precise, and charge it with a dynamism equivalent to your opening count. In a fast prep like this one, breathing becomes ever more important. A strong, sharp, precisely timed inhalation accompanying your hand gesture multiplies the potency of your prep.

The legitimacy of theater songs such as "Make Our Garden Grow" and "Oh, What a Beautiful Morning" calls for traditional initial preparations, as well as beat patterns. At the first readings, you might want to give extra preparatory beats or count out loud as you lead the orchestra in, but by the second or third time through you can reduce your initial preps to what you will use in performance. The first measure of "Oh, What a Beautiful Morning" is in 6/4 meter, in this case two subdivisions of a dotted half.[6] The appropriate beat pattern is an "Italian" six-beat, or a two pattern subdivided in threes. For the first rehearsal you might count a full bar while leading the orchestra in: "*One*-and-a-*two*-and-a" or "*One*-two-three-*four*-five-six" (stressing the italicized syllables, the strong beats), but eventually you will most likely need only one preparatory quarter, and a good breath for the winds. "Make Our Garden Grow," with its broad triple meter, begins on the third beat of a measure, a musically significant pickup to the downbeat. For both rehearsal and eventual performance, you can beat the first two empty half notes of the pickup measure, again counting out loud, if you like ("One-*two*" or "One-and-*two*-and").

Different instruments (and instrumentalists) respond better to different sorts of preparations. When conducting an ensemble, you can combine approaches, or compromise among them. In both of the preceding musical examples, a variety of instruments play on the initial beat. "Make Our Garden Grow" begins with French horn, harp, and woodwinds. The winds have the melody, the horn sustains under them, and the harp punctuates the beginning and the end of the phrase. The woodwind attack will be slower than the harp's; the horn's will be slower still. Woodwind players must, to produce a sound, inhale and blow, after which the air must traverse the tubes of their instruments and reach the listener. The French horn in particular has a very long and twisted pipe, and thus a long delay between the player's attack and the emission of sound. The harpist, by contrast, merely plucks the strings.

---

6. The original cast album does not reflect this; the music has been rearranged so that the first verse is accompanied, and preceded by an introductory vamp in 3/4 time. The published show score begins as described (see Figure 17.3).

The orchestration at the top of "Oh, What a Beautiful Morning" (see Figure 17.3) also features French horns, as well as low strings sustaining a pedal fifth. The horns have the melody, a "horn call" answered by the flute, oboe, and clarinet, suggestive of bird calls. The first horn notes are articulated; the string pedal is merely sustained.[7]

If you follow the rule that a prep is in the character of the entrance, how then to reconcile such different means of attack in your preparatory gesture? Two mechanisms in particular will help.

First, again, is breathing. The winds and horn need to breathe. Therefore, so should you when bringing them in, as they do, deeply. Your breath can help the harp and the strings, too. Though the preparation may not translate as literally as it does with wind instruments, all musicians breathe or otherwise physically prepare before they play (or sing). Your breath is a representation of their preparations, and is universally understood. The specific quality of your breath allows the players to feel as an ensemble the intent of your prep. (As an exercise, try cueing an orchestral chord with breath alone.)

Second is the "rebound" of your ictus. Every conducting field has an imaginary lower limit, a floor, so to speak. It is there that the ictus of your downbeat (and some other beats, as well) will touch, or strike. The floor has resilience: rather than stopping at the ictus, your beat "bounces" before moving toward the next point in the pattern. The bounce of a beat is its rebound. You can feel rebound by beating just a downbeat: you will need to make an effort to stop the pattern from moving at its endpoint. Staccato or *marcato* beats have little or no rebound, while the rebound of a slow *molto legato* may be as wide as the gesture leading to it. Rebound allows room for each individual to play in response to your beat.

In "Oh, What A Beautiful Morning," your initial prep, your single quarter-note upbeat, should be quite broad. On the downbeat, place your ictus at the very bottom of the field, with a large, mostly lateral rebound leading to the second beat (this applies whether you are conducting quarters or dotted halves). This movement will accommodate the bowed, sustained strings and the breadth of the horn call. Your cue to the twittering flutes in m. 2 can be a similar gesture, but in miniature. The harpist will not necessarily play at the precise point of your initial ictus, but instead look for your rebound, where, as he or she knows, the inherent delay of the woodwinds' tone production will place the horn and woodwind entrances.

Sometimes the delay between your beat and an orchestra's response to it can be long and disconcerting. Especially in larger orchestras with large string and brass sections, there can be such a significant delay that you feel as if you are conducting far in front of the ensemble, or that they are playing way behind, at the outer limit of your

---

7. I have removed in my transcription of the original piano-vocal score what I believe to be an errant staccato marking on the eighth note preceding the last quarter note of the first bar. It seems more likely that the first and second groups of three notes in that bar should be articulated the same.

rebound. If you want the orchestra to play closer to your beat, keep your patterns very small, accent each beat slightly, and use very little rebound. The lack of breadth in your gesture disallows the players from coming in too far after the ictus. You can also establish your approach in rehearsal by communicating it verbally to the orchestra: "Please play right with my beat, as opposed to behind it. I want to feel the inner rhythms of the music along with you, and be as much an orchestra member as a leader." You can encourage the orchestra to listen to the rhythm section as well, when there is one.

Like all preparatory beats, preps within songs are in character. When you brought in the bass and drums in "Time Warp" you did so with appropriate zest. If at the end of the first phrase of "Make Our Garden Grow" you want to feature the harp that punctuates the last note, give a preparatory upbeat that is both directed at the player and accented. "Breathe" has an eight-bar introduction, and in the eighth bar (the second bar in Figure 17.4), the guitar walks up a scale into a rhythmic accompanimental pattern that begins in the ninth measure. Because the guitar scale sets the upcoming tempo, you feel the pulse within yourself and accurately communicate it to the guitarist with your prep and subsequent beat pattern. The percussionist also enters in the ninth measure, playing time on the maracas. As you cue the guitarist, you also connect with the percussionist, coordinating the rhythm of the two and further securing the tempo (you might continue conducting for some measures into the section to fully establish the time and feel).

Cutoffs are something like preparatory beats in reverse; the main difference is that continuation does not necessarily rest on them. A cutoff is any gesture that ends a note or phrase. The preparation to a cutoff need not fall within the beat pattern. Often a tiny circular motion is fine, and is easy to place anywhere within the field.

There are two main types of cutoff gesture. First is a simple cutoff, which ends a musical event or passage. A simple cutoff can occur anywhere during a piece, within or at the end of a phrase, or at the end of the piece. Within a piece, it is your reminder to a player that a certain note should end at a certain point, and in a certain way. Most of this information is too fundamental for conductors to attend to. They usually reserve cutoffs for musical moments or groups of performers that require coordination, particularly singers on stage. Second is a cutoff that ends one event and begins another, or a "cut and go," a cut and a prep combined in one beat, where the cutoff gesture continues into the prep.

When conducting for the stage you often coordinate cutoffs with stage events, such as dialogue, a lighting shift, or any physical action. To achieve their dual musical and dramatic purposes, you prepare cutoffs precisely, and represent in them the character of the music and the stage content. Before a gentle cut, for example, you would use a soft, caressing prep with an exact but not overly articulated endpoint, while a sharp cut gets a sharp, angular prep and an accent at the end, with no rebound. Size matters, too; a cutoff's breadth can indicate a dynamic, or simply help its visibility.

Coordinating an articulated cutoff at the end of piece, often referred to as a "button" or, when larger, a "stinger," can be tricky. Make sure that your two hands, or your baton and your hand, or your instrument and your hand, are in sync. Make sure that you are not showing different cutoffs or preps to the cutoff with each hand, with hand and head, or with head and piano attack. Think of a cut not as the end of the music, but as an active part of the music, so that you do not undervalue its execution. Feel the musicality of the cut as much as the time of the cut; that is, feel how it fits in rather than just when it occurs, and the accuracy will follow.

Rests and Holds

Silence is as much a part of music as sound. The spaces between notes are themselves notes, and are invaluable as punctuation marks in the musical syntax. Therefore, like notes, music directors conduct silences and rests. In stage scores the accompaniment often waits, marking time while something happens on stage. Either a musical passage repeats until a cue to proceed, or a note or silence holds in anticipation of moving forward.

During and coming out of holds, stops, and starts, conductors have the performers' attention. All eyes turn to the podium, looking for the signal to wait, or move on. For conductors, there are two parts to these moments: the hold itself, and what ends the hold. Some holds end with a cut and go, some move to another hold, and some move on without a cut. Here are some variants of holds, stops, and starts. There will be some overlap with free tempo and recitative in the ensuing discussion, topics of the subsequent section.

In mm. 67–68a of "What Is This Feeling?" the tempo slows, and the group vocal is interrupted by a solo comment sung in free tempo (Figure 17.8).

FIGURE 17.8 Excerpt from "What Is This Feeling?" from *Wicked*.

A fermata on beat five of the 6/4 measure indicates the interruption. On the sixth beat the soloist has an unaccompanied pickup to a held orchestral chord in the next measure. When her phrase ends, there is a quarter-note pickup in the bass leading the accompaniment and vocals back into tempo. Though unmarked, there is in practice a slight *ritardando* in the 6/4 measure, presumably so that the solo singer's "Well . . ." can be heard clearly without the reverberation of the chorus drowning her out.

This translates to conducting as follows. Broaden your beat pattern in the 6/4 bar to indicate the *ritard*, stopping either on beat four or beat five. (Either a "German" six pattern, a four pattern with an extra beat on each side, or a subdivided 3/2 pattern will work; both communicate the metrical extension of the passage; this is not so much a meter shift as a meter augmentation.) If you stop on beat five, you meet Galinda's spoken "Well?" on beat four, then strongly hold beat five. If you stop on beat four, there is a rest before the prep to the next downbeat, so make sure that this empty beat appears only as pre-preparatory to the actual preparatory beat. To accomplish this, keep the empty beat five beat lateral, rather than an upswing that might suggest an upbeat, and deny the beat an ictus, that is, keep your motion free of click. Simply move your hand(s) outward, then continue with a clear upward pickup beat with a clear ictus. You need only mark the next six quarter notes, m. 68 and the first half of m. 69, in a 4/4 pattern, that is, move through the beats with minimal expression, staying with the singer if desired. Stop and hold on beat two of m. 68a (move clearly to the left to show that beat two is where the hold is, as you would in recitative), then execute a strong beat three to the right as a prep to the quarter note in the bass on beat four. Always avoid any extraneous motion.

To hold a beat, use muscular resistance in your wrist, arm, and shoulder to stop or suspend your pattern mid-movement. Some slight motion usually persists through a hold, especially when holding a note (as opposed to a rest). When holding a note forcefully, you might shake your hand during the hold, like a tremolo, to sustain the power, though this is a somewhat hackneyed conducting gesture, so use it sparingly. Turn your palm upward to "hold" the time and the tone within the gesture. At the end of the hold, release the tension, either with a cutoff or with a motion indicating a new beat, a cut and go.

A passage similar to Figure 17.8 occurs coming out of the verse of "Belle," with slightly different conducting requirements.

In the first 2/4 bar of Figure 17.9, there is a short hold on the first half of beat two. The next bar is *colla voce* (the accompaniment follows exactly the sung melody, sometimes doubling it, as it does here, in the oboe and clarinet). The third 2/4 bar contains

FIGURE 17.9 Excerpt from "Belle," *from Beauty and the Beast.*

in its short span four significant conducting events. There is a hold on the first quarter note; a holdover eighth note in the strings, trumpet, oboe, and flute that requires a cutoff; a caesura in the accompaniment; and an eighth-note vocal pickup ("Bon-[jour]") into the subsequent cut-time allegro.

Here is how the conductor sees it. The hold on beat two of m. 14 entails pausing on the ictus with no click and minimal motion, rather than holding it firmly. In this case your hand is palm down (your left hand, that is, presumably, as your right hand might well be holding a baton), because the hold is very brief and there is a *decrescendo* into it, so already your hand will be indicating the dynamic change in this way. Beat two is effectively subdivided: after the hold you simply continue the beat pattern upward as a prep to the next bar. In the *colla voce* bar you conduct legato with complete attention to the singer; there is no ictus, but there is a clear change of direction as the singer moves to the next note; the instrumentalists (including a cello sliding down a fifth over the course of its half note) will follow you following the singer, and listen to the singer along with you, if they can. In the next measure, you again listen to the singer, and immediately following her cutoff, give a smooth, quick circular cutoff to the players, preferably with the left hand only. This action leaves the right hand ready to move, and reserves it for the more important function of giving a prep into the ensuing *Allegro*. The caesura is very short and your gestures will follow one another immediately, so using just the left hand for the cutoff further prioritizes the prep. Ideally, your pattern in the 2/2 (cut-time) allegro, and your prep for it, should be broader in size than the 2/4 pattern, on the general principle that the more subdivisions a beat can contain, the larger that beat should appear (a 2/2 pattern is thus bigger than a 2/4 pattern), but also because the new feel is vivacious, and *forte*.

Certain conductors will not give a prep following a hold, but expect the orchestra to react to the ictus of the subsequent beat. This idiosyncrasy is a holdover from opera vocal performance, in which money notes were held until the singer ran out of air, and so the durations of those notes varied widely. I do not subscribe to this technique, as an abbreviated prep is all that you need, and is always possible, if you understand the singer, the stage, and the score.

Safeties and Vamps

A safety is a bar-long or multi-bar-long hold, in rhythm, that repeats indefinitely until a cue to continue, or stop. Often the number of times a safety repeats is set in rehearsal, but still the openness of the hold remains, should something change or go wrong on stage—thus the name "safety." In Figure 17.10, there is a dialogue cue to continue, Belle's line, "Thank you very much." At the end of or somewhere during this line, according to how it was rehearsed or at the conductor's discretion, the conductor indicates that the safety is over and the orchestra should move forward.

FIGURE 17.10 Second excerpt from "Belle."

There is a clear way to conduct this safety. At the point where the safety measure begins, hold your left hand still and upright while the right hand continues to beat time, but with minimal emphasis. You might hold up the index finger of the left hand, because a finger pointed up can quickly and clearly be turned downward to indicate the continuation, with little warning. But any indication with the left hand that the music is on hold will do (you can also count down with the fingers of your left hand, when you know the end of a safety is coming). Break the stillness of the left hand only when ready to give the prep to continue. If you choose to give more than one beat of prep out of a safety, de-emphasize any pre-preparatory beats, and save the definitive beat for the actual preparation.

A vamp is a safety that contains a musical pattern whose meaning is more than just the marking of time. The example from "Belle" is a safety. The guitar introduction of "Time Warp" (Figure 17.2) is the epitome of a vamp (it is also a safety). Because there is no change in what the guitar does until after the music continues out of the vamp, and because the vocal entrance is a half-bar pickup, as conductor you need only give a subtle (yet clear) gesture to indicate the continuation. If using your index finger for the hold you can simply turn it downward as the music moves out of the vamp on the singer's cue.

There are also safeties that may not end at their repeat signs, or even at a bar line. These will be marked in a score as "out on any beat" or "continue at any point" or some other printed direction. Other safeties contain a musical cue within them, the most common being a "vocal last time" safety, where the singer begins while still in the safety. The technique for getting out of these holds is no different, but your gestures must be even more vivid and forceful, your beat pattern directions even clearer, and your holds even more vigilant, as the unpredictability of the out cue may be befuddling to anyone needing it, especially if it tends to change from performance to performance. In rehearsal, have the orchestra players mark their parts clearly with the details of

FIGURE 17.11 All eyes on music director James Lowe holding a safety. (*Credit:* Photo by Steve Singer.)

safeties and vamps, and add a note (a hand-drawn pair of eyeglasses is a usual marking) where they should make a special effort to watch the conductor (Figure 17.11).

Free Tempo, Recitative, and Following Singers

Recitative, a holdover from opera, fits well into popular stage performance. Conversational singing and sung dialogue suit the pseudo-realism of musical stage entertainment. Most recitative sections in musicals and popular song are short, and soon modulate to a steady tempo, though a few are quite extensive, including entire musical scenes. One well-known example of musical theater recitative is the verse of "Sit Down, You're Rockin' the Boat" from *Guys and Dolls* (Figure 17.12).

The first upbeat of this number plainly demonstrates that preparatory beats need not be in tempo; you can give a prep of any duration, then specify the tempo with the relation of the first and second beats of the subsequent measure.[8]

The singer has only an eighth-note pickup to the first measure. Therefore, unless you lead the singer in or augment the duration of the pickup note, it is impossible for you to give a quarter-note pickup to the first measure. The solution is simple, as there is no motion in the accompaniment until the third beat of m. 1, so in this case you have two beats to establish the quasi-tempo. Give a prep of any duration you choose, then beat the correct time for the first three beats of m. 1.

---

8. There are many printed orchestrations and reductions of this piece; my comments are specific to this, my own version, an amalgam of several existing ones.

FIGURE 17.12 Excerpt from "Sit Down, You're Rockin' the Boat," from *Guys and Dolls*.

After that it gets more complicated. The singer breathes between beats three and four of m. 1, so you hold on beat three until the singer is ready. Stretch beat three laterally, keeping it moving slowly outward until the singer's fourth beat (two eighth notes, "I got . . ."), then change direction upward, on cue, for the upbeat to m. 2. During the hold, be ready to react quickly and move on. Your tension and alertness translate to orchestral compliance.

In m. 2 there is only a whole note in the accompaniment, but a breath mid-bar for the singer. Hold on beat three, with moderate tension, ready to move into beat four, which will prepare the next bar, in which several instruments enter as a group (including strings, bass, and French horn). Your prep to m. 3 should be stronger, and larger, to accommodate the larger grouping, but you must also predict where the singer will continue. His pickup to m. 3 is only an eighth note, again insufficient for you to fully prep the larger group. Here you think along with the singer; most likely you know his phrasing from rehearsal, and you can begin your prep before he continues (of course this plan will backfire if he pauses unexpectedly).

Forward motion continues into m. 4, where again the singer will breathe between beats three and four. Here the hold is more complex, as the strings and woodwinds play a legato fill on beats three and four, leading into the downbeat of m. 5. As with the *colla voce* section in "Belle," your gesture moves with the singer, but in this example the accompaniment is independent of the melody, so your extended gestures are there only to lead the orchestra, with the singer's melody as your guide. Stretch beat three, move musically into a stretched beat four and, when you hear the singer's pickup (the eighth note "And . . ."), move fluidly into the downbeat. In your beat four, which by design moves in an upward direction, you might leave a small amount of headroom at the apex of the gesture so that as you move into the downbeat, you can hitch, a slight upward acceleration of your gesture, to signify that your motion is transforming from a hold on an upbeat to a functional prep.

In both mm. 5 and 6 the singer breathes after beat three. In m. 5 the entire accompaniment cuts with the end of the singer's phrase. Use only your left hand to show the cut, while your right hand (or baton) holds on beat three, waiting for the singer before you move into the prep to m. 6 with both left and right hands. In m. 6, the winds and violins hold their note past the singer's cut while the lower parts cut off as in the measure before. Make the cut on beat three with both hands, and move on with both hands. Because beat three is *staccato*, you need hit the ictus only as a cutoff. If you wanted to hold beat three a bit longer, you would use a quick circular motion ending on the ictus. In m. 8, hold beat three, and cut the orchestra with the singer, in the same character as the singer cuts off his note.

FIGURE 17.13 Opening section of "What Is This Feeling?"

The recitative section at the top of "What Is This Feeling?" (Figure 17.13) complicates coordination of stage and pit with duet singing. Both leading women sing the first vocal cue ("There's been some confusion . . .") in a somewhat free tempo, their interaction and the amount of freedom most likely having been set in rehearsal. This particular passage moves somewhat regularly, but the actors are free to act, broadly. It is typical of the free tempos found in stage music, reminiscent of classical *recitativo accompagnato*.

Fluidly indicate the meter in a clear pattern, with some resistance, following the singers' pace, marking empty beats, and when there is a hold, wait on the penultimate beat before moving forward. When it is not possible to hold two beats early, as in m. 7, indicate beat four and hold it according to the marked fermata, then give an extra beat out of time as preparation for m. 8, and sort out the tempo in beats one and two of the new measure. So that this recurrent beat four is not confusing, when you first reach it, do not overemphasize it; merely arrive there and pause, holding the beat gently in place.

The problem remains of synchronizing the soloists and the orchestra at the beginning. There are two solutions. One is to agree in rehearsal that you will be the one to bring everyone in together. The other is to have the singers coordinate their entrance themselves, with you following and bringing in the orchestra. Because you will have to anticipate the singers' entrance, you use an out-of-tempo prep, and react quickly to some perceptible indication the singers give that they are about to sing, probably a breath or a slight movement. If need be, you can all agree on a specific timing or physical cue, but usually you can find a way to follow the singers just by observing them and their breathing (assuming you can see them).

As discussed earlier, there is a *ritard* and a hold leading into the chorus of "Oh, What a Beautiful Morning" (Figure 17.7). When the music resumes, you will be conducting a new beat pattern (one instead of the previous three). You will need to give an extra beat as a pickup.

In m. 28, broaden your pattern and decelerate into beat three, where you wait for the singer to finish his note and breathe before the next phrase. To start the new tempo, again, you might work with the singer in rehearsal, or instead follow his breathing and physicality in performance, in which case your prep will be will likely be a quarter note or less, and you set the new tempo as you assume the new beat pattern in m. 29. It might help secure the tempo in mm. 29 and following to lightly indicate quarter-note subdivisions within your dotted half-note pattern, at least for a few measures. Over repeated performances, you might simply grow accustomed to the singer's timing.

Tempo and Tempo Changes

An equation of musical and human elements known as "feel" and "groove" defines tempo (see the next paragraph). Yet the generalized notion of "tempo," viewed by many as purely quantitative—that is, the numerical value that appears on a metronome—occupies such a large portion of a music director's life that it warrants solitary examination. Conductors set tempo from the podium, and at times, a click, metronome, or prerecorded track enforces it. A click can be a music director's best friend, especially when it comes to tempo disagreements, but it is essential to differentiate between metronomic rate and actual tempo.

Metronomes are absolutely, mechanically precise. Grooves and feels, however, the aesthetic motors that underlie rhythmic patterns repeated over time, are not. (They can come extremely close, even without a metronome as a guide.) Moreover, even "steady" tempos are modifiable in real time; that is, the tempo of a song may change from phrase to phrase or even within a phrase. A metronome's aim is faultless timekeeping, but tempo is epitomized by the way each human being subtly and subjectively interprets it, in a groove or feel. The same metronome marking may sound entirely different in different feels, in the same way as an optical illusion can make two lines of the same length appear different. Even when music directors and choreographers agree on and set tempos from the outset, mark them carefully, and perform them consistently, dissension seems to arise.

Click tracks go through the monitoring system. You collaborate with the sound department to rig the click to your and the musicians' specifications. Make sure you that can hear the click as you wish to, but that it is inaudible to the audience. A freestanding metronome should always be on the podium for reference, but its beats are yours alone and cannot be shared, unless you plug it into the monitors.

You can trust your own internal clock only up to a point. After a long career in music, I have developed something like perfect relative tempo memory, using metronome markings that are ingrained in me as references for others. Yet I am aware that my accuracy is compromised by my state of being—fatigue, excitement, caffeine, meals—so I always check my numbers against the metronome's before deploying them, and especially before defending them. Undoubtedly, the most common notes and complaints that music directors receive from directors, stage managers, or performers concern tempo; that is, a number or section is deemed too fast or too slow. Even preset metronome markings will undergo repeated reexamination and resetting.

A click track shared by other members of the orchestra or rhythm section, obviously, keeps you and the orchestra metronomically honest. When you're using a click, your conducting and playing must accurately represent the beat. When you're not using a click, your closest connection should be with those instrumentalists keeping the time. If there is a rhythm section, concentrate on coordinating the tempo with them, and trust their knowledge of it. If the violins play steady staccato notes, work with them to lock in the rhythm. Sing or otherwise feel the beat or subdivisions of it internally, giving yourself a tangible pulse (some older metronomes have a vibrating touch pad, a very handy feature). Rehearse the players so that they understand the purpose behind the desired tempos and adhere to them over repeated performances. A collective approach is superior to a single, fallible authority trying to rein in the variables of several human beings, all subject to the same influences on their internal clocks as you are.

There are two types of tempo changes: first, planned changes, such as a notated and rehearsed *rallentando* or *accelerando*, and second, adjustments of ongoing tempos in real time. In rehearsal, you explain the reasoning and the techniques behind tempo adjustments. "So that the singer has time to breathe, after that *ritard* we need to add an extra lift." "Energize this section. If that means to you that you rush it little bit, that's fine, or just think of it as very bright. We're supporting the ecstatic emotion on stage." You obviously cannot rehearse real-time adjustments, but during rehearsal you develop expectations of where you will need to attend to them (let's say the drummer, for instance, always rushes in the bridge, or the singer tends to slow down more at the cadence than he did in rehearsal).

Many examples of conducting tempo changes appear in earlier examples. The slowing at the ends of the A sections of "Sometimes a Day Goes By" and at the end of "Breathe" (Figure 17.4), the transition from verse to chorus in "Oh, What a Beautiful Morning" (Figure 17.7), the broadening of the last few measures of "Make Our Garden Grow," and the accompanied recitatives in "What Is This Feeling?" (Figure 17.13) and "Sit Down, You're Rockin' the Boat" (Figure 17.12) are all examples of planned, rehearsed tempo variations. The rule is that decelerating beats result in expanded beat patterns, while acceleration entails more compact motions. This is a physical reality as well as a musical translation, applicable to tempo shifts and constant tempos alike.

Feels, Grooves, and Syncopations

Music moves not just in a certain tempo but in a certain fashion. It bounces, it skips, it lilts, it slinks, it cooks. As conductor you embody the "feel" of music in your gestures and attitude. You do not create the feel—it is already there—but you perpetuate it. Because stage music conforms to onstage content, a universe of feels is possible, sometimes within a single production, or even a number. Feel dictates the rate at which music moves, that is, its tempo. A merengue is more animated than a tango, but a tango is tenser. A hard rock song can travel in high gear, or be a lumbering wall of sound. Feel and genre are interconnected as well. Most songs in the rock repertoire, for example, have a backbeat or half-time feel, and swing rhythms, or "shuffles" (variously interpreted triple rhythms) are most common in jazz or jazz-influenced music.

One can further deconstruct the notion of "feel" into groove, a specific rhythmic pattern formed by interacting rhythms in different parts. Musicians usually reserve the term "groove" for feels that are conspicuously solid. One is more likely to refer to the show-folk-rock "feel" of "Sometimes a Day Goes By" than its "groove." "Easy to Be Hard" has a groove that the players themselves create, as the song's performance history shows. Your job as music director is to formulate and codify feels and grooves, initiate them on cue, and maintain them over time.

The insistent hard-rock groove, straight-ahead feel, and furious tempo of "Time Warp" require a great commitment of energy from the conductor. The "Jerry Lee Lewis" style of piano comping (providing a rhythmically interesting but non-melodic accompaniment for a soloist) indicated in the score also encapsulates the energy of the groove. The groove is embodied in your hands and overall physicality, so any bodily movements you make must also be in time. If you're stomping your foot, stomp in tempo. When you reach the half-note chords of the hook ("*Let's do* the *time warp* again"), communicate the depth of the longer notes and their striking contrast to the driving four-beat with precisely placed chords on the piano coordinated precisely with weightier movements of your head and body.

The groove of "Breathe" is a beautifully woven mesh of instruments in counterpoint: gentle rhythm patterns in the guitar and percussion, trumpet and flute counter lines, and support from piano and bass, all underpinning a euphonious vocal arrangement. Because the interaction of the lines forms the musical substance, you simultaneously conduct each of the individual idiomatic elements and coordinate their amalgamation. In Figure 17.4, when the vocal enters, you conduct a precise three-beat to the guitar and percussionist, moving with the root and offbeats of the guitar. Your beat is small, so as not to waste movement, and because the quarter note is quite brisk. When the bass enters on a sustained note eight bars later, you change to a one-beat feel: the first eight bars have established the groove, and the bass entrance confirms the dotted half note as its underlying motor.

Your approach to the traditional feels of "Oh, What a Beautiful Morning" and "Belle" would be similar. Once you have established tempo, your conducting can attend to details of the orchestration while sustaining the feel. Dance along with the music, and enliven your beat with specificity and variety according to the dramatic and comedic moments on stage and in the pit.

Though the stereotype of a "show tune" might suggest a square, on-the-beat feel, by now we know that not to be true. On the contrary, music directors expend a good portion of their conducting energy in dealing with syncopation. The fundamental technique for all syncopations is to accentuate the beats in your pattern after which syncopated notes, or "afterbeats," occur. The strength of your accent depends on the distance of the syncopation to the beat. If the syncopation happens very shortly after the beat, say, a sixteenth note, then your beat is very sharp, to elicit an immediate response. At the other extreme, if the syncopation happens long after the beat, for instance, only a sixteenth note before the subsequent beat, you would only lightly mark the pre-syncopation beat, just enough to announce that something will happen between the current beat and the next one. The same principle applies to syncopated entrances and syncopated beginnings of songs. When giving more than one beat of prep for a cue that begins off the beat, such as the vocal entrance in "Make Our Garden Grow," mark only lightly the beat before the prep, to prevent performers from mistaking it for the real thing.

Syncopated patterns are often the essence of a groove (not so in hard rock songs like "Time Warp"). Progressive pop songs and rhythm-and-blues-influenced material, in particular, as one might categorize "Easy to Be Hard," tend to have more syncopation. In more old-fashioned material such as "Belle," syncopations such as those in the signature introductory measures (mm. 17–18 in Figure 17.9), give variety, character, and uniqueness to otherwise unremarkable feels. When conducting you can highlight the syncopations in "Belle" in your beat patterns and in your body in any number of ways. You can skew the pattern diagonally within the field, which slants and thereby de-emphasizes the downbeats, and do the same with your posture. Your shoulders and hips are especially useful for moving in counter-rhythms to the on-the-beat pattern of your arms and hands.

The repeated treble eighth-note chords that anchor the groove of "What Is This Feeling?" combine with the syncopated stop-time punctuations to produce its standard theater-pop groove. Your conducting can help the song overcome some of its derivativeness (as does the clever orchestration). Keep the eighth notes airtight with exactness of motion, and the accents precise and in character with carefully calculated preparations. As noted, clear beat patterns and a restricted rebound will help to evince precision and character in the feel.

Dynamics and Articulations

Dynamics and articulations also motivate and define beats and preparations, syncopated or otherwise. Their influence is discernible in the shapes of beat patterns, and you can transfer them to your gestures and body movements. Dynamics, as noted, are a measure of perception of loudness, and articulation is the manner in which notes attack, sustain, and release. In the same way as they shape notes, dynamics and articulations shape your conducting motions. Stage music can go to dynamic extremes, and is often very specifically articulated. These musical elements reflect the vivid detail of stage entertainment. For these reasons, as well as for musical ones, dynamics and articulation are often your main focus when conducting.

Dynamics are relative. A *forte* in "Sometimes a Day Goes By" is unlike a *forte* in "Time Warp," or "Make Our Garden Grow." Stage scores tend to omit many dynamic indications, as they are production specific. Simple hand motions can instantaneously and clearly convey desired dynamics and general articulations. Smaller patterns generally indicate relative softness, and larger patterns, loudness. You will use a large, majestic beat pattern to empower the full-volume sing-off and weighty coda of "Make Our Garden Grow," but for "Time Warp" the dynamic is in your beat's intensity, not its size. For the small forces and head conducting of "Sometimes a Day Goes By," your pattern will vary little with the dynamic shifts. When playing and conducting, as in "Sometimes a Day Goes By" and "Time Warp," the dynamic of your playing also "conducts" the group dynamics. When not playing, rotate your palms up and move your hands upward to indicate loudness, or a crescendo, and the opposite, palms down, hands moving downward, to show softness or a diminuendo. Specify the length of a dynamic shift by regulating your upward or downward movement. When not conducting a beat pattern your gestures are freer to indicate dynamics, or in some instances you dedicate your left hand to dynamic indications while your right hand continues to beat time.

As well as the size of your beat, your posture and attitude on the podium can convey dynamics. Yet sometimes it is more important for you to show the character of a dynamic rather than the dynamic itself. In a way, as conductor you "act" the song with the singer to portray its musical context. In "Easy to Be Hard," with its tendency toward restraint (see the earlier analysis), your demeanor is somewhat mild but a bit tense through the verses, and only slightly more passionate during the B sections. In "What Is This Feeling?" you can play the humor with the singers. Your body, facial expressions, and thought process can communicate both the dynamics (which consist mostly of being softer under soloists and louder under the group) and the archness of tone. Certain passages of "Belle" are purely joyous (such as the sections conducted in one), and there you can let your beat pattern soar to reflect exuberance, rather than indicating a specific dynamic. Small conducting gestures and a relaxed demeanor persist throughout "Breathe," regardless of written dynamics, a result of your understanding of the intimate dramatic setting from which the song originates.

On the podium you must often quiet the accompaniment, so as not to drown out singing or dialogue. Many notes you receive from the director will concern the orchestra's being too loud (most of the rest will be about tempo). Sound design has mitigated this problem somewhat, but not entirely; especially in live situations it is incumbent on the conductor to keep the band or orchestra soft enough that it does not interfere with spoken or sung text. Set up drum kits, amplifiers, and other loud sound sources so as to alleviate overloud volumes (see the previous chapter, "Orchestras and Orchestration"). Most instrumentalists are well aware that they will have to attenuate their dynamics when accompanying a stage production.

Like dynamics, articulations in stage music are often generalized and customized. Scores from before the 1990s, those that predate computer copying, are less likely to have complete and consistent articulation markings. For a shortcut, an orchestrator or copyist might have marked articulations only in the original statement of a musical phrase, and assumed the music director and players would interpret it similarly whenever it appeared. You might have to add in articulations or research the writers' intent when preparing scores and parts. Some will be self-explanatory, implicit by style or by extrapolation within a score. Most composers, arrangers, and music directors have fully availed themselves of the capabilities of computer notation to enter articulations more specifically.

The following is a brief listing of articulation marks you will find in stage scores, how to interpret them for the stage, and how to indicate them when conducting.

> Staccato and *marcato*: These are generalized indications of shortness; *marcato* notes are accented as well as short. The beats of a staccato patter are small and stop on each ictus with little or no rebound. A sharper ictus or more forceful gesture indicates more accent. There are two main types of staccato marking, a dot and a wedge, the latter implying a slight accent and extreme shortness.
>
> *Tenuto*: A *tenuto* marking (a straight line over a note) indicates that a note is to be held its full length. If there are several *tenuto* markings in a row, particularly when a note is repeated, a slight space between notes is implicit. The space becomes larger with a combined *tenuto*/staccato marking. A slur appearing over *tenuto* markings ("*louré*" in string terms) gives a combined effect of sustain and separation. For *tenuto*, your gestures have some resistance; you rest slightly on every ictus and move through them with gravity, as if holding a moderately heavy object. Longer stops on ictuses indicate either greater separation between beats or an extended duration, as some *tenuto* markings imply.

Accents: Stage music loves accents, a musical attribute certainly germane to splashy stage choreography. The accent vocabulary is wide and varied, but the conducting gesture for all of them is basically the same, a physically accented beat with minimal bounce. You can develop in your own gestural lexicon some specificity to match each accent and its intent; as always, embodying the purpose of a musical value in your conducting is the most effective approach. The basic accent symbol (>) is shortened by the addition of a staccato (·) or lengthened with a *tenuto*.

Legato: Slurs, or phrase markings, are also contextual. For winds and strings, slurs indicate not only legato but also connection with breath or bow. True legato is not just slurring, but also connection of tones for expressive purpose; the *espressivo* aspect of legato playing might or might not be inherent in the written marking. Strings and winds cannot stay on one bow or one breath forever, so their slurs may interrupt a legato articulation. (You might dictate breaths or bow changes in rehearsal, but the players mostly figure them out on their own.) There are other ways than slurs to notate the connection of notes. A *tenuto* symbol followed by a staccato effects a down-up, long-short slur. A legato beat pattern is, like the articulation it represents, very liquid with slight resistance, moving through beats with no discernible stop, instead using change of direction and speed to define the ictuses.

Cueing and the Stage

Cueing, for a conductor, means initiating a musical event or showing someone where to begin playing or singing. All the preceding techniques, therefore, represent some form of cueing. Though elementary, cueing is essential, because the order and manner in which events happen on stage determine believability. The conducting principles with which I began this chapter—clarity and purpose, with meaningful, economical gestures—apply particularly well to cueing. You cue events for a reason, cue them precisely, and cue them in character.

When possible, make eye contact with whomever you cue; of course, if performers are in character or musicians are engrossed in the music, you may not catch their eyes, but you can still give the cue. It is acceptable to leave the conducting field when cueing; indeed, a gesture outside the field's boundary is particularly explicit (the field itself remains intact). To cue something on stage from below in a pit, extend your arm upward so that it is in clear view (this move may take some contortion, depending on your position). Conducting to a camera makes it difficult to cue individuals, and unfortunately there is no real solution. When possible, try to combine camera cues with live ones.

Most cues are simple preparatory gestures and, as in any prep, breathing is crucial. Inhale with the singer or player in conjunction with your preparatory gesture. Breathe according to the nature of the instrument or voice and the musical character. When you are cueing the twittering flutes in "Oh, What a Beautiful Morning," breathe as a flutist would breathe. You may choose to conduct a singer or player beyond a cue, to continue supporting his or her effort. This flute passage would be one example, as would a chorus's forcefully sustained chord. You can also give a very obvious cue when a performer needs reminding of a certain event or quality of the music. For example, if you think a singer might breathe where he or she shouldn't, then when cueing, conduct the entire phrase. You disallow a breath by prolonging your motion. If a singer or player has a tendency to enter early, then shortly before the cue, hold him or her back with a flat hand, palm out (a "stop" sign), that is, freeze him or her with your conducting, until the correct moment, where you give a very visible cue.

Some cues are only formalities. The actor portraying Curly will not need a prep to start "there's a bright golden haze . . ." but you might cue him nonetheless. You are the traffic director for the show and for the audience. Your cues point the performers and the listeners in the right direction, giving shape to the whole and detail to each moment.

18

From the Studio to the Stage

In the final phases of production rehearsal, the creative team integrates all facets of the work into a form that an audience who will buy tickets to see it, and who will enter into the experience with a certain set of expectations, can apprehend and appreciate. As pivotal as rehearsals are, they are only a facsimile of what eventually will be on stage. Even productions that rehearse in the same venue where they perform lack viewers and listeners as essential ingredients to the recipe. When you're moving a production from rehearsal room to performance venue, your objective as music director, as it was in rehearsal, is to believably fuse the music with stagecraft, text, and movement.

Music directors are overrun with duties during this period, but their work follows the flow more than leads the surge. Almost every rehearsal will require that a musical representative be in attendance, if not you, then someone you designate. You will always be needed somewhere, maybe at the sound board, at a creative meeting, in the rehearsal hall with the musicians or a singer, or at a note session. Long hours are the norm and days off are scarce, with cast rehearsals, tech rehearsals, orchestra rehearsals, load-ins and seatings all amassing within a week or two. This can also be a very lucrative time in commercial production, with overlapping rehearsals that inflate music directors' salaries with overtime premiums.

Run-throughs, Dress Rehearsals, and the *Sitzprobe*

The last weeks of studio rehearsal (or, proportionately, in more hurried circumstances, the last days) are customarily devoted to running scenes and/or numbers in show order, without stopping. At first, no one involved in a studio "run-through," or "work-through," or "stumble-through," or "put-together" stipulates or expects proficiency in any stage discipline: singing, acting, or movement. The purpose of these rehearsals is for creative staff and performers to experience the sequence of events from beginning to end, to find out what needs more rehearsal, and to uncover sections already rehearsed that need alteration now that they have been integrated into the whole. (The notion of "dress" rehearsal is now mostly a vestige of more traditional stage rehearsal practices, its specific connotation of rehearsing in costume lost amongst the many technical demands and add-ons of modern stage production. Now the term refers to any rehearsal in which a show is run in its entirety, with or without full production values, including costumes.)

In stark contrast to the leniency allowed stage performers, at this phase, the standard for the music director, as accompanist or conductor of the accompaniment, and for the accompaniment itself, is perfection. The instrumental contingent in final studio rehearsals must be as fluent, flawless, and consistent as conditions permit. The supportive nature of your work as music director is never more evident, nor more important, than in these final rehearsals. While others grope to find their way, you provide unconditional assistance. A reliable accompaniment helps the director see his or her vision, helps performers fulfill their assignments, and helps all to assess the presentation's performance readiness or worthiness. A faulty accompaniment can only detract from these efforts. The rehearsal accompaniment may not take exactly the same form as the final accompaniment; in many cases, you have probably not yet incorporated the full instrumental ensemble. The rehearsal accompaniment, however, has reached its apex in these final rehearsals, and you can perfect it as a separate entity. In shorter rehearsal periods, this rigor is somewhat relaxed, but the fact remains that the proper execution of many production elements rests upon the accompaniment, so its presentation must be as close to performance level at this point in the process as is feasible.

Indeed, there is no reason for your work, besides time constraints, to be anything less than polished. By this point in the process, you will have had ample practice time on the technical elements of the music, and you will have run increasingly large segments of the show. You now know the arrangements, the strengths and weaknesses of the stage performers and rehearsal musicians, the dramatic or comedic intent and plot of the show, the cues, the pacing, and the staging, and indeed some of this work may be of your own creation. If the rehearsal period has been extensive, you know these things more intimately and profoundly.

The director and stage manager, and sometimes the choreographer, take charge of run-throughs, and might call aloud performance cues and directions, scene and lighting shifts, or costume changes. For example, someone— probably the stage manager—will cue you to start the show (assuming the show starts with music), and call out, "Applause!" at each predicted applause point. Small invited audiences may attend, among them designers, producers, backers, consultants, advisers, technicians, and friends. They form an encouraging and observant group, and can be good barometers of progress or success at a sensitive moment in the production process. The creative staff uses such test audiences to measure reactions and work out timings, yet understands that the sincerity and accuracy of their responses are questionable because of professional bias. One cannot assume, for example, that the thunderous ovation a heartfelt solo ballad receives in a rehearsal room will be duplicated in a large space, without a constituency of automatic sympathizers.

Music directors will no doubt feel some measure of disappointment in the loss of quality or unexpected alterations in singers' performances during these rehearsals. Performers taking steps backward, or sideways, is a natural part of the process, and you should reserve attempts to restore what you might perceive as their having forgotten or ignored until you have made two important judgments. First, do you believe the deficiency or change to be temporary, and something you can overlook until it happens repeatedly, or is it something that will need rehearsing, in the short term or ongoing? Second, is a change a more truthful musical or acting choice, and did it perhaps arise out of a performer's instinct, and is it therefore more believable? If the answer to the second question is yes, you will want to rethink the music direction rather than remind the performer of the existing plan or "correct" what he or she has changed.

Prioritize your adjustments. Devise a plan to fix what urgently needs fixing and that which realistically can be fixed. It is difficult to find music rehearsal time this late in the production, so some of your work with the performers might be impromptu. Dress rehearsals improve through repetition, and many vocal performances return to their earlier levels of proficiency. Within a few run-throughs, you will be able to assess how the larger demands of a production are affecting the vocal performances. Gauge the process to find the right time to address recurrent problem areas. Some issues might be better left until the production has moved into technical rehearsals and is playing in its performance space, as the new venue might entail further adjustments. Again, whenever possible, to lock a musical direction into a performer's routine, connect it somehow to the larger scheme of the production.

With the performers' attention now trained on many elements, it requires strategizing to interest them in musical specifics. Be judicious as well as proactive; it is easy to be overeager when there is so much to be done in such a short time. Let's say that after a run-through, you are concerned with a leading soprano's intonation in a tricky melisma (a group of notes sung to a single syllable). She is relaxing on a chair with a cup of tea. You tell her that she did a great job, except for the penultimate notes of the phrase, which were a little under pitch. She agrees, and informs you of how she was already aware of the problem, and that she had planned to work on it, and thanks for letting her know, and as soon as you've walked away, she forgets that you ever had the conversation, because at that moment, what is occupying her thought process is that she was too far upstage of her costar, her face was invisible to the right side of the house, and that her tea is cold. So that she will better absorb what you have to offer, approach the singer and ask when it would be a good time to discuss your notes from the run-through, perhaps now, or a bit later.

The director and choreographer will also have major concerns arising from run-throughs, and as usual their work takes precedence. During these final rehearsals the director and choreographer will also be more likely to voice their opinions about musical performances, to you or to the performers directly, and some of their notes or comments may contravene what you (or they) have directed. This is the time for cooperation, not resistance. Unfortunately, the trickle-down of pressure on a director can always rain upon a music department. The music director may be a target, and the musical needs seem like mere inconveniences, when so many other important things are going on. (This is not just true of music; any creative element might become a scapegoat or be brushed aside when the stakes are high.)

Holding a sing-through, or *Sitzprobe*, as a final step in the process of rehearsing a musical show, comes from opera, where the conductor, orchestra, and singers would coordinate their musical performance of large, complex scores without interference from onstage matters. In modern commercial stage production, with its lighter music, amplified sound, and primacy of onstage values, a *Sitzprobe* might be only a courtesy, albeit a very welcome and enjoyable one. Most productions make time for one even when it is not needed, and a few use a *Sitzprobe* in place of one orchestra rehearsal. In any case, a *Sitzprobe* is a milestone in a production, marking a nearly completed creative preparatory journey.

Singers and dancers certainly want to hear their accompaniment before it is buried under the stage or in a monitor system, but in reality the difference between what happens in a *Sitzprobe* and when a production moves into a theater is so drastic that it renders what one learns in a studio sing-through almost moot. You can hold the *Sitzprobe* in the performance venue, after the load-in and sound check (see the following section, "Load-ins, Seatings, and Sound Checks"), which is a sensible and efficient strategy when rehearsal time is short, and better approximates the performance relationship of singers and orchestra, as is the objective. In preproduction, you and the contractor, in consultation with the producer, director, and stage manager, schedule the *Sitzprobe* at a desirable time, usually between the final orchestra rehearsal and the first dress rehearsal with orchestra and cast together in the performance venue. Usually you will have time for reading each number of a show only once or twice. When scheduling, allow for a minimum of triple the length of a number (for a five-minute song, schedule at least fifteen minutes).

As music director you will seldom have the undivided attention of every performer as you do in a *Sitzprobe*. Furthermore, unlike run-throughs in a rehearsal room, in this environment you, and the accompaniment, are permitted errors. It is your first crack at listening to the singers while leading the orchestra. Here you can sort out the mechanics of your conducting, and determine what you need to practice or refine in your own performance as well as others'. It is everyone's rehearsal to share in, which makes it exciting, but it is yours to lead, which makes it invaluable to you.

The excitement preceding and during these rehearsals is unmitigated, and their party atmosphere can be so pervasive that they cease to be rehearsals at all and turn into celebrations. Stage performers are utterly energized by the arrival of a larger ensemble playing music that until this point they have heard only in reduced form. After weeks of hard physical work, all the stage performers have to do at these rehearsals is sing with the band, a comparatively easy effort invariably brings out big smiles and charged vocal performances. (Figures 18.1A and 18.1B). Whereas collective appreciation is empowering,

FIGURE 18.1 The *Sitzprobe* for *Dessa Rose*, with (A) music director David Holcenberg at the keyboard, and (B) music director Alex Lacamoire reveling with the cast at the *Sitzprobe* for *In The Heights*. (*Credits:* A: Sara Krulwich/The *New York Times*/Redux; B: Photo by Josh Lehrer.)

you should nonetheless keep things moving. Amidst the gaiety, it is easy to lose time to ecstasy and mutual admiration. It is your rehearsal to lead and organize, and therefore up to you to stay on point. Set the tone at the beginning: "I love everyone's enthusiasm, and let's all enjoy this wonderful union of cast and orchestra to the fullest. Let's also remember we have two hours of music to cover in three hours, so let's work efficiently enough that we can get through the whole score." I must add, neither facetiously nor bitterly, that the extreme glorification that music directors, orchestras, and orchestrations often experience in a *Sitzprobe* might well be only temporary.

Load-ins, Seatings, and Sound Checks

In the days leading up to public performances, the production and its personnel move into the performing venue. As music director you bring with you your work-related gear and items of personal necessity and comfort to a new, probably transient office space, often a dressing room or some other backstage locale. In most productions, music directors have little to do with transporting musical equipment into the playing area, a procedure called the load-in. Musical instruments and their accessories are but one small part of a production's load-in. By the time they arrive, the scenery is likely already on the stage, racks in the dressing rooms are filling with clothes, miles of wiring for sound and electrics have been laid, and so on. The music load-in itself is often technically complex, and must fit within the larger schedule and physical configuration. Thus the typical production model puts ultimate responsibility for it on the stage crew rather than on the music department, though as music director you, along with the music coordinator, are the crew's primary advisers and consultants.

In preproduction you will have discussed with the crew chiefs and designers the space required in the pit or band area, and provided some kind of mock-up of your ideal configuration (Figure 18.2). This will become part of the overall design of the show, and during its construction or preparation you should visit the venue to ensure its progress and workability (if you cannot, you can request photographs taken from several angles). On Broadway the music coordinator will be the music department's primary representative at load-in (especially when you are at rehearsal), and works with the stage crew to achieve the desired layout. A load-in takes several hours, and is often done in phases, over a period of days or even weeks. The customized pits of many new shows, tucked into unusual areas, sometimes require special construction.

The props department sets up such objects as any heavy instruments (drums, pianos, organs, keyboards, harps), the amplifiers, chairs, music stands, music lights (their cables will be run by electricians), risers, shelving, carpeting, acoustic paneling, and, very importantly, your podium. The sound department situates and connects microphones, speakers, audio monitors, headphones, mixers, cables, and sometimes the video equipment, too—the cameras and monitor screens (video may also be handled by

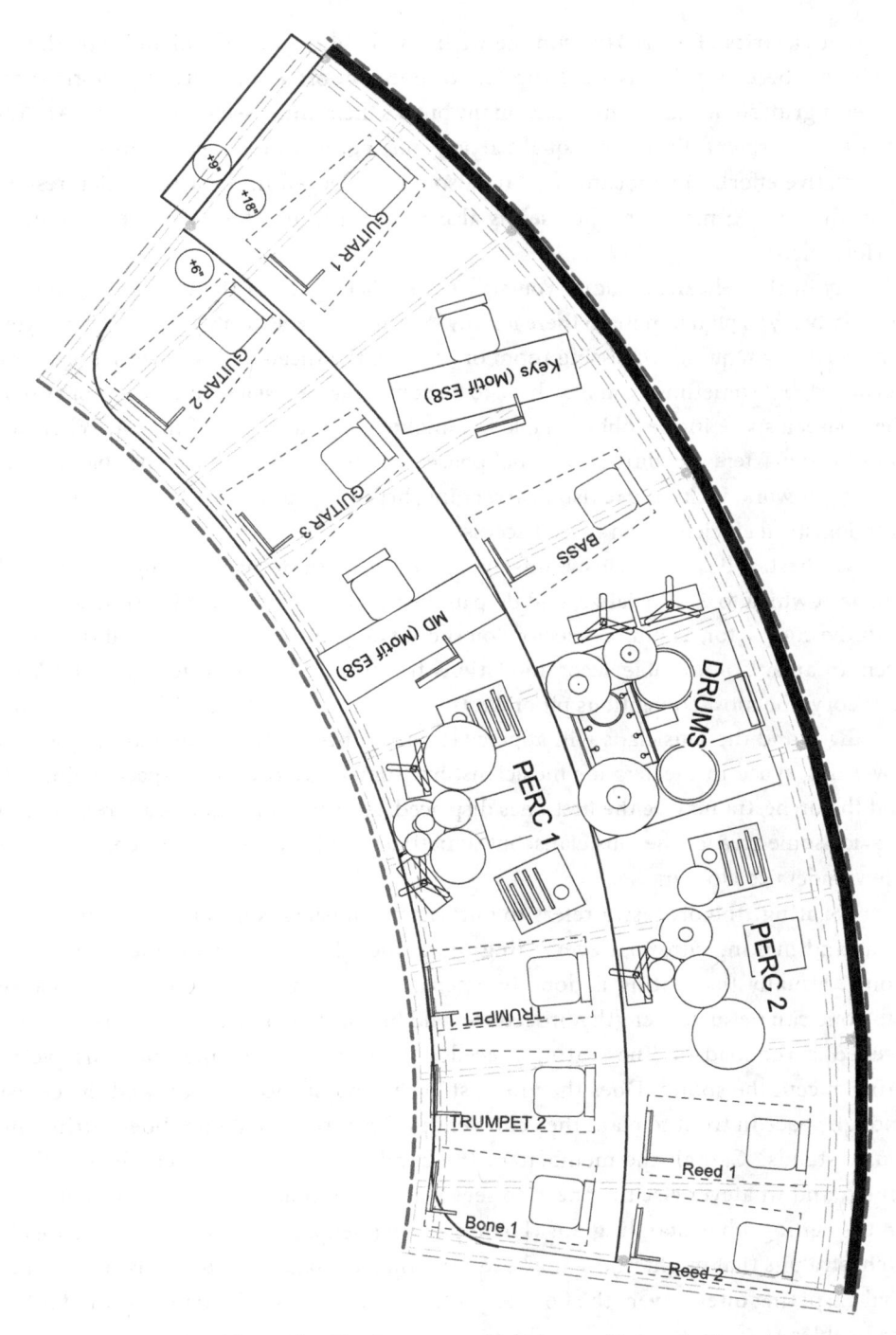

FIGURE 18.2 Stage band layout for *The Capeman* at the Delacorte Theater in Central Park.

props or electrics). Electricians run the wiring and lighting, overhead and stand lighting both. These technicians are dedicated to your comfort and facility of performance, however gruff some may seem or how many breaks their union seems to require. Always treat them respectfully and as equal participants, not just functionaries in support of the creative effort. Most technicians are also quite engaged in the artistry that results from their work; many are themselves also musicians, directors, designers, or stage performers.

As in the rehearsal studio, you will need office space in the performing venue, especially if you plan to remain there for any length of time. Probably you will have (you may certainly request) a dressing room or office in the theater, ideally with a piano or keyboard, but sometimes you may have to be content with just a secluded row or two of the house, a space in the lobby, a table in a nightclub, or a corner of the pit. Wherever your headquarters are, during the final phases of rehearsal you should be able to continue your work, including revising, arranging, brushing up, and giving notes privately, with logistical efficiency and ease of access.

Orchestras deserve exclusive offstage space, too, with storage, a changing area, and a table at which to eat, socialize, and do paperwork, musical and administrative. Along with the contractor, as music director you should do your best to ensure that they have such an area. Comfortable accommodations translate to better performance (at least in theory; the most contentious pit orchestras are sometimes those with the most opulent digs), and the musicians will appreciate your concern. The union has regulations governing space in theaters for musicians, but sometimes backstage space is limited, and the orchestra may be the first ones displaced. All Broadway houses are required to provide some area for the musicians, but sometimes it is little more than a corridor with a few undersized lockers.

"Seating" the orchestra refers to putting the musicians into their playing positions and making sure that everything there, including their instruments, is functional. Usually the seating is done in a separate session from the load-in, because each one can be such a lengthy procedure, and because the musicians are usually not needed at the load-in. The seating precedes the sound check, and concerns everything except the sound. Does the violinist have enough room to bow and the cellist enough space in front to plant the cello's endpin? Are the trombone slides hitting the music stands? Can all the members of the band orchestra see the conductor, their music, and whatever else they need to see? Is the drummer knocking his or her head on the ceiling when standing up? (Foam padding belongs on any protrusions inside orchestra pits that might injure the heads and limbs of passing musicians, and industrial carpeting often covers the floor to protect against passersby tripping and falling over cables.)

There is no reason to call the musicians all at once for the seating, unless the ensemble is very small, or if the orchestration and sound design are entirely acoustic and the music is very traditional and orchestral. With a non-amplified group playing non-electrified music, or with a chamber-sized group using minimal sound reinforcement (such as a mic on the piano, a pickup on the bass, or an onstage amp for the guitar), you can approximate the positions of chairs and stands, invite all the musicians in, and have them shuffle about until comfortable. But whenever a rhythm section or amplified or electrified instruments are involved, you should call each rhythm section player (keyboards, drums, percussion, bass, guitar) for an individual seating. It can take quite some time to situate each player functionally. If you can, schedule an hour or more apiece; thirty minutes is a minimum. Bring in the remainder of the orchestra by section (strings, reeds, brass), or if it is a modestly sized group, bring in the others all at once. Allow at least a half hour for each section.

Sound checks ensure that the audience, the musicians, and you can hear the instruments properly, alone and as a group. A sound check sometimes follows the seating immediately, or on the same day. Connecting the seating and sound check can save time and money; one efficient scheduling practice is to hold the orchestra seating and sound check in the theater in the morning and early afternoon and follow with the *Sitzprobe* later in the day. In scheduling musicians for a sound check, double the amount of time that you had allotted to each player or group of players for the seating. Start the call with the rhythm section. Drummers, guitarists, and keyboard players probably take the longest. Allow extra time for balancing larger groupings, working your way up to *tutti*. The full group also needs sound check time as well; play a few numbers with varying styles or instrumental combinations to check balances. At times you might bring singers into an orchestra sound check to estimate vocal-orchestral balances; this practice can save time and improve quality later on. It also gives singers another chance to hear what it will sound like to them singing in the hall with the orchestra, especially if the *Sitzprobe* is in a separate space.

If an orchestra is mostly or entirely made up of keyboards emulating acoustic sounds (a so-called virtual orchestra), the load-in, seating, and sound check overlap much more. You can combine them into one, as you might with a keyboard section in a larger orchestra. Internal balancing begins with the programmer and continues with you and the player, who set volume levels in orchestra rehearsal and sound check. The sound design and operator then mix the pre-balanced electronic instruments with any real ones and with the voices on stage.

The Broadway and pop music concert models for load-ins, seatings, and sound checks are well thought out and streamlined. With specialists assiduously and creatively fulfilling their tasks under your watchful but non-interfering eye, you are assured of a physical setup that is at the very least utilitarian, and usually much more than that. In amateur and some academic and developmental productions, on the other hand, any or all of these tasks might fall into your lap. Organize a team if you can, and distribute the duties as on Broadway. Your role may be more hands on: moving chairs, connecting cables, screwing in light bulbs. The order in which you do things is important, and common sense can guide you. First construct the playing area, set up the equipment,

FIGURE 18.3 The unusual offstage band setup at *Carrie* (Off-Broadway), with (A) Paul Staroba, music director, and (B) a stage thrust encroaching on the orchestra pit and conductor's podium. (*Credits:* A: Joshua Bright/*New York Times*/Redux; B: Photo courtesy of the Grosse Pointe (MI) Public School System.)

FIGURE 18.4 Mesh ceilings now cover many pits to protect those on stage from falling in, but also enclose the orchestra, acoustically and/or visually, and sometimes physically. (*Credit:* Photo courtesy Falun Dafa Association of Calgary/*Epoch Times*).

and run any wiring, then seat the orchestra. Next, position the microphones and monitors, and, finally, do the sound check.

Things move slowly and methodically in seatings and sound checks, as they should, for this is the only chance to get the setup right. Inevitably problems will surface. Patience and cooperation are preferable emotional stances to panic or finger pointing. Sometimes you may need to make severe adjustments to suit the physical space: cutting a drum kit in half, hanging instruments on a wall when they are not being played, rethinking of some element of the sound design, even re-orchestrating.

All departments are suffering through comparable growing pains, and all are making concessions, as are you. Solve problems creatively, and cooperatively. That there are so many unorthodox orchestral configurations in modern stage productions is testament to the obstacles music directors face and their innovative thinking in overcoming or avoiding them (Figures 18.3 and 18.4).

Music directors are always pleased to mount the podium in the many well-designed, permanent pits (and stages, and rehearsal studios) that have been and are being constructed in performing arts centers, theaters, and concert halls around the world. There, they and the musicians sit comfortably, even luxuriously. Many universities with strong arts programs are paragons in creating well-appointed music performance spaces. In these pits and theaters are amenities like hard-wired, state-of-the-art electrics, lighting, and sound equipment; and spacious warm-up, dressing, and lounge areas. Architects

FIGURE 18.5 A new pit under construction at the Blackfoot Performing Arts Center, Idaho. (*Credit:* Photo reprinted by permission of BPAC.)

design the halls with acoustics and the musicians in mind (Figure 18.5), and the resident professional and faculty crew members, designers, and staff know well the capabilities and operations of their venues. As music director you can harvest their knowledge in feeding your physical and musical needs.

The Podium

Setting up your podium will be done at the load-in, or occasionally, part of constructing the set. (There may be no podium, but wherever the musical leader sits or stands in performance becomes the operative podium.) The podium will be your home in performance, so having what you need within easy reach is indispensable. Unfortunately, there are few available prefabricated podiums or conductors' desks for general sale that provide space adequate to the needs of a modern music director, apart from some double-wide music stands and some with one or two small shelves underneath. Yet you will probably need something more substantial for the chattel that the podium will store, including your scores, full and reduced; the associate and assistant conductors' scores; a spacious, sturdily anchored surface that can withstand the bulk of all those scores, on which you can read and annotate them (a conductor's "desk"); a monitor speaker or two, headphones, a mixer, a video camera, a video monitor, a microphone to talk to the orchestra, one or two telephones connecting you to the stage managers and sound operator, and some means of taking notes (pads and pencil, a laptop, an iPad);

FIGURE 18.6 The author at the conductor's station for *Mask* at the Pasadena Playhouse, CA. Among the visible items, counterclockwise from behind my left shoulder: a laptop running Ableton live (synthesizer patch information), a front fill speaker, the conductor's left monitor speaker, the phone line to stage management, the conductor camera, a loop generator, a speaker selector, the keyboard and music stand, and, barely visible in the extreme lower right, a second laptop to display the loops. (*Credit:* Photo property of the author.)

and a metronome, batons, water bottles, and any number of tchotchkes. This list does not take into account a keyboard or guitar and any associated gear, such as synthesizer modules or computers.

With acoustic music and in productions with little or no amplification, you can make do with a more sparsely furnished podium. You will not need the speakers, the video equipment, the mixers, or anything else that plugs in. You will still need a sizable, stable work surface.

Willing and imaginative property masters might enjoy sinking their teeth into the design and construction of a sumptuous podium with room for and convenient access to all its amenities, but a busy crew member may not always have the time or resources. The stage crew will help make your podium at least serviceable, but having the crew members construct your dream home may take more planning, and supplication. Figure 18.6 shows a very ergonomic conducting workspace.

Regardless of pit configuration, ensure that your sight lines from the podium to the musicians and the stage are clear, whether live or transmitted by video. A live sight line is preferable, without exception. The eye contact you make, the breaths you take, and the facial expressions you exchange with performers are at the heart of conducting, and they are impossible with only a camera and monitor, even if the system is two-way. Much effort goes into replicating this immediacy of contact by electronic means, but nothing can ever replace looking at and conversing with someone in person. Ensure that the pit floor, where the musicians are seated, is not so far below you that they cannot look up to see you. This is a function both of the podium height and the distance from the pit floor to the deck. If the orchestra is buried too deeply, it might as well be in isolation.

Although traditional orchestra seating configurations were designed not just for acoustic purposes but also for visual ones, almost every Broadway musical now has a camera on the conductor. It feeds his or her image to the stage through monitors positioned in the wings and on the front the of the balcony (this ostensibly so that the singers can also keep their heads up and play to the balcony instead of looking down into the pit), and increasingly often to the orchestra, sometimes with a small video monitor mounted on every music stand. The podium should put you at a height where you are visible to all, and from where you can, ostensibly, see and hear everyone equally well. When using a camera and monitor, make sure that the camera frames your conducting properly, or that you are conducting within the camera view, and work toward some combination of real mutual sight lines and those provided by the video equipment. It may take some experimentation to give every member of the orchestra and everyone on stage a clear view of you, and you of each of them (without undue contortions), but it will pay off.

Conducting from behind a keyboard, especially from behind a piano, presents formidable obstacles to sight lines, whether or not you are on a podium. A keyboard between you and the stage blocks the conducting field directly in front of you. If the keyboard is electronic and the music stand is not placed too high, you might be able to see and conduct over the top (you can sit on an elevated stool). But when playing on a podium behind an upright or a grand piano, you may have to tolerate limited visual exchange with the performers, either a partially obstructed view or a view available only when you actively turn toward someone. Uprights and grand pianos each present their own problems. Most high-quality uprights are tall, console-style behemoths, and grand pianos, if they are to be properly heard or amplified, should have their tops open at least partway. Propping open or removing a grand piano top restores at least a partial sight line, but the piano can be too loud. It is possible to position a piano at an angle to the forestage for a less obstructed view, but you will then face mostly in one direction, toward stage left or right. When you're conducting on stage, risers and clever positioning of orchestra members and the piano or keyboard can mitigate many sight line difficulties.

The podium should be easily accessible, so that you can get in and out often and quickly. Especially during dress and tech rehearsals, you will want to circulate through the theater to speak to your collaborators but return to the podium as home base. There should be ample room for you to wave your arms, play your instrument, and have some freedom to move your feet. Some podiums will end up restrictive despite your best efforts. The hard metal grate over the *Tommy* orchestra pit at Broadway's St. James Theatre through which my head and shoulders protruded and the very short distance between me and the apron (the front facing of the stage) caused dozens of cuts and bruises on my hands and arms, and quite a few broken batons. (I wound up using a baton only six inches long, and took care not to extend my wingspan too far in any direction while I was conducting the stage, lest I sacrifice some flesh to the grating.)

Just as important as your sight lines is how you hear the orchestra and the stage. Unlike the visual element, listening live may not be the ideal way to hear a show when conducting. This is obviously true of productions using electronic instruments, which may emit no live sound at all, but can also apply to acoustic instrumental and vocal groups, whose amplitude, for whatever reason, may not be enough to hold its own in the bigger monitoring soundscape. Interestingly, there are some acoustic orchestras I have conducted that I would have heard better through headphones, and I have led some rock orchestras whose sound I would have preferred to hear live, but had access to only through headphones or a speaker monitor.

In most cases some combination of live and enhanced monitoring is best. With both means at your disposal, you can modify your monitoring in real time, a great asset when you consider the variables of live performance. Of course, if you are on a podium in a pit, chances are you will hear at least some live sound (unless you somehow deliberately block it), because you will, in effect, be in the very first row of the house with the audience. What comes out of Broadway "front fills," speakers built into the apron, may be your loudest sound source on the podium. Because vocals often dominate their output, they can be effective vocal monitors, but they can also drown out everything else for anyone in their path.

Multichannel monitor mixers allow you to control and customize your mix, and are now relatively affordable. You can easily manipulate levels and panning, and mute or solo individual channels. In rehearsal and sound check, work out with the sound department how the instruments, vocals, and effects will be assigned to monitor channels. For listening, you may have a choice of speaker monitors or headphones (or both, or neither). Headphones assure immediacy and clarity of sound but can be unwieldy, especially when you are playing, and, depending on the type and how you wear them, isolate the conductor from the room. Many music directors have custom-made in-ear earpieces that fit snugly and comfortably. (Wireless headphones for conductors present their own set of problems; with so many devices in the theater already competing for radio frequencies, they have not been explored.) Near-field monitor speakers of the kind used in recording studios or small, powerful monaural monitor speakers are good alternatives to headphones. A single speaker will do when you want only one element of the sound, such as the vocals, louder in the mix; for a full mix a two-speaker stereo system is much preferable.

The same basic principles of positioning, sight lines, and audibility apply to an offstage or backstage band as well as a pit orchestra, except that you may be able to see and hear only by way of electronic transfer. Even when an orchestra is offstage, I recommend not splitting it up into disparate spaces, except if you expressly desire acoustic isolation. Instead, try to keep the musicians nearby one another so that the experience of collective performance is not lost; their remote placement already undermines their immediacy.

Technical Rehearsals, Previews, and Brush-ups

In technical rehearsals, or "tech," directors and designers incorporate technical elements of a production—lighting, scenery, costumes, sound, and any specialty elements—into the creative work. The stage manager, technical director, crew chiefs, and director jointly administer tech rehearsals.

At first, technical rehearsals have little to do with music, yet they require reliable, accurate musical accompaniment. You can delegate the task to an associate or rehearsal pianist, as long as he or she is well versed in the score and has a direct line of communication to you in case of questions or necessary musical adjustments. Technical issues discovered in tech rehearsals often entail alterations to the score, such as adding or subtracting measures to synchronize with revised blocking or a scene shift. Hiring a tech rehearsal pianist is more cost effective for a union production, as your pay scale well exceeds the pianist's. Orchestra rehearsals often coincide with tech, and you and your preferred rehearsal pianist might be otherwise engaged. Anticipate this conflict and recruit a tech rehearsal accompanist who is not an orchestra member, keep him or her updated throughout the rehearsal process, and keep the hot line open while you are separated. The props crew might move a piano in the house to accompany tech, particularly when the orchestra is remotely positioned or mostly electronic, but part of tech will involve sorting out the sound. You or your associate can sit on the podium and conduct the accompanist in the pit or the house (this can be a chance to practice conducting), or if a keyboard is part of the podium setup, accompany from there. Tech and dress rehearsals are occasionally combined, mostly in brief production schedules, and the orchestra may be called throughout. Otherwise, having musicians at tech is an unnecessary financial burden.

Technical rehearsals usually, but not always, proceed in show order. Most move at a snail's pace, moment to moment and cue to cue, crafting every one in at least some small way. Again, stock theaters and special events with tight schedules tech in a matter of hours, skimming over all but the essential. A "cue to cue" is a rehearsal that skips everything except technical cues, and is a common practice in tech, for the music and other departments. In a music cue to cue, you start a number, then jump to the end of that number or any significant internal juncture within it, go on to the next, and repeat the process until the desired endpoint. In a technical cue to cue, the music director follows the stage managers or tech director, and accompanies as needed or requested, as they advance through their lighting, scenic, costume, and sound cues. A clearly written score with clear measure numbering and rehearsal markings is highly advantageous in tech. You might create a master tech rehearsal copy of the score that includes notes on all technical cues that affect or correlate significantly with the music; this score can stay on the piano at tech and be used by all tech rehearsal accompanists.

As the technical functioning of a show improves through repetition and adaptation, as the pieces fit together in increasingly longer sequences, your presence as music director on the podium becomes more essential. The technical elements are now dependent on your conducting. The stage manager calls cues by watching your beat. The conducting plot becomes part of the technical plot (it probably was in rehearsal, too, but now it is codified). The consistency and clarity of your gestures take on renewed importance, as you are now communicating information to non-musicians, players, and singers alike. It also becomes increasingly important that any conductor other than you on the podium embraces the same approaches and techniques that you set forth. The way that you conduct the show encapsulates the music direction.

Again at this point in the rehearsal process, you might be shocked at how the musical work on stage seems to have degenerated. Tech is not, I repeat, about music. The director will probably be less worried about a performer singing a quarter tone flat than about his not standing in his light. A performer will be more concerned about a button on her costume being too tight than she will about the correct notes of her harmony part. Be patient. Stay out of the way during tech, unless music becomes the subject of the rehearsal, or if technical aspect of the show requires coordination with the music. If the proceedings are slow, you might be able to sneak in a note to or hold a mini-rehearsal with a performer (Figure 18.7). Of greater concern to you during tech should be how to add sixteen bars to a transition during

FIGURE 18.7 The author consults with an actor onstage during the tech for *Mask*. (*Credit:* Photo by Barry Mann.)

FIGURE 18.8 Score pages litter the podium during previews of Broadway's *If/Then*. (*Credit:* Photo by Carmel Dean.)

the dinner break, because the curtain takes sixteen more bars to rise than the director had predicted, or how the left channel of your podium monitor system is much louder than the right, or that there is a half-second sound delay between the stage and the podium.

"Previews" are paid public presentations of shows that performers and audience acknowledge are still unfinished, nearing their final form, but not quite there yet. Critics (professional and armchair both) and theater buffs love attending previews of musicals, and performers appreciate the interested and committed audience. Preview tickets are also usually discounted, so less well-heeled theatergoers, including students and fellow artists, can find relief from high retail prices.

Despite the extremely short hours available for rehearsing (Equity guidelines permit limited afternoon rehearsals during Broadway previews, and producers sometimes budget for extra because of the importance of the work done there), preview periods sometimes involve making, or at least trying out, sweeping changes in a score, a script, or staging. After all, this is the creators' last chance to get it right. Musical numbers composed or arranged during an afternoon rehearsal or meeting may go into the show that night (Figure 18.8), and it is not uncommon at all to see one or more songs cut.[1] (If you have used themes

---

1. Perhaps the most often told legend is the last-minute addition of the title song from *Oklahoma!*, a change that purportedly rescued the show during its New Haven tryout.

from cut songs elsewhere in the score, reconstructive surgery may be needed.) At the same time, music rehearsal time disappears almost entirely, unless prescribed by the director, in which case it will become a priority. As well as rehearsing new material, the director might think a key is wrong for the singer, or that you should redo a dance arrangement. You can count on accomplishing only the music direction goals that sit very high atop your priority list, because fixing problems less vital or less connected to the stage so late in the process is unrealistic. (Equity also requires that shows "freeze" shortly before opening, precisely to prevent directors and producers from tinkering with their work ad infinitum, and to the physical detriment of the performers.)

You might have to rehearse any new or revised orchestral material by grabbing a few moments immediately before a show, or maybe just by talking musicians through the music in the lounge when they arrive at the theater. The musicians' union allows for short orchestra calls before Broadway shows as a provision for this sort of work, but they too are costly, and can be complicated to coordinate with crew calls, especially now that many orchestras are dependent on the sound equipment and a sound operator to make any sound at all, and their "noise" may be unwelcome because of coinciding stage preparations.

You and the creative team evaluate preview spectators for the effectiveness of the cueing and pacing, as well as for the overall progress of the material. As conductor, you learn typical audience reactions and calibrate your conducting accordingly. With each subsequent performance your predictive abilities deepen. You can, for example, specify the reactions of different age groups, and pace the show slightly differently for a summer matinee audience of restless adolescents (brighten the tempos, pick up the cues) and a Saturday night date crowd (relax and let them enjoy the ballads). You might learn that your lead singer has better breath control after a good night's sleep, or that your drummer drags tempos at the matinee after a two-show day.

Extended preview periods are limited to the higher echelons of commercial theater, or shows with complex technical plots. With shorter runs or standard productions of repertory shows, previews are not as crucial, though helpful under any circumstances. It is natural to want to try out one's work in front of an audience before facing the verdict of the general public. For music directors, it is a fine way to work out nerves and gain confidence and fluency in leading a large-scale performance in which so many people trust in your precise execution. In stock, academic, and amateur theaters, an invited dress rehearsal might replace previews. This is a full performance done in the theater for invitees only, known also as a "gypsy run." Broadway shows have gypsy runs, too, sometimes more than one, immediately before previews begin.

Giving and Receiving Notes

Once a production runs without having to stop, each individual or unit functions autonomously. Neither the director nor stage manager, nor the music director conducting the performances, dictates to those working around him or her how to do their work, as he or she did somewhat in rehearsal. The purpose of simulated performance has been met: all the performers, musicians, and technicians are now aware of their directions and the resulting actions, how to carry them out, and in what order. From the podium, you coordinate the execution of these actions. As rehearsals reach their conclusion, giving notes replaces practicing and drilling. Using notes, the creative triumvirate of director, choreographer, and music director correct and adjust stage performances, technical elements, and all production values, continually fine-tuning what began as a conception and is now an organism. During all dress rehearsals and previews, whether conducting or observing, as music director you take notes, by any means of your choosing.

Not unlike production meetings, note sessions are gathering places in which the participants in a production exchange information, air issues, and solve problems. The primary purpose of note sessions, though, is to allow the directors to direct when there is little or no opportunity to rehearse. A note is a direction. For this reason, many stage directors insist that all participants in a production attend note sessions, even if they themselves are not the recipient of notes. One slight adjustment might affect the entire group.

Music directors are on both the giving and receiving ends of notes. They give notes to stage performers, orchestra and rehearsal musicians, sound designers and operators, orchestrators and arrangers, synthesizer programmers, and associates and assistants. They receive notes from the director, and possibly the choreographer and stage manager. Stage performers (except star performers) will not, or at least should not, give music directors notes—they are not directors—but they will often ask for an adjustment from you or the music; issues of tempo, as usual, seem to dominate their requests.

Directors and choreographers dominate group note sessions during dress rehearsals and previews, but you can seize note-giving opportunities. Note sessions follow almost every run-through or performance until a few days before opening night, and sometimes beyond. If you need time to give the cast notes, request it, but you may be granted only the leavings of the director and choreographer's share. I have guiltily sidestepped this injustice by asking the director if I might start off the note session, and promising I'd only take a few minutes, and then maybe running a few minutes overtime. Regardless, because of the ascendancy of stage directors in these sessions, the performers may be disinclined to absorb what you have to say. The director's comments may seem to a performer more overriding and immediate than a missing final consonant or a half step becoming a whole step or an unwanted riff sneaking into a melody. Be creative and adaptive to the production and the people in it, and employ different means of giving notes to cement the material into the performers' onstage work. Once again, the best way to give notes is to connect them with some other aspect of the staging or the production, by the reasoning that the music is only one part of a much bigger production picture.

There are three reasons to give a note. First is that a performer has done something in error or that conflicts with the direction, for example, he or she is singing a wrong note or wrong rhythm, singing out of tune, phrasing inconsistently, or breathing in the wrong place. Second is that something the performer is doing requires coordination with another element of the production, in which case the right creative representative should also hear the note. You might ask a singer to face downstage when he or she has an important solo line, a request that the choreographer or director will have to approve. You might exchange two singers' vocal lines because of their stage placement; this note would also have to go to the sound operator. You might note that a singer sings an important harmony line offstage while making a costume change—can the costume change be postponed and the area near the singer silenced during the important passage? The third reason is a change in the direction or the material. You might want to add a singer to a part, or eliminate one. You might want to try a lower key, because a high note sounds strained, or give a tempo a boost. A director might change the intention of a scene, requiring changes to the dynamics, or the orchestration.

Though the object of notes is improvement, they sometimes meet with resistance. This is understandable. For one thing, in rehearsal performers have adopted patterns and routines for themselves that they are reluctant to amend. Moreover, criticism or change under any circumstances, even those devoted to collective excellence, can be hard to accept. It is important for music directors to deliver notes constructively, respectfully, and positively. This considerateness increases the likelihood that the performer will digest and consistently abide by the direction, and upholds the favorable relationship between music director and performer. Some highly respected, seasoned performers might be allowed more leeway and receive fewer notes; star performers can do pretty much what they like, though most will welcome a music director's thoughts. In the end, you cannot force any performer to do something a certain way if he or she chooses not to, you can only do your best to protect the music and the vision of the production, and encourage others to do the same. You can appeal a hard case to the director, but eventually you may have no choice but to relent, or to reserve your most fervent efforts for the most pressing issues.

Most notes that you give will not, thankfully, meet with contention, as long as you are thoughtful in giving them. Again, before giving any note, make sure that it is feasible and desirable: maybe you are asking too much that the soprano belt a high G while doing a split, or that the guitarist switch from electric to acoustic in two measures, and maybe the "wrong" rhythm a singer was singing is, in performance, more effective. If you have any concern whatsoever that a note you give may conflict with the overall direction, check with the director or stage manager before giving it.

As a recipient of notes, do not take up undue time in a note session with discussing or, worse, questioning a note the director gives you. If a note you get is problematic, just take and execute it as best you can, and reserve any discussion of it for a private moment. As a giver of notes, do not elaborate too deeply on any one, or engage in too much analysis. If a note requires that much discussion, it probably needs rehearsal, or examination outside the note session. If a note you give is not getting through, speak to the recipient alone in greater depth. Choose your timing and the setting carefully (don't jump on performers with notes from the previous night the moment they arrive at work). Again, never criticize the performer, only the performance.

Another means of giving notes is to put them in writing. Some stage performers and musicians respond well to written notes, while others do not. As long you express yourself positively, lucidly and unambiguously, they can do no harm. Misunderstanding of a written note, however, can make matters worse, so read your written notes before as if you were a performer reading them, and try to anticipate any misinterpretation. Format your notes so that they are readable at a glance. Be succinct, yet descriptive.

Written notes lose impact if they are too abundant or persistent. Other music directors and I have been guilty of handing out so many notes that after a while singers and musicians cease to read them with their initial keenness. In a long-running show, constant noting may be demeaning to a weary performer giving his or her all nightly. I have also been guilty of posting written notes phrased in a negative or critical manner, and they were invariably counterproductive. One compounds the ill effects of negativity by writing it down. I urge other music directors not to make my mistakes. In addition, do not share written notes to soloists with the whole group; print them separately, unless the note affects others' performances. You can post written notes on actors' call boards and distribute copies to their dressing room, but performers will best absorb them when you accompany them with a verbal explanation. When giving notes orally in a note session, have a written handout ready to reinforce the improvements and perpetuate them beyond rehearsal.[2]

Director Michael Greif and others use a system of giving notes that is simple yet surprisingly effective, and one I have expropriated. Either an assistant taking notes for me or I myself write each note on a separate sheet of paper on a small pad. I deliver the note orally, then tear off the piece of paper and give it to the recipient. For some reason, having notes on separate sheets upgrades the importance of each one, and increases the likelihood that performers will attend to all of them. Perhaps it is because they hold in their hands not one page listing several directions, but rather a handful of discrete thoughts. Often I see these single sheets taped prominently to performers' dressing room mirrors the next day.

In a perfect world, directors would not give music notes directly to singers or instrumentalists, because of the confusion it can cause. Nonetheless, it is permissible for a director to do so, and some do. A note they give may conflict with your music direction, and a performer may view the director as the musical authority. You can't tell a director not to give a note to a singer, but you can ask that you be there when he or she gives it. Preferably a director will have you pass the note on to the performer, or will give

---

2. I had intended to include an example of written notes, but in the end decided not to. Using an example from a real production was impossible because it showed individuals in a critical light, and a mock-up seemed unnecessary—the reader could make one up, based on the information I have provided, as illustrative as mine would be.

the note in a group session where open discussion is the protocol. If a note does present musical problems, speak privately with the director about the conflict of interest, then work with the performer to satisfy both the director's needs and yours.

We are about to come full circle, back to the moment the curtain rises on the first performance. Though this will be the end toward which you and the production staff have worked, the experience has already been creatively satisfying. Effective rehearsal translates to good performance, but performance entails new challenges of its own.

PART VI

Performance

19

Conducting in Performance

In a rehearsal scene in the marvelous 1948 film *The Red Shoes*, the music director–composer of a dance company pounds on the podium with his baton, carping at the neophyte prima ballerina (also his clandestine lover) to stay in time with the music. Later in the film, as the opening night curtain approaches, he pokes his head into her dressing room and tells her, "Dance whatever tempo you like. I'll follow you." In many ways, this dichotomy of attitude sums up the relationship between a music director and the stage.

Although what you conduct in performance largely refers to what you taught and learned in rehearsal, you also react to what is happening in real time. The reason for rehearsing, and the goal of your work as music director, was to ready the music for a production. Assuming you have accomplished this task, in performance you are the catalyst of the music and the facilitator of the people you have rehearsed. You continue to make choices of what elements of the music and the production are most important to display in your conducting. The default conducting position of beating time is sometimes all you need, or even less than that, but what ultimately regulates the content of your conducting is what the stage performers and instrumentalists need from you in order to give an effective and believable performance.

Your function is unique, and in performance it is more indispensable than in any other phase of production. This is not hyperbole; a music director, assuming he or she is the conductor, can be absent—temporarily—from any part of the production process other than a performance. I refer the reader to the opening paragraph of the introduction to this book. Without someone to make the music happen, the musical production is inoperative. As in rehearsal, you lead the cast and orchestra through a performance, but at least in the eyes of the audience, the cast now leads the show. In reality you both lead and follow. The technical aspects of the production, too—indeed, the entirety of the production—are similarly within your musical domain, where you are at once a monarch and a functionary.

The Pre-Show Routine

An old musician's adage says that if you are not a half hour early for a gig, you're late. This saying may be an exaggeration, but it speaks to the way musicians like to prepare for performance, and music directors are no exception. Musicians know that if they are comfortable, relaxed, and focused, they will perform better, and wise use of the time leading up to performance helps induce these states. In performance you shouldn't have to worry whether you're properly warmed up, where you've left your smartphone, if your water bottle is full, or if an understudy is on in a leading role. You address these matters beforehand, and dealing with them becomes your pre-show routine, which, naturally, will differ in each production you work in.

Each musician has his or her idiosyncratic pre-show systems and rituals. Before conducting, I always stretch a bit (more as I get older). I like to be physically ready on the podium; conducting is, to varying degrees, athletic, so raising one's heart rate and loosening one's muscles makes sense—an athlete would never play a sport cold. When I am conducting and playing both, especially if a keyboard part is difficult, I also warm up at the keyboard before a show with simple exercises that limber and strengthen my fingers. Preparing at the piano (or your given instrument) is also important because the conducting is usually more crucial to the production than playing, but the playing is imperative as well. With the technical exercises, I improve my dexterity (in the short term and the long), allowing me in performance to be less aware of and concerned about playing and concentrate more on conducting. When I conducted *In The Heights* on Broadway, the extraordinarily challenging piano part required that I be at the keyboard one hour before every performance for a full warm-up and run-through of the most difficult portions of the score. For a simpler keyboard part, a few minutes' warm-up is probably plenty. For *The Lion King*, with no piano part, a little limbering and a little quiet time were my goal, but the half hour before that massive production's curtain was often so frantic that it prevented even those minimal routines.

In a show running on Broadway, a music director's job really begins at the half-hour call, and often earlier. First stop might be your office or dressing room, followed by a visit to stage management for updates on the current performance and the production as a whole. On your to-do list could be among many other things, to find out which performers are out for that performance, assign musicians to rehearsals, ask for production news that might be of interest (Performer A took a new job and we'll have schedule a casting call for a replacement; Performer B is going on vacation for two weeks) and chime in with your own (three subs in the brass section tonight and there's a new drum part for the big dance break), review rehearsal or performance reports, sharpen pencils, and stock up on sticky notes. There may be quick and sometimes unofficial brush-up rehearsals around the half-hour call, or notes that you need to give, either by posting them or delivering them in person, or both. A performer, particularly an understudy or a sub, might want to review something musical with you. Texting has become a common means for giving last-minute notes and direction, and for arranging quick meetings. Actors' Equity bylaws officially prohibit stage performers from receiving notes after the half-hour call (their own untouchable preparation time), but most do not mind, especially if the alternative is being called in early or for additional rehearsal. Do not give a note after half-hour without permission from a stage manager and the performer.

Even you're when not giving notes, it's good to visit periodically with performers in their dressing rooms, mostly just to connect in person before you connect in performance. Though mostly a formality, your visits reaffirm to the performers that you are thinking about them and are there to support them. Often, conversations about how to improve the performance or about one another's approach to performance arise informally. Feel free to participate in performers' pre-show rituals. Company gatherings or "magic circles" backstage immediately preceding shows are the custom of many performing groups; hokey as you may find them, join in. You are a performer, too.

The stage manager's pre-show countdown comes over the backstage public address system: "fifteen minutes, five minutes. . . ." After changing into show garb (tuxedos have given way almost entirely to "casual blacks"), I usually then go to the pit, or playing area, or the musicians' lounge. There I visit the musicians, as I did the stage performers. I find out who is subbing and go through the score in my head for any adjustments, based on the subs or the stage understudies, I will need to make. As I did upstairs, as it were, I give notes to musicians and connect with them both on issues related to the show and as a matter of conviviality. I like to get out on the podium early; particularly, early in a run when I can be a bit anxious, and seeing the audience, sometimes greeting people in the front rows, puts me at ease. If I am playing, I do a few last-minute noodles at the keyboard. Again, these are my own rituals and patterns, not advice on how to spend your pre-performance moments.

"Five minutes . . . ," then . . . "Places, please." ("Thank you, five; thank you places," are the actor's traditional responses, an indication to the stage managers that they have heard the call.) On Broadway, several minutes usually elapse between the places call and the start of a show; most shows go up between four and seven minutes after the scheduled hour, giving the musicians and all the performers plenty of time to settle into place. Some musicians can be lax about start times, and their indifference, feigned or real, can cause delays. You can set in-house policies (in association with the music coordinator and in-house contractor, but the union may not sanction your rules or help you in enforcing them), such as requiring that musicians arrive at the theater by a certain time, be in the pit by a certain time, or be prepared to play at the scheduled curtain time.

"Places" is my final call to the podium, if I have not arrived sooner. I check my gear—baton, keyboard, click tracks, monitors—to make sure everything is there and working. I call the sound operator on the house phone to check in. (Music director to sound operator: "Watch out for Man number three in the ensemble; he's a dancer covering a singer and goes flat. Maybe you should duck his level a few dB [decibels] for the whole show." Sound operator to music director: "The sub drummer always hits the overhead mic with his stick when he goes for the crash cymbal. Can you have him move the mic two inches higher, or tell him to be careful?") A minute or two before the actual start, the stage manager who is calling the performance contacts me to check that the orchestra is ready. A minute or so later, there is the house announcement about photographs and cell phones and candy wrappers. Conductors often have a cue light on the podium, which is lit as a warning, and turns off as an indication to start the show. Or maybe there is a click-track lead-in, a sound cue, or a line of dialogue. By some predetermined cueing sequence, the show begins.

I bring the orchestra to attention, and on cue, raise my baton (or my hand or head) for the initial preparation. The much anticipated moment, the event that my colleagues and I have so long prepared for, has at last arrived. If all goes as planned—and it most often does—when I bring the baton down to indicate the first beat of the music, the performance is under way.

Showtime

In performance your job as music director is to coordinate or control any part of a production that is musicalized, but in truth you are no longer in control. That is not to say you should relinquish control, or be passive; quite the opposite. Your approach and your mechanics should go on as though they made the show operate. Still, whatever happens on stage or in the pit will happen, independent of your participation and authority. For the most part, almost without fail, things go according to plan. Inevitably, though, they also occasionally go wrong. Dancers dance the wrong steps, musicians play wrong notes, actors forget their lyrics, a singer spontaneously rewrites a melody, a microphone fails, a spotlight lights the wrong person at the wrong time, a piece of scenery does not move when it should, the theater floods, or the sky falls. And you, as music director, usually just keep on conducting as if nothing has happened (unless, of course, someone is injured or in danger), keeping the accompaniment lined up with the stage. In the reality of the onstage world, as far as the accompaniment is concerned, nothing went wrong. I wish I had written this: the show must go on.

When conducting in performance you project the persona of the show to the performers on stage, the musicians in the pit, and the audience in the house. On a podium in a traditional pit, you might indeed be very close to the audience. Some pit designs open the downstage pit wall in the center, so that the conductor protrudes slightly into the house. If the orchestra is on stage, you are in full view of the audience. Wherever you are, even backstage, your demeanor must always be in line with the material, and reflect your dedication to the tasks at hand. For the "life" of the performance, you commit your intellect, your feeling, and your physical being to the music and the stage. Just as one performer out of character on stage will jeopardize the believability of the whole, so will your lack of absolute, unilateral involvement endanger the effectiveness of the music, and thereby the production. At best, your endeavor ceases to be a job and becomes experiential, rather than occupational. If your involvement is true and not superficial, this transformation occurs naturally. The music channels through you to the stage and the pit. At times it almost seems easy, as if the group that learned the music together and now know it so well reunited daily to sing and play it. The orchestra members becomes one with you; they are your instrument, the accompanimental instrument of the production.

A description of the mechanics of conducting a performance reads like the assembly instructions for a piece of furniture. Therefore, I have relegated them to Appendix A, where there are detailed accounts of conducting the opening numbers of the Broadway musicals *In The Heights* and *The Lion King*.

Repeated Performances: Variations on a Theme

In an academic production or a special event, there may be only one or just a few performances. Most productions perform more than once. With the huge effort and expense it takes to mount a production, it makes sense to present it before multiple (paying) audiences, nightly for an indefinite run, as on Broadway, nightly in a proscribed run, as in a regional or stock theater, or periodically over time, as with a nightclub act that tours or repeats weekly at a certain venue. Repeated performances are one of the professional charms of music direction. Once you learn and rehearse a show, keeping it going is a far less overwhelming task than building it from nothing.

Your best performances may be hard to recall in any detail. If you are truly "in the moment," unified with the music and with the other performers and the production, your self-awareness dims and you do not necessarily record specific occurrences. Instead, it is the whole of the experience that makes an impression and stays with you after the curtain falls or the lights go out. I can barely recall the actual performances of many opening nights; the flurry of activity and the fascination of the moment blur their memories.

With repetition, performing becomes more conscious and less ethereal, but hopefully not mechanical. There will be inevitable variations in each performance because human beings are involved, and a stage reality is unfolding in real time. Still, Broadway shows are remarkably consistent in duration from night to night, even with different actors, conductors, and audiences as variables. Slow or fast tempos matter quite little in how long a show or a song lasts. Taking a five-minute number a few clicks more slowly or faster will result in only a few seconds of lengthening or shortening. Yet all the factors of pacing taken together—like dialogue, cueing, improvisations, tempo, and tech—can indeed change the actual and perceived duration of a production. From your central position, you read a show's pace and react accordingly over repeated performances. You can intensify or relax tempos, pick up cues, and manipulate the overall energy with your attitude, and your conducting.

The perception of one performance being better or worse than another can differ from person to person. After a show a singer may come to you and proclaim that he or she really nailed the big climax in the ballad—the money note was powerful and right on pitch and the whole room felt it. A moment later, the trumpet player may approach you with a long face and apologize for the big clunker he or she made in the middle of the tender ballad—it must have ruined the entire show for everyone. You are thinking about how the electric bass seemed much louder than usual and the upright much softer, how the dancers seemed unhappy with the tempo of the ballet even though you used a metronome, and how before tomorrow's show you wanted to post a note about a choral cutoff that was repeatedly late despite your clear gesture. Yes, the singer did nail the big song, but that was true every night, as far as you were concerned, and yes, the trumpeter did bleat the note in the ballad, but it certainly did not ruin the evening.

Most performances are neither perfect nor horrible, and most shows, once they are running, mostly run themselves, with daily ups and downs, and the occasional triumph or crash. Not just for you, but for everyone, doing a show repeatedly is a job like any other, with responsibilities and, one would hope, pride in one's work. Everyone counts on himself or herself and his or her colleagues to do right by the job, and for the most part, everyone delivers. It is up to you to maintain your opening-night energy and absorption in the show at all times and encourage the same in other performers. Although every performance will be slightly different, your presence on the podium embodies, and your conducting gestures confirm, the musical values and the director's vision as rehearsed and previously performed. Your musical leadership inhibits deviation from the plan, and prevents error, carelessness, or extemporization.

On Broadway, performers and musicians rotate regularly. Soon after the opening night of any Broadway show (and sometimes before), there will be understudies on every stage and substitutes in every orchestra. As with principal players, the key to evincing good performances from standbys and subs is to train them well. In performance you cannot support them as you can in rehearsal; the onus is on them to give a performance that has not had the benefit of rehearsing extensively with others. Subbing and swinging are not for the faint of heart, and often the jobs are entrusted to the most proficient and confident of stage performers and instrumentalists. Even in academic and amateur productions, there may be subs in the orchestra (the preferred concertmaster may be available only one of the two days of the show, so you allow the principal second violin to move up for that day) or on stage (quite often academic and community theaters double-cast roles so that everyone gets a chance to be in the show).

For you on the podium, the presence of an onstage understudy doesn't usually make a huge difference in the conducting plot. You might throw a few extra cues an understudy's way, just to be helpful, but you will be most supportive by carrying on as if nothing was different. A substitute in the orchestra might need a little more attention, particularly a rhythm section player whose part might make more of a difference in the whole.

One of my favorite conducting anecdotes involves a substitute conductor of a well-known Broadway production, who conducted only once in a great while, but who was a masterful musician easily able to handle the pop-rock score with absolute aplomb. One night, after about a month away from the show, he was called in to conduct. On his arrival at half hour, the stage managers besieged him in panic. The leading lady's standby was on, they told him; she had never done the role before and rehearsed only the first act, but all the other covers were out sick or on vacation. Also, four chorus members had the flu, and would be covered by only two swings, so only half of the four-part harmonies could be sung. On top of that, they said, the regular crew person who ran the automation had a family emergency, so all the traveling scenery cues might be off by a few seconds. Could the conductor please make sure that everyone got his or her parts and entrances right, and that the leading woman got all her second-act cues with extra clarity, and make sure the two-part harmony was working, and keep an eye out for the extra stage transition time, and so on? The conductor, having no opportunity to coach the singer on her Act II song, reduce the choral parts, or otherwise prepare for all these unexpected "crises," conducted the same show he always had, giving the same cues, listening to and for the same things he always did, watching the scene changes, all as he had been taught by the original music director, and leading with his customary poise and musicianship. At the end of the performance, stage management was effusive. The conductor had saved their lives. He was their hero. Thank goodness he was there to so capably see the show through such rocky circumstances.

When Things Go Wrong

The goal of every department in a stage production is a perfect show. With repeated performances, though, comes greater possibility of error, simply because there are more chances for things to go wrong and more changes of personnel. Big mistakes are more common early in a run, before the kinks have been completely ironed out. Short runs may come with shorter rehearsal periods, however, so when a production only plays once or a few times, things can, and probably will, go wrong.

I have stressed the importance of errorless musical accompaniment, and music directors and musicians share in the quest for flawlessness. Of course, musicians make mistakes, plenty of them, but most are small and go unnoticed. The major ones are less frequent, but they can be conspicuous—and sometimes amusing—and therefore disruptive. Conductors make mistakes, too, but they are mostly inaudible. If you deliberately conduct something very differently, it will not appear as a conducting mistake. Rather, you make apparent in your demeanor that the change is purposeful and that the orchestra should heed it.

When you or someone in the band does make an egregious error, it is best to move past it without fuss, hard as it may be not to noticeably react, because most errors are forgotten within moments. There are conductors who have reputations as "scowlers"—I fear that at times I have been among them—who react noticeably to musical mishaps. Whereas it is human nature to flinch at the unexpectedly discordant, a wince from the conductor usually only makes the offending players feel worse than they already do, and the mistake more conspicuous than it already was. Players are aware of their flubs, and are usually appropriately contrite. A nervous or inexperienced player will be even more sensitive to a conductor's apparent irritation, which can increase the possibility of further error. If a player destroys an important moment with a careless clam or an obviously wrong tempo, you have every right to be perturbed, particularly if the music was properly rehearsed. Still, performance is not the time to voice your dissatisfaction. Even intermission may be too soon; better yet, wait until after the performance to speak up, if at all.

Only rarely does an orchestra or orchestra member seriously jeopardize a performance. One show for which I was the music director suffered through a nightmarish performance when a sub drummer who confidently proclaimed his readiness to perform, and whom we had auditioned by taking him through the main grooves of the show, was not, it turned out, ready at all. He did not read music well and had learned the songs from a demo, failing to understand that we had revised the stage score extensively. Moments into his first performance, as soon as added bars inserted to accommodate the staging began to appear, it became obvious that something was very wrong. The gallant associate conductor on the podium spent much of the evening miming the feels of the new material, simulating repeat signs and holds with improvised signals, and indicating where the drummer could just remain tacet to avoid further damage. The drummer also received ongoing verbal direction from the bassist and keyboard players, sitting next to the kit (which was behind a plexiglass wall). Fortunately, he was a topnotch player, and when he and the score were in the same place, the music rocked. From that day on, I have run all rhythm section players through their entire show before allowing them to perform publicly.

Musical problems often stem from circumstances of the production. At a special event I did as a keyboard player (not as music director), a charity concert at a nightclub in Manhattan, the stage was far too small for the nine-piece band and multiple singers to fit (the producer should have flagged this problem in advance; the music director was hired after the venue was chosen and the performers and band were contracted), and the keyboards and half of the sound equipment were on a truck whose tire blew out on the New Jersey Turnpike (the unforeseeable yet apparently inevitable sort of problem that can plague a one-off event). The sound check for the full band that had been scheduled for 11:00 AM began at 3:30 PM with only the house piano, guitar, and drums. The rest of the gear arrived at 5:00. We were set up by 6:00, for an 8:00 show. Even the tech crew gave up their normally sacrosanct one-hour dinner break. To replace lost rehearsal time, the very patient music director took performers aside at the piano to rehearse their numbers, then communicated any relevant results of the rehearsal to the rest of the band and the sound man. When the sound check at last got under way, the music director quickly put out a new schedule, proportionately shortening everyone's time on stage, and favoring those numbers he had not rehearsed privately. He gave the two celebrities who were appearing their full sound-check times (and a little extra). He and the band members and I hastily simplified arrangements and talked through introductions and interludes and endings and song forms of numbers that were on the rehearsal schedule but not rehearsed. (The show went well, with no errors conspicuous enough to prevent the audience's gratification. In attendance were some very discerning musician friends of mine, who perceived some rockiness but avowed that it in no way hindered their enjoying the show.)

Onstage, there are also errors and problems, and changes over time that lead to new errors and problems. As in the pit, most of them make little difference in the convincingness or effectiveness of the whole. As noted in earlier chapters, even when audiences are aware of mistakes, they can absorb them as part of their theatrical experience, and not allow their state of suspended disbelief to be disturbed. The most damaging problems come from lack of believability: a gross miscasting, subpar singing or acting, awkward or poorly executed staging, and the like. These sorts of problems are seldom part of any conscientious production organization beyond the secondary school level, but sometimes they are unavoidable, and as music director you can often see them coming, and prepare to weather them (you are the music director of *Victor/Victoria* or *Smokey Joe's Cafe* at a camp for girls). There is little you can do in performance but to remain as supportive as you would be if things were going better, and keep your musical house in order.

From the podium you are able to control, or at least influence, some performance issues in real time. If someone on stage or in the pit is not in time with the rest, or if you want to speed or slow a tempo, you can do so by turning your conducting to that player as an insistence to follow it. With a pronounced gesture you can indicate to someone to sing or play more loudly or softly, or enforce an articulation. Your attempts will not invariably yield results, but they will enough of the time that they are worthwhile. For the most part, you design your conducting on the basis of your anticipation of these needs, but still you are proactive and reactive in performance.

Many large problems will not be in your power to solve or manage from the podium, yet it may still be up to you to save the day, or at least coordinate the rescue effort. Problems originating with sound amplification plague modern productions. They can be relatively small, such as a sound operator picking up the wrong singer, or a microphone going out on stage. Immediately in this latter event, you should bring the orchestra down to their softest possible dynamic under the onstage performer, who may not know that his or mic has failed (Broadway sound design has no onstage vocal monitoring, to avoid feedback; singers hear only themselves live). Significant problems obviously arise when synthesizer systems fail or computers crash. Electronics that make up a significant part of a show's accompaniment should be redundant and backed up by an available piano sound for emergency accompaniments. Entire sound systems have been known to die mid-performance, and the show turns into an impromptu acoustic mix, balanced by, appropriately, the music director on the podium.

The opening night of my first major national tour was tainted for me by a wayward thirty-two-measure mid-song click track with prerecorded voices, which did not trigger despite my repeated attempts. (I started the click, which played at the sound board remotely, by pushing a button.) After waiting a few uncomfortable moments of silence, I went on without it. And then the track started. The band and the prerecorded vocals were apart by several bars, and a fraction of a bar. Half the singers on stage went with the prerecord, and half went with the band and me. There was no way out. If I stayed where I was (which is what I did), I would be off from the prerecorded voices until they ended thirty-two bars later (by the time I could make the decision we were already eight or more bars into the prerecord), and I would have to count on the sound operator having the good sense to see that I was staying put and shut the track down. On the other hand, if I had adjusted the band to the click I would have left the other singers behind, as well as wasting time and risking possible further confusion in making the shift. Clicks have become more reliable since then.

So-called train wrecks, such as that incident, are rare but not unheard of. Many are not musical, but technical. The central set piece of *The Lion King* is Pride Rock, which on Broadway is a massive, mechanically intricate helical promontory that rises like a corkscrew from the deck. When the set piece and the trapdoor it emerges through do not line up properly, as has happened once or twice in performance, the resulting cracking of wood and squealing of gears and rattling of chains is terrifying. But almost every time it happened, the show went on—on one occasion, playing the remainder of the first act with a crippled Pride Rock resting forlornly upstage in the half-light. Such technical issues are, unsurprisingly, more commonplace now that stage technology has become so elaborate.

Onstage performers are sometimes the cause of major problems, usually by skipping material or beginning to sing much earlier or later than intended. This situation is one in which an accompanimental unit's connection to the stage becomes especially crucial. If a singer omits a large section, or enters (or doesn't enter) unexpectedly, a band accustomed to the correct cues will adjust automatically, or look to the music director to make sure that he or she wants the adjustment. From the podium, in a mild emergency such as this one, all you will most likely need is to make eye contact with an attentive band (again the importance of live contact is clear) to alert the musicians to or confirm to them that there is a problem, then indicate with your expression and gesture what the solution will be: to hold, to continue, to jump to a new place, to go backward or forward, whatever is necessary. During rehearsal, give the orchestra important lyric cues as guideposts, and explain the structure of musical material and how it relates to what is happening on stage. Having a microphone on the podium connected to the monitoring systems of each player is very useful in any emergency, as you can simply state the solution to the problem into the mic. Rehearse your orchestra well and trust them to respond, under your calm guidance, in time of crisis. Memorizing the score is important for music directors conducting a show, but the possibility of trouble demands that you keep a copy of the score on the podium and open to the number being played, so that if calling out measure numbers and lyrics is your only deliverance, that information is close at hand.

Music directors make occasional mistakes, too. An obvious error, such as cueing a singer or instrumentalist in the wrong place, will probably be ignored, and the singer or instrumentalist will enter as he or she should. It is not that the conductor is being disregarded or his or her authority doubted. Rather, the performers know that nobody is perfect, not even the one who is supposed to be. A conductor, though, can sometimes cause major problems with an unexpected gaffe. I was not the only one to start a click track prematurely in one of my first performances conducting *In The Heights*. I was bailed out by a very forgiving and quick-thinking Lin-Manuel Miranda, who simply skipped a few (important) lines of dialogue, and by a band who understandably took a bar or two to figure out how I had screwed up, and how badly, but within moments were back on track, as it were. Because of the click, we had no alternative in those circumstances but to follow it and move on. It would have been too much to try to stop it, back up, and restart, and the delay and confusion would have been much more destructive to the show's believability than jumping ahead. Lin was not the slightest bit angry with me for what I perceived as grounds for termination; when I went to his dressing room at intermission to apologize he laughed off the whole thing. That's showbiz.

20

Maintaining a Production and Preserving a Show

The first days of performance, from previews into opening night, are hectic, exhilarating, and often euphoric. Short runs and one-nighters may come with proportionately less elation, a consequence of their limited production processes, and occasionally a production will have soured, with the realization that it is not the artistic achievement everyone had hoped, or worse, it is an unmitigated flop. In any situation, once the first night curtain has come down, perhaps after a brief sense of relief, reality sets in. A gala opening night turns for some performers to something not unlike post partum depression the next morning, perhaps with the realization that the production is a job, and not just a chance to shine. This reaction is not usually the case with active professionals, for whom each job is another episode in a long career.

A Day in the Life

Performance does not necessarily dictate, or dominate, your daily regimen as a music director. Your workday may begin in the afternoon, with some sort of rehearsal, or sometimes earlier, with a staff meeting, an audition, or, in the bigger picture of your career, another job or an interview for another job. On some days, you may only conduct the show. Some of your work will involve managing your staff to assist in the ongoing production effort. Invest some time in taking care of yourself, getting proper rest, exercise, and nutrition, as physical conditioning will enhance your work, which to some extent is physical. Your dedication to perpetually improving as a musician must also never wane. Many music directors I know supplement their professional pursuits by continuing their education: studying composition; researching music in unfamiliar styles; learning new instruments even taking singing, acting, and dance lessons; and always continuing to practice, study, and learn new repertoire. Whereas some musicians' veneer can seem quite casual, and their attitude toward their work almost cavalier, most of the good ones are anything but, and the coolness is purely outward. Music is a demanding discipline and a competitive profession, and for the most part, only the strong survive. Musicians know this, and train diligently to gain and maintain their professional status.

Unlike the other musicians in the orchestra, music directors must arrive early before a performance, going through their agendas as described in the previous chapter, "Conducting in Performance," and more. When the final curtain comes down, most theaters clear out quickly—it's late, and the work is done—but music directors may have to stay on to finish the day's tasks and plan for tomorrow's. There is probably an equal balance among people working on a Broadway show, music directors included, between those who socialize after work, going out to eat or drink or view other entertainments, and those who go home to their families, or just go home. In other situations, with shorter runs and energetic participants, there may be celebrations every night. Stock theaters throw some lively cast parties, as do colleges, and the high spirits can carry over from the performance into the wee hours. Many working music directors keep a night owl's schedule, and for some the idea of an early morning call is anathema. Others never seem to rest at all.

Regardless of how you spend your hours off, the next day, it's back to work. Full days off are scarce, and precious. Musicians don't really think in terms of days off; rather, music is ongoing in their lives; it is simply what they do daily. Holidays often have added performances (some paid at overtime scales). Whether you're working on one or more shows, preparing for the next one or more, or just practicing, listening, or reading, you and your job may become indistinguishable. This, however, is the ostensibly desirable professional state; it is certainly the best way to make a living. Indeed, the most successful music directors are tireless and diligent, and only sometimes take very relaxing and luxurious vacations, when the payoff and their schedules allow.

Keeping the Performance Fresh

As music director you are among the only members of the creative staff who remains on site after opening night. Therefore it is up to you, to a great extent, to prolong the glow of that noteworthy consummation. In your presence and attitude as a leading member of the company, and on the podium with your conducting, you maintain the music, carry the creative torch, and uphold the production's vision. You also charge anyone who takes your place to do the same.

Depending on how long a production runs, you will have some tangible role in its ongoing quality control. Single-engagement productions such as concerts obviously require no upkeep, and in short runs, your post-opening duties may be limited to giving a few notes that prevent repeating any major missteps of previous performances. Long runs and multiple productions of the same show, however, require maintenance, and as the resident creative team representative, you will find that maintenance becomes a large part of your job post-opening. Stage managers are the producer's and director's official onsite designates, but they may not always be as attuned to the creative aspects of a production as are music directors.

Repetitive performances can sometimes make concentration difficult to muster, especially when you have technically mastered and memorized the score. Boredom, though not a typical problem for performing music directors, can creep in whenever you repeat a piece many times. Yet in the vanguard of the podium you must retain your resolve and strength of character, even if it is partially only exterior. Most single performances will require enough concentration, and most repeated shows will have enough novelty from performance to performance, to keep your attention. Particularly in a show with a short run, you are more likely to over-conduct (justifiably; the show may still be underrehearsed) than give a perfunctory performance.

Most of the time, conductors leading long runs bring a magnificent presence and command to their performances nightly, without fail. Unfortunately, though, it is not uncommon to find a professional music director merely going through the motions, even on Broadway, or perhaps especially on Broadway. I know it's true because I have been guilty of it on occasion (eventually I fired myself for this transgression), and I have witnessed other Broadway music directors and conductors doing it as a matter of course. It is obviously inappropriate for a conductor to chew gum, or snack, or text-message during a performance (unless the need to do so is somehow dire), yet it happens. Broadway is supposedly the paragon of stage performance, and sets the example for all stage performance. Anything less than full involvement in the task at hand is unconscionable. If as music director you reach a point where restlessness is hampering the quality of your performance, either find new elements of the score or the story to love, or else take time off. A show that earns a long run should by nature be profound enough or interesting enough or spontaneous enough that there are many levels on which you can appreciate and re-appreciate it, and sufficient challenges to keep every musician engaged, particularly the music director, who should be hyperaware of every musical detail, and more.

What might be mildly tedious for you can more easily become stale for an instrumentalist. The union CBA for Broadway allows musicians to take off half of their shows, as well as allowing for virtually unlimited leaves of absence, with the conductor's approval.[1] The same does not hold true for onstage performers, though

---

1. Other music directors and I would much prefer more restrictive subbing policies, but we realize that, in reality, musicians would probably find ways around them. We all agree that, in principle at least, subbing is healthy in a long run.

Equity and other stage unions do permit some personal days and time off for other jobs. For the most part, music directors appreciate, or at least tolerate, the variety of personnel in the pit, provided that the subs play as well as the principals, as most do, and sometimes do with more enthusiasm and care than a regular who plays the same music over and over. Some principal players take off too often or use too many subs, and music directors are within their rights to replace a consistent absentee, or limit their substitutions. More on subbing will follow in the section Subbing in the Orchestra.

Rehearsing after Opening

A music director's maintenance of a running production falls under five main headings: rehearsing singers and orchestra members, giving notes, new casting and contracting, training conducting replacements, and score notation. In addition, of course, as music director you maintain a production with your conducting, by delivering consistent, specific, and energetic leadership from the podium.

In rehearsal, you train new singers, those who cover roles from within the cast, and those you and the creative team hire as replacements for original cast members. The guidelines listed earlier for auditions and rehearsal time still apply, but the rehearsal process for replacements is obviously quite different, and auditions may be ongoing. On Broadway, by contract, there are three types of covers on stage: standbys, understudies, and swings. A standby covers a specific principal role or roles but does not perform otherwise. An understudy performs in the show, usually in the ensemble, and covers principal parts as cast. The standby usually goes on before an understudy. A swing covers many parts, ensemble and principal both, but performs only when needed (which on Broadway is often; swings are on all the time, especially because they also cover understudies who are covering principals).

When working into a running show, most new onstage performers begin rehearsal in isolation, learning their music and dance, then their staging. Gradually the current cast joins the new performers. If the trainees are in the ensemble, they rehearse with other ensemble members whose parts intersect with theirs, and if they are principals, with other principals and ensemble members with whom they share songs, scenes, or important staging or stage time. Music directors often delegate at least the initial training of replacements, especially those in the ensemble, to an associate or designated rehearsal pianist or vocal teacher. At some point, music directors will coach all new principal performers, as well as all understudies and standbys for all principal roles.

Training new Broadway stage performers culminates in a "put-in" rehearsal, at which most principals, or their understudies, run through the entire show with the new performers. (To save time, the stage managers might devise an abridged version that includes only the portions of the show in which the new performers appear.) Music directors attend almost all put-ins, and sometimes conduct them, though they are a good opportunity to put a substitute conductor on the podium (see the later section "Subbing on the Podium"). Equity also requires that understudies get their turn, and periodically all Equity shows have understudy rehearsals, in which principal covers get a chance to work together on stage. Both put-ins and understudy rehearsals use limited technical elements, perhaps not even microphones, again unless the personnel being rehearsed are more elite. Only occasionally, perhaps when a major principal player is being put in (a Phantom, perhaps, or a Jekyll-Hyde or a Mama Rose), or perhaps a star performer, will the orchestra be called for a put-in—the cost is otherwise prohibitive—but the smaller rehearsal unit that appeared in studio rehearsals may reconvene to accompany.

The advantage for music directors of working with new stage performers one on one is the ability to teach the values of the music in depth from the outset, as there is nothing to interfere with delving deeply and intensively into the material in rehearsal (and for the performer, outside of rehearsal). Furthermore, by this time the music direction has been fully codified. A replacement's mastery of the musical material is thereby also usually hastened, coming in a matter of days rather than weeks. The clear disadvantage for the performer is not being able to learn as part of the group. The onstage community supersedes any individual, and working one's way into a show without the aid of group learning is challenging. This is the reasoning behind holding put-in rehearsals.

As music director of a production, you are entitled to call brush-up rehearsals for either ensemble or principal onstage players, whose salaries include a certain number of rehearsal hours per week, but not usually for the orchestra, whose hourly rates would amount to significant extra expenditure. You can correct most accompanimental problems with notes. If enough onstage musical issues need addressing, or if one or two or a few larger musical problems arise, a brush-up session with the cast can correct them, though perhaps not permanently—in which case, call another one. Principals need restorative work such as this less frequently. You can usually accomplish what you need to with a note, and only if something has diverged markedly from the original direction is rehearsal necessary.

Group brush-ups can be quite enjoyable, similar to a *Sitzprobe*. They, as well as put-ins, sometimes feel like rehearsal reunions, and cast members usually appreciate them (though most prefer not to rehearse too often once a show opens, and some will creatively evade rehearsal calls). The rewards of re-rehearsing music that is completely familiar are many. Matters that the rapid pace of production rehearsal might have precluded now have a chance for further airing, things such as musicality and expression, dramatic connection, and more. Still, it is a good idea to keep brush-up rehearsals relatively brief and to the point. The performers will be grateful for the respect you show for their time, and for their comprehension of the material.

The complexities of administrating post-opening maintenance, particularly scheduling and hiring, as well as the musically repetitious nature of the work, lead many music directors to delegate these responsibilities to an associate. The benefit for associates is the increased involvement and responsibility, which puts them in a more upwardly mobile position, should they hope to be promoted. They can also schedule themselves for as much of the rehearsal as they like, providing additional income. Music directors and associates receive the same salary premiums in rehearsal as they do in production and in performance, so producers prefer that music directors not dominate rehearsal hours, and count on music directors and their assignees to help in allocating rehearsal funds frugally. Music directors handing over rehearsals or rehearsal coordination to a designate should still supervise the work, and participate to some extent.

As in production rehearsal, all musicians you engage for post-opening rehearsals should be familiar with the stage content as well as highly proficient with the accompaniment. Often these musicians play in the pit, as principals or subs, but some may come from outside the production. Stage managers might express a preference for some rehearsal musicians over others, either in general or for specific types of rehearsal, and there is usually no reason you should not honor their choices. You can train rehearsal musicians yourself, or delegate their training to a music staff member. In any case, however, the training is unpaid for all, and you are ultimately responsible for it. If you do not want to play all rehearsals yourself, you'll have to show others how you want it done. Furthermore, you (or a delegate under your supervision) are responsible for disseminating all new or modified information about the music and the production (including score changes, cast changes, and tempo changes) to all rehearsal musicians. As in production, you can set up an information exchange system such as a shared calendar or an email distribution chain that allows you to quickly send out any updates to all those who need to know. Be explicit with whomever you delegate about when they should report to you and what they can do autonomously.

It's a good idea to follow up all post-opening rehearsals, except individual replacement rehearsals, with accompanying written notes, as reminders of what was covered in rehearsal. You might also post or distribute notes on a predetermined schedule, so that they become part of the performers' routines, maybe even a welcome one. ("Note Fridays?") Periodically, as a matter of form and when necessary, you should communicate with the stage director, especially if you feel that the direction or vision is somehow compromised and that his or her intervention would help (the stage managers might be your first counsel in such a situation).

Subbing in the Orchestra

Unlike onstage covers, substitutes in the orchestra, or subs, take responsibility for their own learning, and their training time is uncompensated. They might also have limited access to the performing area, so getting comfortable, and getting comfortable while playing an entire show with others who play it regularly, can be quite problematic. Substitute musicians must be willing to devote considerable time to learning something they will perform only on occasion. As noted, they must be highly skilled, collected under pressure, and very well prepared; indeed, subs in Broadway pits are some of the most expert musicians on the scene.

Music directors have the option of entering a sub's training process at their discretion, and can set subbing policies for any pit that they oversee, with the approval of the union. In professional orchestras the principal players train their own subs, probably on a far greater level of detail than you would ever get to. It is, after all, the principal's chair and the principal's name in the program. If you find that a principal is training subs inadequately, you may enforce guidelines on how you want it done, or insist that the subs comprehend the flaws in the principal's training process and make up the shortfall themselves. In nonprofessional or nonunion situations, you should fully audition and/or train all subs before they are allowed to perform, as you have no guarantee of their abilities.

Conductors of Broadway shows, according to the union CBA, have absolute power over who may sub in the orchestra. They can simply turn thumbs up or down at will to decide a replacement musician's fate. If they chose to, they could bypass the union's generous substitution rules simply by disallowing every sub, though according to the CBA, "The disapproval of a substitute by a Conductor shall not be arbitrary or capricious."[2] On the other hand, "No substitute shall have the right to render any services if at any time the Conductor should find him or her unacceptable. The Conductor shall have the right to maintain the musical integrity at all times."[3] It is understandable for a music director to want every performance to have the exact musical qualities as the original performance, or the best performance, but that is unrealistic. Subs bring their own personalities, and like all human elements that go into a stage production, they make valuable creative contributions. In practice, many music directors personally approve or disapprove every sub through an exhaustive vetting or rehearsal process, while others turn over administration of subs entirely to the principal players or in-house contractor, and sometimes to an associate or assistant conductor.

There are a few standard and useful music direction practices related to subbing worthy of mention. First is a music director's "designation" of subs. Designated subs are

---

2. AFM Local 802, *Collective Bargaining Agreement*, 2003, p. 15, VIII K 4a.
3. Ibid., p. 16, VIII K 6.

those you consider to be equivalent in proficiency to the principal. After a few performances by a substitute, you decide if he or she is worthy of designation, and if so, he or she will from then on be permitted to play with undesignated subs. Many music directors devise a policy, and the CBA supports it, that limits the number of undesignated players in a section. As music director you determine what comprises a section. Usually the categories will be conventional, such as strings, brass, and woodwinds, but with new hybrid orchestrations, sections can take on new configurations, or overlap (strings and the keyboard playing synthesized strings, for example). You might also institute a rule that all subs get two or three chances before they are disapproved, so that if an imperfect first or second performance is the result only of inexperience or nerves, the player has a chance to recover.

Subs playing complicated, virtuosic, or stylistically specific music and those with the largest parts in the orchestration certainly need more pre-performance testing and rehearsal from a music director than those playing familiar or simpler material. Pay special attention to any players whose parts are consequential enough that an inferior performance will jeopardize the entire production. I learned the hard way from the sub drummer crisis described above that working through the entire score with subs such as these is essential, and it is entirely up to you to judge a player's readiness. Your contractual "right to maintain musical integrity at all times" can come in very handy. A player who plays the book perfectly may, in your opinion, lack the feel, or the confidence, or even the experience, that you deem necessary to perform in front of an audience. Subs with less crucial roles in the orchestration (there are fewer of these as orchestras get smaller) can pass muster under their own supervision, or that of their section leader. Another efficient training method is to draw up a list of excerpts that each instrumentalist must work on with you before approval for performance. (Each chair's excerpt list will be different.)

Subbing on the Podium

Associate and assistant conductors also train independently, by watching you, often by going through the production rehearsal process, and by covering you when you are not conducting. They may well add something of themselves to the conducting plot; how much they should add is up to you. You may want a replica of yourself on the podium, or you may prefer to give your associates and assistants free rein, or probably something in between. No two conductors are alike, so you cannot force your personality or your precise gestures on your substitutes, but you should insist on the intent behind those gestures. Whoever covers you on the podium should conduct "your" show, that is, go through a similar thought process and deliver what you deliver—the same cues, indications, beats, phrasing—when you are conducting. (If there are only a few performances of a show, you may not even have a cover, though having one is always a good idea in case of catastrophe.)

Look for opportunities to have your subs conduct, in rehearsals, and when possible, in performance. Tech rehearsals, put-ins, and understudy rehearsals are excellent opportunities for associates to take the baton. So are certain dress rehearsals and perhaps a preview; these events might also allow you the opportunity to listen to the show as an audience member in the house and take notes on sound, balance, and diction. Delegating to your covers some of the orchestra substitute training eases your workload, and at the same time assists in their training. Subs who are new to a production will also gain from by being at the podium for an understudy rehearsal or put-in, but will require several sessions with you (or an associate) to explain and analyze the score, go over the mechanics of the conducting, and discuss the subtleties and variables of the production. With longer runs and longer rehearsal periods in particular, the time and effort your associates and assistants put into mounting a production and learning the score certainly warrants some podium time as a reward.

You may be concerned that your associate's or assistant's work is somehow less skilled, or inspired, or confident, than yours, but performances can easily survive a conductor not as polished or commanding or self-assured, particularly with an accompanimental ensemble that knows the show well. Furthermore, like any sub, an associate or assistant conductor's proficiency, command, and self-assurance will increase with each performance. Training your covers and replacements can be as exhaustive or as minimal as the situation dictates. If you are working with someone with very limited conducting experience, take more time with his or her induction. You can allow more experienced and trusted associates and assistants, and those who have been through the production rehearsal process, to conduct with far less preparation, perhaps even just a talk-through of the score to assure that all the beats are in place.

On Broadway, the pecking order of associates and assistants can be very confounding. If you are the principal conductor, you should be on the podium for most, if not all, of at least the first several performances of any extended run. After that, it is at your discretion who conducts, with approval from stage managers, the director, and producers, who will rarely question your choices. There may be performances that you ought to conduct, such as those when a new principal performer is taking the stage for the first time, or immediately following a check-in rehearsal with a show's director. You should keep in mind who will be playing in the orchestra; for instance, you might not want to pair an inexperienced assistant conductor with a first-time rhythm section player. The union assumes the same rules for conducting subs as for all pit musicians, so according to the bylaws you should have five subs. However, this is necessary only in shows with extended runs, and I have never seen the rule enforced.

Observe your substitutes as they conduct their first few performances, and take notes. Once you feel comfortable, you can leave them in charge, but their conducting may still be subject to the reactions of others working on the productions, and chances are you will hear any negative feedback before they do. Stage performers, for example, may characterize one conductor's show as brighter or lazier than another's. A stage manager might need a clearer cue from the cover conductor for a certain event, or someone in the orchestra may want the cover conductor to omit a gesture that he or she finds confusing. As music director, you are the clearinghouse for these notes and comments.

Disputes

It seems unconscionable that professional performers should have cause to gripe; rather, they should be grateful to be paid for doing what they love. Nevertheless, they do complain, and argue, and stubbornly at times. The best approach to resolving disputes, of course, is preemptive. When you cast and contract a production you look for people who will get along, and will function in the workplace without conflict.

Dissent in stage productions has two main causes: something having to do with the performance (artistic or technical) or something behavioral. Most artistic complications are resolved in rehearsal, and by opening night there is little left to argue over. Personal disputes are considerably more thorny. Even once they're resolved, there may be residual animosity or hard feelings, which can fester. Other issues arise over time, with repeated performances, as performances and perceptions evolve, or devolve.

Most disputes, thankfully, are small. Members of a rhythm section might haggle over a feel, or a dancer and music director might lock horns over a tempo. Singers might think that other singers are drowning them out, or upstaging them, or otherwise hindering their performance. Day-to-day moods and tempers can lead to ruptures in the harmonious mood of most productions, but many heal in the light of the next day, or week. When small problems occur, you as music director should not get flustered. Many are best left ignored, and others you can let sit for a while and wait for them to resolve themselves. Don't unnecessarily put yourself in the line of fire; you are already there. Simply monitor conflicts that do not directly involve you or the music, and step in only if they seem to be growing and encroaching on your territory. If you do get involved, deploy your communication skills and good humor to defuse the situation. As the creative and administrative head of a department that is one of several departments in a larger organization, you don't exclusively own every problem, but you will need to resolve the musical ones.

If there is a serious breach of behavioral correctness, such as sexual harassment, bigotry, or bullying, involving anyone whom you oversee, broach the matter with the company managers, stage managers, or producers, who will take over the matter with you as an advisor. Broadway orchestras have grievance processes clearly dictated by the CBA to deal with such problems and to arbitrate disputes between musicians and employers and between musicians and other musicians (including conductors).

Working conditions can cause significant consternation. For years the Broadway *Beauty and the Beast* orchestra fought with producers over decibel levels and suffocating haze in the pit. Several Broadway orchestras have had orchestra members on non-speaking terms, and a few physical altercations have broken out over the years. Onstage performers occasionally throw tantrums, and sometimes their huffs persist over time. They hate their opposite performer on stage; he or she blows the lyrics, or wears too much cologne, or misses his or her marks. The choreography is sending them to the orthopedist. They hate the conductor; he or she is out to get them by slowing down the tempos. Again, if the issue is nonmusical, stay out of it unless it threatens the musical performance. Weather others' outbursts with composure. If the music is threatened, then you, along with stage managers, company managers, and music contractors, are responsible for identifying the problem and if necessary reprimanding the offender, according to the official procedures provided to you. If a problem persists after your intervention, you can appeal to the producers for support. If things get bad enough, you will turn the entire issue over to them, and turn from prosecutor to witness.

When major musical conflicts arise, stand behind the philosophy that production is a collaborative effort, and therefore it is best to solve problems as a group, with mutual assent rather than autocratic decrees. Gather the orchestra, or the section, or just the combatants, and take the time to talk or rehearse the problem through (in a situation like this the music coordinator, a management representative, might not be welcome, unless the conflict has reached a head). Exert your authority and decision-making power fairly and gently but firmly, and always in support of the production rather than any individual. Explain to the musicians that the stage is where your ultimate loyalty lies, and so should theirs, and base your actions upon this allegiance.

Original Cast and Other Recordings

Late in the 1990s, major record labels began to succumb to the onslaught of online sales and streaming music. They survived by merging or downsizing, or simply folded. Among the first to surrender were classical labels or the classical divisions of major labels. It was these companies, such as Columbia, RCA, and Polydor, that produced many of the Broadway cast albums of the Golden Age and through the second half of last century. Recorded show music was never a big generator of profits, but the records sold enough copies, and the prestige factor was sufficient, to warrant continuing to make what were called "original cast albums" (often confused with "soundtracks," which are recorded movie or TV scores). These recordings memorialized great performances and gave modern music directors a tool for researching shows from the repertoire in their original form and with their original visions.

Some large companies do still produce records for hit Broadway musicals, but any show album that is not guaranteed to sell well will no longer bear a multinational label. As in the popular music industry, independent companies have filled the gap, and a few classical labels, including Nonesuch, continue to record stage music. Under the current model, smaller labels such as PS Classics, Varese Sarabande, Original Cast, and Sh-K-Boom Records and its subsidiaries now record many shows, concerts, stage productions, and other theatrical material, but do not finance the recordings, with the knowledge that sales are not likely to reimburse the substantial outlay required for a high-end recording of an hour or more of music. Thus they are not labels in the traditional sense; they act more like distributors, and thereby are able to stay financially afloat.

With or without a label deal, or a label's backing, affordable computer software has made a good recording of almost any production possible. You can take a feed from the sound board, and record a show live. If a production is acoustic, you can set up some good microphones, push the record button on Logic or ProTools or GarageBand, and take a clean digital musical snapshot. Or, you can record one part at a time, allowing each musician and singer to work at his or her convenience and pace, and gradually assemble the pieces into a whole. School productions often engage a videographer to provide parents and participants with a souvenir of the event. Making an audio version is even simpler and more editable.

Some of the original conventions of making cast recordings for professional productions endure. Most cast albums are recorded early in the run of a show, while the original cast is in place and fresh, and so that the album can be a tool to promote ticket sales. Many Broadway shows still record on the first day off after opening night. The only drawback to this practice is that voices are often tired after the opening night buildup of rehearsals, performances, and parties. But most cast recordings are imperfect, anyway. They are thriftily budgeted, and recorded quickly. Musicians, including music directors, receive union session rates, on low- and high-budget scales, depending on the production and the producer, from about two hundred dollars per three-hour session upward per session, plus the usual overages. Each session can accommodate three or four songs at best (there are also union limits on how many songs can be recorded in one session). Therefore, a twenty-piece orchestra for three hours runs up a bill of several thousand dollars. Actors' Equity has a particularly lucrative deal for their membership: each cast member receives a week's salary for each day in the recording studio, and receives their entire recording fee again once a year for as long as the original production runs.

Some music directors produce or coproduce the cast albums for shows they originate, but this is mostly a recent development, another byproduct of the accessibility of digital recording technology. Experienced music directors of the past might have been able to negotiate additional fees for conducting cast albums, but record production, which involves at least knowledge of engineering and mixing, used to be the sole province of technical experts. The best record producers were also musically intelligent and had masterful interpersonal and advisory skills. They knew how to draw the best performances from each individual and group, and could capture it in recorded sound. Now, with home recording software available and affordable to the public, a music director is more likely to take on such a role. The parallel between record producers and music directors is again obvious: both work with performers and musicians collaboratively, yet from a position of leadership, to evince the most effective possible performance.

The scores of most productions exceed the capacity of storage media such as LPs or CDs, as well as the attention span of most listeners. Furthermore, people listening to cast albums are mostly interested in the primary musical material of a show, not the interstitial music or smaller pieces such as reprises and interludes. Therefore, in preparation for making a cast recording, music directors work with composers, directors, record producers, and sometimes the performers to cut a score down to recordable size. You can shorten safeties and vamps, eliminate any transitional material, truncate introductions and dialogue sections, even reshape a song structure, so that a score fits into a package that a buyer-listener can appreciate outside of the theater. Many cast-album producers, though, will try to keep some sense of the live quality of a show in the recording, and tell the story of a show or otherwise bring to the fore the spirit of the stage. They are not necessarily out to make a studio version of a show's songs. Depending on where and how the recording takes place, a cast-album producer may record fewer takes, use less isolation, and is apt to accept small imperfections that do not interfere with the overall listening experience. When budget permits, many shows expand their orchestras for recording, giving the music a fuller sound in a sonic environment more revealing and exacting than a live venue. (This practice is not without irony in an age of dwindling orchestras.)

Constructing and recording click tracks and prerecords is a new addition to music directors' agendas. The sound department helps you record these to your specifications during preproduction or during cast rehearsals, so that they are available when tech begins. Keep in mind that when you are generating a click track, the decisions you make at an early phase of production may be immutable—you can alter tracks later, but the changes will incur time and money. You can customize a click track to suit the groove of a song, with slight variations, or with a "humanizing" plug-in (random, microscopic deviations). Clicks are the same as any other digital recording, and tempo is very easy to manipulate when there is no accompanying audio. You might find that one segment of a song needs relaxation, while another feels slow with the same metronome marking.

Repeatability and the Rehearsal Score

By nature, productions cannot be reproduced exactly, just as no two performances can be alike. With additional productions of a show as well as with extended runs, the written score is one of the ways that a production can be preserved and repeated with the same intent in the music direction (and, to some extent, the stage direction). As home recording technology did with cast albums and engineers, notational software has allowed music directors to create their own high-quality written scores without necessarily engaging a copyist. Specific dynamics, articulation, feel, and other musical values that were once prohibitively time consuming when entered on paper by hand are now far simpler. Music directors can, to some degree, write down their music direction in the piano-vocal or piano-conductor score, the score that will be used in future rehearsals.

It is up to you to decide what to include and what to omit in a written score. Only elements that are germane to the score itself, not to a certain production, are worthy of permanent entry, but ultimately it is all at your discretion. Some shows will benefit from production-specific information in the score, such as important dialogue and staging cues, metronome markings, or other written indications without which the musical meaning would be unclear, while others require only general musical and staging information. In any case, avoid overcrowding a score with information, as it becomes too hard to read at a glance, and your specificity might only confuse music directors of future productions.

Obviously, in any written score there must be some indication of melody and accompaniment. Most scores contain a complete vocal arrangement, as they are used to rehearse singers. There are scores whose accompaniment is a piano arrangement of a larger ensemble, and others with some combination of instrumental parts that add up to something resembling an accompaniment. In the latter case a rehearsal pianist will need to weave the different instrumental threads into a playable and useful accompaniment. Choose a notational system that is appropriate to the musical style and content. A rock score can be a glorified lead sheet with cues, while shows with orchestra might be made up of piano parts plus one or more additional staves containing instrumental cues. All orchestral scores will need some type of reduction for rehearsal accompanying.

Because notation software makes entering musical detail so convenient, there is no reason not to do it, as these values can be just as crucial to effective performance. Don't be afraid to mark every note with an articulation and every phrase with a dynamic if it will make for a better performance. Make your tempo indications characteristic and descriptive. Instead of "Adagio," try "Romantically, gently," along with specific metronome settings, or "With playful energy" in place of "Brightly."

Enter lyrics carefully, correctly, and precisely as the writers and director dictate, with such details as proper hyphenations, punctuation, and contractions. The text is as much a part of the score as the music. For this reason, some dialogue should probably also appear in most scores, at least when there is music along with it, though of course scores do not usually make space for an entire libretto (some do). Reprinting in the score entire scenes that take place with music under may be unnecessary, but you should certainly include key segments of dialogue, especially "hit points" (a term borrowed from film scoring), points at which the music and a word or stage action are meant to converge.

The following examples show the progression of two rehearsal scores from their origins to their final versions. Figure 20.1 is (A) an excerpt from my original hand-copied score of "Go to the Mirror, Boy" from *Tommy* (I still used a ruler for beams) and (B) the published version of the same section. The changes are not extensive. I do not recall why we omitted chord symbols in the printed version. One mistake in the printed version is that the treble clef in the vocal line at m. 20 and following and again at m. 36 and following should have a subscript "8" indicating that it transposes down an octave.

Figure 20.2 shows three versions of "Grasslands" from *The Lion King*: (A) an anonymous early sketch (including a scribbling of the stage costume); (B) a hand-notated transcription (by Karl Jurman, original associate conductor and now music director of the Broadway production); and (C) the final piano-vocal-rehearsal score version.

Lastly, Figures 20.3A and 20.3B show the composer's sketch and my final version of the rehearsal score for the opening number of the musical *Mask*. Composer Barry Mann and lyricist Cynthia Weil would give me material that took three forms: rough written vocal arrangements with some chord symbols, abbreviated piano takedowns, and well-produced demos representing the composer's ideal notion of the sound and feel of the songs. Through a long series of developmental productions, I worked out the rehearsal accompaniments and refined the rehearsal score. The handwritten notes on the original version are associate music director Paul Ascenzo's. In several presentations we used the demo tracks as accompaniment, and some of Paul's more cryptic indications refer to settings on the primitive CD playback system, which he operated masterfully and musically.

FIGURE 20.1A Author's draft of an excerpt from the piano-vocal score of "Go to the Mirror Boy," from *Tommy*.

FIGURE 20.1B The same excerpt, final version from the piano-vocal score.

FIGURE 20.2 Three phases of developing the piano-vocal score for "Grasslands," from *The Lion King*: an early sketch, the first rehearsal transcription, and the final version. (© 1997 Walt Disney Music Company.)

FIGURES 20.2 Continued

FIGURES 20.2 Continued

FIGURE 20.3 (A) Early sketch of the vocal arrangement of an excerpt from "Come Along for the Ride," from *Mask*.

FIGURE 20.3A Continued

FIGURE 20.3B The same excerpt, final version from the piano-vocal score.

FIGURE 20.3B Continued

Considering the time and care that music directors put into preparing, rehearsing, and performing the music for a show, it is gratifying that they can leave a permanent record of their creative effort in a document that will outlast a single production. It is also encouraging that as stage music history moves onward, every new show or revision of a show can be properly chronicled and archived as an entry as part of an ever increasing repertoire, and one whose music future music directors can now far more faithfully reproduce. Piano-vocal scores were once the province of copyists, but now that computers have streamlined their creation, music directors have understandably and rightly staked a greater claim in the process. The written score of a show may be the best—indeed, one of the only—tangible and enduring testaments to a music director's considerable efforts.

21

Working as a Music Director

Starting Out

In preparing to write this book, I interviewed several working music directors about their pathways into music direction, and spoke to several others who hoped to be employed as music directors in the future. Consistent with the findings about music direction throughout the book, their backgrounds and routes into the profession differ widely. Most are well-trained, formally educated musicians who began at an early age and have more than one musical skill. Most went to colleges or music conservatories and studied either serious (classical) music or jazz, or both. Almost all are excellent sightreaders, score readers, and accompanists, and have a wide knowledge of music literature, history, style, and performance practice in multiple genres. Naturally, there are divergences from these generalities. Some music directors are self-taught, some started music later in life, and some arrived at the profession from nontraditional musical origins. Some do not even read music, and do not need to (such as the music director of an improvised comedy show or experimental dance concert).

Perhaps the greatest commonality among everyone I spoke with was the piano, both as a foundation and as a means to an end. Accompanying at the piano is music direction in microcosm, and to those who have not read this book, accompanying at the piano seems perhaps equivalent to music direction. Indeed, many Broadway music directors have astounding mastery of the piano, and were first noticed for their pianistic abilities.

Some music directors working on Broadway, including me, got their best positions through working as an audition pianist. That is how I got my job on *Tommy*—I was playing auditions for *Tommy* orchestrator Steve Margoshes's musical *Fame*, and the scheduled *Tommy* music director dropped out shortly before the La Jolla production. Audition piano is also what brought music director Alex Lacamoire to New York City from Boston, where he had studied at Berklee College of Music. I went to Boston on an audition junket for *The Lion King*. Alex was the pianist there, and I was so impressed with his skill at the piano that I approached him and offered him a job as rehearsal pianist on the show. He arrived in New York, cheerily, some weeks later, and within a year or two, he had taken the musical theater scene by storm with his work on several shows, among others *Wicked, Batboy,* and *In The Heights*. Music director Kevin Stites, a superb pianist, was an accompanying major at the University of Illinois, studying under the great John Wustman, at the same time as I was there as a choral conducting student (he directed a production of the musical *Sugar* for which I was music director. Coincidentally, I recently worked on Broadway alongside a young music director, a marvelous pianist, who had studied under a university professor who was my conducting classmate at Illinois).

Early on, to support myself in my pursuit of theatrical music direction jobs, I played piano wherever I could. I played not only auditions, which became something of a specialty and a wonderful learning aid (mastering the repertoire, following and bailing out singers, transposing, sightreading all sorts of scores), but also piano bars and concerts, and as a keyboardist in theatrical and legitimate orchestras, mostly as a substitute. (Having been an undisciplined pianist when I was younger, I found that this constant work at the keyboard was finally forcing me to advance my skills to a more competitive level.) Accompanying singers and acts in clubs and concerts can be a career in itself, or a steppingstone to more elaborate productions. Orchestra size reductions and the shift in musical style have brought more combined piano-conductor chairs into modern orchestration, so more job opportunities will exist for those who can both play and conduct well.

Playing the piano, however, is not the only inroad to a career in the field. There are now some university music-direction training programs that address the wider music-direction skill set represented in this book. Some Broadway music directors have had conducting training at an advanced level, as did I, and others are educated as composers. Stage composers are often multi-skilled musicians, and many are also experienced music directors, among them Tom Kitt, Scott Frankel, and Jason Howland. Several other working music directors I know began as singers and stage performers. A few have come from Hollywood and the film industry, and some from popular and recorded music. Guitarists, bassists, and drummers also work as music directors, mostly in clubs, concerts, and special events, rather than in musical theater.

Arranging, transcribing, and copying are other specialties that line up well with music direction as an ultimate goal, as they all have a place in music direction, and each one can provide income independently from music direction. Earlier I mentioned music assistantships as an avenue to the podium; there too is an excellent proving and training ground. The pay may be negligible, but the knowledge and connections you earn by being a functional member of a working music department may easily compensate for the loss. Internships are another route, though as an intern you may be less active in important musical and administrative work.

Career Philosophy

Music direction can be one of several jobs you do as a musician, or it can be a career choice. Those aspirants who hope to conquer the higher echelons of the profession know that it is difficult to get there, and just as difficult to stay there once they arrive. As did I, and as I still do, they pound the pavements; make phone calls and write emails; look for opportunities to network with colleagues, composers, producers, and contractors; distribute their résumés; and design their websites—all essential steps. What makes one person move up while another does not cannot be reliably measured. Most people wanting to enter the field are quite talented and very diligent. There is certainly some luck involved, often in the form of being in the right place at the right time. One can easily draw the conclusion that it is advisable to work successfully in many different jobs, thus increasing the odds that you will be somewhere at some moment that will turn out to be the right place at the right time.

The most contented music directors I know think of music direction work not as an exclusive professional pursuit, but as part of a larger musical life. By nature, music direction spills into other areas, so why not work in these areas as well as holding the title of music director (or supervisor)? The conglomeration of skills that makes up music direction varies, and your particular expertise may lie somewhere within. When starting out, you might first practice professionally those skills at which you are most competent, and use the funding to improve on the others.

In my case, one of these abilities was teaching, and academics factored heavily in my upward (and sideways, and downward) career course, beginning with my college *West Side Story* that I spoke of in the Introduction: The View from the Podium (and even earlier, with high school music and theater projects). As a student, I had no notion of a career as a stage music director. Rather, I assumed that my classical background would lead me to a university professorship somewhere, probably in theory or composition (that I came from a family of academics also seemed to factor into my destiny; in high school I even held a seminar for my classmates in rock history). My sights were most set on being a composer of both serious and popular music, and of something in between that I had yet to discover (another *West Side Story*, perhaps?), and most composers were based in academia.

Music direction began for me as a summer job to make money. It was the student producer of *West Side Story* who first intimated that I could get paid to conduct and play for the stage (as I remember, I received $500 for *West Side Story*). I landed my first stock job that summer, and kept at it for the next few summers. Once I had started to build a résumé as a music director, and had added references from colleagues and former employers, finding and booking additional work became easier. All the while, and following my college graduation and a master's in choral conducting, I continued to teach (privately, mostly, but also in classes), coaching singers, teaching ear training and beginning piano, and later coaching other music directors and composers. It was a steady source of income, and one that I could control. I parlayed the money I made as a music director and teacher into periods of composing, a pursuit I knew was very unlikely to provide a living on its own; if it did, it could be a good living. But music direction jobs continued to come in, and got better, with higher profiles and better pay, and my ultimate goal, composition, proved an uphill climb. Notwithstanding, the composition work and study I did while working my way up the music direction ladder, and that I continue to do now, have greatly informed and improved my work as a music director. I returned to school in the mid-1990s for a doctorate in composition, continuing the educational thread and maintaining my fallback profession. Since then I have been able to balance music direction, scholarship, and composition, adding up to a very fulfilling musical life.

My greatest regret now is that early on, once I had had a small taste of success in music direction, I fell too deeply under its spell, and the spell of its paycheck. Instead of enjoying a continuum of jobs that included many excellent positions, some that paid adequately, many that did not, I thought of employment as an object of need, competition, and even desperation. Motivated by a strong desire for marriage and family and a misplaced sense of mid-1980s yuppie-ism, I shouldered the burden of the expensive New York City cost of living, lived from job to job, and tallied income against outgo. I rejected composing because the reward always seemed too distant and the potential for income too tenuous. In retrospect I know that accumulating entries for one's curriculum vitae is important, but not as important as the privilege of working as a musician, being paid to make music in any way one can, living in the moment of each job, even when only scratching out a living, leading a true artistic life. Now, later in my career, as I find myself less attracted to the massive responsibilities of music direction, I sometimes yearn for the sorts of work I once thought of as the means to the end of being a music director, particularly playing, arranging, and composing, which, because I am now known as a music director, or I appear overqualified, are harder for me to find.

A steady gig (which music directors might delineate as one lasting longer than a few months) can be a music director's bread and butter, if he or she so chooses. The kinds of salaries offered on Broadway and tours and in some local theaters are unusual in any arts profession, so musicians' attraction to them is understandable. The downside of a long-term job lies in performing the same material repeatedly, which can become monotonous for a creative mind, and lead to musical and intellectual stagnation. Music directors with steady jobs therefore often complement them with other work. Union agreements on Broadway and elsewhere stipulate leaves of absence in part to alleviate so-called long run-itis, and so that musicians can maintain their professional profiles, though producers may not be as lenient in allowing music directors time off. (A customary provision in music directors' contracts states that all terms are subject to the union's CBA. Therefore, as conductor, protected by the union, a music director is entitled to leaves of absence, but your side agreement with the producer as music director may prohibit them. When negotiating a contract for what could be an extended run, keep this constraint in mind.) Like many creative professionals, music directors use the salaries of the higher-paying commercial projects they work on to finance the low-budget, more artistically satisfying work they do on the side.

The new divisions of labor apparent in several recent Broadway production music departments may be rewriting the rules of music direction. Music supervisors of many new Broadway shows are music directors like those described in this book, but do not necessarily lead the orchestra in performance. They may do the bulk of their work in preproduction and rehearsal, and after opening night become just an occasional visitor. Often they combine their music supervision of a production with orchestration or arranging. This approach complies with the often ignored union bylaw that the conductor of a Broadway production cannot also be the orchestrator (the rationale is in providing as many jobs as possible), and highlights the appeal of receiving a Tony award for one's musical work, so far available only to orchestrators. This trend effectively splits music direction as I have described it in two, and in doing so gives music director–supervisors more flexibility to work on more productions, as they are not tied to a single production as conductor and daily maintainer. (Is this perhaps a modern incarnation of the transformation in symphony orchestra leadership from conductor to music director?)

If this book has been biased toward professional music direction situations based in New York, it is because I have spent my life and based my career here. Yet many music directors will never work in New York, and many who make New York their home base will, as did I, work extensively in other locations. Music direction opportunities exist everywhere, in urban, suburban, and rural areas, and on the road, and if you are able to, there is no reason not to accept work everywhere. I have also enjoyed working as a music director overseas, both for American-based shows and those originating in foreign countries. One of the charms of an active music direction career can be subsidized travel for work. There are some music directors who have spent years as touring conductors of Broadway productions, making an excellent living, seeing the world, working on first-rate productions, and amassing bountiful pensions.

Disappointment over not getting a gig, and feeling envy of someone other than you getting a job that you wanted, are normal emotions. They should neither deter you nor upset you to a point where they cause you rancor or resentment. At times you will need a thick skin, or at least the ability to stay cool when things are stressful, both in your career and in your music direction work. As is true in many professions, artistic and otherwise, the professional realm of music direction is not a meritocracy. The finest musicians will probably attain some form of career success, provided that they get along with others at least functionally. The cream does inevitably rise to the top. Regardless, a lesser musician might enjoy as much success, or more. Undoubtedly, working hard at your musical skills, industriousness in job hunting, and making wise career choices will help you make your mark, but do not guarantee sustained prosperity, and others who have not worked as hard may out-succeed you. They may indeed have worked very hard at being successful, as opposed to being the best at their craft, an effort that sometimes seems to carry more weight in an artistic climate skewed in favor of promotion over substance. Are the producers and writers and arrangers of the gazillion-selling dance or pop or even musical theater songs of today truly the finest and most creative musicians? No, by no means, though they may be highly gifted or adept at what they do, and what they do has clearly struck a cultural nerve. If their success is disproportionate, it is symptomatic of the commercial music world, of which music direction is a part.

Maintaining a Career

Perhaps harder yet than starting out in music direction is prolonging your career for a lifetime. In the 2010s the general public probably associates the phrase "a career in music" mostly with pop and hip-hop artists and producers, or perhaps with a member of a major symphony orchestra, or with music education. There are, unbeknownst to them, occupations in stage music, and in music direction: the low profile of music directors also conceals the continually burgeoning opportunities in the field. Primarily a freelance career, music direction is a conglomeration of jobs and productions over time, and I mean the openmindedness I endorsed in "Career Philosophy" to be completely inclusive. With alacrity and dedication and some good fortune on your side, you can find a career's worth of work. Your level of commitment is up to you; the good fortune is not, except insofar as trying to be at the aforementioned right place at the right time.

Idealistic though I may sound, I believe that all artists who wish to succeed professionally should simply commit to doing the finest work they can, and to perpetually improving on their abilities. Eventually, as long as they do not hide in a cave or show their work only to their spouses and/or pets—in other words, if they at least put themselves "out there" on the scene even minimally—their reputations will assure that they will be able to find some gainful employment. This axiom should hold true throughout a career. But as new artists enter the scene and capture the interest of employers as you once did, you may have to put greater effort into finding work and keeping your desirability and assets current and visible.

Each job leads to another. A member of one production team will bring your name into consideration for another, assuming you have done your job well. Doing your job well is measured by your colleagues at quite an elementary level, mostly by your making everyone you work with happy and secure, and by executing a reliable accompaniment from night to night. Going along and getting along, however sycophantic they may sound, will engender others' trust in you. (Being dutiful and staying in line do not mean, of course, that you cannot work to improve a production's flaws.) If employers find you trustworthy in one situation, they are confident in promoting you for another. Your musical skills are largely presumptive in the eyes of your nonmusical production colleagues; only when something sounds very wrong to them will they question your musicianship or musical leadership. Your musical teammates will hold you to higher musical standards, but music directors get their jobs from directors and producers as often as or more than they do from musicians. There is nothing wrong with expressing your personality fully in your work, but it is essential to accentuate the positive, and be a problem solver rather than a source of friction. Always keep in mind the fundamental notion of accompaniment: that it is woven into a larger fabric and is not itself the object of attention. This musical truth extends to the whole of music direction. Your job will often be thankless, despite the production's and the other performers' dependence on you, but you would be out of place in asking for thanks.

Ideally, over time you will develop associations with production organizations, directions, performers, choreographers, orchestrators, contractors, instrumentalists, and many other people in the entertainment industry who will sustain your working life. There may be lean times and busy times. There will, one would hope, be periods that are so busy that you deem your workload unmanageable, and reach out to your musical colleagues to share it. This too is an extremely productive career practice, as your colleagues will as a result more likely consider you as an option when their workloads exceed their capabilities. Music directors are quite friendly with one another, even if they are competing for the same jobs, and your friendships too will turn into work associations. Your workplace reputation develops out of the history of your personal interactions. Mounting a production entails people spending many hours in one another's company, working on the production, reflecting on the production, and hanging out after the show, so being good company over long hours and many weeks is very important.

A defining moment in your career as a music director might be getting fired from a job, or excluded from an opportunity that it seemed you were in line for. Sometimes such events are gratuitous, but they might be an indication that there is something you can improve in either your musicianship or your interpersonal skills. Even if you are able to ask of someone the reason for your firing or your exclusion from consideration, you cannot be assured of an unequivocal reply, because of the politics involved and the possibility that your firer or excluder must in some way save face or protect his or her colleagues or superiors. Draw your own rational conclusions and make the appropriate adjustments.

Filling in the blanks of your skill set is also decisive in so competitive a field. Do not be content with being a fair conductor, or pianist; work at getting good at both. If you don't know about all the idiomatic sounds, fingerings, and playing positions of the instruments of your orchestra, research them. If you are unfamiliar with the song literature of a certain style, do some intensive listening. If you can't play rock piano, or jazz piano, or can't read music, take lessons. Self-teaching, computer software, tutors, and institutional music programs are available everywhere, and with the Internet, you could conceivably study any musical discipline, including conducting, remotely, with your preferred mentor in a distant location. Keep your mind and docket open to opportunities that do not fit your current agenda; they may end up taking you to a musical, intellectual, or financial place you did not expect.

The movement in stage production toward electronica is now unstoppable. A survey of the posts in the Facebook group TheatreMusicDirectors.org clearly shows that many of the problems music directors face concern the best way to integrate the available technologies into their productions. It would seem that studying Mainstage and Ableton Live and other performance software is now as important in preparing to be a music director as are conducting training or score analysis. The music directors currently working on Broadway are perhaps not as updated on the latest technologies as are the generation behind them, and are doing just fine without necessarily being experts in extreme synthesis of stage scores. Most productions, though, have more limited budgets, and digitized music has found a strong foothold in them. Music directors of those productions have no choice but to keep up. Furthermore, if music directors are to have control of the music as it passes through a sound system, it behooves them even more to be up on the machinery that processes the music.

From the point of view of someone who has been a music director for forty years (I'm counting my high school shows) I can also advise you to exercise good financial judgment over the course of a freelance career, in the interest of long-term security. Freelance workers everywhere are familiar with the difficulties in getting insurance coverage and acceptable credit ratings, and in setting aside savings and retirement funds. A young music director may not have these challenges in mind, but as he or she matures they take on greater importance. Union music jobs come with pension contributions, but the union's pension fund, though well vested, no longer bestows on union retirees the generous payouts it did those who worked in the second half of the 1900s; too many financial crises since the 1990s made sure of that, as it has in all occupations. It is wise to set up a savings plan for the long term, even if it is meager at first, as soon as you can.

You should also retain a representative, if your work is sufficiently lucrative, to negotiate your contracts and act as a liaison between you and producers. An agent or manager, who will take a share of your income, usually 10 percent, or a lawyer, who will charge a hefty hourly rate up front, but whom you will only pay once, will look after your needs, offer counsel, and separate you from any dickering over money. An agent or manager offers longer-term care than a lawyer, but any representative might also be helpful in finding you additional work. Some music directors incorporate themselves as businesses as a way of deflecting taxes, but there are many tax advantages available to all freelance musicians. Make sure any accountant or business manager you engage is familiar with the entertainment industry.

Keep your contacts in the industry alive by using social media, by making a good website and résumé (actually several résumés, of different lengths and with differing emphases), and make periodic phone calls and send email greetings to potential employers (do not overdo it—see the following section, "How to Get a Gig"). Attend other events in your field and greet your colleagues when you can. If you are working or want to work as a Broadway music director, you should see almost every musical that comes into New York (this is difficult when you are working, but also more affordable). To save money, take your friends up on their offers of complimentary tickets, see shows in previews, and, when you can, attend rehearsals or run-throughs. Go see all sorts of music, and theater, and dance. There is something to be learned from every viewing of every type of performance at every level, and perhaps there is a contact to be made there. Gently promote the best work you are doing. You needn't—indeed, you shouldn't—post every gig you do on Facebook, especially the high-profile ones, which your colleagues will already know about, but it is important to advertise regularly. The question "What have you done?" is not so important as "What have you done lately?" Many music directors of my generation, those in their middle age, who have had some professional success, still follow the same rules of job hunting and career preservation that they have throughout their musical lives.

How to Get a Gig

If you find out, please call me, okay? I'm free as of two weeks from Sunday....

And that's sort of how it starts. As I continue to piece together a living as a musician I am repeatedly humbled by the truth of artistic professions: that they were not meant to be professions; they were meant to be art. To make a living as an artist, you must not only perfect your art to the degree that it is worthy of exposure to the world at large, but you must also publicize it and manage it, when you first start out and throughout your career, and hope that someone buys it. Recently, a lucrative job I had for three months from this writing unexpectedly fell through. After coming to terms with the effect that this loss would have on my cash flow, I made some phone calls and sent some emails to people I thought might be overloaded or looking for subs and covers. I also contacted some composer friends. I count myself very lucky that within two days I had managed to overbook myself for the next month, making a significant dent in the financial shortfall that resulted from the lost gig. It was only a result of my having built a network and a reputation over time that I was able to secure employment merely by picking up the phone and offering my services, and I'm not sure I'd get the same positive result on another occasion.

Always be open to working for little or no pay, especially if it means getting in on the ground floor of a project that you believe has a chance for a successful commercial future. The only problem with such willingness is that, because nonpaying jobs may entail just as much or more effort than paying ones, your nonpaying workload might disqualify more profitable work. Furthermore, as I have now repeatedly asserted, you should also have no objection to working in only one area of music direction—teaching, arranging, composing, conducting, working as an associate or assistant, subbing—rather than doing the whole job.

The main tools for finding jobs as a music director are, consistent with the previous career summary, first, working effectively in the jobs you do, and second, networking.

No less important is your readiness to do a job when you are hired for it. I learned its importance when I was young by being let go from a job as an associate conductor at a stock theater. The position, it turned out, was primarily for an accomplished pianist, and I failed to prepare and practice music I thought I could sightread. My playing on the first day of rehearsal was clumsy at best, and I did not return for a second day. This termination was a defining event for me.

Networking takes all sorts of forms, from the training programs you went through and the students and professors you met there, to your relationships with every person on every production team and creative team and in every cast and orchestra you have worked with. The best way of networking is to work. This is, of course, a paradox: you cannot find work until you network, and you cannot effectively network until you have a job. It highlights the importance of accepting entry-level positions; any foot in the door is helpful, and any tiny opportunity can develop into a great one. By following several small opportunities, you increase your likelihood of success. It is possible to network without having a job, but having something substantial to present is always preferable. When you work on a production that shows your work in a good light, offer complimentary tickets to anyone who can help you find additional work. If you can, make a video of you conducting, make audio recordings of your work (when it is permissible), and track down any recordings others have made. YouTube, MySpace, SoundCloud, and similar sites are at your disposal to supplement and distribute your curriculum vitae.

You can mail or email your résumé with a well-written cover letter to contractors, producers, theaters, directors, and other music directors. In all likelihood, the recipients of these notes and credentials will not act on them, and more than likely they will not even respond. If you do choose to write such a letter, keep it brief, friendly, businesslike and to the point (Figure 12.1). Do not ramble, do not digress, do not be unduly friendly with anyone you have not met, and do not rely on your computer to check spelling and grammar.

Ms. Proscenia Scena

Artistic Director, Playhouse-In-The-Hills

Dear Ms. Scena,

I am writing at the recommendation of our mutual friend Dionysus Terpsichord, who mentioned to me that you might be seeking musicians for your upcoming season. I would be particularly interested in a position a music director, but would consider working in any musical capacity you might need. My skills include conducting, vocal coaching, composing, arranging, and accompanying at the piano, and I am comfortable in most musical styles. My résumé is attached, and my website address and contact information appear below.

Please feel free to contact me at your convenience if you would like to schedule an interview or if you require further references or information. Thank you very much for your attention and consideration.

Sincerely,

FIGURE 21.1 Sample cover letter.

Ideally, in any initial contact, find someone who can introduce or recommend you to the person you are contacting. Always ask permission to use someone as a reference; you cannot assume that he or she will want to, or will give you a positive report, just because he or she is an old friend or liked your work on the last production you did together. Never ask someone with whom you have not had a good working relationship for a reference. (I have been the uncomfortable victim of both of these improprieties.) Use any resource or intermediary you may have to find a phone number or an email address of someone you think might be helpful, and drop a line, but avoid namedropping. Restrict your correspondence to one email, perhaps one more a year or so later, but nothing more. Never inundate a potential employer with unsolicited mail or calls. Furthermore, do not put anyone from whom you hope to get employment on your news update list, your automatic six-month check-in, or any other uninvited advertising, unless the recipient has specifically requested that you do so. The constant contact can serve only as a deterrent: employers do not want employees who they fear will be constantly promoting themselves when working together.

More effective than this sort of emailing or "cold calling," however, is personal contact. The AFM offers outreach programs in New York and elsewhere for musicians wanting to work in the theater industry at which they can meet and question working professionals. Organizations such as ASCAP (American Society of Composers, Authors and Publishers) and BMI (Broadcast Music, Inc.) offer workshops of various kinds in theatrical and popular music that, while they may not discuss music direction outright, provide information and networking opportunities useful to music directors. There are some class opportunities, and private teachers; trade papers and union journals advertise these. Trade papers and websites also have job listings for music directors and related work; Playbill.com, Backstage, and Theater Communication Group's ArtSearch are among many publications and websites that run classified ads for stage music employment. Their offerings may be sparse, but it takes only a few good jobs to get your career rolling.

Best of all, as is true for instrumentalists and music directors alike, is to get to know others in your field. Use the networking inherent in your educational program; in other words, keep in touch with your classmates and your teachers, and consider continuing your training or lessons after any degree is complete. Contact other music directors you'd like to work for or with and offer your apprenticeship, or ask if there's any chance you might observe a performance he or she is conducting (Figure 21.2). It's not usually a good idea to offer to take music directors out for coffee or a drink so you can "pick their brains." In doing this you are, in essence, asking for free advice, and from someone who is potentially the competition. Always show respect for age and experience; early in your career, most of the people hiring you will be older than you and will have been around the block many more times. Begin any correspondence or conversation formally, and with humility. And always do your due diligence before writing; make sure that you are up to

Dear Mr. Church,

Please forgive any imposition. My name is Jose Iglesia, and I am an aspiring music director who recently moved to New York City from Barcelona, Spain. I am writing at the recommendation of our mutual friend Giuseppe Chiesa, who was my teacher at [name of Music Festival], to ask if I might observe you conducting your production of [name of show] one night from the orchestra pit.

Like you, I have a degree in conducting, and I am a solid accompanist and arranger. I am hoping to meet people in New York and familiarize myself with the musical environment here, and eventually I hope to develop a career in music direction. It would be very helpful to watch you in action.

Please contact me anytime if you might be able to accommodate me. My résumé and contact information are attached and reprinted below. Thank you for your time and attention.

Sincerely,

FIGURE 21.2 Sample letter of introduction to a music director.

date on the activities of the person you are writing to. I have received several letters from people asking if they might sub for me on productions for which I no longer work. Stay up to date, and keep your correspondence polite and succinct, as in Figure 21.2.

Observing shows from the orchestra pit is how substitute instrumentalists learn their parts, in addition, of course, to practicing them on their own. On and Off-Broadway, keyboard subs watch an associate or assistant conducting play his or her keyboard book, and hope for the opportunity to work into the rotation. It is quite acceptable to invite yourself to watch even if the player does not need subs at that time. Often the player will allow you to make a photocopy of the part, and you can learn it, and be ready on the slim chance that you will be called; as it did for my idol, Maestro Bernstein, with the New York Philharmonic, such fortuitous happenstances have been known to lead to great careers. There are many fine musicians who do not hold chairs in Broadway orchestras who supplement their incomes by subbing, and often subbing on a keyboard chair is an excellent avenue to conducting. This happens more, of course, on shows with longer runs, so it is not as useful a route toward work in music direction, where subbing opportunities are fewer. The CBA's requirement that the conductor have five subs has opened a few doors for aspiring Broadway conductors.

One question I am frequently asked is whether a music director should be selective in accepting work or should take every job that comes along in the hope of its leading to something better. There is no simple answer. One music director friend of mine has a brash recommendation: accept every job, and if you find something better, quit the job you first took. This approach can work out if the career significance of the new job far outweighs the one you let go, but as a rule, quitting on a job, or "bailing," is frowned upon. Avoid burning bridges. I made a faux pas early in my career after being offered a position (associate conductor) on a major national tour by a major contractor. At the same time, a small show I had written songs for and for which I was the music director was about to go into production Off-Broadway, and I was reluctant to leave New York. I made the contractor wait a few days for my decision, and then turned the job down. He never called me again. (And my show failed miserably.) Some music directors simply crowd their schedules with projects. Whereas I endorse pursuing multiple opportunities, if your pace is too frenetic, you run the risk of selling one job short in favor of another or damaging your reputation by not being able to give every project the attention it deserves.

If you adhere to the conviction of doing your work for the work's sake, then it becomes easier to balance selectivity with practicality. Accept the jobs that you want to do and need to do, those that fulfill both your artistic and pragmatic wishes. It is understandably difficult to trust that the world of music will do right by you, and the unavoidable downward turns of a life in music might further entrench your cynicism. Nonetheless, it is your choice, perhaps your only choice, to pursue this career. Artistic vocations are notorious for their financial and emotional fluctuations, and one can only hope that the creative rewards will outweigh the heartbreak and frustration. Persistence and patience usually pay off, and practice, too, but making music because you love to is the real prize. If you can make a living doing it, I offer a sincere "Bravo!"

CampusExplorer.com, a website that students visit to investigate baccalaureate training programs and occupations, paints a bleak picture of music direction as a career choice:

> Music directors and composers generally work part-time during the nights and weekends and intermittent unemployment and audition rejections are common. For this reason, it is common for music directors and composers to supplement their income with other jobs. Usually, a passion for music drives these individuals to begin their training early by studying an instrument or training their voice. There is a fierce competition for jobs because of the many individuals who wish to enter this field. . . . Many can only find part-time or intermittent work.[1]

I refuse to share the pessimism of this outlook. Rather, I contend that music directors who view their work as fluid, as malleable, and as an ever-growing skill set will find more employment in the 21st century than ever before. With music and theater and singing and all stage performance so much more popular and visible than ever, more job opportunities are sure to follow. The competition has always been tough, and that is as it should be; the work of music directors and the music they produce should be held to a high standard. It is a cliché, but true: if it were easy, everyone would do it. And stage music has not yet become so mechanized as to eliminate human music directors from the picture: we're still here, even if sometimes we're the ones mechanizing the music. Either way, live or on track, we're going to get it right, and we're going to make it sound good.

---

1. "Music Directors and Composers Overview," Campus Explorer, http://www.campusexplorer.com/careers/EA22DFFB/music-directors-and-composers/.

APPENDIX A

Putting It Together

A music direction text as exhaustive as this one would surely benefit from multiple case studies describing the details of conducting many pieces from many shows. Because of space limitations, however, I have selected two, *In The Heights* and *The Lion King*. They are both exemplary of modern production, and in combination they contain a rich lode of information relevant to the topics at hand. I have conducted both shows on Broadway many times, one as music director and supervisor, one as associate conductor, so I speak with great familiarity with the material. As a replacement conductor for one, I am able to share the conducting thought processes and direction of a fellow music director (and one of the finest, Alex Lacamoire). I will discuss the opening number of each show: in *In The Heights*, "In The Heights" and the start of its playout, "Back to Work," and in *The Lion King*, "The Circle of Life."[1] "In The Heights" is multipartite, quite varied in style, and complex in content, whereas "The Circle of Life" is considerably simpler, at least after its wild opening vocal counterpoint. The conducting chair at *In The Heights* is also the primary keyboard part, both as a rhythm book and in an orchestral role. As mentioned, the part is extremely challenging to play, and its styles are very specific and unfamiliar to many musicians. The conducting is just as challenging. The conductor's focus is on the execution of the accompaniment as opposed to the vocals. In *Lion King*, the conductor attends more to the stage than the orchestra. The conducting is simpler, and does not have the added burden of a keyboard part.

There were cameras on the conductor in both shows, as well as direct sight lines from the conductor to the stage and most of the band, and a combination of live and video feeds for the orchestra and singers. Both use(d) Aviom mixers on each instrumental chair in the pit and on the podium for individualized monitoring. For *Heights*,

---

1. This account refers to the original production of *The Lion King* at the New Amsterdam Theater; since then, the Broadway version of the show, now at the Minskoff, has undergone some changes, though these two numbers have remained largely intact.

conductors wore closed headphones or earpieces (much of the sound is not audible live), or open-ear phones (or closed phones with one ear on and one off) for a mix of live and monitored sound. In *Lion King*, they listen live, through the house and stereo vocal monitors on the podium.

As opposed to describing in prose every musical minutia related to conducting, I have made a list of the most salient events in the conducting plot or process for each song, with occasional editorial addenda. Whereas I have tried to be thorough, I did not go into every subtlety of each moment, much as I would have liked to, and as much as they might have been relevant.

Measure numbers refer to the conductor's score, available from the publishers, and I will use lyric cues as markers as well. The songs as I describe them may be heard intact on the original cast recordings of each show (there is a tiny cut in "In The Heights" on the recording, but it is irrelevant to this description).

On a personal note, I must add that both of these numbers (and shows) are marvelous to conduct. The audience's enjoyment of them is palpable, and the craft, wit, and emotion that went into creating them are extraordinary. As conductor you are channeling music and accompanying theatrical entertainments that are engaging, intelligent, and smartly produced. You both emit and feed off the energy of the material, the stage, the band, and the audience. While conducting, you feel privileged, and the huge responsibility on your shoulders lightens in the enraptured atmosphere of skillful creation and performance. The satisfaction that comes with the experiences of conducting these pieces and others like them in a first-class performance setting are the motivation for many a career in music direction. Note: in these descriptions, the commentary in brackets ([]) is secondary, explanatory, or production-specific information.

In The Heights #1: "In The Heights"

- Clave pattern is running as a click track at top. When Usnavi is ready to begin, he puts his hand on his rear pants pocket. Give a three-four gesture [the three-four is actually two half notes; the meter is 4/4 but in a cut-time feel] to the camera and slightly to the stage, in a clear pattern (out-up), cueing the spotlight on Usnavi and his lyric "Lights up on Washington Heights . . ." (Usnavi's entrance has an eighth-note anticipation.) [The actor does not need a cue, but your connection with him ensures the simultaneous entrance, and cues the lights.]
- Cue the *guiro* (in the drum kit part) at m. 11 with a clear half-note prep; the player will play a pattern in half notes. [Mm. 11–12 are always played four times.]
- Going into m. 13, clearly cue the bass, guitar, keyboard 2 (an electric piano), and live clave (percussion 2). The prep is for a clearly articulated, *tenuto* quarter note on the subsequent downbeat, played precisely together; the prep must convey this articulation and precision.

- Cue the same group a few times more in the same manner, at your discretion, as the sparse accompaniment continues.
- Give a small cue to the alto sax and trumpet at m. 20. Cue the conga (percussion 1) at m. 21, and indicate the accent on that downbeat. Cue the guitar entrance at m. 24, and *tutti* at m. 29. [One of the purposes of this series of cues is to reinforce the buildup of instrumental forces in the accompaniment. This buildup reflects the scene on stage, in which, as in the orchestration, new characters enter one by one, increasing the density of the visual texture. Altogether this adds up to the musical-dramatic believability of a neighborhood waking up and coming to life.]
- In m. 29, count out loud (optionally into the conductor microphone), "One-two-three-four." (The click is out by this point, and the clave is now live.) [This is the original music direction, an enforcement of strict time and absolute accuracy of the ensuing downbeat and tempo.]
- At m. 38, push the button to trigger the new click. Though there is almost no latency between your push of the button and the start of the track, the action of pushing the button requires that you anticipate the beat slightly so that the first click lands precisely in tempo. [Any click system may have startup idiosyncrasies, which is why I mention this here.]
- Safety at m. 46, waiting for a clear end to Abuela's line, "Pacencia y fe." (Do not anticipate the end of the line; err on the safe side and wait one extra repeat if the timing is tight.)
- At m. 48, trigger the new click, which also contains prerecorded hip-hop loops and effects.
- Optionally conduct lightly until click goes out at the downbeat of m. 70 ("(It's) *got*-ten mad expensive..."). Optionally cue drum fill at m. 67 ("Our neighbors started [packin' up]..."). [Cues such as these, unnecessary but fun, also serve to point up events that might not normally be perceived by a listener. I have always asserted that even if only a few listeners' experience is enhanced only minimally by giving such a cue, it is a worthwhile effort, and in this case, it also reinforces the synchronization of conductor and drummer.]
- Cue the onstage ensemble singing the hook melody "In The Heights..." at m. 71. The melody begins after beat 3, in an eighth-note syncopation. Big breath and sharp cue on beat three.
- Beginning on the next downbeat, play the piano *montuno* (a repeated, arpeggiated phrase typical of piano parts in Afro-Cuban music), continuing to the downbeat of 87, a full band stop. [While you're playing this phrase and other very rhythmically driven keyboard parts, the playing is as effective a keeper of the beat as your conducting gestures.]
- At. m. 88 ("Next up to bat, the Rosarios..."), conduct in four, to the camera. The four-beat assures that the tempo remains constant or even stretches a little through

this short, accompanied recitative-style section, and sets up a contrast to the gentler two-beat feel to follow at m. 96.
- Conduct the stop at m. 94, and while resuming playing at m. 95, coordinate the entrance by leading the band in with the head (the main theme, now in two, conducting half notes), synchronizing the upbeat gesture with the rolled piano chord, and reaching the top of the chord exactly on the downbeat.
- Both hands to the piano at mm. 95–96. Cue the guitar, which enters after beat 2 of m. 97, with the left hand. In mm. 98–102, rest or keep time lightly, in two (the clave returns at m. 96).
- Play piano both hands from mm. 103–111 (sung dialogue between the Rosarios).
- Lightly conduct the more aggressive two-beat feel beginning at m. 112. Optional cues to the saxes at m. 114, 116, and 124, and other brass and wind entrances through this section.
- Cue the accented stops on the second eighth note of beat four at m. 118 and the second eighth note of beat two at m. 124.
- Play the piano arpeggio at m. 126 *leggierissimo* (very lightly) [under "... liquor store," a laugh line on stage—the precision helps the joke land]. Likewise, conduct the arpeggiated echo in keyboard 2 and percussion/drums at m. 128 in a precise four.
- With the downbeat of m. 129, cue the precise guitar chord entrance rolled into beat two (before "Thanks, Usnavi," a musical dialogue punctuation).
- Play the piano arpeggio in m. 130 again very evenly, but this time poise your left hand on the click button, ready to start it precisely on the downbeat of m. 131. Change patch with foot pedal. Double-check that patch has changed properly.
- In m. 134, conduct the crescendo and accent on the second half of beat four.
- Play brief synth cue at m. 139 ("... too darn hot ..."), then change patch by hand and check that patch has changed. Optionally conduct lightly through m. 150.
- Play synth part beginning at m. 150 ("'One dollar ...'"). Coordinate the rhythm carefully, listening to the click and drums and the keyboard 2 and brass/sax accents on beat four of each measure. [This is another example of where you're playing leads as much as your conducting gestures, and as a player you must respond correctly to your own conducting, and in this case, a click.] After downbeat of m. 158, change patch with footswitch.
- Resume playing (organ patch) at m. 159; continue to monitor tempo of the pattern (don't rush). At m. 166, change patch with footswitch and cue stage ensemble after beat three (again, "In The [Heights]..."). (The click goes out at m. 165.)
- Play the *montuno* in mm. 167–181, then change patch with footswitch during bar of rest. Do not turn page yet [this is a relatively fast page turn; it is not unusual for conductors to deal with these rapid turns, but this one became part of the conducting choreography, so I mention it here]. On the next downbeat (m. 183), trigger the new click/effects track, and simultaneously begin the right-hand pattern

on synth piano in the new feel. Then turn the page with left hand. Throughout this sequence, keep very strict time, in line with the hip-hop style, even while not conducting, with the chords (the click is off).
- Optionally cue the keyboard 2 string punctuation at m. 191. [This cue has no particular purpose but to connect with, to "have a moment" between, the conductor and keyboard 2 player; the entrance is obvious and deliberately simplistic. Such interactions are mostly a diversion to alleviate the tedium of repeated performances, and to musically fraternize with bandmates.]
- Continue quarter-note piano pattern through m. 205; optionally conduct lightly in two with left hand. During m. 206, change patch with footswitch.
- In mm. 207–212R (Vanessa's verse, beginning with "No . . ."), play the electric piano footballs with a hard attack (these soft chords are the main tonality in the orchestral texture, so they need to be heard, and the patch is soft), and conduct lightly by grooving along with head or body. The click speeds up slightly in these measures.
- Optionally cue the trombone at m. 212K ("No, n-n-no, I won't . . .").
- Turn page to be ready to play next keyboard cue with two hands. At end of m. 212R, change patch. (The click goes out at the end of this bar.)
- Play *dolce* piano part m. 212DD ("You owe me a bottle . . . I'll see you later, so . . ."). Continue light time with body, and in demeanor and playing express the warmth of the scene on stage, and note the foreshadowing in the story.
- Clearly conduct mm. 212EE–212FF ("[I'll see you] later, so/Ooh . . ."), in two, to coordinate keyboard 2, flute and drums. [A very exposed, plain syncopation such as this one is more reliably accurate when conducted]. Prep the downbeat of m. 213 with the head, and play the downbeat tightly with the band, off the prep.
- Resume the high register hip-hop quarter note chords at m. 215 ("[Yo] bro, take five . . ."). Stop and change patch at m. 221 while indicating *subito piano* and crescendo in mm. 221–222, mostly with head and face, and while positioning right hand for tricky synth string arpeggio at m. 223. Focus on playing right-hand arpeggio figure.
- Conduct mm. 225–229 ("Yeah, I'm a streetlight . . .") clearly, in four, to coordinate the downbeat hits in every other bar.
- In m. 230 (". . . rolling down the street . . ."), play the synth effect on the second eighth note of the second beat with right hand at full key velocity, and hold until the next downbeat, then release precisely. On the same downbeat (m. 231), trigger the click with the left hand. In m. 232, play the synth effects on beats three and four with the left hand, then change patch with the right hand (or footswitch), and check that the patch has changed. [Yes, it's just as complicated as it sounds, and treacherous, too.]
- Conduct mm. 233–240, holding back the tempo with the slightly slowed click.

- Optionally cue the chorused guitar chord at m. 237 ("[it's] all about the legacy..."). [Possibly an important cue because the orchestration is highlighting an important plot point, and another foreshadowing.]
- In m. 240, cue the stage ensemble on the second half of beat three as before (another "In The Heights..." entrance).
- Play right hand (orchestra bells) in mm. 241–247, while continuing to conduct lightly, in two, with the left hand. Continue to monitor the tempo, and keep it on the back side of the click. [You can also express this as "sitting back" on the beat or playing "behind" the click.]
- Change patch on the downbeat of m. 248, and play the rhythmic string part. Continue to monitor the time, now using the playing as a guide.
- At m. 254, lift left hand from keyboard and cut the ensemble with a large, strong gesture on beat three ("[to]-*day*!").
- Quick patch change on the downbeat of m. 256A (the last "[(In The) Heights...]", then play the *montuno* until m. 256M, ("[And to]-night is so far a-[way]...").
- At m. 257 (the coda), indicate *subito piano*, then the crescendo to the end, again while playing, using your head, body, and facial expression. Stretch the tempo slightly (click is off) to accommodate the lyrics and counterpoint. Think of an eighth-note pulse to keep the tempo in check, and work with the drummer to enforce the time.
- Stretch the rest before the final orchestral stinger at m. 265 very slightly; the additional milliseconds before the button emphasize its finality.
- Wait for the peak of the applause, then count off, aloud and into the conductor microphone, a full bar into the playout ("Back to Work") in the same tempo.
- Allow the energy and dynamic to dissipate through the transition by conducting less and by making a conspicuous *diminuendo* in the piano part at mm. 5–6, going under dialogue and into the next scene.

The Lion King #1: "Circle of Life"

- To cue the first Rafiki vocal (Figure A.1), wait until the rising curtain reveals the top of her headpiece (she is downstage left), then give her a clear (but not forceful) prep, approximately an eighth note in the eventual tempo, with the right hand, and an equivalent breath.
- Optionally, keep time lightly through the first measure: the note tends to shorten in repeated performances, but should remain its full length. [Subtle timekeeping may not prevent the singer from shortening the note, but will discourage it. Anything more than subtle is inappropriate in a stage moment when the stage and the performer are so strikingly the focal points.]
- Off the last syllable of Rafiki's first line in m. C ("[ba]-ba"), the "call," give a strong eighth-note prep and clear breath to the camera (ensemble singers are offstage

and in the front of house, watching on video monitors) for the "response," "Sithi hu ngonyama." [Beat patterns and metrical orientation are irrelevant; what is important are togetherness, articulation, correctness of diction, dynamic, and spirit; therefore, you dictate rhythms and phrases rather than use beat patterns.] The prep and last eighth note (two sixteenth notes on "Si-thi") form the pickup to m. D (see Figure A.1).

- Conduct the first two quarter notes of m. D (a 4/4 bar) for the half note "-hu," then dictate the eighth-quarter-eighth rhythm of "ngo-nya-ma." On the last eighth note, while the left hand holds the chord through the next downbeat (and implicitly, though not explicitly, beyond: five beats in all, plus the anticipatory eighth note), the right hand springs into a preparation for the secondary response in m. E, "Ngonyama, Nengw'ebo."

- Dictate this response phrase as well, though not every note, and with the right hand only: dotted eighth ("Ngon-ya)-sixteenth ("ma"). The sixteenth-note gesture is also an eighth-note rest/breath/prep to a quarter plus a sixteenth ("Neng [quarter]-we [sixteenth]"), followed by an indefinite hold on "bo" (there is an unwritten fermata on the first quarter note of the SATB parts in m. F). At the same time, with the left hand, cue the tertiary response, "Ngonyama," beginning on beat two of m. E.

FIGURE A.1 "The Circle Of Life," opening measures, annotated with conducting beats. (© 1994 Disney Walt Disney Music Company.)

Dictate the outline of this phrase as well, with an eighth note ("Ngo-"), an eighth tied to a dotted eighth ("-nya-"), and a sixteenth tied to an indefinite hold ("-ma"). As the score and conducting diagram show, the left hand and right hand are a sixteenth-note apart at beat two of m. E, but meet on the second sixteenth of beat two in the same measure. (The conducting hands may in this case be reversed without loss of communication.)

- The hold continues with the left hand, while the final right-hand gesture of m. E preps a cue to the soloist marked as "Lebo," positioned high in the rafters to the conductor's right.
- Give the ensemble cutoff strongly to the camera, near the downbeat of m. G, with a sweeping downward gesture that represents the long vocal pull-off.
- The entire passage (mm. A–G) repeats in mm. H–N, but with a different solo responder, the character "Faca"[2] in the rafters on the opposite side; cue him with the left hand. Optionally cue Rafiki's two subsequent entrances at m. H and again at m. N, using the last two eighth notes of each soloist's chant as a quarter-note prep.
- Again, the passage repeats beginning at m. O, but now there are no secondary and tertiary responses; only the main choral grouping remains. In mm. R–V (the repeated "Ngonyama"), begin by dictating with both hands the eighth-quarter-eighth tied to half rhythm, each followed by a long half-note gesture and breath that also prepare each next statement.
- At the full cadences (cadences on the tonic D major), at mm. R–S and m. T–U, shorten the sustained half note to a quarter, for a longer breath. Indicate the cutoffs clearly, in tempo, and breathe and prep during the (unwritten) quarter-note rests for the re-entrances at mm. S and U.
- In m. V, the last bar before the tempo kicks in, switch to a standard, grooving, widely lateral four-beat. Cue the orchestra on beat four, or with a three-four prep.
- Starting in the next measure, sing or mouth along with the chant, "Ingonyama nengw'e nama bala," as it begins its long cycle of repetition.
- Think about the meaning of the words (loosely translated, "behold the lion and tiger") and the majesty and significance of the theatrical and dramatic moment. Uphold the correct pronunciation [drilled exhaustively in rehearsal]. Work on coordinating the many voices now scattered throughout the theater, entering the stage from all sides, wielding elaborate puppetry of all sorts. Do not underestimate the difficulty of singing under these circumstances, and maintain energy and precision, as well as visibility, throughout. Register the audience reaction to the

---

2. "Lebo" and "Faca" were the names of the actors who originally played these singing antelopes, and Lebo was, of course, also the vocal arranger and choral director for the South African material in the show.

sights and sounds, and maintain their connection to the music as the visual effects become more engrossing.
- Cue the back-and-forth calls of the soloists in the rafters in mm. 1–9D. The audience will be looking at the animals, so continued cueing of this musical element keeps it present in both the soundscape and the landscape.
- Continue coordinating the chant as the singers gradually reach the stage. Check the tempo to make sure it is not too fast or slow; connect with the chant as a motor rhythm. [Once the groove kicks in, the accompaniment is relatively straightforward and otherwise needs little attention.]
- In m. 9D, indicate a decrescendo to the camera, stage, and orchestra.
- Cue Rafiki's first lyric, "From the day we arrive . . . ," on the last beat of m. 9D, and stay with her into m. 10–11. She may have difficulty hearing over all the tumult, and a clear cue keeps her in the groove and prevents an early or late entrance.
- Cue the strings at m. 18.
- Indicate a big crescendo in m. 25, leading into the chorus.
- In mm. 26–27, cue and conduct the *forte* vocal step-out, "Balek'ingonyam'i ya ga le." Give a clear cutoff to stage and camera with the left hand on beat four of m. 27 (the end of "le") with a slight sweep to indicate a slight pull-off.
- The overall dynamic is *forte*, but leave headroom for a larger climax to come.
- At mm. 40–41, indicate decrescendo to *piano*. Cue pan flute solo entrance on the second half of beat four of m. 41, with a pre-prep on beat three.
- Continue to mouth the words and keep the chant intact through the break. The actors are tiring and value the conductor's energy.
- In mm. 56–57, indicate a large crescendo to *fortissimo*.
- As before, cue the step-out in mm. 58–59. Keep in mind that this time the passage is in response to the iconic staging of Mufasa proudly holding out the baby Simba at the top of Pride Rock, and the animals bowing in fealty to the new prince, so it has even more weight.
- In this second chorus some ensemble singers join Rafiki on the melody, and more join in as the chorus progresses. Conduct the melody to the camera and the stage with the left hand (the right hand continues to beat time), all the way to the end of the piece. Give clear, medium-sized preps and cutoffs so that they are visible both on stage and in the camera. Dictate the subdivided and syncopated melodic rhythms, and mark the beats through the sustained notes until their cutoffs.
- Indicate the crescendo into the key change at m. 65, and maintain the peak dynamic from m. 66 to the end.
- Slow applause segue to the next piece; the audience response to the opening can be quite protracted. Wait at least a few seconds into the peak of the applause before continuing.

Bibliography, Suggested Reading, and List of Musical Works Cited

BOOKS ON CONDUCTING

Durant, Colin. *Choral Conducting: Philosophy and Practice.* New York: Routledge, 2003.

Ehmann, Wilhelm. *Choral Directing.* Translated by George D. Wiebe. Minneapolis: Augsburg Pub. House, 1968.

Jordan, James, Giselle Wyers, and Meade Andrews. *The Conductor's Gesture: A Practical Application of Rudolf von Laban's Movement Language.* Chicago: GIA Publications, 2011.

Leinsdorf, Erich. *The Composer's Advocate: A Radical Orthodoxy for Musicians.* New Haven, CT: Yale University Press, 1981.

Linton, Stanley. *Conducting Fundamentals.* Englewood Cliffs, NJ: Prentice-Hall, 1982.

Meier, Gustav. *The Score, the Orchestra and the Conductor.* New York: Oxford University Press, 2009.

Nicholl, Matthew, and Richard Grudzinski. *Music Notation: Preparing Scores and Parts.* Boston: Berkelee Press, 2007.

Rudolf, Max. *The Grammar of Conducting: A Comprehensive Guide to Baton Technique and Interpretation.* 3rd ed. New York: Schirmer Books, 1995.

Schuller, Gunther. *The Compleat Conductor.* New York: Oxford University Press, 1997.

BOOKS ON ORCHESTRATION

Adler, Samuel. *The Study of Orchestration.* 3rd ed. New York: W. W. Norton, 2002.

Heussenstamm, George. *The Norton Manual of Music Notation.* 1st ed. New York: W. W. Norton, 1987.

Piston, Walter. *Orchestration.* New York: W. W. Norton, 1955.

Read, Gardner. *Style and Orchestration.* New York: Schirmer Books, 1979.

Rimsky-Korsakov, Nikolay. *Principles of Orchestration: With Musical Examples Drawn from His Own Works.* New ed. New York: Dover Publications, 1964.

Sebesky, Donald. *The Contemporary Arranger.* Rev. ed. Van Nuys, CA: Alfred Pub., 1975.

Stone, Kurt. *Music Notation in the Twentieth Century: A Practical Guidebook.* New York: W. W. Norton, 1980.

MISCELLANEOUS BOOKS RELEVANT TO MUSIC DIRECTION

Beeching, Angela Myles. *Beyond Talent: Creating a Successful Career on Music.* 2nd ed. New York: Oxford University Press, 2010.

Block, Geoffrey. *Enchanted Evenings: The Broadway Musical from Show Boat to Sondheim.* New York: Oxford University Press, 2011.

Boyd, Jenny. *Musicians in Tune: Seventy-Five Contemporary Musicians Discuss the Creative Process.* New York: Simon & Schuster, 1992.
Cohen, Allen, and Steve Rosenhaus. *Writing Musical Theater.* New York: Palgrave MacMillan, 2006.
Engel, Lehman. *Planning and Producing the Musical Show.* Rev. ed. New York: Crown Publishers, 1966.
Engel, Lehman. *Words with Music: Creating the Broadway Musical Libretto.* 2nd ed. New York: Applause Theater & Cinema Books, 2006.
Frankel, Aaron. *Writing the Broadway Musical.* Millennium ed. Cambridge, MA: Da Capo Press, 2000.
Frith, Simon. *Performing Rites: On the Value of Popular Music.* Cambridge, MA: Harvard University Press, 1996.
Klickstein, Gerald. *The Musician's Way: A Guide to Practice, Performance, and Wellness.* New York: Oxford University Press, 2009.
Laird, Paul. *Wicked: A Musical Biography.* Lanham, MD: Scarecrow Press, 2011.
Levitin, Daniel. *This Is Your Brain on Music: The Science of a Human Obsession.* New York: Plume, 2007.
Levitin, Daniel. *The World in Six Songs: How the Musical Brain Created Human Nature.* New York: Dutton, 2008.
Nally, Donald. *Conversations with Joseph Flummerfelt: Thoughts on Conducting, Music and Musicians.* Lanham, MD: Scarecrow Press, 2010.
Spencer, David. *The Musical Theatre Writer's Survival Guide.* Portsmouth, NH: Heinemann, 2005.
Stempel, Larry. *Showtime: A History of the Broadway Musical Theater.* New York: Norton, 2010.
Suskin, Steven. *The Sound of Broadway Music: A Book of Orchestrators and Orchestrations.* New York: Oxford University Press, 2009.
Swain, Joseph P. *The Broadway Musical: A Critical and Musical Survey.* Lanham, MD: Scarecrow Press, 2002.

MUSICAL WORKS CITED

Bernstein, Leonard, and Richard Wilbur. "Make Our Garden Grow." *Candide.* Boosey & Hawkes, 1989. Distributed by Hal Leonard, Milwaukee, WI. Originally published in 1955.
Bernstein, Leonard, and Stephen Sondheim. "Balcony Scene." *West Side Story.* New York: G. Schirmer, Inc., and Chappell & Co., Inc., 1957.
Church, Joseph, and Randy Newman. "Stabbing of Valentine." *Faust.* Unpublished. Reprinted by permission of Alfred Music.
Church, Joseph, Frank Wildhorn, and Jack Murphy. "Underscore." *Havana.* Unpublished. Property of the author.
Guns 'N' Roses. "Welcome to the Jungle." *Appetite for Destruction.* Geffen, 1987.
Hamlisch, Marvin, and Edward Kleban. "Opening," *A Chorus Line.* 1975.
John, Elton, Tim Rice, et al. "The Circle of Life." *The Lion King.* Walt Disney Music Company, 1997.
Kander, John, and Fred Ebb. "Sometimes a Day Goes By." *Woman of the Year.* 1981.
Lennon, John, and Paul McCartney. "And I Love Her." *A Hard Day's Night.* Parlophone, 1964.
Loesser, Frank. "Sit Down, You're Rockin' the Boat." *Guys and Dolls.* 1951. Transcribed by author.
M, Lebo, and Hans Zimmer. "Nants' Ingonyama." *The Lion King.* Walt Disney Music Company, 1994.
M, Lebo. "Grasslands." *The Lion King.* Walt Disney Music Company, 1997.
Mann, Barry, and Cynthia Weil. "Come Along for the Ride," *Mask.* 2008.
Menken, Alan, and Howard Ashman. "Belle," *Beauty and the Beast.* 1994.
Menken, Alan, and Howard Ashman. "Skid Row." *Little Shop of Horrors.* 1982.
Miranda, Lin-Manuel. "Back to Work." *In The Heights.* 2007.
Miranda, Lin-Manuel. "Blackout." *In The Heights.* 2007.
Miranda, Lin-Manuel. "Breathe." *In The Heights.* 2007.
Miranda, Lin-Manuel. "In The Heights." *In The Heights.* 2007.
O'Brien, Richard. "Time Warp." *The Rocky Horror Show.* 1973.
Porter, Cole. "I Get A Kick out of You." *Songs for Young Lovers,* Frank Sinatra. Los Angeles: Capitol, 1954.
Rodgers, Richard. "Alleluia." *The Sound of Music.* 1959.
Rodgers, Richard. "Morning Hymn." *The Sound of Music.* 1959.
Rodgers, Richard, and Oscar Hammerstein II. "Julie and Carrie Sequence." *Carousel.* 1945.

Rodgers, Richard, and Oscar Hammerstein II. "Opening Act 1." *Oklahoma!* 1943.
Schwartz, Stephen. "What Is This Feeling?" *Wicked.* 2003.
Simon, Paul. "The Boxer." *Bridge over Troubled Water.* New York: Columbia, 1969.
Sondheim, Stephen. "Being Alive." *Company.* 1970.
Townshend, Pete. "Go to the Mirror, Boy." *The Who's Tommy.* 1993.
Willson, Meredith. "Sincere." *The Music Man.* 1957.

Index

42nd Street, 175
academic theater, 63–65; author's experience in, 2; brief runs in, 327; creation of recordings of, 345; economics of, 75; in examples, 148, 153; invited dresses in lieu of previews in, 315; load-ins in, 305; producers in, 75–76; production meetings in, 123; scheduling rehearsal time in, 125, 185; reconstructions of shows in, 155; resident musical directors in, 16; subs and double-casting in, 328; synthesized orchestras in, 106; vocal coaching in, 189; warm-ups in, 225; working with instrumentalists in, 264
Academy Awards, 63
accompaniment, 199–200; complexity of, 34, 156; fundamental notion of, 365; in examples, 200–202; in rehearsal, 96, 140, 208, 212, 226–27; in run-throughs and *Sitzprobes*, 298, 300; interpretation of vocal scores, 347. *See also* rehearsal musicians
accordions, 250, 257
acting: in song, 203–6, 220–21
actors. *See under* performers
Actors' Equity: as part of Tony Awards Administration Committee, 18; casting regulations of, 128; freezing of shows mandated by, 315; pay rates for recording set by, 345–46; proscription of notes close to curtain by, 325; regulation of workshops by, 67; rehearsal rules of, 185, 314; stage managers in, 77; support of musician's strike by, 25; time off allowed by, 337; understudy rules of, 338
After Midnight, 32
Ain't Misbehavin', 14
American Idiot, 157, 159
American Idol, 44, 66–67, 115, 126n1

American Repertory Theater, 53
American Theater Wing, 17
Anything Goes, 171
arranging, 154–59; as an extension of music direction, 360, 363, 367; as storytelling, 159; conceptualization of, 156–59; dance arrangers, 103–4, 176–78; dance arranging, 176–78, 228; definition of, 8, 154; for cabaret acts, 58; on *American Idol*, 126n1; relation to orchestration, 98–100; technical aspects of, 159–64; vocal arrangers, 100, 103–4; vocal arranging, 88, 136–137, 164–74
Ashman, Howard, 170, 273
auditions, 110, 126–32; pianists, 130, 132, 359–60
Avenue Q, 74

bassists. *See under* instrumentalists
baton, 269–71; case studies, 373–81; choruses, 221–22; instrumentalists, 264–67; monitors, 269–270, 308, 310–11, 373; podiums, 308–11; techniques, 271–96
 articulations, 294–95; cutoffs, 281–82; dynamics, 293–94; following singers, 286–89; recitative, 286
 grooves, 291–93
 feels, 291
 meters, 272–78; preparatory beats, 278–81; rests and holds, 282–84; safeties and vamps 284–86;
 syncopations, 292; tempo (*see* tempo)
Beauty and the Beast, 273, 344
Berlin, Irving, 4, 83
Bernstein, Leonard: as composer, 2, 38, 83, 148–49, 151; as conductor, 263, 370
blocking, 224–25

Bohème, La, 74
Book of Mormon, The, 27–28, 141n2, 253
bows and exit music, 240
brass. *See under* instrumentalists
Bridges of Madison County, The, 29
Bring It On: The Musical, 155
Broadway, 2, 4–5, 7–8, 45–49, 336; history of musicals, 40–41; modern state of, 5, 41–44; music directing practices on, 182–83, 185, 223, 268, 302, 304–5, 311, 314–15, 324–25
Brown, Jason Robert, 29, 36
Bye Bye, Birdie, 48

Cabaret, 41, 165, 171
Camelot, 85
Candide, 148–53
Capeman, The, 46, 303
Carousel, 75, 113
casting, 115–17, 121, 126–32
casting agents, 116–17, 128–32
Chenoweth, Kristin, 30
Chicago, Illinois, 8, 51, 53, 165
Chicago, 69, 141n2, 175, 190n4
choral technique, 213–21
choreographers, 88–90, 155–56; auditions with, 130–31; choice of orchestrators by, 100; in rehearsals, 223–29; in run-throughs, 298–99; note sessions with, 316–17; suggestions for bows music by, 240; union, 18; work with dance arrangers, 104. *See also* arranging: dance arranging
Chorus Line, A, 43, 48; movie adaptation, 33; opening vocal arrangement, 166–68, 171
Cirque du Soleil, 33, 62
Clark, Dick, 35
click tracks, 289–90; conducting to, 268; in rock music, 157; mishaps involving, 332–33; pre-show, 325–26; production of, 346–47
Closer Than Ever, 49
Clurman, Harold, 85
Coleman, Shepard, 16–17, 27
community theater, 65–67; invited dress in lieu of previews, 315; load-ins in, 305; orchestra subs in, 328; producers in, 75–76; warm-ups in, 225; working with instrumentalists in, 243–45, 264
Company, 48, 172–173
company managers, 79
composers, 81–84, 115; as compared to songwriters, 83–84; free rein to write incidental music given by, 237–8; in attendance at rehearsals, 188; in examples, 13, 42; in preproduction, 122, 142; of new shows, 144; of pop music, 21, 38, 69, 237; recommendations for jobs by, 73, 93; relation to orchestration, 93, 99–100, 106; who also music direct, xiv, 14, 360; writing for specific performers, 114
concerts, 43, 59–61
conducting, 262–64; cueing, 231–35, 295–96; handling mistakes, 329–30; importance of, 323; in performance, 326–27; observing, 370; preparation for 140–41; relation to music directing, 15; technical aspects of, 267–96
conductors, 94–96; assistant & associate, 94–95, 185, 209–10, 226, 339–43, 370; inspirational, 263; supervision of instrumental subs by, 340; subs, 341–43
copyists, 80, 100–103, 126, 163, 245, 258; as an extension of music directing, 15, 347, 358; misleading work by, 142–43, 294
cruise ships, 1, 7, 50, 55, 69
cuing. *See under* conducting

Dallas, 51
dance, 88–90, 111, 174–78, 227–29
dance arranging. *See under* arranging
dancers. *See under* performers
De La Guarda, 49
Denver Theater Center, 53
designers, 42, 90–92, 122
directors, 15, 42, 73, 84–88, 121, 155–56; adaptation of music to shows by, 103–4, 165, 174, 230, 232–33, 235, 237, 240; choice of orchestrators by, 100; in comparison to music directors, 15, 73; in rehearsal, 96, 182, 188, 223–29; in run-throughs, 298–300; note sessions with, 315–19; post-opening involvement with, 339, 342; recommendations for jobs by, 73
Dreamgirls, 43
drummers, *see under* instrumentalists

Ehmann, Wilhelm, 211
Engel, Lehman, 7, 42
exit music. *See* bows and exit music

Fantasticks, The, 256n2
Fiddler on the Roof, 44, 162
Follies, 41, 75
Footloose: The Musical, 33
Forbidden Broadway, 49
Fosse, Bob, 89, 224
Fuerza Bruta, 49

Gemignani, Paul, 139, 251
general managers, 79
Gershwin, George and Ira, 83, 132, 265
Glass, Philip, 84

Glee, 44, 63
Gondoliers, The, 158–59
Goodman Theater, 53
Goodspeed Opera House, 53, 67
Grammy Awards, 38
Grease, 44, 126, 171
Greif, Michael, 318
guitars, *see under* instrumentalists
Guthrie Theater, 53
Guys and Dolls, 115, 202, 240, 286–87

Hair, 40, 48, 189, 192, 194, 200
Hairspray, 175, 268
Hamlisch, Marvin, 10, 84, 166
Harper, Wally, 59
Hartenstein, Frank, 76
Hartford Stage, 53
Havana, 237
Hedwig and the Angry Inch, 49
Hello, Dolly!, 16, 115
High School Musical, 63
Holmes, Rupert, 84
house managers, 80
Howard, Peter, 16–17
Hunchback of Notre Dame, The, 159
In The Heights: difficulty of piano part, 324; in examples, 176, 210, 260, 274–75, 373; star casting in, 115; vocal arrangements in, 169. *See also* Lacamoire, Alex; Miranda, Lin-Manuel

incidental music, 235–39: transitional music, 238–39; underscoring, 235–38
industrials. *See under* revues
instrumentalists: bassists, 132–33, 251–52; brass players, 185; 253–55; 267; brass parts, 260; disappearance of strings, 255–56; drummers, 96, 250–52, 305; drum parts, 258–59; guitarists, 96, 252–53, 305; guitar parts, 258–59; keyboardists (*see* synthesizers); percussionists, 134, 250–51; percussion parts, 258; positioning of (*see* orchestras: positioning of instrumentalists in); strings, 134–35, 185, 295, 341; string parts, 260; synthesizers (*see* synthesizers); woodwind players, 253–55, 279; woodwind parts, 260

Jackson, Michael, 230
Jekyll and Hyde, 41, 159, 338
Jersey Boys, 41, 141n2, 145, 158
jukebox musicals, 41, 141n2, 157–58

Keller, Michael, 108
Kennedy Center, 53

keyboards. *See* synthesizers
King and I, The, 114, 189
Kosarin, Michael, 170, 276

Lacamoire, Alex, 360, 373
LaChiusa, Michael John, 49
Lady Gaga, 33
La Jolla Playhouse, 87, 158n1
Las Vegas, 1, 8, 45, 57, 62, 159
League of Regional Theaters (LORT), 52, 55
Lerner and Loewe, 29
Les Miserables, 69, 166
Light in the Piazza, The, 33
Lincoln Center, 31, 53, 149
Lion King, The, 2, 62n2,141n2, 148; casting of, 116; conducting of, 269, 324; dance arranging of, 96; the discovery of Alex Lacamoire through, 360; in examples, 123–24, 348, 373–74; opening cues in, 231; orchestration in, 254, 257; set malfunctions in, 332; translation of, 116; vocal rehearsals for, 211
Little Night Music, A, 44, 171
Little Shop of Horrors, 170
Lloyd Webber, Andrew, 40, 157, 190
load-ins, 302–7
London, 18n6, 51, 62
Los Angeles, 8, 47, 51, 130
LORT, *see* League of Regional Theaters
lyricists, 42, 81–82, 122, 188

MacDermot, Galt, 188, 194n10, 200–201
Madonna, 33
Mamma Mia!, 141n2, 155
Margoshes, Steve, 87, 158n1, 359
Marry Me a Little, 49
Marshall, Rob, 224
Mask, 348
Matilda, 33, 141n2
McAnuff, Des, 87, 158
Menken, Alan, 170, 273, 276
Merman, Ethel, 30
metronomes, 229, 289–90
Minnelli, Liza, 58, 165
Miranda, Lin-Manuel, 114, 333
Miss Saigon, 5, 41
Mitchell, Brian Stokes, 30
monitors, audio: for conductors, 308, 311, 314, 325; for instrumentalists, 248, 290, 302
monitors, video. *See under* conducting
Monty Python's Spamalot, 233
Motown: The Musical, 141n2, 145
movie musicals, 69
Movin' Out, 46, 175

music contractors, 96–98, 117, 244, 304; hiring criteria of, 109; in rehearsals, 245, 267, 300; networking with, 361, 365, 368, 370; recommendations for jobs from, 73
music coordinators, 96–98, 108, 185, 302, 344
music direction, xiii-xiv, 1–2, 6, 13–22; as a career, 5, 359–71; associates (*see* conductors: associate); cuing (*see* conducting: cuing); definition of, 13; examples of score analysis, 148–53, 171–74, 191–93; handling mistakes, 329–33; in rehearsal, 181; indispensability in performance of, 323; learning scores, 139–41; networking, 367–69; note sessions, 315–19; over the course of a run, 334–37; score preparation, 138–45; settling disputes, 343–44; through history, 19–22; working with singers, 112–14. *See also* vocal coaching
Music Man, The, 165–66, 175, 233
music supervisors, 8, 13n2, 94, 361, 363; awards for, 18n6; of tours, 51
musician's union: advent of, 21; at regional theaters, 53–55; copyists in, 103; lack of recognition for music direction, 15, 17–19, 46–47, 51, 94; lack of recognition for synthesizer programmers, 106; Local 802, 17, 19n7, 94; minimums enforced by, 25, 157; music coordinators as representatives of, 96–97; overseeing industrials and revues, 63; pay scale of, 46–47, 91, 132, 312, 345; pensions, 366; petitioning for new Tony Award categories, 17–18, 155; proscription of auditions by, 98; proscription of conductors orchestrating shows, 363; protection of orchestra members, 109, 244; protection of right of first refusal, 68; regulation of backstage space, 304; rehearsal rules of, 185, 267, 315; sub policies of, 94, 336, 340, 342; time off permitted by, 336, 362
My Fair Lady, 41

Nashville, 51
Newman, Randy, 46, 91, 238
nightclubs and cabaret, 30, 57–61, 247, 258, 327
Nixon in China, 33

Of Thee I Sing, 40
Off-Broadway, 46–49, 69, 97, 370
Oklahoma!, 40–41, 162, 175, 274–75, 314n1
On Your Toes, 175
Once, 257
opera, 37–39, 84
orchestras, 108–9, 243–61; call times for, 325; 328–32; disputes in, 108–9, 343–44; effect of designers on, 90–92; estimation of rehearsal time for, 185, 245–46; librarians, 245; location of, 9, 23, 311–12, 326; offstage space for, 304; parts, 257–61; positioning of instrumentalists in, 98, 248–57; rehearsals, 244–46, 264–67, 332, 338; seating, 304–5, 307; sightlines for, 310–11; *Sitzprobes,* 185, 300–302, 305, 338; size of, 22–28, 62, 132, 134–37, 346; subs, 94–95, 328–29, 336n1, 340–41, 370; volume of, 294
orchestrations, 8–9, 98–103, 132–35, 142–43, 156; as the purview of the music director/supervisor, 14, 141n2, 155, 363; effects of transposition on, 161–62; for specific performers, 114–15; reduction of, 28, 49, 136–37; writing and copying of, 257
orchestrators: arrangements created by, 143, 238, 240; awards for, 17, 18n6, 27, 145, 155; in attendance at rehearsals, 96, 245; for concerts, 59; notes given by, 316; work with composers, 83, 93; work with synthesizer programmers, 104, 106, 108; writing of idiomatic parts by, 253–4, 258
overtures, 239–40

Passing Strange, 49
percussionists. *See under* instrumentalists
performers, 37, 46, 110–17; actors, 110, 113–16, 203n16, 204–5; arranging for, 162, 165, 171; casting (*see* casting); covers, 337–38; cues for, 296; dancers, 110–12, 130, 229, 343; disputes amongst, 333–34; in nightclubs, 57–61, 225; in rehearsal, 183–86, 205, 217, 220, 224, 226; in run-throughs and *sitzprobes* 297–300; learning speed, 125; mistakes made by, 332–33; notes from, 290; notes to 313, 315–19; pre-show routines with, 324–25; put-ins, 337–38; singers, 30, 110–14, 130–31, 170–71, 188–90, 317. *See also* vocal coaching; stars (*see* star performers); union (*see* Actor's Equity)
Peter Pan, 143n3, 230, 233
Phantom of the Opera, The, 141n2, 157, 268, 338
piano-vocal scores, 141–44; creation of, 347–58
pianos, 247–48, 310, 359; practice, 139–40
P!nk, 33
Pippin, Don, 166
pop music, 30, 35–36, 40, 82, 157, 305; employment of music directors in, 21
Porgy and Bess, 40, 268
Porter, Cole, 29, 133, 136, 145–46
preproduction, 121–26, 142, 176, 208, 302, 363; creation of musical material during, 144, 176; estimation of rehearsal time, 125, 183–85; scheduling, 123–26, 300; score preparation in, 141–45

previews, 314–16
Prince, Harold, 24, 149
producers, 48–50, 54–55, 74–76, 80, 93–97, 115, 190n5, 314, 345, 362; as employers, 73, 80, 92–93, 97, 100, 104, 116, 364, 366; casting of stars by, 115; handling conflicts, 344; in examples, 133–35; in preproduction, 122–23, 185, 300; in rehearsals, 165, 182, 226, 245, 298, 315; networking with, 361, 368; orchestral reductions due to, 24–25, 28, 31, 251; past vs. present, 41–44. *See also* academic theater: producers in; community theater: producers in
Producers, The, 233
production meetings, 90, 121–23
Puccini, Giacomo, 38, 83

Randy Newman's Faust, 238
recitative, 232, 286; conducting (*see* conducting: following singers)
recordings: original cast, 344–46
reeds. *See under* instrumentalists: woodwind players
regional theaters, 51–56, 75; development of new shows at, 67, 69; rehearsals at, 187
rehearsal musicians, 64, 96, 183, 226–28, 347; choice to use, 140, 208, 226, 312; dance arrangers as, 104; in note sessions, 316; non-pianists as, 96, 104, 251; payroll designation of music directors as, 47; post-opening, 337, 339
rehearsal spaces, 98, 125
rehearsals, 139, 181–229, 323; cue-to-cues, 312; dance rehearsals, 175–76; ensemble music rehearsals, 208–13; final, 297–302, 315–16; industrial and special event rehearsals, 62–63, 123; music director salaries for, 47; musicians (*see* rehearsal musicians); orchestra rehearsals (*see* orchestras: rehearsals); overview of, 181–86; post-opening 337–39, 363; run-throughs, 297–99; scheduling (*see* preproduction: estimation of rehearsal time); technical rehearsals, 312–14; voicing complaints in 88; with singers (*see* vocal coaching); with directors and choreographers, 223–30
Rent, 47–48, 74
revivals, 31, 53, 141n2; popularity of 42, 48; scaled-down versions of, 136; star casting in, 115
revues, 36, 49, 62–63, 133–34n3, 135n4; dance arrangements for, 175; industrials, 62; transitions in, 230, 234
Rittmann, Trude, 96, 169
Riverdance, 62
Robbins, Jerome, 89
Rock of Ages, 48, 78, 141n2, 157–58
Rocky Horror Show, The, 273–74

Roundabout Theater, 53, 158
Rodgers and Hammerstein, 29, 96, 114

scheduling. *See under* preproduction
Schwartz, Stephen, 84, 190
score preparation. *See under* preproduction
Seller, Jeffrey, 74–75
singers. *See under* performers
singing competitions, 66–67
Sister Act: The Musical, 41, 91, 115, 255
Sitzprobes. *See under* orchestras
Smokey Joe's Cafe, 62, 331
Sondheim, Stephen, 28, 40, 49, 83, 171–72
sound checks, 305–7, 311
sound design, 29–32, 88, 91–92; at load-ins, 304–5; at orchestra rehearsals, 245; importance of collaboration in, 122, 125, 317; isolation of instruments in, 250, 256; management of bad singers with, 218; Tony Awards for, 18
sound operators, 91–92, 94, 122, 171, 245; example of communication with, 325–26; note sessions with, 316–17; telephones to, 308
Sound of Music, The, 44, 116, 168–69, 171
South Pacific, 31–32
Spring Awakening, 33, 157
stage managers, 18, 76–79; approval of conducting subs by, 342; in preproduction, 122–23, 125; in rehearsals, 223, 225; in run-throughs and *sitzprobes*, 298, 300; in technical rehearsals, 312–13; management of disputes by, 344; note sessions with, 315–17; pre-performance, 308, 325; post-opening, 336, 339; replacement of producers in smaller productions by, 80
star performers, 110, 115–16, 223, 338
Starlight Express, 41, 268
Starting Here, Starting Now, 49
Steel Pier, 190n4
Stites, Kevin, 360
stock theaters, 55–56, 244; intense workloads at, 123, 183, 226, 312; invited dress in lieu of previews at, 315; re-orchestration at, 99
Streisand, Barbra, 30, 58
strings. *See under* instrumentalists
Stroman, Susan, 224
Strouse, Charles, 83
Sunday in the Park with George, 48, 113, 162
Suskin, Steven, 7, 17
Sweeney Todd, 65, 136–37
synthesizers, 104–5, 134, 247; in *American Idiot*, 157; in *Book of Mormon*, 27–28; parts, 258–59; programmers, 104–8, 185, 316; sectionals, 185; supplanting orchestras, 23–25, 49, 135–36, 244, 253, 257; supplementing string sections, 255–56, 267, 341

tempos, 90, 163, 195–98, 199n12; conducting of, 289–91, 327, 331; in dance rehearsals, 227–29
Tesori, Jeanine, 49
Tharp, Twyla, 46, 156
Timberlake, Justin, 33
Tony Awards, 23, 63; for music direction, 16–18; for orchestrations, 27, 145, 155, 363
tours, national, 49–51
Townshend, Pete, 87, 158
transcription, 145–47, 155, 163, 360
Tune, Tommy, 224

unions, 17–18, 47, 77; breaks, 185, 267; comparison to nonunion work, 50, 55, 136, 340; journals, 369; minimums, 24–25, 158n1; SDC, 18; technician's, 304; TMA, 50. *See also* Actor's Equity; musician's union

Victor/Victoria, 115, 331
vocal arrangements, *see under* arrangement
vocal coaching, 112–13, 187–206; definition of, 187; diplomacy in, 189–90; for acting, 203–6; key, 194–95; song-specific examples of, 191–93, 203, 205–6

vocal technique, 198–99

War Horse, 155
warm-ups: acting, 225–26; dance, 227–28; piano, 324; vocal, 217
Wedding Singer: The Musical, The, 33
Weill, Kurt, 83, 114
West Side Story, 2, 41, 88, 175, 361; musical examples, 236–37
Who's Tommy, The: arrangements in, 96, 158–59, 158n1, 169; creation of, 87–88; dispute over dance arrangement in, 228; employment as music director on, 359; 124; in examples, 129, 348; injuries caused by set of, 310; synthesizer patches used in, 106
Wicked, 44, 141n2, 210, 268, 360
Wildhorn, Frank, 237
Woman of the Year, 187, 190
woodwind players. *See under* instrumentalists
workshops, 43, 67–69, 134, 247
World Goes 'Round, The, 188

You're A Good Man, Charlie Brown, 65